view from the

telecosm

George Gilder

AMERICAN | HERITAGE
CUSTOM | PUBLISHING

A DIVISION OF FORBES INC.
60 FIFTH AVENUE
NEW YORK, NEW YORK 10011

Custom Publishing also acknowledges the research assistance of the Discovery Institute (206-287-3144), which is based in Seattle and manages the official Gilder Archives at http://www.discovery.org/ggindex.html.

CIP Data is available.
Printed in the United States of America
10 9 8 7 6 5 4 3 2 1

ISBN 0-8281-0962-1

CONTENTS

1

Into the Fibersphere

Philip Hope, divisional vice-president for engineering systems at Dallas-based Electronic Data Systems Corp., has an IQ problem. His chief client and owner, General Motors, wants to interconnect thousands of three-dimensional graphics and computer-aided engineering (CAE) workstations with mainframes and supercomputers at headquarters with automated assembly equipment at factories in Lordstown, Ohio, and Detroit, with other powerful processors at GM's technical center in Warren, Mich., at its Opel plant in Ruesselheim, Germany, and at its design center outside San Diego. On behalf of another client, Hope wants to link multimedia stations for remote diagnostics, X-ray analysis and pharmaceutical modeling in hospitals and universities across the country.

Any function involving 3D graphics, CAE, supercomputer visualization, lossless diagnostic imaging and advanced medical simulations demands large bandwidth or communications power. Graphics workstations often operate screens with a million picture elements (pixels), and use progressive scanning at 60 frames, or images, per second. Each pixel may entail 24 bits of color. That adds up fast to billions of bits (gigabits) per second. And that's for last year's technology in a computer industry that is doubling its power and cost-effectiveness every year.

What Hope needs are bandwidth and connections. The leading bandwidth and connections people have always been the telephone companies. But when Hope goes to the telephone companies, they want to tell him about intelligence: their "advanced intelligent network," which will be coming on-line over the next decade or so and will solve all his problems. For now, what are called DS-3 services are available in many areas, operating T-3 lines at 45 megabits (millions of bits) per second. These facilities are ample for most computer uses, and working together with several different regional Bell operating companies (RBOCs), Hope should be able to acquire these services in time for a General Motors takeover by Toyota. DS-3 is only one-twentieth of the required gigabit-per-second rate.

Hope has been through this before. In the early 1980s, he actually wanted DS-3 services. Then, he was interconnecting GM facilities in southeast Michigan with plants in Indiana and Ohio. But Michigan Bell could not supply the lines in time. EDS had to build a network of microwave towers to bear the 45-megabit traffic. Later in the decade, the phone companies offered him even higher capacity fiberoptic lines, with the requirement that the optical bits be slowed down and run periodically through an electronic interface so the telco could count the number of "equivalent channels" being used.

What Hope and others in the systems integration business need is not intelligent networks tomorrow but dumb bandwidth that they can deliver to their customers flexibly, cheaply and now. To prepare for future demand, they want the network to use fiberoptics. It so happens that America's telephone companies have some 2 million miles of mostly unused fiber lines in the ground today, kept as redundant capacity for future needs. Hope would like to be able to tap into this "dark fiber" for his own customers. Futhermore, for those fiber strands in use, the telephone companies actually use less than 1 percent of the available bandwidth.

As a leader in the rapidly expanding field of computer services, EDS epitomizes the needs of an information economy. With a backlog of $22 billion in already-contracted business, EDS is currently a $7 billion company growing revenues at an annual rate of 15 percent, some three times as fast as the phone companies. EDS will add $1 billion or so in new sales in 1992 alone. If the company is to continue to supply leading-edge services to its customers, it must command leading-edge communications. To EDS, that means dumb and dark networks.

THE "DARK FIBER" CASE

That need has driven EDS into an active role as an ex parte pleader in Federal Case 911416, currently bogging down in the United States Court of Appeals for the District of Colombia as the so-called "dark fiber" case. On the surface, the case—known as *Southwestern Bell et al. v. the Federal Communications Commission and the U.S. Department of Justice*—pits four regional Bell operating companies against the FCC. But the legal maneuvers actually reflect a rising conflict between the Bells and several large corporate clients over the future of communications.

Beyond all the legal posturing, the question at issue is whether fiber networks should be dumb and dark, and cheap, the way EDS and other customers like them, or whether they should be bright and smart and "strategically" priced, the way the telephone companies want them.

On the side of intelligence and light are the phone companies—Southwestern Bell, U.S. West, Bell South and Bell Atlantic. The forces of darkness include key officials at the FCC and such companies as Shell Oil, the information services arm of McDonell Douglas and long-distance network provider Wiltel, as well as EDS.

Most of the four-year course of the struggle has passed unnoticed by the media. In summary, the issue may not seem portentous. The large corporate customers want dark fiber; the FCC mandates that it be supplied; the Bells want out of the business. Despite the obscurity of the proceedings, they raise what for the next 20 years will be the central issue in communications law and technology. The issue, if not the possible trial itself, will shape the future of both the computer industry and the telephone industry during a period when they are merging to form the spearhead of a new information economy.

Dark fiber is simply a glass fiberoptic thread with nothing attached to it—no light being sent through it. In this "unlit" condition, it is available for use without the intermediation of phone company electronics or intelligent services.

In the mid-1980s, the Bells leased some of their dark-fiber lines to several large corporations on an individual-case basis. These companies learned to love dark fiber. But when they tried to renew their leases with the Bells, the Bells clanged no—why don't you leave the interconnections and protocols to us? Why don't you use our marvelous smart network with all the acronyms and intelligent services? Why don't you let us meter your use of the fiber and send you a convenient monthly bill for each packet of bits you send?

EDS and the other firms rejected the offer; they preferred the dumb fiber to the intelligent network. When the Bells persisted in an effort to deny new leases, the companies went to the FCC to require the Bells, as regulated "common carrier" telephone companies, to continue supplying dark fiber.

In the fall of 1990, the FCC ruled that the phone companies would have to offer dark fiber to all comers under the rules of common carriage. Rather than accept this new burden, the phone companies petitioned to withdraw from the business entirely under what is called a Rule 214 application. Since the FCC has not acted on this petition, the Bells are preparing to go to court to force the issue. Their corporate customers are ready to litigate as well.

It is safe to say that none of the participants fully comprehend the significance of their courthouse confrontation. To the Bells, after all is said and done, the key problem is probably the price. Under the existing tariff, they are required to offer this service to anyone who wants it for an average price of approximately $150 per strand of fiber per mile per month. As an offering that competes with their T-3 45-megabit-per-second lines and other forthcoming marvels, dark fiber threatens to gobble up their future as vendors of broadband communications to offices, even as cable TV preempts them as broadband providers to homes. Since the Bells' profits on data are growing some 10 times as fast as their profits on voice telephony, they see dark fiber as a menace to their most promising markets.

The technological portents, however, are far more significant even than the legal and business issues. The coming triumph of dark fiber will mean not only the end of the telephone industry as we know it but also the end of the telephone industry as they plan it: a vast intelligent fabric of sophisticated information services. Dark fiber also could mean a thoroughgoing restructuring of a computer industry increasingly dedicated to supplying "smart networks." Indeed, for most of the world's communications companies, and for professors of communications theory and designers of new computer networks, the triumph of dark and dumb means back to the drawing board, if not back to the Dark Ages.

But the new dark ages cannot be held back. Springing out the depths of IBM's huge T. J. Watson Research Center, spread across Westchester County, N.Y., is a powerful new invention—the all-optical network—that will soon relegate all bright and smart executives to the troglodyte file and make dumb and dark the winning rule in communications.

THE WRINGER EFFECT

From time to time, the structure of nations and economies goes through a technological wringer: a new invention radically reduces the price of a key factor of production and precipitates an industrial revolution. Before long, every competitive business in the economy must wring out the residue of the old costs and customs from all its products and practices.

The steam engine, for example, drastically reduced the price of physical force. Once wrested at great expense from human and animal muscle, power now pulsed cheaply and tirelessly from machines burning coal and oil. Throughout the world, dominance inexorably shifted to businesses and nations that reorganized themselves to exploit the suddenly cheap resource. Eventually every human industry and activity, from agriculture and sea transport to printing and war, had to centralize and capitalize itself to take advantage of the new technology.

Putting the world through the technological wringer over the last three decades has been the integrated circuit, the IC. Invented by Robert Noyce of Intel and Jack Kilby of Texas Instruments in 1959, the IC put entire systems of tiny transistor switches, capacitors, resistors, diodes, and other once-costly electronic devices on one tiny microchip. Made chiefly of silicon, aluminum, and oxygen—the three most common substances in the earth's crust—the microchip eventually reduced the price of electronic circuitry by a factor of 1 million.

As industry guru Andrew Rappaport has pointed out, electronic designers now treat transistors as virtually free. Indeed, on memory chips, they cost some 400-millionths of a cent. To waste time or battery power or radio frequencies may be culpable acts, but to waste transistors is the essence of thrift. Today, you use millions of them to slightly enhance your TV picture. If you do not use transistors in your cars, your offices, your telephone systems, your design centers, your factories or your missiles, you go out of business. If you don't waste transistors, your cost structure will cripple you. Your product will be either too expensive, too slow, too late or too low in quality.

Endowing every engineer or PC hacker of the Information Age with the creative potential of a factory owner of the Industrial Age, the microchip reversed the centralizing thrust of the previous era. All nations and businesses had to adapt to the centrifugal law of the microcosm, flattening hierarchies, outsourcing services, liberating engineers, shedding middle management. If you did not adapt your business systems to the new regime, you would no longer be a factor in the world balance of economic and military power.

During the next decade or so, industry will go through a new technology wringer and submit to a new law: the law of the telecosm. The new wringer—the new integrated circuit—is called the all-optical network. It is a communications system that runs entirely in glass. Unlike existing fiberoptic networks, which convert light signals to electronic form in order to amplify or switch them, the all-optical network is entirely photonic. From the first conversion of the signal from your phone or computer to the final conversion to voice or data at the destination, your message flies through glass on wings of light.

Just as the old integrated circuit put entire electronic systems on single slivers of silicon, the new IC will put entire communications systems on seamless webs of silica. Wrought in threads as thin as a human hair, this silica is so pure that you could see through a window of it 70 miles thick. But what makes the new wringer roll with all the force of the microchip revolution before it is not the purity but the price.

Just as the old IC made transistor power virtually free, the new IC—the all-optical network—will make communications power virtually free. Another word for communications power is *bandwidth*. Just as the entire world had to learn to waste transistors, the entire world will now have to learn how to waste bandwidth. In the 1990s and beyond, every industry and economy will go through the wringer again.

The impact on the organization of companies and economies, however, has yet to become clear. What is the law of the telecosm? Will the new technology reverse the centrifugal force of the microchip revolution . . . or consummate it? To understand the message of the new regime, we must follow the rule of microcosmic prophet Carver Mead of the California Institute of Technology: "Listen to the technology and find out what it is telling us."

THE SHANNON-SHOCKLEY REGIME

The father of the all-optical-network—the man who popularized the phrase, built the first fully functional system and wrote the definitive book on the subject—is Paul E. Green, Jr., of Watson Research Center at IBM. Now standing directly in the path of Green's wringer is Robert Lucky, who, in April 1985 at a Cornell Centennial Symposium in Newton, Mass., first gave Green the idea that an all-optical network might be possible. The leading intellectual in telephony, Lucky recently shocked the industry by shifting from AT&T's Bell Laboratories, where he was executive director of research, to Bellcore, the laboratory of the regional Bell operating companies. There he will soon have to confront the implications of Green's innovation.

Contemplating the new technology, Lucky recalls a course on data networks that he taught for several years on late 1970s with Green. As a computer man, Green relished the contrast between the onrushing efficiencies in his technology and the relative dormancy in communications. Indeed, for some 25 years, while computer powers rose a millionfold, network capacities increased about a thousandfold. It was not until the late 1980s that most long-distance data networks much surpassed the Pentagon's ARPANET (Advanced Research Projects Agency Network) running at 50 kilobits (thousands of bits) per second since the mid-1960s.

Dominating the entire post-World War II era of electronic communications were the powerful mathematic visions and theories of Claude Shannon of the Massachusetts Institute of Technology and Bell Labs. Shannon was the reclusive genius who, in the mid-1940s, invented information theory to ascertain the absolute carrying capacity of any communications channel. Whether wire or air, channels were assumed to be narrow and noisy, the way God made them (sometimes with help from AT&T). Typical were the copper phone lines that still link every household to the telephone network and the airwaves that still bear radio and television signals and static.

The all-purpose remedy for these narrow, noisy channels was powerful electronics. Invented at Bell Laboratories by a team headed by William Shockley and then developed by Robert Noyce and other Shockley protégés in Silicon Valley, silicon transistors and integrated circuits engendered a constant exponential upsurge of computing power.

Throwing ever more millions of ever faster and cheaper transistors at every problem, engineers created fast computers, multiplexers and switches that seemed to surmount and outsmart every limit of bandwidth or restriction of wire. This process continues today with heroic new compression tools that allow the creation of full video conferences over 64-kilobit telephone connections. Scientists at Bellcore are now even proposing new ways of using the Motion Picture Engineering Group (MPEG) compression standard to send full-motion movies at 1.5 megabits per second over the 4-kilohertz twisted-pair copper wires to the home. Using ever faster computers, Bellcore is saying it can give you pay-per-view movies at VCR resolution without installing fiber, or even coaxial cable, to the home.

In the Shannon-Shockley era, the communications might be noisy and error-prone, but smart electronics could encode and decode messages in complex ways that allowed efficient identification and correction of all errors. The Shannon channel might be narrow, but fast multiplexers allowed it to be divided into time slots accommodating a large number of simultaneous users in a system called time-division multiplexing. The channel might clog up when large numbers of users attempted to communicate with each other at once, but collision detectors or token passers could sort it all out in nanoseconds. Graphics and video might impose immense floods of bits on the system, but compression technology could reduce the floods to a manageable trickle with little or no loss of picture quality. If all else failed, powerful electronic switches could compensate for almost any bandwidth limitations. Switching could make up for the inadequate bandwidth at the terminals by relieving the network of the need to broadcast all signals to every destination. Instead, the central switch could receive all signals and then route them to their appropriate addresses.

To this day, this is the essential strategy of the telephone companies: compensate for narrow, noisy bandwidth with ever more powerful and intelligent digital electronics. Their "core competence," the Bells hasten to tell you, is switching. They make up for the shortcomings of copper wires by providing smart, powerful digital switches.

The Bells' vision for the future is to join the computer business all the way, making these switches the entering wedge for ever more elaborate information services. Switches will grow smarter and more sophisticated until they provide an ever-growing cornucopia of intelligent voice and fax features, from caller ID and voice mail to personal communications systems that follow you and your number around the world from your car commute to your vacation beach hideaway. In the end, these intelligent networks could supply virtually all the world's information needs, from movies, games and traffic updates to data libraries, financial services, news programs, and weather reports, all climaxing with yellow pages that exfoliate into a gigantic global mall of full-motion video where your fingers walk (or your voice commands echo) from Harrods to Jardines to Akihabara to Century 21 without your leaving the couch.

At the time when Green and Lucky taught their course, this strategy for the future was only a glimmer in the minds of telephone visionaries. But the essence of it was already in place. As Green pointed out, telephone companies' response to sluggishness in communications was to enter the computer industry, where progress was faster. The creativity of digital electronics would save the telephone industry from technical stagnation.

Lucky, however, protested to Green that it was unjust to compare the two fields. Computers and telecom, as Lucky explained them, operate on entirely different scales. Computers work in the microscale world of the IC, putting ever more thousands of wires and switches on single slivers of silicon.

By contrast, telecommunications operates in the macroworld, laying out wires and switches across mostly silicon landscapes and seabeds. It necessarily entails a continental, or even intercontinental, stretch of cables, microwave towers, switches and poles. "How was it possible," Lucky asked, "to make such a large scale system inexpensive?" Inherent in the structure and even the physics of computers and telecommunications, so it seemed to Lucky two decades ago, was a communications bottleneck.

As Lucky remembers it, Green was never satisfied with Lucky's point. Green believed that someday communications could achieve miracles comparable to the integrated circuit in computing.

THE BANDWIDTH SCANDAL

Today, as Lucky was the first to announce, fiberoptics has utterly overthrown the previous relationship between fast computers and slow wires. Now it is computer technology that imposes the bottleneck on the vast vistas of dark fiber. A silicon transistor can change its state some 2.5 billion times per second in response to light pulses—bundles of photons— hitting a photodetector. Since a human being would need a thousand years or so of 10-hour workdays even to count to 2 billion, 2 billion cycles in a single second—2 gigahertz—might seem a sprightly pace. But in the world of fiberoptics, running at the speed and frequencies of light, even a rate of 2 billion cycles per second is a humbling bow to the slothful pace of electronics. Since optical signals still have to be routed to their destinations through computer switches, communications now suffers from what is known as the "electronic bottleneck."

It is this electronic bottleneck—the entire Bell edifice of Shannon and Shockley—that Paul Green plans to blow away with his all-optical networks. Green is targeting what is a secret scandal of modern telecommunications: the huge gap between the real capacity of fiberoptics and the actual speed of telephone communications.

In communications systems, the number of waves per second, or hertz, represents a rough measure of two things about a transmitted signal: its center frequency and its bandwidth about that center frequency. The bandwidth, not the center, or carrier, frequency, is what expresses the ultimate carrying capacity. Your AM radio dial, for example, runs from around 535 kilohertz (535,000 hertz) to 1,705 kilohertz, and each station uses some 10 kilohertz. With an ideal receiver, the AM passband might carry 117 stations. The 10 kilohertz of bandwidth allowed each station suffices for speech and music, but the fidelity is poor. It is much better with FM radio, in which the bandwidth set aside for each station is 200 kilohertz, 20 times the AM number.

By contrast, the intrinsic bandwidth of one strand of dark fiber is some 25,000 gigahertz in each of three groups of frequencies—three passbands—through which fiber can transmit light over long distances. This bandwidth might accommodate some 25,000 supercomputer "stations" at a gigahertz per terminal (or 2.5 billion AM stations).

For comparison, consider all the radio frequencies currently used in the air for radio, television, microwave and satellite communications—and multiply by 1,000. The bandwidth of one fiber thread could carry more than 1,000 times as much information as all these radio and microwave frequencies that currently comprise the "air." Expressed another way, one fiber thread could bear all the traffic on the phone network during the peak hour of Mothers' Day in the United States (the heaviest load currently managed by the phone system).

Yet, even for point-to-point long-distance links, let alone connections to homes and telephones and computer networks, engineers now turn their backs on this immense capacity and use less than 1 percent, or one 25-thousandths, of it. Deferring to the electronic bottleneck, the telephone industry uses fiber merely as a superior replacement for the copper wires, coaxial cables, satellite links and microwave towers that connect the local central-office switches to one another for long-distance calls.

Over the last 15 years, the Bell Labs record for fiberoptics communication has run from 10 megabits per second over a 1-kilometer span to 10 gigabits per second over nearly 1,000 kilometers. But all the heroic advances in point-to-point links between central offices continued to use essentially one frequency on a fiber thread, while ignoring its intrinsic power to accommodate thousands of useful frequency bands.

In a world of all-optical networks, this strategy is bankrupt. No longer will it be possible to throw more transistors, however cheap and fast, at the switching problem. Electronic speeds have become an insuperable bottleneck obstructing the vast vistas of dark fiber beyond. So-called gigabit networks planned by the telephone and computer companies will not do. What is needed is not a 1-gigabit spread among many terminals but a large network functioning at 1 gigabit per second per terminal.

The demands of EDS offer a hint of the most urgent business needs. Added to them will be consumer demands. True high definition television, (HDTV), comparable to movies in resolution, requires close to gigabit-per-second bandwidth, particularly if the program is dispatched to the viewer down the fiber in burst mode all at once in a few seconds, or if the user is given a chance to shape the picture, choose a vantage point, window several images at once or experience three dimensions. When true broadband channels become available, there will be a flood of new applications comparable to the thousands of new uses of the IC.

No foreseeable progress in electronics can overcome the electronic bottleneck. To do that, we need an entirely new communications regime. In the form of the all-optical network, this regime is now at hand.

LAW OF THE TELECOSM: NETWORK "DUMB AS A STONE"

The new regime will use fiber not as a replacement for copper wires but as a new form of far more capacious and error-free air. Through a system called wavelength-division multiplexing and access, computers and telephones will tune into desired messages in the fibersphere the same way radios now tune into desired signals in the atmosphere. The fibersphere will be intrinsically as dumb and dark as the atmosphere.

The new regime overcomes the electronic bottleneck by altogether banishing electronics from the middle of the network. But, ask the telcos in unison, what about the switches? As long as the network is switched, it must be partly electronic. Unless the network is switched, it is not a true any-to-any network. It is a broadcast system. It may offer a cornucopia of services, but it cannot serve as a common carrier like the phone network, allowing any party to reach any other. Without intelligent switching, it cannot provide personal communications nets that can follow you wherever you go. Without intelligent switching, the all-optical network—so they say—is just a glorified cable system.

These critics fail to grasp a central rule of the telecosm: bandwidth is a nearly perfect substitute for switching. With sufficient physical bandwidth, it is possible to simulate any kind of logical switch whatsoever. Bandwidth allows the creation of virtual switches that to the user seem to function exactly the way physical switches do. You can send all messages everywhere in the network, include all needed codes and instructions for correcting, decrypting and reading them, and allow each terminal to tune into its own messages on its own wavelength, just like a two-way radio. When the terminals are smart enough and the bandwidth great enough, physicist George Keyworth points out, your all-optical network can be "as dumb as a stone."

Over the last several years, all-optical network experiments have been conducted around the world, from Bellcore in New Jersey to NTT in Yokosuka, Japan. British Telecom has used wavelength-division multiplexing to link four telephone central offices in London. Columbia University's Telecom Research Center has launched Teranet, which lacks tunable lasers or receivers but can logically simulate them. Bell Labs has generated most of the technology and has experimented with networks in the laboratory but, as a long-distance specialist, has focused on the project of sending gigabits of information thousands of miles without amplifiers. The only fully functional system is the Rainbow I created by Paul Green's team at IBM.

As happens so often in this world of technical disciplines sliced into arbitrary fortes and fields, the large advances come from the integrators. Green is neither a laser physicist nor an optical engineer nor a telecommunications theorist. His work at IBM has ranged from overseeing speech-recognition projects at the Watson Research Center to shaping company strategy at corporate headquarters in Armonk. His most recent success was triggering the initial development of the new APPN (Advanced Peer-to-Peer Network) protocol. According to an IBM announcement in March, APPN will replace the venerable SNA (Systems Network Architecture) that has been synonymous with IBM networking for more than a decade.

Green took some pride in this announcement, but by that time the project was long in his past. He was finishing the copy editing on his magisterial tome, *Fiber Optic Networks* (published by Prentice Hall). And he was moving on to more advanced versions of the Rainbow, which he and his team had introduced in October 1991 at the Telecom 91 Conference in Geneva and which has been installed between the various branches of Watson Research Center.

As Peter Drucker points out, a new technology cannot displace an old one unless it is proven at least 10 times better. Otherwise the billions of dollars worth of installed base and thousands of engineers committed to improving the old technology will suffice to block the new one. The job of Green's eight-person team at IBM is to meet that tenfold test.

Green's all-optical network creates a fibersphere as neutral and passive as the atmosphere. It can be addressed by computers the same way radios and television sets connect to the air. Consisting entirely of unpowered glass and passive spitters and couplers, the fibersphere is dark and dumb. Any variety of terminals can interconnect across it at the same time using any protocols they choose.

Just as radios in the atmosphere, computer receivers connected to the fibersphere do not find a series of bits in a message; they tune into a wavelength or frequency. Because available Fabry Perot tunable filters today have a lower cost and a larger tuning range than tunable lasers, Green chose to locate Rainbow's tuning at the receiver and have each transmitter operate at a fixed wavelength. Future networks can use any combination of tunable equipment at either end.

When Green began the project in 1987, the industry stood in the same general position as the pioneers of radio did in the early years of that industry. They had seemingly unlimited bandwidth before them, but lacked transmitters and receivers powerful enough to use it effectively. Radio transmitters suffered "splitting losses" as they broadcast their signals across the countryside. Green's optical messages lose power every time they are split off to be sent to another terminal or are tapped by a receiver.

The radio industry solved this problem with the development of the audion triode amplifier. Green needed an all-optical amplifier to replace the optoelectronic repeaters that now constitute the most widespread electronic bottleneck in fiber. Amplifiers in current fiber networks first convert the optical signal to an electronic signal, enhance it and then convert it back to photons.

Like the pioneers of radio, Green soon had his amplifier in hand. Following concepts pioneered by David Payne at the University of Southampton in England, a Bell Laboratories group led by Emmanuel Desurvire and Randy Giles developed a workable all-optical device. They showed that a short stretch of fiber doped with erbium, a rare-earth mineral, and excited by a cheap laser diode can function as a powerful amplifier over the entire wavelength range of a 25,000-gigahertz system. Today, such photonic amplifiers enhance signals in a working system of links between Naples and Pomezia on the west coast of Italy. Manufactured in packages between two and three cubic inches in size, these amplifiers fit anywhere in an optical network for enhancing signals without electronics.

This invention overcame the most fundamental disadvantage of optical networks. You can tap into an electronic network as often as desired without weakening the voltage signal. Although resistance and capacitance will weaken the current, there are no splitting losses in a voltage divider. Photonic signals, by contrast, suffer splitting losses every time they are tapped; they lose photons until eventually there are none left. The cheap and compact all-optical amplifier solves this problem.

Not only did Green and his IBM colleagues create a working all-optical network, they also reduced the interface optoelectronics to a single microchannel plug-in card that can fit in any IBM PS/2-level personal computer or RS/6000 workstation. Using off-the-shelf components costing a total of $16,000 per station, Rainbow achieved a capacity more than 90 times greater than FDDI (Fiber Distributed Data Interface) at an initial cost merely four times as much.

Just as Jack Kilby's first ICs were not better than previous adders and oscillators, the Rainbow I is not better in some respects than rival networks based on electronics. At present it connects only 32 computers at a speed of some 300 megabits per second each, for a total bandwidth of 9.6 gigabits. This rate is huge compared with that of most other networks, but it is still well below the target of a system that provides gigabit rates for every terminal. More seriously, the tunable lasers and receivers currently switch too slowly for some supercomputer and mainframe applications accessing several programs at once in "packets."

A more serious limitation is the lack of packet switching. Rather than communicating down a dedicated connection between two parties, as phones do, computer networks send data in small batches, called packets, each bearing its own address. This requires switching back and forth between packets millions of times a second. Neither the current Rainbow's lasers nor its filters can tune from one message to another more than hundreds of times a second. This limitation is a serious problem for links to mainframes and supercomputers that may do many tasks at once in different windows on the screen and with connections to several other machines.

As Green shows, however, all these problems are well on the way to solution. A tide of new interest in all-optical systems is sweeping through the world's optical laboratories. The Pentagon's Defense Advanced Research Projects Agency (DARPA) has launched a program for all-optical networking. With Green installed as the new President of the IEEE

Communications Society, the technical journals are full of articles on new wavelength-division technology. Every few months brings new reports of a faster laser with a broader tuning range or a filter with faster tuning or an ingenious new way to use bandwidth to simulate packet switching. Today lasers and receivers can switch fast enough, but they still lack the ability to cover the entire 25,000-gigahertz bandwidth needed.

The key point, however, is that, as demonstrated both in Geneva and Westchester, the system showed the potential efficiency of all-optical systems. Even in their initial forms, they are more cost-effective in bandwidth per dollar than any other network technology. Scheduled for introduction later in the decade, Rainbow III will comprise 1,000 stations operating at 1 gigabit per second, with the increasingly likely hope of fast packet-switching capability. At that point, the system will be a compelling commercial product at least hundreds of times more cost-effective than the competition.

Without access to dark fiber, however, these networks will be all but worthless. If the telephone companies fail to supply it, they risk losing most of the fastest-growing parts of their business—the data traffic that will soon contribute some 50 percent of their profits.

THE CHALLENGE TO THE TELCOS

For the telephone companies, the age of ever smarter terminals mandates the emergence of ever dumber networks. This is a major strategic challenge: it takes a smart man to build a dumb network. But the telcos have the best laboratories and have already developed nearly all the components of the fibersphere.

Telephone companies may complain of the large costs of the transformation of their system, but they command capital budgets as large as the total revenues of the cable industry. Telcos may recoil in horror at the idea of dark fiber, but they command webs of the stuff 10 times larger than those commanded by any other industry. Dumb and dark networks may not fit the phone company self-image or advertising posture. But they promise larger markets than does the current phone company plan, which will choke off their future in the labyrinthine nets of an "intelligent switching fabric" that will always be behind schedule and full of software bugs.

The telephone companies cannot expect to impose a uniform network governed by universal protocols. The proliferation of digital protocols and interfaces is an inevitable effect of the Promethean creativity of the computer industry. IBM's Green explains, "You cannot fix the protocol zoo. You must use bandwidth to accommodate the zoo."

Robert Pokress, a former systems engineer at Bell Labs and now head of Unifi Corp., Burlington, Mass., points out that telephone switches—now 80 percent software in development costs—are already too complex to keep pace with the ever-changing computer technology on their periphery. While computers become ever more lean and mean—turning to reduced instruction set processors—networks need to adopt reduced instruction set architectures. The ultimate in dumb and dark is the fibersphere now incubating in the telcos' magnificent laboratories.

The entrepreneurial folk in the computer industry may view this wrenching phone company adjustment with some satisfaction. But the fact is that computer companies face a strategic reorientation as radical as the telcos do. In a world where ever smarter terminals require ever dumber communications, computer networks are as gorged and glutted with smarts as phone company networks, and even less capacious. The nation's most brilliant nerds, commanding the 200-MIPS Silicon Graphics superstations or Macintosh Quadra multimedia power plants, humbly kneel before the 50-kilobit lines of the Internet and beseech the telcos to upgrade to 64-kilobit basic ISDN (Integrated Services Digital Network).

Now addicted to the use of transistors to solve the problems of limited bandwidth, the computer industry must use transistors to exploit the opportunities of nearly unlimited bandwidth. When home-based machines are optimized for manipulating high-resolution digital video at high speeds, they will necessarily command what are now called super-computer powers. This will mean that the dominant computer technology will first emerge not in the office market but in the consumer market. The major challenge for the computer industry is to change its focus from a few hundred million offices already full of computer technology to a billion living rooms now nearly devoid of it.

Cable companies possess the advantage of already owning dumb networks based on the essentials of the all-optical model of broadcast and select—of customers seeking wavelengths or frequencies rather than switching circuits. Cable companies already provide all the programs to all the terminals and allow them to tune in to the desired messages. Uniquely in the world, U.S. cable firms already offer a broadband pipe to 90 percent of American homes. These coaxial cables, operating at 1 gigahertz for several hundred feet, provide the basis for two-way broadband services today. But the cable industry cannot become a full-service supplier of telecommunications until it changes its self-image from a cheap provider of one-way entertainment services into a common carrier of two-way information. Above all, the cable industry cannot succeed in the digital age if it continues to regard the personal computer as an alien and irrelevant machine.

MASSIVELY PARALLEL NETWORKS

Analogous to the integrated circuit in its economic power, the all-optical network is analogous to the massively parallel computer in its technical paradigm. In the late 1980s in computers, the effort to make one processor function ever faster on a serial stream of data reached a point of diminishing returns. Superpipelining and superscalar gains hit their limits. Despite experiments with Josephson Junctions, high electron mobility and cryogenics, usable transistors simply could not be made to switch much faster than a few gigahertz.

Computer architects responded by creating machines with multiple processors operating in parallel on multiple streams of data. While each processor worked more slowly than the fastest serial processors, thousands of slow processors in parallel could far outperform the fastest serial machines. Measured by cost-effectiveness, the massively parallel machines dwarfed the performance of conventional supercomputers.

The same pattern arose in communications, and for many of the same reasons. In the early 1990s the effort to increase the number of bits that could be time-division multiplexed down a fiber on a single frequency band had reached a point of diminishing returns. Again, the switching speed of transistors was the show-stopper. The architects of all-optical networks responded by creating systems that can use not one wavelength or frequency but potentially thousands in parallel.

Again, the new systems could not outperform time-division multiplexing on one frequency. But all-optical networks opened up a vast vista of some 75,000 gigahertz of frequencies potentially usable for communications. That immense potential of massively parallel frequencies left all methods of putting more bits on a single set of frequencies look as promising as launching computers into the chill of outer space in order to accelerate their switching speeds.

Just as the law of the microcosm made all terminals smart—distributing intelligence from the center to the edges of the network—so the law of the telecosm creates a network dumb enough to accommodate the incredible onrush of intelligence on its periphery. Indeed, with the one-chip supercomputer on the way, manufacturable for less than $100 toward the end of the decade, the law of the microcosm is still gaining momentum. The fibersphere complements the promise of ubiquitous computer power with equally ubiquitous communications.

What happens, however, when not only transistors but also wires are nearly free? As Robert Lucky observes in his forward to Paul Green's book, "Many of us have been conditioned to think that transmission is inherently expensive; that we should use switching and processing wherever possible to minimize transmission." This is the law of the microcosm. But as Lucky speculates, "The limitless bandwidth of fiberoptics changes these assumptions. Perhaps we should transmit signals thousands of miles to avoid even the simplest processing function." This is the law of the telecosm: use bandwidth to simplify everything else.

Daniel Hillis of Thinking Machines Corp., Cambridge, Mass., offers a similar vision, adding to Lucky's insight the further assertion that massively parallel computer architectures are so efficient that they can overthrow the personal computer revolution. Hillis envisages a power-plant computer model, with huge Thinking Machines at the center tapped by millions of relatively dumb terminals. All these speculations assume that the law of the telecosm usurps the law of the microcosm. But, in fact, the two concepts function in different ways in different domains.

Electronic transistors use electrons to control, amplify or switch electrons. But photonics differ radically from electronics. Because moving photons do not affect one another on contact, they cannot readily be used to control, amplify or switch each other. Unlike electrons, they cannot be trapped in a capacitor to serve as a memory. For computing, photons are far inferior to electrons. With single-electron electronics now in view, electrons will keep their advantage. For the foreseeable future, computers will be made with electrons.

What are crippling flaws for photonic computing, however, are huge assets for communicating. Because moving photons do not collide with each other or respond to electronic charges, they are inherently a multichannel medium. They are immune to lightning strikes, electromagnetic pulses or electrical power surges that destroy electronic equipment. Virtually noiseless and massless pulses of radiation, they move as fast and silently as light—they are light.

Listening to the technology, as Caltech prophet Carver Mead recommends, one sees a natural division of labor between photonics and electronics. Photonics will dominate communications and electronics will dominate computing. The two technologies do not compete; they are beautiful complements of each other.

The law of the microcosm makes distributed computers—smart terminals—more efficient regardless of the cost of linking them together. The law of the telecosm makes dumb and dark networks more efficient regardless of how numerous and smart are the terminals. Working together, however, these two laws of wires and switches impel ever more widely distributed information systems.

It is the narrow bandwidth of current phone company connections that explains the persistence of centralized computing in a world of distributed machines. Narrowband connections require smart interfaces, complex protocols and expensive data. Thus you get your on-line information from only a few databases set up to accommodate queries over the phone lines. You limit television broadcasting to a few local stations. Using the relatively narrowband phone network or television system, it pays to concentrate memory and processing at one point and tap into the hub from thousands of remote locations.

Using a broadband fiber system, by contrast, it will pay to distribute memory and services to all points on the network. Broadband links will foster specialization. If the costs of communications are low, databases, libraries and information services can specialize and be readily reached by customers from anywhere. On-line services lose the economies of scale that lead a service such as Knight-Ridder's Dialog to attempt to concentrate most of the world's information in one set of giant archives.

By making bandwidth nearly free, the new integrated circuit of the fibersphere will radically change the environment of all information industries and technologies. In all eras, companies tend to prevail by maximizing the use of the cheapest resources. In the age of the fibersphere, they will use the huge intrinsic bandwidth of fiber—all 25,000 gigahertz or more—to replace nearly all the hundreds of billions of dollars worth of switches, bridges, routers, converters, codecs, compressors, error correctors and other devices, together with the trillions of lines of software code, that pervade the intelligent switching fabric of both telephone and computer networks.

The makers of all this equipment will resist mightily. But there is no chance that the old regime can prevail by fighting cheap and simple optics with costly and complex electronics and software.

The all-optical network will triumph for the same reason that the integrated circuit triumphed: it is incomparably cheaper than the competition. Today, measured by the admittedly rough metric of MIPS per dollar, a personal computer is more than a thousand times more cost-effective than a mainframe. Within 10 years, the all-optical network will be millions of times more cost-effective than electronic networks. Just as the electron rules in computers, the photon will rule the waves of communication.

The all-optical ideal will not immediately usurp other technologies. Vacuum tubes reached their highest sales in the late 1970s. But just as the IC inexorably exerted its influence on all industries, the all-optical technology will impart constant pressure on all other communications systems. Every competing system will have to adapt to its cost structure. In the end, almost all electronic communications will go through the wringer and emerge in glass.

This is the real portent of the dark-fiber case wending its way through the courts. The future of the Information Age depends on the rise of dumb and dark networks to accommodate the onrush of ever smarter electronics. At stake is nothing less than the future of the computer and communications infrastructure of the U.S. economy, its competitiveness in world markets and the consummation of the Age of Information. Although the phone companies do not want to believe it, their future will be dark.

2

The New Rule of Wireless

At first glance, Vahak Hovnanian, a homebuilding tycoon in New Jersey, would seem an unlikely sort to be chasing rainbows. Yet in the converging realms of computers and communications that we call the telecosm, rainbows are less a matter of hue and weather than they are a metaphor for electromagnetism: the spectrum of wavelengths and frequencies used to build business in the Information Age.

An Armenian Christian from Iraq, Hovnanian ran a business building high-quality "affordable" housing. His first coup came on Labor Day in 1958 when, together with his three older brothers, he bought an apparently undesirable property near the waterfront in Tom's River for $20,000. From this modest beginning has arisen not only one of the nation's largest homebuilding enterprises (divided among the four immigrant brothers), but also a shattering breakthrough on some seemingly bleak frontiers of the electromagnetic spectrum. Together with maverick inventor Bernard Bossard, Hovnanian has launched a wireless cellular TV business in frequencies once thought usable only in outer space.

Perhaps the reason Hovnanian feels comfortable today pioneering on the shores of the telecosm is that some 35 years ago he was an engineer at Philco Semiconductor following in the theoretical steps of AT&T Bell Laboratories titan William Shockley. Shockley led the team that plunged into the microcosm of solid-state physics and invented the transistor. At the heart of all-digital electronics, this invention still reverberates through the world economy and imposes its centrifugal rules of enterprise.

This law of the microcosm dictates exponential rises in computer efficiency as transistors become smaller. It is this law that drives the bulk of the world's computations to ever-cheaper machines and pushes intelligence from the center to the fringes of all networks. Today the microcosm is converging with the telecosm and igniting a new series of industrial shocks and surprises.

The convergence of microcosm and telecosm in an array of multimedia industries—from personal intelligent communicators to video teleputers to digital films and publishing—is now the driving force of world economic growth. John Sculley, chairman and CEO of Apple Computer, has projected that by 2002 there will be a global business in multimedia totaling some $3.5 trillion—close to the size of the entire U.S. economy in the early 1980s.

This new world of computer communications will break down into two domains— the fibersphere and the atmosphere. The fibersphere is the domain of all-optical networks, with both communications power—bandwidth—and error rate improving by factors in the millions. In "Into the Fibersphere" (*Forbes ASAP*, December 7, 1992), we saw that the potential capacity for communications in the fibersphere is 1,000 times greater than all the currently used frequencies in the air—and so radically error-free that it mandates an entirely new model of wired telecommunications. Now we will discover that the atmosphere will offer links as mobile and ubiquitous as human beings are. It thus will force the creation of an entirely new model of wireless networks.

In one sense, Sculley's $3.5 trillion dream can be seen as the pot of gold at the end of Maxwell's rainbow. In 1865, in a visionary coup that the late Richard Feynman said would leave the American Civil War of the same decade as a mere "parochial footnote" by comparison, Scottish physicist James Clerk Maxwell discovered the electromagnetic spectrum. Encompassing nearly all the technologies imagined by Sculley, Maxwell's rainbow reaches from the extremely low frequencies (and gigantic wavelengths) used to communicate with submarines all the way through the frequencies used in radio, television and cellular phones, on up to the frequencies of infrared used in TV remotes and fiberoptics, and beyond that to visible and ultraviolet light and X-rays. In a fabulous feat of unification, Maxwell reduced the entire spectrum to just four equations in vector calculus. He showed that all such radiations move at the speed of light—in other words, the wavelength times the frequency equals the speed of light. These equations pulse at the heart of the information economy today.

Virtually all electromagnetic radiation can bear information, and the higher the frequencies, the more room they provide for bearing information. As a practical matter, however, communications engineers have aimed low, thronging the frequencies at the bottom of the spectrum, comprising far less than one percent of the total span.

The vast expansion of wireless communications forecast by Sculley, however, will require the use of higher frequencies far up Maxwell's rainbow. This means a return to the insights of another great man who walked the halls of Bell Labs in the late 1940s at the same time as future Nobel laureate William Shockley, and who left the world transformed in his wake.

In 1948, the same year that Shockley invented the transistor, Claude Shannon invented the information theory that underlies all modern communications. At first encounter, information theory is difficult for nonmathematicians, but computer and telecom executives need focus on only a few key themes. In defining how much information can be sent down a noisy channel, Shannon showed that engineers can choose between narrowband high-powered solutions and broadband low-powered solutions.

FROM LONG & STRONG TO WIDE & WEAK

Assuming that usable bandwidth is scarce and expensive, most wireless engineers have strived to economize on it. Just as you can get your message through in a crowded room by talking louder, you can overcome a noisy channel with more powerful signals. Engineers therefore have pursued a strategy of long and strong: long wavelengths and powerful transmissions with the scarce radio frequencies at the bottom of the spectrum.

Economizing on spectrum, scientists created mostly analog systems such as AM radios and televisions. Using every point on the wave to convey information and using high power to overcome noise and extend the range of signals the long and strong approach seemed hugely more efficient than digital systems requiring complex manipulation of long strings of on-off bits.

Ironically, however, the long and strong policy of economizing on spectrum led to using it all up. When everyone talks louder, no one can hear very well. Today, the favored regions at the bottom of the spectrum are so full of spectrum-hogging radios, pagers, phones, television, long-distance, point-to-point, aerospace and other uses that heavy-breathing experts speak of running out of "air."

Shannon's theories reveal the way out of this problem. In a counterintuitive and initially baffling redefinition of the nature of noise in a communications channel, Shannon showed that a flow of signals conveys information only to the extent that it provides unexpected data—only to the extent that it adds to what you already know. Another name for a stream of unexpected bits is noise. Termed Gaussian, or white, noise, such a transmission resembles random "white" light, which cloaks the entire rainbow of colors in a bright blur. Shannon showed that the more a transmission resembles this form of noise, the more information it can hold.

Shannon's alternative to long and strong is wide and weak: not fighting noise with electrical power but joining it with noiselike information, not talking louder but talking softer in more elaborate codes using more bandwidth. For example, in transmitting 40 megabits per second—the requirement for truly high-resolution images and sounds—Shannon showed some 45 years ago that using more bandwidth can lower the needed signal-to-noise ratio from a level of one million to one to a ratio of 30.6 to one. This huge gain comes merely from increasing the bandwidth of the signal from two megahertz (millions of cycles per second) to eight megahertz That means a 33,000-fold increase in communications efficiency in exchange for just a fourfold increase in bandwidth.

Such an explosion of efficiency radically limits the need to waste watts in order to overcome noise. More communications power comes from less electrical power. Thus, Shannon shows the way to fulfill Sculley's vision of universal low-powered wireless communications.

This vision of wide and weak is at the heart of the most promising technologies of today, from the advanced digital teleputer sets of American HDTV to ubiquitous mobile phones and computers in so-called personal communications networks (PCNs). Shannon's theories of the telecosm provide the basic science behind both Sculley's dream and Hovnanian's video spectrum breakthrough.

Shannon's world, however, is not nirvana, and there is no free lunch. Compensating for the exponential rise in communications power is an exponential rise in complexity. Larger bandwidths mean larger, more complex codes and exponentially rising burdens of computation for the decoding and error-correcting of messages. In previous decades, handling 40 megabits per second was simply out of the question with existing computer technology. For the last 30 years, this electronic bottleneck has blocked the vistas of efficient communication opened by Shannon's research.

In the 1990s, however, the problem of soaring complexity has met its match—and then some—in exponential gains of computer efficiency. Not only has the cost-effectiveness of microchip technology been doubling every 18 months but the pace of advance has been accelerating into the 1990s. Moreover, the chips central to digital communications—error correction, compression, coding and decoding—are digital signal processors. As we have seen, the cost effectiveness of DSPs has been increasing—in millions of computer instructions per second (MIPS) per dollar—some tenfold every two years.

This wild rush in DSPs will eventually converge with the precipitous plunge in price-performance ratios of general-purpose microprocessors. Led by Silicon Graphics' impending new TFP Cray supercomputer on a chip, Digital Equipment's Alpha AXP device and Hewlett Packard's Precision Architecture 7100, micros are moving beyond 100-megahertz clock rates. They are shifting from a regime of processing 32-bit words at a time to a regime of processing 64-bit words. This expands the total addressable memory by a factor of four billion. Together with increasing use of massively parallel DSP architectures, these gains will keep computers well ahead of the complexity problem in broadband communications.

What this means is that while complexity rises exponentially with bandwidth, computer efficiencies are rising even faster. The result is to open new vistas of spectrum in the atmosphere as dramatic as the gains of spectrum so far achieved in the fibersphere.

ATTACKING THROUGH THE AIR

Hovnanian's campaign into the spectrum began when a cable company announced one day in 1985 that under the Cable Act of 1984 and franchise rights granted by local governments, it had the right to wire one of his housing developments then under construction. Until that day, Hovnanian's own company could package cable with his homes through what are called satellite master antenna TV systems. In essence, each Hovnanian development had its own cable head end where programs are collected and sent out to subscribers.

When the cable company, now Monmouth Cable Vision, went to court and its claim was upheld by a judge, Hovnanian sought alternatives. First he flirted with the idea of having the phone company deliver compressed video to his homes. In 1986, in the era before FCC Commissioner Alfred Sikes, that was both illegal and impractical. Then he met

Bernard Bossard and decided to attack through the air. An early pioneer in microchips who had launched a semiconductor firm and eventually sold it to M/A COM, Bossard was familiar with both the soaring power of computers and the murky problems of broadband noise that have long restricted the air to a small number of broadcast AM TV stations.

Air delivery of cable television programming had long seemed unpromising. Not only was there too little spectrum available to compete with cable, but what spectrum there was, was guarded by the FCC and state public utilities commissions.

Nonetheless, in the early 1990s "wireless cable" did become a niche market, led by Microband Wireless Cable and rivals and imitators across the land. Using fragments of a frequency band between 2.5 and 2.7 gigahertz (billions of cycles per second), Microband, after some financial turmoil, now profitably broadcasts some 16 channels to 35,000 New York City homes in line of sight from the top of the Empire State Building. As long as they are restricted to a possible maximum of 200 megahertz and use AM, however, wireless firms will not long be able to compete with the cable industry. Cable companies offer an installed base of potential gigahertz connections and near universal coverage.

Having spent much of his life working with microwaves for satellites and the military, Bossard had a better idea. He claimed he could move up the spectrum and pioneer on frontiers of frequency between 27.5 and 29.5 gigahertz, previously used chiefly in outer space. That would mean he could command in the air some half a million times the communications power, or bandwidth, of typical copper telephone links, some ten times the bandwidth of existing wireless cable, some four times the bandwidth of the average cable industry coaxial connection, and twice the bandwidth of the most advanced cable systems.

The conventional wisdom was that these microwaves (above about 12 gigahertz) are useless for anything but point-to-point transmissions and are doubtful even for these. For radio communication, the prevailing folklore preferred frequencies that are cheap to transmit long distances and that can penetrate buildings and tunnels, bounce off the ionosphere or scuttle across continents along the surface of the earth. The higher the frequency, the less it can perform these feats essential to all broadcasting—and the less it can be sent long distances at all.

Moreover, it was believed, these millimeter-sized microwaves not only would fail to penetrate structures and other obstacles but would reflect off them and off particles in the air in a way that would cause hopeless mazes of multipath. Multipath would be translated into several images, i.e., ghosts, on the screen.

Finally, there was the real show-stopper. Everyone knew that these frequencies are microwaves. The key property of microwaves, as demonstrated in the now ubiquitous ovens, is absorption by water. Microwaves cook by exciting water molecules to a boil. Microwave towers are said to kill birds by irradiating their fluids. Microwave radar systems won't work in the rain. Mention microwaves as a possible solution to the spectrum shortage, and everyone—from editors at *Forbes* to gurus at Microsoft, from cable executives to Bell Labs researchers—laughs and tells you about the moisture problem.

So it was no surprise that when in 1986 Bossard went to M/A COM and other companies and financiers with his idea of TV broadcasting at 28 gigahertz, he was turned down flat. Amid much talk of potential "violations of the laws of physics," jokes about broiling pigeons and warnings of likely resistance from the FCC, he was spurned by all. In fairness to his detractors, Bossard had no license, patent or prototype at the time. But these holes in his plan did not deter Vahak Hovnanian and his son Shant from investing many millions of dollars in the project. It could be the best investment the Hovnanian tycoons ever made.

NEW RULE OF RADIO

For 35 years, the wireless communications industry has been inching up the spectrum, shifting slowly from long and strong wavelengths toward wide and weak bands of shorter wavelengths. Mobile phone services have moved from the 1950s radio systems using low FM frequencies near 100 megahertz, to the 1960s spectrum band of 450 megahertz, to the current cellular band of 900 megahertz accommodating more than 10 million cellular subscribers in the U.S.

During the 1990s, this trend will accelerate sharply. Accommodating hundreds of millions of users around the world, cellular communications will turn digital, leap up the spectrum and even move into video. Shannon's laws show that this will impel vast increases in the cost-effectiveness of communications.

In general, the new rule of radio is the shorter the transmission path, the better the system. Like transistors on semiconductor chips, transmitters are more efficient the more closely they are packed together. As Peter Huber writes in his masterly new book, *The Geodesic Network 2*, the new regime favors "geodesic networks," with radios intimately linked in tiny microcells. As in the law of the microcosm, the less the space, the more the room.

This rule turns the conventional wisdom of microwaves upside down. For example, it is true that microwaves don't travel far in the atmosphere. You don't want to use them to transmit 50,000 watts of Rush Limbaugh over 10 midwestern states, but to accommodate 200 million two-way communicators will require small cells; you don't want the waves to travel far. It is true that microwaves will not penetrate most buildings and other obstacles, but with lots of small cells, you don't want the waves to penetrate walls to adjacent offices.

Microwaves require high-power systems to transmit, but only if you want to send them long distances. Wattage at the receiver drops off in proportion to the fourth power of the distance from the transmitter. Reducing cell sizes as you move up the spectrum lowers power needs far more than higher frequencies increase them. Just as important, mobile systems must be small and light. The higher the frequency, the smaller the antenna and the lighter the system can be.

All this high-frequency gear once was prohibitively expensive. Any functions over two gigahertz require gallium arsenide chips, which are complex and costly. Yet the cost of gallium arsenide devices is dropping every day as their market expands. Meanwhile, laboratory teams are now tweaking microwaves out of silicon. In the world of electronics—where prices drop by a third with every doubling of accumulated sales—any ubiquitous product will soon be cheap.

The law of the telecosm dictates that the higher the frequency, the shorter the wavelength, the wider the bandwidth, the smaller the antenna, the slimmer the cell and ultimately, the cheaper and better the communication. The working of this law will render obsolete the entire idea of scarce spectrum and launch an era of advances in telecommunications comparable to the recent gains in computing. Transforming the computer and phone industries, the converging spirits of Maxwell, Shannon and Shockley even pose a serious challenge to the current revolutionaries in cellular telephony.

THE NEW PC REVOLUTION: PCN

Many observers herald the huge coming impact of wireless on the computer industry, and they are right. But this impact will be dwarfed by the impact of computers on wireless.

In personal communications networks (PCN), the cellular industry today is about to experience its own personal computer revolution. Just as the personal computer led to systems thousands of times more efficient in MIPS per dollar than the mainframes and minicomputers that preceded it, PCNS will bring an exponential plunge of costs. These networks will be based on microcells often measured in hundreds of meters rather than in tens of miles and will interlink smart digital appliances, draining power in milliwatts rather than dumb phones using watts. When the convulsion ends later this decade, this new digital cellular phone will stand as the world's most pervasive PC. As mobile as a watch and as personal as a wallet, these PICOs will recognize speech, navigate streets, take notes, keep schedules, collect mail, manage money, open the door and start the car, among other computer functions we cannot imagine today.

Like the computer establishment before it, current cellular providers often seem unprepared for this next computer revolution. They still live in a world of long and strong—high-powered systems at relatively low frequencies and with short-lived batteries—rather than in a PCN world of low-power systems at microwave frequencies and with batteries that last for days.

Ready or not, though, the revolution will happen anyway, and it will transform the landscape over the next five years. We can guess the pattern by considering the precedents. In computers, the revolution took 10 years. It began in 1977 when large centralized systems with attached dumb terminals commanded nearly 100 percent of the world's computer power and ended in 1987 with such large systems commanding less than one percent of the world's computer power. The pace of progress in digital electronics has accelerated sharply since the early 1980s. Remember yesterday, when digital signal processing (DSP)—the use of specialized computers to convert, compress, shape and shuffle digital signals in real time—constituted an exorbitant million-dollar obstacle to all-digital communications? Many current attitudes toward wireless stem from that time, which was some five years ago. Today, digital signal processors are the fastest-moving technology in all computing. Made on single chips or multichip modules, DSPs are increasing their cost-effectiveness tenfold every two years. As radio pioneer Donald Steinbrecher says, "That changes wireless from a radio business to a computer business."

Thus, we can expect the cellular telephone establishment to reach a crisis more quickly than the mainframe establishment did. The existing cellular infrastructure will persist for vehicular use.

As the intelligence in networks migrates to microcells, the networks themselves must become dumb. A complex network, loaded up with millions of lines of software code, cannot keep up with the efflorescent diversity and creativity among ever more intelligent digital devices on its periphery. This rule is true for the broadband wire links of fiber optics, as intelligent switching systems give way to passive all-optical networks. It is also true of cellular systems.

Nick Kauser, McCaw Cellular Communications' executive vice-president and chief of technology, faced this problem early in 1991 when the company decided to create a North American Cellular Network for transparent roaming throughout the regions of Cellular One. "The manufacturers always want to sell switches that do more and more. But complex switches take so long to program that you end up doing less and less," says Wayne Perry, McCaw vice-chairman. Each time Kauser tried to change software code in one of McCaw's Ericsson switches, it might have taken six months. Each time he wanted to add customer names above a 64,000 limit, Ericsson tried to persuade him to buy a new switch. The Ericsson switches, commented one McCaw engineer, offer a huge engine but a tiny gas tank. The problem is not peculiar to Ericsson, however; it is basic to the very idea of complex switch-based services on any supplier's equipment.

When McCaw voiced frustration, one of the regional Bell operating companies offered to take over the entire problem at a cost of some $200 million. Instead, Kauser created a Signaling System 7 (SS-7) network plus an intelligent database on four Tandem fault-tolerant computers, for some $15 million. Kauser maintains that the current services offered by North American Cellular could not be duplicated for 10 times that amount, if at all, in a switchbased system. Creating a dumb network and off-loading the intelligence on computer servers saved McCaw hundreds of millions of dollars.

The law of the microcosm is a centrifuge, inexorably pushing intelligence to the edges of networks. Telecom equipment suppliers can no more trap it in the central switch than IBM could monopolize it in mainframes.

Kauser should recognize that this rule applies to McCaw no less than to Ericsson. His large standardized systems with 30-mile cells and relatively dumb, high-powered phones resemble big proprietary mainframe networks. In the computer industry, these standardized architectures gave way to a mad proliferation of diverse personal computer nets restricted to small areas and interlinked by hubs and routers. The same pattern will develop in cellular.

COULD 'CHARLES' UPEND MCCAW?

Together with GTE and the regional Bell operating company cellular divisions, McCaw is now in the position of DEC in 1977. With its new ally, AT&T, McCaw is brilliantly attacking the mainframe establishment of the wireline phone companies. But the mainframe establishment of wires is not McCaw's real competition. Not stopping at central switches, the law of the microcosm is about to subvert the foundations of conventional cellular technology as well. Unless McCaw and the other cellular providers come to terms with the new PC networks that go by the name of PCNs, they will soon suffer the fate of the minicomputer firms of the last decade. McCaw could well be upended by its founder's original vision of his company—a PICO he called "Charles."

Just as in the computer industry in the late 1970s, the fight for the future is already underway. Complicating the conflict is the influence of European and Japanese forces protecting the past in the name of progress. Under pressure from EEC industrial politicians working with the guidance of engineers from Ericsson, the Europeans have adopted a new digital cellular system called Groupe Speciale Mobile (GSM) after the commission that conceived it. GSM is a very conservative digital system that multiplies the number of users in each cellular channel by a factor of three.

GSM uses an access method called time-division multiple access (TDMA). Suggestive of the time-sharing methods used by minicomputers and mainframes to accommodate large numbers of users on centralized computers, TDMA stems from the time-division multiplexing employed by phone companies around the world to put more than one phone call on each digital line. Thus, both the telephone and the computer establishments are comfortable with time division.

Under pressure from European firms eager to sell equipment in America, the U.S. Telephone Industry Association two years ago adopted a TDMA standard similar to the European GSM. Rather than creating a wholly new system exploiting the distributed powers of the computer revolution, the TIA favored a TDMA overlay on the existing analog infrastructure. Under the influence of Ericsson, McCaw and some of the RBOCs took the TDMA bait.

Thus, it was in the name of competitiveness and technological progress, and of keeping up with the Europeans and Japanese, that the U.S. moved to embrace an obsolescent cellular system. It made no difference that the Europeans and Japanese were technologically well in our wake. Just as in the earlier case of analog HDTV, however, the entrepreneurial creativity of the U.S. digital electronics industry is launching an array of compelling alternatives just in time.

Infusing cellular telephony with the full powers of wide and weak—combining Shannon's vision with computer advances—are two groups of engineers from MIT who spun out to launch new companies. Qualcomm Inc. of San Diego is led by former professor Irwin Jacobs and telecom pioneer Andrew Viterbi. A Shannon disciple whose eponymous algorithm is widely used in digital wire-line telephony, Viterbi now is leading an effort to transform digital wireless telephony. The other firm, Steinbrecher Corp., of

Woburn, Mass., is led by an inventor from the MIT Radio Astronomy Lab named Donald Steinbrecher.

Like Bernie Bossard and Vahak Hovnanian, the leaders of Qualcomm and Steinbrecher received the ultimate accolade for an innovator: They were all told their breakthroughs were impossible. Indeed, the leaders at Qualcomm were still contending that Steinbrecher's system would not work just weeks ago when PacTel pushed the two firms together. Now they provide the foundations for a radical new regime in distributed wireless computer telephony.

SIGNALS IN PSEUDONOISE

Ten years ago at Linkabit, the current leaders of Qualcomm conceived and patented the TDMA technology adopted as the U.S. standard by the Telephone Industry Association. Like analog HDTV, it was a powerful advance for its time. But even then, Viterbi and Jacobs were experimenting with a Shannonesque technology.

A classic example of the efficacy of wide and weak, CDMA exploits the resemblance between noise and information. The system began in the military as an effort to avoid jamming or air-tapping of combat messages. Qualcomm brings CDMA to the challenge of communications on the battlefronts of big-city cellular.

Rather than compressing each call into between three and 10 tiny TDMA time slots in a 30-kilohertz cellular channel, Qualcomm's CDMA spreads a signal across a comparatively huge 1.25-megahertz swath of the cellular spectrum. This allows many users to share the same spectrum space at one time. Each phone is programmed with a specific pseudonoise code, which is used to stretch a low-powered signal over a wide frequency band. The base station uses the same code in inverted form to "despread" and reconstitute the original signal. All other codes remain spread out, indistinguishable from background noise.

Jacobs compares TDMA and CDMA to different strategies of communication at a cocktail party. In the TDMA analogy, each person would restrict his or her talk to a specific time slot while everyone else remains silent. This system would work well as long as the party was managed by a dictator who controlled all conversations by complex rules and a rigid clock. In CDMA, on the other hand, everyone can talk at once but in different languages. Each person listens for messages in his or her own language or code and ignores all other sounds as background noise. Although this system allows each person to speak freely, it requires constant control of the volume of the speakers. A speaker who begins yelling can drown out surrounding messages and drastically reduce the total number of conversations that can be sustained.

For years, this problem of the stentorian guest crippled CDMA as a method of increasing the capacity of cellular systems. Spread spectrum had many military uses because its unlocalized signal and cryptic codes made it very difficult to jam or overhear. In a cellular environment, however, where cars continually move in and out from behind trucks, buildings and other obstacles, causing huge variations in power, CDMA systems would be regularly swamped by stentorian guests. Similarly, nearby cars would tend to dominate faraway vehicles. This was termed the near-far problem. When you compound this challenge with a static of multipath signals causing hundreds of 10,000-to-1 gyrations in power for every foot traveled by the mobile unit—so-called Rayleigh interference pits and spikes—you can comprehend the general incredulity toward CDMA among cellular cognoscenti. Indeed, as recently as 1991 leading experts at Bell Labs, Stanford University and Bell core confidently told me the problem was a show-stopper; it could not be overcome.

Radio experts, however, underestimate the power of the microcosm. Using digital signal processing, error correction and other microcosmic tools, wattage spikes and pits 100 times a second can be regulated by electronic circuitry that adjusts the power at a rate of more than 800 times a second.

To achieve this result, Qualcomm uses two layers of controls. First is a relatively crude top layer that employs the automatic gain control device on handsets to constantly adjust the power sent by the handset to the level of power received by it from the base station. This rough adjustment does not come near to solving the problem but it brings a solution into reach by using more complex and refined techniques.

In the second power-control step, the base station measures the handset's signal-to-noise and bit error ratios once every 1.25 milliseconds (800 times a second). Depending on whether these ratios are above or below a constantly recomputed threshold, the base station sends a positive or negative pulse, either raising or lowering the power some 25 percent.

DYNAMIC CELLS

Passing elaborate field tests with flying colors, this power-control mechanism has the further effect of dynamically changing the size of cells. In a congested cell, the power of all phones rises to overcome mutual interference. On the margin, these high-powered transmissions overflow into neighboring cells where they may be picked up by adjacent base station equipment. In a quiet cell, power is so low that the cell effectively shrinks, transmitting no interference at all to neighboring cells and improving their performance. This kind of dynamic adjustment of cell sizes is impossible in a TDMA system, where adjacent cells use completely different frequencies and fringe handsets may begin to chirp like Elmer Fudd.

Once the stentorian voice could be instantly abated, power control changed from a crippling weakness of CDMA into a commanding asset. Power usage is a major obstacle to the PCN future. All market tests show that either heavy or short-lived batteries greatly reduce the attractiveness of the system. Because the Qualcomm feedback system keeps power always at the lowest feasible level, batteries in CDMA phones actually are lasting far longer than in TDMA phones. CDMA phones transmit at an average of two milliwatts, compared with 600 milliwatts and higher for most other cellular systems.

A further advantage of wide and weak comes in handling multipath signals, which bounce off obstacles and arrive at different times at the receiver. Multipath just adds to the accuracy of CDMA. The Qualcomm system combines the three strongest signals into one. Called a rake receiver and coinvented by Paul Green, currently at IBM and author of *Fiber Optic Networks* (Prentice Hall, 1992), this combining function works even on signals from different cells and thus facilitates hand-offs. In TDMA, signals arriving at the wrong time are pure interference in someone else's time slot; in CDMA, they strengthen the message.

Finally, CDMA allows simple and soft hand-offs. Because all the phones are using the same spectrum space, moving from one cell to another is easy. CDMA avoids all the frequency juggling of TDMA systems as they shuffle calls among cells and time slots. As the era of PCN microcells approaches, this advantage will become increasingly crucial. Cellular systems that Spurn Qualcomm today may find themselves in a quagmire of TDMA microcells tomorrow. Together, all the gains from CDMA bring about a tenfold increase over current analog capacity. In wireless telephony above all, wide and weak will prevail.

Like any obsolescent scheme challenged by a real innovation—and like minicomputers and mainframes challenged by the PC—TDMA is being sharply improved by its proponents. The inventors of the Linkabit TDMA patents at Hughes and International Mobile Machines Corp. (IMMC) have introduced extended TDMA, claiming a 19-fold advance over current analog capacity. Showing a conventional cellular outlook, however, E-TDMA fatally adopts the idea of increasing capacity by lowering speech quality. This moves in exactly the wrong direction. PCN will not triumph through compromises based on a scarce-spectrum mentality. PCN Will multiply bandwidth to make the acoustics of digital cellular even better than the acoustics of wire-line phones, just as the acoustics of digital CDS far excel the acoustics of analog records.

Riding the microcosmic gains of digital signal processing, CDMA inherently offers greater room for improvement than TDMA does. Bringing the computer revolution to cellular telephony, CDMA at its essence replaces frequency shuffling with digital intelligence. Supplanting the multiple radios of TDMA—each with a fixed frequency are digital-signal-processing chips that find a particular message across a wide spectrum swath captured by one broad band radio.

With the advance in digital electronics, the advantage of CDMA continually increases. As the most compute-intensive system, CDMA gains most from the onrushing increases in the cost-effectiveness of semi-conductor electronics. Qualcomm recently announced that it has reduced all the digital signal processing for CDMA into one application-specific chip.

For all the indispensable advances of CDMA, however, Qualcomm cannot prevail alone. It brilliantly executes the move to digital codes, but proprietary mainframe computer networks are digital, too. As presently conceived, CDMA still aspires to be a cellular standard using the same mainframe architecture of mobile telephone switching offices that now serve the analog cellular system. In itself the Qualcomm solution does little to move cellular toward the ever cheaper, smaller and more open architectures that now dominate network computing and will shape PCN.

HEARING FEATHERS CRASH AMID HEAVY METAL

Consummating the PCN revolution—with its millions of microcells around the globe and its myriad digital devices and frequencies—will require a fundamental breakthrough in cellular radio technology. In the new Steinbrecher minicell introduced early this month at the Cellular Telephone Industry Association show, that breakthrough is at hand. The first true PC server for PCN, this small box ultimately costing a few thousand dollars will both replace and far outperform a 1,000-square-foot base station costing more than a million dollars.

Once again, in an entrepreneurial economy, crucial innovations come as an utter surprise to all the experts in the field. Donald Steinbrecher began in the Radio Astronomy Lab at MIT in the 1960s and early 1970s, creating receivers that could resolve a random cosmic ray among a mass of electromagnetic noise. This required radios with huge dynamic range—radios that could hear a feather drop at a heavy metal rock concert. He and his students solved this intractable problem by creating unique high-performance receivers and frequency "mixers." These could process huge spans of spectrum with immense variations of power and translate them without loss into intermediate frequencies. Then, computer systems convert the signals from analog to digital and analyze them with digital signal processors.

Moving out to begin his own company in 1973, Steinbrecher and his colleagues made several inventions in the fields of radar and digital signal analysis. At first, most of their customers were national security contractors in the intelligence field. For example, Steinbrecher supplied the radios for the ROTHR (remote over the horizon radar) systems that became famous for their role in the war against airborne drug traffic. Then in 1986, the company was asked if its equipment could work in the cellular band.

After cosmic rays and battlefield radar, the cellular band was easy. When he saw that the digital signal processors at the heart of his systems were dropping in price tenfold every two years, Steinbrecher knew that his esoteric radios could become a consumer product.

Translated to cellular, this technology opens entire new frontiers for wireless telephony. Rather than tuning into one fixed frequency as current cellular radios do, Steinbrecher's cells can use a high-dynamic-range digital radio to down-convert and digitize the entire cellular band. TDMA, CDMA, near or far, analog cellular, video, voice or data, in any combination, it makes no difference to the Steinbrecher system. His minicell converts them all at once to a digital bit stream. The DSPs take over from there, sorting out the TDMA and CDMA signals from the analog signals and reducing each to digital voice. To the extent the Steinbrecher system prevails, it would end the need for hybrid phones and make possible a phased shift to PCN or a variety of other digital services.

Hoping to use Qualcomm chipsets and other technology, Steinbrecher could facilitate the acceptance of CDMA. For CDMA, the minicell provides a new, far cheaper radio front end that offers further relief to the near-far problem and is open to the diverse codes and fast-moving technologies of PCN. For the current cellular architecture, however, Steinbrecher offers only creative destruction, doing for large base stations what the integrated circuit did for racks of vacuum tubes in old telephone switches.

In essence, the new minicell replaces a rigid structure of giant analog mainframes with a system of wireless local area networks. Reconciling a variety of codes and technologies, the Steinbrecher devices resemble the smart hubs and routers from SynOptics Communications and Cisco Systems that are transforming the world of wired computer networks.

Best of all, at a time when the computer industry is preparing a massive invasion of the air, these wide and weak radios can handle voice, data and even video at the same time. Further, by cheaply accommodating a move from scores of large base stations to scores of thousands of minicells per city—on poles, down alleys or in elevator shafts—the system fulfills the promise of the computer revolution as a spectrum multiplier. Since each new minicell can use all the frequencies currently used by a large cell site, the multiplication of cells achieves a similar multiplication of bandwidth.

Finally, the Steinbrecher receivers can accommodate the coming move into higher frequencies. Banishing once and for all the concept of spectrum scarcity, these high-dynamic-range receivers can already handle frequencies up to the "W band" of 90 gigahertz and more.

BOUNDLESS BANDWIDTH

The future of wireless communications is boundless bandwidth, accomplished through the Shannon strategy of wide and weak signals, moving to ever smaller cells with lower power at higher frequencies. The PCN systems made possible by Qualcomm and Steinbrecher apply this approach chiefly to voice and data. Recent announcements by Bossard and Hovnanian extend the concept to television video as well. Last December, they disclosed that their company, Cellular Vision, was already wirelessly delivering 49 cable television channels to 350 homes near Brighton Beach, Long Island, in the 28-gigahertz band. They declared a plan to soon sign up some 5,000 new customers a month all over New York.

Among engineers in cellular and cable firms, Cellular Vision evokes the same responses of incredulity and denial familiar at Qualcomm and Steinbrecher. Like them, Bossard is resolutely on the right side of the Shannon and Shockley divide. In answer to the multitude of qualms and objections and demurrals, all three companies cite the huge benefits of more bandwidth. Qualcomm can assign some 416 times as much bandwidth to each call as a current cellular or TDMA system. Steinbrecher's minicell receivers can process 4,160 times as much bandwidth as an analog cell site or TDMA radio.

Hovnanian achieves some 300 times the bandwidth of a broadcast TV station and some three times the bandwidth of even a typical cable head end. For Hovnanian's so-called multipoint local distribution system, the FCC has allocated a total of two gigahertz between 27.5 and 29.5 gigahertz—one gigahertz for TV and one gigahertz for experimental data and phone service. This large swath of spectrum allows Cellular Vision to substitute bandwidth for power. Using FM rather than the AM system of cable, Cellular

Vision gains the same kind of increased fidelity familiar in FM radio. Assigning 20 megahertz to each channel—three times the six megahertz of an analog system—Cellular Vision proves the potency of wide and weak by getting 20 decibels—some 10 times—more signal quality. These extra decibels come in handy in the rain.

With a radius of three miles, Cellular Vision cells are about 100 times smaller than telephone cells. Transmitting only 10 milliwatts per channel over a three-mile radius, the system gets far better signal-to-noise ratios than the three-watt radios of cellular phones or the multikilowatt systems of AM radio or television broadcasts. The millimeter wavelengths at 28 gigahertz allow narrowband highgain antennas that lock onto the right signal and isolate it from neighboring cells. At 28 gigahertz, small antennas command the performance of much larger ones (for example, a six-inch antenna at 28 gigahertz is equivalent to a three-foot antenna at 4 gigahertz or a 300-foot antenna at broadcast television frequencies).

In Brighton Beach the receiving antennas, using a fixed-phased-array technology, are just four inches square, and the transmitting antennas deliver 49 channels from a one-inch omnidirectional device on a box the size of a suitcase. Between cells, these transmitters can send programming and other information through a conventional point-to-point microwave link.

SINGING IN THE RAIN

So what happens in the rain? Well, it seems that Cellular Vision does better than conventional cable. When you have small cells in geodesic lowpower wireless networks using the full computational resources of modern microchips, you have plenty of extra decibels in your signal-to-noise budget to endure the most violent storms. Indeed, the 350 Brighton Beach customers of Cellular Vision received continuous service during the November 1992 near hurricane in New York, which brought floods that interrupted many cable networks for hours. One competitive advantage of Cellular Vision over cable seems to be less vulnerability to water.

Moving television radically toward the regime of wide and weak, Bossard and the Hovnanians have changed the dimensions of the air. However, they cannot escape the usual burdens of the innovator. Any drastic innovation must be some 10 times as good as what it replaces. Otherwise, the installed base, engineering momentum and customer loyalty of the incumbents will prevail against it.

Cellular Vision faces a wired cable system with some $18 billion in installed base. Already deploying fiber at a fast pace, cable companies plan to move within the next year toward digital compression schemes that increase capacity or resolution by a factor of between six and 10 (depending on the character of the programming). That means some 500 digital channels or more. TCI, the leading cable company, has ordered some one million cable converter and decompression boxes from General Instruments' Jerrold subsidiary for delivery late in 1993. In the U.S. cable industry, Hovnanian faces an aggressively moving target. Most cable experts doubt he can make much of a dent.

This view may be shortsighted. Clearly, Cellular Vision—and its likely imitators—can compete in the many areas with incompetent cable systems, in areas yet unreached by cable or in new projects launched by developers such as the Hovnanians. In the rest of the world, cable systems are rare. Cellular Vision is finding rich opportunities abroad, from Latvia to New Zealand. Most of all, as time passes, Cellular Vision might find itself increasingly well positioned for a world of untethered digital devices.

Such a cellular system could be adapted to mobile telephone or computer services. With a bit-error rate of one in 10 billion, it could theoretically transmit computer data without error correction. With one gigahertz of bandwidth, the system could function easily as a backbone for PCN applications, collecting calls from handsets operating at lower frequencies and passing them on to telephone or cellular central offices or to intelligent network facilities of the local phone companies.

The future local loop will combine telephone, teleputer and digital video services, together with speech recognition and other complex features, in patterns that will differ from neighborhood to neighborhood. Easily customizable from cell to cell, a system like Bossard's might well offer powerful advantages.

In an era of bandwidth abundance, the Negroponte switch—with voice pushed to the air and video onto wires—may well give way to this division between fibersphere and atmosphere. With the fibersphere offering virtually unlimited bandwidth for fixed communications over long distances, the local loop will be the bottleneck, thronged with millions of wireless devices. Under these conditions, a move to high-frequency cellular systems is imperative to carry the increasing floods of digital video overflowing from the fibersphere.

In any case, led by Qualcomm, Steinbrecher and Cellular Vision, a new generation of companies is emerging to challenge the assumptions and structures of the existing information economy. All these companies are recent startups, with innovations entirely unexpected by international standards bodies, university experts and government officials. They are the fruit of an entrepreneurial America, guided by the marketplace into the microcosm and telecosm.

WHY IMITATE EUROPEAN FAILURES?

Meanwhile, the European and Japanese experiences with government-guided strategies should give pause to proponents of similar policies here. Thirty years of expensive industrial policy targeting computers has left the Europeans with no significant computer firms at all. The Japanese have done better, but even they have been losing market share across the board to the U.S.

In the converging crescendos of advance in digital wireless telephony and computing, progress is surging far beyond all the regulatory maps and guidebooks of previous years.

If the entire capacity of the 28-gigahertz band, renewed every three miles, is open to telephony and video, bandwidth will be scarcely more limiting in wireless than it is in glass.

In this emerging world of boundless bandwidth, companies will prevail only by transcending the folklore of scarcity and embracing the full promise of the digital dawn. In an era of accelerating transition, the rule of success will be self-cannibalization. Wire-line phone companies are not truly profitable today; their reported earnings all spring from slow depreciation of installed plant and equipment that are fast becoming worthless. As George Calhoun of IMMC demonstrates in his superb new book, *Wireless Access and the Local Telephone Network* (Artech, 1992), new digital wireless connections are already less than one-third the cost of installing wire-line phones. For the RBOCS, aggressively attacking their own obsolescent enterprises is their only hope of prosperity.

As Joseph Schlosser of Coopers & Lybrand observes, self-cannibalization will not appear to be in the financial interests of the established firms; it will not prove out in net-present-value terms. There will be no studies to guarantee its success. Executives will have to earn their pay by going with their gut. As semiconductor and computer companies have already learned, phone and cable companies will discover that self-cannibalization is the only way to succeed in this era—the only way to stop others from capturing the heart of your business.

This is the lesson of the last decade. When Craig McCaw sold his cable properties and plunged into cellular telephony and $2 billion of Michael Milken's junk bond debt, there was no way to prove him right. Today AT&T is preparing to launch him as a rival to Bill Gates as the nation's richest man. Yet McCaw cannot rest on his laurels; the hour of the cannibal is at hand.

In theory, the transition should not be difficult for this resourceful and ingenious entrepreneur, who has long been a leading prophet of ubiquitous wireless phones and computers—his predicted personal digital assistant, "Charles." But a company that has paid billions for its 25-megahertz national swath of long and strong frequencies faces especially acute dilemmas in moving toward a regime of wide and weak. As a man—and company—that has made such transitions before, McCaw is favored by history and by AT&T. As a giant pillar of the new establishment, though, McCaw may find it as difficult to shift gears as did the computer establishment before him. The stakes are even higher. The next decade will see the emergence of fortunes in ever-changing transmutations of PCN, digital video, multimedia and wireless computers that dwarf the yields of cable and cellular. The window of opportunity opens wide and weak.

3

The Issaquah Miracle

In the spring of 1989 when Michael Bookey first visited the Middle School in Issaquah, Wash., to help the school system with its computers, he was reminded of his early ventures into Communist China. "After 20 years of working with computer networks, to enter Issaquah seemed to me like encountering an exotic tribe of primitives untouched by the modern world." The only sign of modern technology was a forlorn computer room full of Radio Shack TRS-80 machines, most of which had broken down.

Then he learned that as a remedy for this problem, the district had recently voted a levy of $2.7 million for outlays on "high technology." Lacking any better ideas, the school system had decided to distribute the money equally among the teachers, to spend as they wanted. What they wanted turned out to be VCRs, incompatible CD-ROM drives and a random selection of computers, printers and other gear to be scattered through the schools under the influence of a flock of computer salespeople attracted to the site by the pool of mandated money. To Bookey, this remedy seemed worse than the disease. It meant that the bulk of the money would be wasted, further estranging both taxpayers and students from the most powerful technologies of their era. Bookey wanted school officials to know that the most powerful technology is not computers, but computers joined in networks. Explaining the magic of networks, Bookey asks you to imagine a car plumped down in the jungle. Checking it out, you might find it a very useful piece of equipment indeed. A multipurpose wonder, it would supply lights, bedding, radio communications, tape player, heat, air conditioning, a shield against arrows and bullets, and a loud horn to frighten away fierce animals. In awe of the features of this machine, you might never realize that the real magic of a car comes in conjunction with asphalt.

For the first 10 years of the personal computer era, according to Bookey, we have used our computers like cars in the jungle. We have plumbed their powers for processing words and numbers. All too often, home computers have ended up in the closet unused. We have often failed to recognize that most of the magic of computing stems from the exponential benefits of interconnection.

In the microcosm, the interconnections come on individual chips, as ever smaller transistors crammed ever closer together work faster, cooler and cheaper, enhancing both the capability and the speed of the processor. The microcosm strewed some 100 million personal computers around the world and endowed individuals at workstations with the creative power of factory owners of the Industrial Age.

Just as the microcosm generates exponential gains from increasing connections on chips, the telecosm generates exponential gains by increasing connections *between* chips—powerful microcomputers in themselves. These links between increasingly potent microchips will soon dominate the world of communications. The networking industry therefore faces a drastic transition from a people-to-people regime to computer-to-computer. This change is so radical that it resembles a mutation that creates a new species.

People communicate in domains of time and space entirely alien to the world of computers. To a person, a one-second delay on a voice line seems hardly noticeable; to a computer, one second may mean a billion computations that would take hundreds of human lifetimes to accomplish by hand.

Most important, people can transmit or receive only a small stream of information at a time. They want relatively narrow bandwidth connections for a relatively long period—a 64-kilobit-per-second voice link, for example, for a 10-minute phone call. Computers, on the other hand, can handle hundreds of millions or even billions of bits a second. They often need many millions of bits of bandwidth for a short time—fractions of seconds.

As industry shifts from a human scale of time and space to a computer scale, the systems and structures in existing telephone and broadcast networks become almost irrelevant. Essentially, all other forms of networks—voice, text, video and sound—are rapidly giving way to various new forms of multimedia computer networks.

Driving this overwhelming force of change is the alchemy of interconnections, working in the telecosm with the same logic and feedback loops as connections in the microcosm. While dumb terminals such as phones and TVs use up bandwidth without giving anything back, computers are contributors to bandwidth, not consumers of it. In general, the more computers, the more bandwidth.

Not only is the network a resource for each new computer attached to it, but each new computer is also a resource for the network. Each new computer expands the potential switching and processing capacity of the system by a large multiple of the increasing demands it makes on other switches and processors. As ever more powerful computers are linked ever more closely, whether in digital cellular microcells or in webs of fiber and coaxial cable, usable bandwidth expands explosively.

Governing the expansion of networks, the law of the telecosm is just as potent as the law of the microcosm. Indeed, in enhancing the productivity of organizations, the telecosm consummates the microcosmic miracle.

MICROSOFT WINDOWS FOR JUNGLE CARS

The creator in the early 1970s of what may have been the world's first fully func tioning system of corporate electronic mail, Bookey was quick to foresee this radical shift from person-to-person to computer-to-computer communications. Pursuing his vision of networks, Bookey in 1982 spurned a possible job at Microsoft on the grounds that the company was outfitting cars for the jungle—a decision that probably cost him several million dollars. Instead, he joined Seafirst Bank in Seattle, where he made history (in the form of a reference in John Sculley's autobiography, *Odyssey*) by pushing the purchase of a thousand Macintosh computers for bank networks at a crucial time for Apple.

In 1986 Bookey left the bank to join Doelz Co., a startup in Irvine, Calif., that built advanced computer network equipment that he had used at Seafirst. For Doelz, Bookey designed software and spearheaded marketing. A so-called cell-based network, the Doelz system broke up a stream of data into short, equal-sized packets, each with its own address, to be sent through the nodes of the net in nanoseconds, like letters accelerated a trillionfold through the branches of the post office.

Bookey was not necessarily wrong in choosing this technology over Microsoft's. In the form of asynchronous transfer mode (ATM) systems, this essential approach, based on short, uniform packets that can be switched at gigabit speeds in hardware, is now the rage of planners in the computer networking industry. ATM is seen as the crucial enabler for digital networks combining voice, data and video in so-called multimedia applications. Bill Gates now calls multimedia the future of his industry.

Although many observers still see ATM as a futuristic technology, Bookey believes its future is nearly now. From the humblest personal digital phone to the most advanced supercomputer, computer-to-computer links will dominate the entire universe of telecommunications, and ATM will dominate network switching. Doelz, however, was ahead of its time and failed to survive a tangled legal imbroglio with AT&T in 1988.

So Bookey took a big profit on his California residence and returned with his wife Robin and daughter Erin to Seattle, where he had grown up and set records in the mile on the track at the University of Washington. He bought his dream house on the top of Cougar Mountain in Issaquah—with a view of the very Twin Peaks made famous in the television series—and put out his shingle as a network consultant under the name Digital Network Architects (DNA). Almost as an afterthought, the Bookeys sent Erin to Issaquah Middle School.

Having designed networks around the world, Bookey had often seen their powerful impact on business organizations, such as banks. Bookey believed that networks could have a similar revitalizing impact on schools. Like banks, schools are essentially information systems that have brought their Industrial Age hierarchy into the Information Age.

Creating networks in schools, however, posed many special problems. Most school systems, like Issaquah, were largely unaccustomed to managing technology. The system would need to create a large MIS (management information services) organization just to keep the network functioning.

Then, as the teachers at Issaquah hastened to point out to Bookey, there was the problem of students. Impulsive, mischievous and messy, they in no way resembled the disciplined employees of a corporation. Speaking from grim experience, some of the teachers told Bookey that his network plans would succeed only if the computers were reserved exclusively for teachers and if students were barred entirely.

Bookey, however, thought there had to be a way to bring the magic of networks to America's increasingly troubled school systems. The secret would be to recognize that, just as computers are not consumers of but contributors to bandwidth, students should be seen not as a problem—but as a precious resource in launching the networks that inform the Information Age.

NETWORKS AS PRODUCTIVITY ENGINES

Ever since Adam Smith first maintained that the division of labor, the spread of specialization, is the catalyst of the wealth of nations, economists have seen the breakdown of functions into subfunctions and specialties as the driver of efficiency and growth. The key force expanding specialization in the contemporary capitalist economy is networks. Indeed, networks, by their nature and purpose, refine the division of labor.

In the financial industry, for example, networks allowed the proliferation of specialized institutions. In the ever-shifting kaleidoscopes of American finance, some institutions went local, some global. Some managed car loans, credit cards or other consumer services; some handled mortgages, mutual funds or real estate trusts; still others stressed computer leases, junk bonds, venture capital or large corporate accounts.

The pell-mell fragmentation of American finance during the 1980s into an ever more refined division of labor enabled the U.S. to lead the world in levels of capital efficiency, with more economic growth per dollar of savings than any other country. Each financial business did not have to repeat all the work of all the rest, and each became more efficient at a particular task. Bookey believes that networks can have a similar effect on that other great information-processing industry: education.

Why should every school have an all-purpose library and a French teacher and a calculus scholar and a health center and an administrative office? Why should every school have an entire complement of buildings? With all the schools on networks, individual schools could specialize in particular subjects, functions and resources, as financial companies do. Education would not have to happen exclusively, or even mostly, in schools.

The explosive spread of networks is now the prime mover of the U.S. economy, allowing all industries to break down into patterns of specialization unbound by place and time.

And now the government wants to get into the act.

SUPERHIGHWAYS IN THE SKY

Zoom through tax-hike tollgates and glide out onto data superhighways—this is the new mantra of American industrial policy. Add the further fillip of investment for educational infrastructure and you can sweep up the ramp toward the federal treasury and drive out with a bonanza.

In this new era of the "big bands," there are now some 10 bills before Congress to foster vast new networks with large bandwidth, or communications capacity. Some $2 billion has already been authorized and $765 million appropriated this year for various programs related to a National Research and Educational Network (NREN). Candidate Bill Clinton presented the concept of NREN as "a national information network to link every home, business, lab, classroom and library by the year 2015." President Bill Clinton, vice-president Albert Gore and a raft of advisors all celebrate the highway as the metaphor for the future information economy. Gore points out that his father was a leader in building the Interstate Highway System in the early 1950s; Albert Jr., wants to play a key role in building the information highways of the 1990s.

Indeed, data superhighways would seem to be the fulfillment of the fibersphere—the way to create the vast new infrastructure of fiber-optic lines that will bring the full promise of digital video and multimedia communications to all citizens.

Why, then, is Mike Bookey so worried? He would seem to be the perfect NREN champion. Bookey has pursued networks through most of his career and now is focusing on networks for education. In explaining the importance of computer connections, he has even long used Gore's favored highway metaphor.

Bookey thinks that the federal superhighwaymen do not grasp the nature of networks and how they grow. "In systems work we have a rule: You design top down, but you build bottom up." Bookey sees the creation of networks as an organic process, driven by public demand, shaped by human needs and rooted in a moral universe of growth through sharing. It is the experience of building the network that creates the expertise to maintain and use it.

In all these processes, big government is nearly irrelevant.

NONE OF THE ABOVE

For the past 10 years, Washington, D.C. experts have been wringing their hands over the supposedly unbearable costs of building broadband networks and the urgent need for large federal funding. Analysts have been ruminating over the question of who would spearhead the creation of broadband nets—the phone companies, the cable television companies or the government.

Before any of these forces could act, however, it became clear that the answer would be none of the above. The hardest part of the job was accomplished, with astonishing speed, by computer and networking companies. The rest of the work is well under way, as cable and phone companies adopt the computer technologies.

As recently as 1989, only seven percent of America's personal computers were connected to local area networks. By 1991 45 percent were connected, and by 1993, close to two-thirds were linked to LANs. Growing even faster than LANs is the internetworking business: the interconnection of existing local area nets in wide area networks. Building internetworking gear or accessories, such companies as Cisco Systems, Cabletron, Wellfleet, 3Com and SynOptics are among the highest flyers in the technology stock market boom. Cisco, for example, is growing some 50 percent a year and commands a market value of almost $6 billion, comparable to that of Digital Equipment Corp. Cabletron has hiked its revenues some 16-fold in the last five years.

Most of these connections run at some 10 megabits per second, enough for high-resolution digital video but inadequate for the more exotic traffic in images predicted for use later in the decade. Increasingly, however, the connections are fiberoptic lines or are broadband coax, which is nearly as good as fiber for short-distance transport. The potential of fiber is almost unlimited (see "Into the Fibersphere," *Forbes ASAP*, December 7, 1992).

Although moving more slowly than the computer firms, telephone and cable companies are rushing to lay fiber ever deeper into the nation's neighborhoods. Spending some $2 billion (as much as NREN), Telecommunications Inc. (TCI) vows, according to CEO John Malone, to have 90 percent of its subscriber households served by fiber to the curb by 1995. Bringing fiber into the local loop at a slower pace, the telephone companies, led by Bell Atlantic, also are forging ahead with ingenious new ways to make their twisted-pair copper connections carry as much as six megabits per second of digital information. Wireless technology is also moving into the local loop for video delivery (see "New World Wireless," *Forbes ASAP*, March 29, 1993).

The U.S. networking industry is not in need of fixing. The U.S. currently commands some three-fourths of all the world's LANs and perhaps 85 percent of its internetworks. Although Gore and others justify their industrial policies by referring to the imperious plans of Japan, the U.S. currently commands about three times the computer power per capita as Japan, some 10 times as many computers attached to networks, and an installed base of broadband fiber and cable nearly 10 times as large.

The remarkable thing is that the U.S. government is so eager to fix a fabulously flourishing system that is the envy of the world. The electronic and photonic networking industries actually resemble highways in only the most superficial way. The highway construction trade has not advanced substantially in 50 years. By contrast, the networking trade is the fastest-moving part of the ever-accelerating computer industry and doubles its cost-effectiveness every year.

Although interconnecting government laboratories, contractors and supercomputer centers with fiber is desirable, a massive government network is not. Issaquah offers better guidance for the future. . . . But first it will be necessary to deal with the abiding menace of the student problem.

OVERCOMING THE STUDENT PROBLEM

"What do you think you are doing? Answer me," the voice insisted with the I've-got-you-squirming-now confidence of a teacher who has caught a pupil red-handed.

"Just lookin' around," grumbled Lee Dumas, the red-headed 13-year-old, trying to sound natural. Glimpsing a telltale red screen of network management among the array of blue displays used in the keyboarding class, the teacher had walked up silently behind Dumas as he broke into the student lists, software programs and grades, and was on the verge of entering the administrative server.

Dumas was a bad kid. No one at Maywood Middle School (one of the 16 campuses in Issaquah) doubted that. His teachers called him "obnoxious" or even "brain-dead." He set what he believes was an all-time record at Maywood by being detained after class some 60 times for insubordination. Using the approved psychobabble, he says, "I had problems with authority. I couldn't accept teachers ordering me around."

After being caught breaking into the computer system, Dumas was dragged up to the principal's office. Neither the teacher nor the principal could figure out the nature of the crime or judge its seriousness. For help, they summoned Don Robertson, the administrator assigned to Issaquah's Technology Information Project (TIP). He considered the situation gravely and recommended severe punishment. Toward the end of the meeting, however, he turned to Dumas and said, "With your talent, you should become the sheriff rather than the outlaw. Why don't you come down and join TIP?"

Since no one had previously detected any talent in Dumas, this comment made a sharp impression. About a week later, he showed up sheepishly at Robertson's door.

To school administrators, kids like Dumas might be a problem, but to Bookey, Issaquah's 9,000 students seemed a wonderfully cheap resource. By training the students to build and maintain the networks, he could make the $2.7 million the foundation of an enduring educational resource. In the end, the Issaquah network was almost entirely built by students between the ages of 12 and 17. Using students to solve the problems of network maintenance and support and thus reduce the real costs by some 80 percent was Mike Bookey's solution to the perplexing problem of computers in schools.

The first step in the Issaquah networking venture, in the spring of 1990, cost no money and arose from pure necessity. Just as in businesses across the country, the initial motive for networking was the arrival of laser printers from Hewlett Packard. Bookey began by giving his 10-person TIP team a pile of manuals and having them install a basic network connecting two PCs, an Apple II and a Macintosh to a laser printer. This step enhanced the value of all the computers at a small fraction of the cost of buying new dot-matrix printers for each.

Four of the ten students managed to cobble together the network in about a month. They learned the intricacies of pulling twisted-pair wiring for 10baseT Ethernet computer connections running at the standard rate of 10 million bits (megabits) per second. The next step was to add a hard disk containing school files and software programs.

Using both Apples and IBM PCs, the Issaquah network from the beginning, had to handle a variety of communications protocols. If the network was to connect to anything outside itself—to the school's administration building or the school system's libraries, for example—Issaquah would have to install equipment that could sort out messages from different computers. This meant Issaquah joined the market for multiprotocol routers. A router is a device that sits on a computer network and reads the addresses on all the message packets that pass by. If the address is on another network with a different protocol, the router creates a new envelope for the packet and sends it to the other network.

Nonetheless, with all their routers and Ethernet wiring, the Issaquah networks slowed to a crawl as soon as they had to connect outside a building. There, they had to depend on what is known as the Public Switched Telephone Network, where everything turns to analog and drowses down to some 2,400 bits per second.

Bookey demonstrated that the school could save money on its voice communications by buying a digital T-1 line that multiplexes 24 phone circuits onto a 1.544-megabit-per-second system. Since 12 of the 24 circuits would be enough to satisfy the school's internal voice needs, the rest of the T-1 line—some 760 kilobits per second—could be devoted to the data communications needs created by the school's new Ethernets. Thus, while getting a cheaper solution for its voice traffic, the school increased its data bandwidth by some sevenfold for free.

Once these connections were in place, the students acquired a Microsoft Mail program to incorporate E-mail in the system. Soon, this became the heart of the network, with both students and teachers using it constantly to handle papers, consult teachers in other schools in the system, make reports to the state and interact with parents and students. E-mail became so central to the functioning of Issaquah that when the computers were down teachers would talk of canceling classes.

To E-mail were added connections to Internet, the global research and education network launched some 33 years ago as DARPA Net (the Pentagon's Defense Advanced Research Projects Agency). Since Internet was civilianized in 1983, adopting the TCP/IP networking standard, it has been expanding its traffic at a pace of some 15 percent per month. Between 1981 and 1992 the number of computers connected to Internet rose from 281 to 1.1 million.

Through Internet, the students could search through a variety of databases for material for a paper or connect to Japan for help in learning Japanese. Along with several other Issaquah students, Aaron Woodman, Jr.—a burly boy with his long blonde hair in a ponytail—became so adept at using Internet that he now gives speeches to national conferences on the subject. The speechmaking needs that grew out of the Issaquah project have imparted valuable lessons in English communications for the students.

All these developments did not occur without administrative resistance. But the administration eventually became a prime beneficiary.

Soon, the computer networks in the Issaquah system were connected by a T-1 line to the Washington Schools Information Processing Cooperative (WSIPC) 20 miles north in Redmond, where attendance and other student records were kept for the entire state. To make these WSIPC services more readily available to schools across the state, Bookey proposed the creation of a statewide educational network running on T-3 lines (45 megabits per second), now known as WEDNET. This provides links all over Washington, from Shaw Island and Stehekin to Seattle and Issaquah, with a rogue line down to Portland, Oreg.

As for Lee Dumas, according to his mother, his situation has changed completely, "both in his attitude toward school and in the school's attitude toward him." After joining TIP, Dumas became one of its most active and enthusiastic members. Last summer, he got a job at the Computer Store in Seattle teaching the Macintosh HyperCard program to a student body consisting, yes, of public school teachers. According to Dumas, they had no problem accepting his authority as a fledgling computer guru.

No longer one of the outlaws, Dumas became an official beta tester for the new Microsoft DOS 6.0 and Windows NT operating systems, specializing in their security procedures. Following the path of another student who found the "Issaquah bug" in Microsoft's LAN Manager program, Dumas believes he found three or four bugs in NT.

Having just finished his sophomore year, Dumas has gone to work this summer at Microsoft for the company's network development chief, Brian Valentine, who regards this once brain-dead punk as a valued employee with high promise for the future. This student who floundered in the usual educational system flourished when his individual specialization was discovered. The Issaquah economy released his energies just as the national economy releases its own energies through the specialization and division of labor in computer networks.

Since there are millions of Lee Dumases in the schools of America—many of them being given up for lost by analysts such as Labor Secretary Robert Reich, because they are not adept at the usual curriculum for "symbolic analysts"—Dumas' redemption by technology bears crucial lessons. The lessons are Bookey's: Students are a resource, not a rabble; specialized practical experience is more edifying than most textbook learning; networks are the critical technology both for economic growth and for educational renewal. To these insights should be added Lewis Perelman's view, in his book "School's Out" (1992, Morrow), that teachers should increasingly abandon their role as a "sage on the stage" in favor of service as a "guide on the side," steering their students through a global cornucopia of educational resources.

EDUCATION AS A NETWORK DRIVER

It may seem peculiar that Bookey, a network guru for large corporations like U.S. West, should focus his attentions on such problems as interconnecting school children in Issaquah with libraries in Bellevue, parents on Squaw Mountain, teachers across town and administrators at the Washington State Information Processing Cooperative. Yet Bookey believes that the educational application may well drive the creation of a true national infrastructure of digital networks. The networking problems of schools closely resemble the networking problems of a nation full of diverse systems.

To achieve their full promise, school networks must link computers of many varieties owned by parents, students and teachers, to administrative servers owned by state and local governments, to printers, libraries and databases. School networks must connect LANs to IBM SNA (Systems Network Architecture) links, to a variety of telephone technologies, from T-1 lines of 1.5 megabits per second to T-3 lines at 45 megabits per second and, soon, to ATM switches and other potential gigabit systems. In all its dimensions, including an acute financial constraint, this challenge is altogether as difficult as interconnecting supercomputers over fiber in an NREN. Bookey relished this challenge at Issaquah.

Advocates of NREN might disparage Issaquah as a relatively low-grade network. After all, it currently has no fiber outside of the fiber links in the telephone network that it uses. Without fiber, the network will not be able to accommodate collaborative learning in multimedia forms across the country.

Bookey demurs. Buying a fiber-optic network before personal computer technology can manage broadband flows of data is premature. In five years, fiber-optic links will probably cost about one-fifth of what they cost today. When the network is needed, Issaquah will be able to purchase it and, more important, also use it. Moreover, TCI recently offered to install fiber throughout the Issaquah school system for nothing as part of its general program of fiber to the curb. The fact is that big-band technology will come to Issaquah in due course, with or without NREN money.

Critics, of course, will carp that Issaquah is a special case—a relatively rich community that could afford to levy $2.7 million for technology. Yet the Issaquah example is galvanizing schools across the state of Washington and even in California and Arkansas, where Bookey and his colleague Mason Conner have been consulting with education officials. Emulating Issaquah, other districts in Washington have since raised some $140 million for network ventures.

GLASS CEILING FOR NETWORKS?

The lesson of Issaquah is that data highways and superhighways, driven by the convergence of microcosm and telecosm, are indeed emerging in America, and at an astonishing pace. They already are revitalizing the economy and society, and are helping to reform the system of education. The only federal initiatives that will significantly assist the process are lower taxes, accommodation of Internet growth and use, and further deregulation of telecommunications.

Communication must begin locally, with access to the community. From these local roots can emerge the great branching systems that can interconnect an information economy. By starting from the top, the government risks paving over the pullulating fabric of networking enterprise with a glass ceiling of expensive and misplaced fiber.

In 1993 an estimated 37 million personal computers will be sold worldwide. The same forces that impelled the networks of Issaquah will drive the owners of these new PCs to interconnect them to other networks and will induce the owners of the networks to link them together. As the centrifugal force of the microcosm, multiplying and distributing intelligence through the world, converges with the integrating power of the telecosm, the exponential miracles of specialization and growth will gain new momentum.

How far can this spiral reach? Internet will soon approach some interesting limits. According to International Data Group, the number of users has risen from 9,800 in 1986, all in the United States, to 4.7 million around the world today. At this pace, Internet will embrace the entire world population by the year 2001. That's one limit. As the system's trunking backbone rises to 45 megabits per second on T-3 lines and above, the sky is the limit for the amount of message traffic. In the first month after the enlargement to T-3 lines in October 1992, usage rose from 3.5 trillion bytes to 4 trillion bytes.

All these networks are dominated by text and still pictures. But the miracles of Internet and Issaquah are about to be joined with a new miracle of growth in digital video connections in the local loop.

BOMBSHELL FROM TIME-WARNER

How soon can this happen? Advocates of NREN speak of this technology being consummated in 2015. But to most politicians and businessmen, a projected date more than five years ahead is essentially a synonym for never-never land—a way of saying, "Forget about it. I'll be retired."

The fact is that a widespread system of two-way broadband networks reaching most American homes, schools and offices is less than five years away. All U.S. business planners must come to terms with this transforming reality.

Announcements this spring from leading cable, telephone and computer companies—from TCI and U.S. West to IBM and Silicon Graphics—bring the shape of this network into clear focus. Exemplary among plans announced by a variety of firms is Time-Warner's projected system in Orlando.

As described by Jim Chiddix, the company's college-dropout technical guru, the Time-Warner showcase venture will be a giant client/server computer network, suggestive of the arrangements now ubiquitous in corporate computing. The wires will be a combination of fiber to the curb and coax to the home. Much of the system's hardware and software will be supplied by computer companies (allegedly including IBM and Silicon Graphics). The "client" computers will be digitized TVs or teleputers linked to powerful database computers that use a parallel-processing architecture to access hierarchical memory systems, from DRAM caches to optical disk archives. These memories will contain terabytes (trillions of bytes) of digital video movies, games, educational software and other programming.

Perhaps the most dramatic breakthrough, though, will come in the switches. While much of the computer and telephone world continues to dither about the future of ATM (many consigning it to the pits of 2015), Time-Warner is committed to installing ATM switches, built by AT&T, beginning next year in Orlando. The ATM system will allow Time-Warner to offer telephone, teleputer and multimedia services together, as soon as the regulators allow it. Chiddix predicts that ATM will soon gravitate to local area networks and ultimately become ubiquitous.

But the most portentous announcements of all have come from the telephone companies, who have the most to lose from this cable-oriented network design. Both U.S. West and Pacific Bell have disclosed that they are adopting a combination architecture of fiber and coaxial cable closely resembling the Time-Warner and TCI projects. This unexpected action by two leading Baby Bells of turning their backs on their millions of miles of twisted-pair copper wires shows both the boldness of the new telephone company leadership and the imperious power of this digital technology. From all sides the telecommunications and computer industries are converging on one essential configuration of advanced parallel-processing hardware, client/server database software and ATM switching.

As microcosm and telecosm converge in the living room, with interactive digital video and supercomputer image processing, the leading edge of the digital revolution moves from millions of offices toward billions of homes. Just as Michael Milken, then of Drexel Burnham Lambert, and the late William McGowan of MCI in 1983 rescued long-distance fiber optics from the never-never lands of the year 2015 to which AT&T had consigned it, John Malone of TCI, Gerald M. Levin of Time-Warner and Richard D. McCormick of U.S. West in 1993 have burst open the floodgates for fiber and ATM in the local loop.

Again, the force behind this revolutionary development was fierce business and technical rivalry in the marketplace. In the real world the ruling principle of network development is not imposed standardization by government but spontaneous order. It springs from the interplay of human creativity and entrepreneurship with the inexorable laws of physics and technology.

These dynamics of interconnection in the Information Age will continue well into the next century. The microcosm will yield chips containing billions of transistors, equivalent to scores of supercomputers on single slivers of silicon. The telecosm will yield bandwidth exploding into the terahertz of all-optical networks and the gigahertz of millimeter waves in the air.

Provided that rulers and regulators do not stifle this spiral of opportunity, the human spirit—emancipated and thus allowed to reach its rarest talents and aspirations—will continue to amaze the world with heroic surprises. The Issaquah miracle of Mike Bookey and Lee Dumas and all the others, and the continuing miracle of American networks, which was entirely unexpected by the world, will repeat themselves again and again in new forms of entrepreneurship and technology.

4

Metcalf's Law and Legacy

The world of networks breaks into two polar paradigms. Most familiar is the Public Switched Telephone Network. From the tiniest transistor flip-flop on a modem chip through labyrinthine layers of rising complexity on up to a 4ESS supercomputer switch linking 107,520 telephone trunk lines (itself consisting of millions of interconnected transistors), the public network is a vast, deterministic web of wires and switches. Once you are connected in the public network, your message is guaranteed to get through.

In the public network, bandwidth constantly expands as you rise in the hierarchy. At the bottom are the twisted-pair copper wires of your telephone that function at four kilohertz (thousands of cycles per second). At the top are fiberoptic trunk lines that function at rates close to the 2.9-gigahertz speeds of the electronic transistors that feed the glass wires. In *The Geodesic Network*, writer Peter Huber has described the five tiers of the telephone switching system as a structure with "the solidity, permanence and inflexibility of the Great Pyramid of Cheops, which on paper it resembled." Although the pyramid has suffered erosion and change in recent years, it remains mostly in place today: the public network pyramid.

That is one network paradigm. The other paradigm is Robert Metcalfe's. It germinated in his mind in 1970 as he read a paper by Norman Abramson of the University of Hawaii given at a computer conference that year. Abramson told of another paradigm. He called it Aloha. With Aloha, there were no guarantees.

AlohaNet was a packet radio system used for data communications among the Hawaiian Islands. Packets are collections of bits led by a header, which is a smaller collection of bits, bearing an address; they proceed through a communications system rather like envelopes through a postal system. The key feature of AlohaNet was that anyone could send packets to anyone else at any time. You just began transmitting. If you didn't get an acknowledgment back, you knew the message had failed to get through. Presumably your packets had collided with others. In Metcalfe's words, "They were lost in the ether."

At that point, you would simply wait a random period (to avoid a repeat collision as both parties returned to the channel at once). Then you would retransmit your message.

To Metcalfe, AlohaNet seemed a beautifully simple network. But Abramson showed that, because of collisions and other problems, it could exploit only 17 percent of its potential capacity. A student of computer science searching for thesis ideas, Metcalfe believed that by using a form of advanced mathematics called queuing theory he could drastically improve the performance of AlohaNet without damaging its essential elegance and simplicity. What Metcalfe, then a graduate student at Harvard, eventually discovered would bring such networks up toward 90 percent of capacity and make the Aloha concept a serious threat to the entire structure of the public network pyramid.

Metcalfe's discovery is known as Ethernet. Twenty years later, Ethernet is the world's dominant local area network and, at 47, Metcalfe is known and celebrated as its inventor. He was also founder in 1981 of 3Com Corp. of Santa Clara, Calif., the leading producer of Ethernet adapter cards and a major communications products company. In this era of networking, he is the author of what I will call Metcalfe's law of the telecosm, showing the magic of interconnections: connect any number, "n," of machines—whether computers, phones or even cars—and you get "n" squared potential value. Think of phones without networks or cars without roads. Conversely, imagine the benefits of linking up tens of millions of computers and sense the exponential power of the telecosm.

Indeed, the power of the telecosm reproduces on a larger scale—by interconnecting computers—the exponential yield of the microcosm, a law describing the near magical effect of interconnecting transistors on chips of silicon: As increasing numbers of transistors are packed ever closer together, the transistors run faster, cooler, cheaper and better. Metcalfe's law suggests that a similar spiral of gains is available in the telecosm of computer communications.

Already the world economy is beginning to reap these gains. Ethernet now links more than half of the world's 40 million networked computers, extending Metcalfe's paradigm and his law. Indeed, the law would suggest that in addition to his some $20 million of personal net worth from 3Com, Metcalfe's concept has fostered scores of billions of dollars in global wealth. Led by Novell Inc., with an equity capitalization of more than $8 billion, the top 15 publicly traded computer networking companies have a total market value of some $22 billion. Add to that sum the productivity value derived from the world's 100 million computers as they are increasingly linked in networks, and you may sense the power of the Metcalfe paradigm.

Today, 20 years after Metcalfe conceived it at Xerox's Palo Alto Research Center, Ethernet is still gathering momentum, gaining market share and generating innovations. Between 1989 and 1993, the percentage of America's computers on LANs rose from less than 10 to more than 60, and most of these gains were in Ethernets.

ETHER MOVES TO CABLE

The telecosm's powers could end up saving the American economy from itself. In an era when the new payroll taxes and regulations of Clintonomics could end up driving millions of mind workers back into their homes, Digital Equipment Corp. is now extending Ethernet's range from its current two-mile limit to some 70 miles. Called Channelworks, the DEC system can run Ethernet on the some 50 million miles of cable television coax. This will enable potential scores of millions of telecommuters to access their familiar office LAN, tap their company E-mail and their corporate databases, and generally make themselves feel at work while at home. Deployed at a profit and extended to customers at a flat monthly rate, Ethernet in the neighborhood could become a massive growth business for the cable industry over the next decade.

As Ethernet spreads and faces the challenge of remote work teams using digital images, simulations, maps, computer-assisted design schematics, visualizations, high-fidelity sounds and other exotic forms of data, the system is constantly adapting. From 3Com spin-offs Grand Junction Networks and LAN Media Corp. to smart hubmaker David Systems, from Kalpana to Synernetics, from National Semiconductor to Hewlett Packard, from Cabletron to SynOptics, from AT&T even to Token Ring leader IBM, scores of companies are pushing Ethernet into new functions and performance levels. It is emerging in full-duplex, multimedia, fast, fiberoptic, shielded, unshielded, twisted, thin, thick, hubbed, collapsed, vertebrate, invertebrate, baseband, broadband, pair, quartet, coaxial and wireless versions. It now can run at 2.9, 10, 20 and 100 megabits per second. It has moved from 2.9 megabits per second to 100 megabits per second and from a few hundred to several million users in some 10 years. At its present pace of progress, Ethernet will someday run isochronous (real-time) gigabits per second on linguine.

ALOHA, ATM, GUSHING CASH

So why is its boyish-looking inventor—over Metcalfe's anguished protests, think of Ted Kennedy some 10 years ago—giving up on his baby just as it enters its roaring 20s? Why is he ready to abandon his basic paradigm in favor of a return to the public network vision of massive, intelligent switching systems? Why is he now talking of Ethernet as a "legacy LAN"?

Discoursing this summer from a deck chair on his yacht (a converted lobster boat) as he breezed down from his Maine retreat to a dock on the Charles River for his 25th MIT reunion, Metcalfe has the air of an elder statesman. Though humbly grateful for the benisons of Ethernet, he has seen the future in a poll of experts prophesying the universal triumph of a powerful new switching system called asynchronous transfer mode (ATM). "I have found," Metcalfe solemnly intones, "an amazing consensus among both telephone industry and computer networking experts that ATM is the future of LANs." Aloha, ATM.

Metcalfe is not alone among Ethernet pioneers flocking back to Ma Bell's pyramid of switches. Also leaving Ethernet behind is his onetime nemesis, Leonard Kleinrock of UCLA, a leading guru of gigabit networks who helped define the mathematical limits of Ethernet, and is given credit (or is it blame?) for naming its Carrier Sense Multiple Access/Collision Detection protocol (CSMA/CD). Preparing to defect to ATM is Ronald Schmidt, the brilliantly ebullient technical director of SynOptics, who created the latest Ethernet rage—sending the signals over telephone wire under the 10baseT standard (10 megabits of baseband data over twisted pair).

There has not been such a stampede to a new standard since the global rush to ISDN (Integrated Services Digital Network) in the early 1980s. Offering digital phone lines at 144 kilobits per second, ISDN is just now coming on-line in time to be aced by the megabits per second of Ethernet over cable.

In a prophetic memo launching the concept in 1973, Metcalfe foreshadowed the secret of Ethernet's success. He wrote: "While we may end up using coaxial cable trees to carry our broadcast transmissions, it seems wise to talk in terms of an ether, rather than 'the cable'. . . . Who knows what other media will prove better than cable for a broadcast network: maybe radio or telephone circuits, or power wiring, or frequency-multiplexed cable TV or microwave environments, or even combinations thereof. The essential feature of our medium—the ether—is that it carries transmissions, propagates bits to all stations." In other words, it is the stations, rather than the network, that have to sort out and "switch" the messages.

The word Ethernet may be capitalized to signify the official standard of CSMA/CD. Or it may be lowercased to suggest a medium without switches, routers and other intelligence. In either case, the word "ether" conveys the essence of the ethernet. An ether is a passive, omnipresent, homogeneous medium. Long believed essential for the propagation of electromagnetic waves, the literal existence of an ether was disproven in the late 19th century by the famous experiments of Albert Michelson and Edward Morley. But the concept of a figurative ether—a dumb medium of propagation—survives in modern communications.

The enduring magic of ethernets stems from the law of the microcosm, favoring distributed terminals over centralized hierarchies, peer networks of PCs over mainframe pyramids. The microcosm's relentless price/performance gains on chips have endowed Metcalfe's peer-to-peer scheme with ever more powerful peers, at ever lower prices. Medium-independent from the outset, the Metcalfe systems do not require central switching. In an ethernet system the intelligence is entirely in the terminals, not in the network itself, and most of the bandwidth is local (where some 80 percent of traffic resides).

Although this ATM is expected to gush jackpots of cash for gaggles of network companies and investors, it is unrelated to its acronymic twin, automatic teller machines. Think of ATM rather as an automated postal center that takes messages (of any size or addressing scheme), chops them up, puts them into standardized little envelopes and figures the best routes to their destinations in billionths of a second. The magic of ATM comes from restricting its services to those uniform envelopes (called cells) of 53 bytes apiece (including a five-byte address) and creating for each envelope what is called a virtual circuit through the network. These features make it unnecessary for intermediate switches in the network to check the address; the cell flashes through the system on a precomputed course.

A compromise defined by phone companies as the longest packet size that can handle voice in real time, 53-byte cells are also short enough to be entirely routed and switched in cheap hardware; i.e., microchips. This means that the ATM postal center can function at speeds of up to 155 megabits per second or even higher. Perhaps most attractive of all, ATM can handle multimedia data, such as digital movies or teleconferences, with voice, text and video that must arrive together at the same time in perfect sync. As the world moves toward multimedia, the industry is flocking toward ATM, the innovation that can make it possible.

ETHERNET: A LEGACY LAN?

By contrast, Ethernet seems old and slow: the vacuum tube of computer communications. Think of it, crudely, as a system where all the messages are cast into the ocean and picked up by terminals on the beach which scan the tides for letters addressed to them. Obviously, this system would work only if the beach terminals could suck up and filter tremendous quantities of sea water. The magic of ethernet comes from the ever growing power of computer terminals. The microcosm supplies sufficiently powerful filtering chips—chiefly digital signal processors improving their powers some tenfold every two years—to sort mail and messages in the vasty deep. This is quite a trick. To the experts, it seems unlikely to prevail for long against the fabulously swift switching of ATM.

True, there is some confusion about just how, where and when this miracle cure will arrive. The industry's leading intellectual, Robert Lucky of Bellcore—a paragon of long-distance networks—predicts that ATM will come first in local area networks, while Metcalfe, of local area network fame, thinks it will come first in wide area networks. James Chiddix of Time-Warner Cable is probably right in predicting digital cable pay-per-view as the first big ATM customer, using it for broadcasting films in his 500-channel digital cable TV project in Orlando. But most experts agree that one way or another ATM will blow away Ethernet during the next decade or so.

Nonetheless, as usual, conventional wisdom is wrong. Ethernet is quietly preparing for a new era of hegemony in the marketplace for computer connections.

The reason Ethernet prevailed in the first place is that, in the words of Ronald Schmidt, "it was incredibly simple and elegant and robust." In other words, it is cheap and simple for the user. Customers can preserve their installed base of equipment while the network companies innovate with new transmission media. When the network moves to new kinds of copper wires or from one mode of fiber optics to another, Ethernet still looks essentially the same to the computers attached to it. Most of the processing—connecting the user to the network, sensing a carrier frequency on the wire and detecting collisions—can be done on one Ethernet controller chip that costs a few dollars.

As Metcalfe described the conception of this technology in 1981, "I explored the advantages of moving the transceiver down out of the ceiling onto the adapter board in the host computer. I had seen many actual Ethernet installations in which our brick transceivers were not up in the ceiling tapping into the ether cable, as they were supposed to be . . . but instead were on floors behind computers, dropped in the centers of neatly coiled transceiver cables. . . . We were discovering that the people buying personal computers and workstations in those days were not generally the same kind of people who were allowed to remove ceiling tiles and string cables through conduits. . . . The personal computer revolution was taking place in organizations from the bottom up. . . . It was time for Ethernet to be re-invented for bottom-up proliferation among the personal computer work group revolutionaries."

Using "silicon compiler" design tools to radically reduce the time to market, Seeq Technology created an Ethernet chip for PCs in time for a single-board version of the interface unit. Putting the transceiver on the adapter board eliminated a special transceiver cable and drastically simplified the system. There is no bulky connection between the coding device preparing information for the network and the transceiver sending or receiving the signals on the net. All this processing is done in the computer, on one printed circuit board, now reduced to the size of a credit card. While its rival from IBM—Token Ring—requires a mostly proprietary array of token-passing managers, clocking assignments and other complexities, Ethernet is an open system. Relative to the alternatives, it offers the possibility of something near plug-and-play. So advantaged, Ethernet has overcome IBM's Token Ring, 20 million nodes to 8 million in installed base.

But this does not persuade Ethernet pioneers Bob Metcalfe, Leonard Kleinrock and Ronald Schmidt. Because ATM can handle all kinds of data fast, Metcalfe sees it as the "grand unifier" bringing together WANs and LANs and effecting a convergence of television, telephony and computing in turbulent multimedia bit streams bursting into our lives early next century. "And of all the variations of multimedia," he writes in Infoworld—Metcalfe is now its publisher—"the one that will drive ATM is personal computer video conferencing—interactive, two-way, real-time, integrated digital voice, video and data." Although Ethernet will persist as a "legacy LAN," he says, it cannot compete with ATM in these crucial new roles. Schmidt makes the same essential case, stressing the need for switch-based architectures in a world of exotic new media.

KLEINROCK'S FORMULA

Why the pessimism on Ethernet? Bringing mathematics to bear on the argument, Kleinrock declares that the collision-detecting functions of Ethernet bog down with large bandwidths, short packets and long distances. Thus, the system must fail with the onset of fiber highways across the land. The oceans of Ethernet will simply grow too large to allow efficient detection of collisions in its depths. With large bandwidths, more packets can be pumped into the wire or glass before a collision is detected; by that time, most of the transmission is finished. When the distances get too long, collisions can occur far from the transmitting computer and take longer to be detected. The shorter the packets, the worse these problems become.

As Kleinrock computes these factors, the efficiency of Ethernet is roughly a function (a), computed as five times the length of the line in kilometers times the capacity of the system in megabits per second, divided by the packet size in bits. When a exceeds a certain level (Kleinrock sets it at 0.05), Ethernet's efficiency plummets.

With ATM packet sizes needed for voice traffic—or even at the minimum Ethernet packet size of 72 bytes—any Ethernet with a capacity much higher than 10 megabits per second exceeds this tipping point. Therefore, high-speed Ethernets must either use packets too long for voice or shrink in extent to far less than three kilometers. This is what Howard Charney's Grand Junction and its rival LAN Media propose with Fast Ethernet. Noticing that 10baseT hubs have reduced the length of Ethernet connections by a factor of 10, Ron Crane, founder of LAN Media, suggests that this change allows acceleration of the system by an equal amount: to 100 megabits per second.

But this seems a one-time fix that fails to address the multigigabit world of fiberoptics. At some point, Kleinrock, Schmidt and Metcalfe agree, ad hoc fixes will begin to fail and ATM (or possibly some other system) will begin to prevail. Using Kleinrock's formula, that point is here today, with 100-megabit-per-second Ethernet lines.

As an increasing share of network traffic takes the form of pictures, sounds, simulations, three-dimensional visualizations, collaborative work sessions, video teleconferences and high-resolution medical images, the Ethernet model already seems to be foundering, according to many expert projections. The triumph of ATM, so it would seem, is just a matter of time.

Time, however, is precisely what is absent from all these projections. Ethernet is a system based on the intelligence of terminals; ATM is a system based on the intelligence of switches and networks. All the arguments for ATM miss the law of the microcosm: the near annual doubling of chip densities, the spiraling increase of computer power surging on the fringes of all networks as transistor sizes plummet over the next decade.

THE POWER OF EXPONENTS

Amazingly, most technology prophets fail to come to terms with the power of exponents. You double anything annually for long—whether deforestation in ecological nightmares or transistors on silicon in the awesome routine of microchip progress—and you soon can ignite a sudden moment of metamorphosis: a denuded world or a silicon brain.

Shortly after the year 2000, semiconductor companies will begin manufacturing microchips with more than a billion transistors on them—first as memories, and soon after as processors. A billion transistors could accommodate the central processing units of 1,000 Sun workstations or 16 Cray supercomputers. This means roughly a millionfold rise in the cost-effectiveness of computing hardware over the next decade or so.

Intelligence in terminals is a substitute for intelligence in networks; switching and routing functions migrate from the center of the web to the increasingly powerful computers on its fringe. Looming intelligence on the edge of the network will relieve all the current problems attributed to ethernets and will render the neatly calculated optimizations of ATM irrelevant.

Meanwhile, the law of the telecosm is launching a similar spiral of performance in transmission media, ultimately increasing their bandwidth, also by a factor of millions. Bandwidth is a replacement for switches. If you can put enough detailed addressing, routing, prioritization and other information on the packets, you don't have to worry about channeling the data through ATM switches. The emergence of dumb, passive all-optical networks with bandwidths some ten-thousandfold larger than existing fiber optics will obviate much of the pressure on switches. Combining microcosm and telecosm in explosive convergence makes it nothing short of ridiculous to expect a system optimized for 1995 chip densities and fiber capacities to remain optimal in 2013, when Metcalfe foresees the final triumph of ATM, or even in 2001.

Of course, ATM will be useful in various applications before then. Sun and SynOptics envisage putting ATM ports in future workstations where ISDN ports mostly languish today. AT&T, MCI, Sprint and Wiltel will incorporate ATM switches in their long-distance networks. Time-Warner may indeed use them for distributing movies. In general, however, companies that rely on an apparent trend toward centralized switches will be disappointed.

Cable firms will do better by sticking to the ethernet paradigm of dumb bandwidth that has made them the envy of all in the emerging era of digital video. IBM and other computer firms with powerful ethernet and fiber technologies should not rush to adopt the public network paradigm. Telephone companies in particular should maintain an acute interest in their ongoing experiments with all-optical networks and other passive optical technologies. Any near-term successes of ATM, afflicted with the many glitches and growing pains of any new technology, are likely to come too slowly to deflect the continuing onrush of ethernets.

Ethernet prevails because it is dumb. In the old world of dumb terminals—whether phones, IBM displays or boob tubes—a network had to be smart. There was time even to put human operators into the loop, and a need to concentrate programming at one central location. But in the emerging world of supercomputers in your pocket or living room, networks will have to be dumb bandwidth pipes. What the coming array of desktop supercomputers and cheap massively parallel servers will need is passive dark fiber, mostly unlit by switching intelligence. Dark fiber can allow for the huge variety of data forms and functions, protocols and modulation schemes that is emerging in the new era of convergence between phones and computers.

Ethernet is the protocol for a dumb pipe, a passive ether. That is why it fits so well on a cable TV line and why it will fit even into the multigigabit world of a multimedia future.

THE RETURN OF ALOHA

The dumb networks of the fibersphere will be ethernets. These all-optical links that have been made possible by the creation of erbium-doped amplifiers and other passive devices give access to the full 25,000-gigahertz bandwidth of fiber optics (see "Into the Fibersphere," December 7, 1992). In these networks, fiber changes from a substitute for copper to a substitute for air. Just as the microcosm put entire computer systems on single slivers of silicon, the telecosm will put entire communications systems on seamless webs of silica. Terminals will tune into the infrared colors of the fibersphere like radios tuning into the frequencies of AM or FM.

As chips and fiber are hugely expanding their performance and bandwidth, information traffic is rapidly migrating from the wires to the air. Although many experts contend that the radio frequencies in the air—the electromagnetic spectrum—are running out, communications systems now use only a tiny sliver of spectrum, well under one percent of the usable span. As shown by Cellular Vision's success in sending cable TV signals over the air at 28 gigahertz, it is now possible to move up the spectrum into the vast domains of microwaves; other experiments show that network traffic in these portions of the spectrum can be accommodated with error rates of less than one in a billion, enough to avoid extensive error correcting.

At the same time, the replacement of today's 30-mile cells with tomorrow's closely packed microcells means an exponential rise in available spectrum and an exponential reduction in power usage. The replacement of analog systems with digital systems using code division multiple access (CDMA) will allow the reuse of all frequencies in every cell, thus further expanding available spectrum (see "New Rules of Wireless," March 29, 1993). A company called ArrayCom in Santa Clara, Calif., is developing a new system, called spatial division multiple access (SDMA), based on smart antennas that can follow an individual communicator as it moves through a cell. This technology would allow the use of all the available spectrum by each "phone."

BACK TO THE REAL "ETHER" NET

Inspired by a radio network, ethernet is well adapted for this new world of wireless. The increasing movement of data communications into the air—the real ether—will give new life to Metcalfe's media-independent system. Cellular systems already operate with protocols similar to CSMA/CD. As microcells fill up with digital wireless traffic, all networks will increasingly resemble the most popular computer networks. In the ether, links will resemble ethernets far more than ATMs.

The coming age of bandwidth abundance in glass and in air converges with an era of supercomputer powers in the sand of microchips. We should build our systems of the future—the cathedrals of the Information Age—on this foundation of sand. It will not disappoint us.

Whether in glass or in air, the basic protection of Ethernet is not smarts but statistics. Ethernet is a probabilistic system. This fact has caused endless confusion. Because a probabilistic system cannot guarantee delivery of data on a specific schedule, or at all, many experts have concluded that Ethernet is unsuited for critical functions, or for isochronous data inherent in multimedia—with voice and video that must arrive in real time. When and whether anything arrives is a stochastic matter.

Nonetheless, if there is enough bandwidth for the application, ethernets work just as reliably and well as their deterministic rivals, even for advanced video traffic. As Kleinrock observes, for many image applications, very long packets can be as effective as very short ones. The long packets become a virtual circuit connection, somewhat like a phone call. It is likely that perhaps 80 percent of all multimedia will be sent in burst mode, with a store-and-forward protocol, rather than isochronously in real time. Broadband ethernets will be better for burst mode than ATM's short packets.

In any case, the combination of intelligence at the terminals and statistics in the network is more robust than the mechanistic reliability of Token Rings or ATM switches. As Metcalfe points out in explaining the triumph of his vision over Token Ring, Ethernet is a simple system that is stabilized by its own failures. The CSMA/CD algorithm uses collision detection in a negative feedback loop that delays retransmission in exponential proportion to the number of collisions, which is a reliable index of the level of traffic. Thus thriving on a worst-case assumption of frequent failure, Ethernet has outpaced all rivals that guarantee perfect performance and depend on it.

METCALFE'S LAW: TRANSCENDING HIS OWN DOUBTS

Now, in ATM, Ethernet is faced with a new paragon of determinism offering high speeds and rigorous guarantees, a new version of the public network paradigm, a new pyramid of switching power. But Metcalfe's law and legacy may well win again, in spite of his own defection.

As Metcalfe explains, "Ethernet works in practice but not in theory." The same could be said of all the devices of the microcosm and telecosm. Both of the supreme sciences that sustain computer and communications technology—quantum theory and information theory—are based on probabilistic rather than deterministic models. They offer the underpinnings for an age of individual freedom and entrepreneurial creativity.

Humankind's constant search for deterministic assurance defies the ascendant science of the era, which finds nature itself as probabilistic. To Einstein's disappointment, God apparently does throw dice. But chance is the measure of human ignorance and the mark of divine knowledge. Chance thus is the paradoxical root of both fate and freedom.

Nations and networks can win by shunning determinism and finding stability in a constant shuffle of collisions and contentions in ever expanding arenas of liberty.

Because of an acceptance of setbacks, capitalist markets are more robust than socialist systems that plan for perfection. In the same way, successful people and companies have more failures than failures do. The successes use their faults and collisions as sources of new knowledge. Companies that try to banish chance by relying on market research and focus groups do less well than companies that freely make mistakes and learn from them.

Because of an ability to absorb shocks, stochastic systems in general are more stable than deterministic ones. Listening to the technology, we find that ethernets resonate to the deepest hymns and harmonies of our age.

5

Digital Dark Horse—Newspapers

Media mirror on the wall, who is the fairest of us all? The perennial question of all suitors of fate and fortune now whispers and resounds through conference resorts, executive retreats and consulting sessions across the land as business leaders from Hollywood to Wall Street pose with pundits and ponder the new world of converging technologies. Symbolized in a famous mandala by MIT's Media Lab, this grand fondue of information tools—to be served la carte on a flat-panel screen—is foreseen to be a $3.5 trillion feast for American business sometime early next century. Few would guess that crucial to the emerging mediamorphosis—as king of the flat panel—will be a slight, graying, bearded man with some 30 teddy bears, Roger Fidler.

Fidler coined the term mediamorphosis as the title of his forthcoming book. His office in Boulder, Colo., looks out on the panorama of a picturesque downtown of red brick and neo-Gothic, surrounded by the Rocky Mountain foothills and sepia sandstone buildings of a mile-high Silicon Valley. Down the hall is an Apple Computer media center which is developing graphical forms of AppleLink, the company's on-line network. Down the block is Cablelabs, John Malone's research arm, which is designing the future of the cable industry.

Roger Fidler, though, is a newspaperman, a veteran of some 32 years in a business little known for technology. Beginning as an 11-year-old paperboy in Eugene, Oreg., Fidler went on to serve as a reporter, science columnist and art director before launching what is now Knight-Ridder Tribune Graphics. A multimillion-dollar business and reliable profit center, this venture provides digital graphics for newspapers and video animations for TV stations across the country over a dedicated network called PressLink, also launched by Fidler. Now Fidler and his allies working in Knight-Ridder's Information Design Laboratory are concocting an audacious plan to make the lowly newspaper the spearhead of the information economy.

Most information companies and executives are betting on him to fail. Barry Diller, the former ruler of 20th Century Fox, recently circled the planet of technology on a celebrated pilgrimage from Hollywood to find where the money would be made in the new information economy. Shunning Fidler's little lab, he arrived at nearby Cablelabs and resolved on home shopping through cable TV. He bought into QVC for some $20 million and went into business with John Malone. After a more corporate investigation, featuring polls and customer surveys, Robert Allen of AT&T settled to a remarkable degree on the $14 billion market in electronic games. Since launching an alliance with Sega, AT&T has been collecting game companies as compulsively as your kid collects games. It has bought shares of Sierra Online, 3DO, Spectrum HoloByte and PF Magic.

Moving toward the news trade is IBM. But rather than collaborating with one of the thousands of newspapers that use its equipment, the computer giant is trysting with General Electric's NBC in a kind of elephants' waltz into the sunset of old broadcast media.

Most of these leaders in the new gold rush toward multimedia are getting it wrong. Fixated by market surveys that map demand for existing video, they are plunging down dead ends and cul-de-sacs with their eyes firmly focused on the luminous visions in their rearview mirrors. Blockbuster, Nintendo and other game and video vendors have good businesses, for the moment, but they are ballast from the past.

NEWS IN THE MICROCOSM

The leader who best comprehends the promise of the next phase in information technology may be Fidler of Knight-Ridder. A student of electronic technology, he has grasped an amazing and rather obscure fact: of all the information providers, only newspapers are fully in tune with the law of the microcosm.

Based on the constant rise in the computing power of individual microchips relative to systems of chips, the law of the microcosm dictates that power will continually devolve from centralized institutions, bureaucracies, computer architectures and databases into distributed systems. On the most obvious level, it caused the fall of the mainframe computer and the companies that depended upon it, and assured the ascent of personal computers and workstations. In the next decade, the law of the microcosm will assure the displacement of analog television, with its centralized networks and broadcast stations, by computer networks with no center at all. While offering a cornucopia of interactivity, computer networks can perform all the functions of TV.

With the cost-effectiveness of chips still doubling every 18 months, the law of the microcosm is not going away. Now it dictates that of all the many rivals to harvest the fruits of the information revolution, newspapers and magazines will prevail.

The secret of the success of the newspaper, grasped by Roger Fidler, is that it is in practice a personal medium, used very differently by each customer. Newspapers rely on the intelligence of the reader. Although the editors select and shape the matter to be delivered, readers choose, peruse, sort, queue and quaff the news and advertising copy at their own pace and volition.

In this regard, newspapers differ from television stations in much the way automobiles differ from trains. With the train (and the TV), you go to the station at the scheduled time and travel to the destinations determined from above. With the car (and the newspaper), you get in and go pretty much where you want when you want. Putting the decision-making power into the hands of the reader, the newspaper accords with the microcosmic model far better than TV does. Newspaper readers are not couch potatoes; they interact with the product, shaping it to their own ends.

Computers will soon blow away the broadcast television industry, but they pose no such threat to newspapers. Indeed, the computer is a perfect complement to the newspaper. It enables the existing news industry to deliver its product in real time. It hugely increases the quantity of information that can be made available, including archives, maps, charts and other supporting material. It opens the way to upgrading the news with full-screen photographs and videos. While hugely enhancing the richness and timeliness of the news, however, it empowers readers to use the "paper" in the same way they do today—to browse and select stories and advertisements at their own time and pace.

Until recently, the expense of computers restricted this complementarity to newsrooms and pressrooms. The news today is collected, edited, laid out and prepared for the press by advanced digital equipment. Reporters capture and remit their data in digital form. But the actual printing and distribution of the paper remain in the hands of printers and truckers.

Now the law of the microcosm has reduced the price of personal computers below the tag on a high-end TV and made them nearly coextensive with newspapers. Newspapers and computers are converging, while computers and televisions still represent radically different modes. It is the newspaper, therefore, not the TV, that is best fitted for the computer age.

Newspapers can be built on foundations of sand—the silicon and silica of microchips and telecom. Not only does the computer industry generate nearly three times the annual revenues of television but computer hardware sales are growing some eight times faster than the sales of television sets. By riding the tides of personal computer sales and usage, newspapers can shape the future of multimedia.

High-definition PC displays will benefit text far more than images. The resolution of current NTSC (National Television Standards Committee) analog television—62 dots per inch—is actually ample for most images, particularly the studio-quality forms that can be converted for digital delivery over fiberoptic lines. Even the conventional interlaced TV screen—in which alternate lines are filled in every second—easily fools the eye for video. But for fully readable text you need the 200 to 300 dots per inch of a laser printer or super-high-resolution screen. Such screens are now being developed. Overkill for most images, they could supply the first display tablets with screens as readable as paper.

FAT PANEL'S DIGITAL NEWSPAPER

After the "Rocky Mountain High" panorama, the first thing you see in Roger Fidler's office is a more modest tableau. At a round table in the corner is a huge teddy bear he calls Fat Panel. Fat Panel is poised to read a tablet that looks very much like a newspaper, but in fact is a flat-panel screen some nine inches wide, a foot high and a half-inch thick. Weighing a little over a pound, far less than the Sunday edition of your local newspaper, this device—call it a newspanel—might contain a trove of news, graphics, audio and even video, representing more than a year of Sunday papers. Through fiberoptic lines and radio links, it might connect to databases of news and entertainment from around the world.

On the face of this tablet is something that looks a lot like the page of a newspaper. It contains headlines for featured stories followed by their first few paragraphs and a jump to an inner page. The jump, unlike that in your usual newspaper, is electronic and immediate. You click an arrow with a pen or a mouse—or in the near future, say the word—and the rest of the story almost instantly appears. If your eyes are otherwise engaged, you can click on an audio icon and have the story read aloud to you.

Discreetly placed on the bottom of the panel are three sample ads. Since ads currently supply some 80 percent of the revenues of many newspapers and magazines, the entire system will rise and fall on the effectiveness of the ads. However, electronics promises a more total revolution in advertising than in any other facet of the newspaper outside of printing. This change comes none too soon. As shown by a general drop in margins from 30 percent in the mid-1980s to close to 10 percent last year, newspapers are suffering a sharp decline in conventional advertising revenues, only partly compensated for by an influx of funds from blow-in coupons and inserts.

In a 1988 prophecy at the American Press Institute in Reston, Va., Fidler envisaged electronic newspanel ads in the year 2000: "When you touch most ads, they suddenly come alive. More importantly, advertisers can deliver a variety of targeted messages that can be matched to each personal profile. An airline ad offering discount fares to South America attracts me with the haunting music of an Andean flute. I'm planning to take some vacation time in Peru next month [Fidler's wife is a Peruvian recording artist], so I touch the ad to get more information. Before I quit, I'll check the ad indexes to see if any other airlines are offering discount fares. With the built-in communicator, I can even make my reservations directly from the tablet if I choose. The airline's reservation telephone number is embedded in the ad, and my credit card numbers and other essential data are maintained in the tablet, so all I would have to do is write in the dates and times that I want to travel and touch a button on the screen. The information is encrypted as well as voice-print protected, so there is no risk of someone else placing orders with my tablet.

Contrary to the usual notion, the electronic newspaper will be a far more effective advertising medium than current newspapers, television or home shopping schemes. Rather than trying to trick the reader into watching the ad, the newspaper will merely present the ad in a part of the paper frequented by likely customers. Viewers who are seriously interested in the advertised item can click on it and open up a more detailed presentation, or they can advertise their own desire to buy a product of particular specifications.

In deference to Fidler, who currently combs the world looking for the best flat-panel screens, Fat Panel appears to be perusing a story on field emission displays (FEDs). Even cathode ray tubes with VGA graphics command only 72 dots per inch of resolution. This has been shown to slow down reading by some 25 percent compared with paper. Readers of Voyager Co.'s tomes on Mac PowerBooks quickly discover that even Susan Faludi's breezy *Backlash* or Michael Crichton's compulsive *Jurassic Park* or James Gleick's normally riveting biography of Richard Feynman bog down in subtle but insidious typographical fuzz. A newspaper with more than one item on the screen would be worse. The age of electronic text entirely depends on the development of screens with the definition of a laser printer. For this purpose, FEDs offer great long-term promise.

While the prevailing liquid crystal displays (LCDs) merely reflect or channel light, FEDs emit light like a cathode ray tube. Indeed, as currently envisaged by a Micron Display Technology process, FEDs will array millions of tiny cathode light emitters that allow bright displays with high resolution and full-motion video. Although today's FEDs require too much power for full portability with current battery technology, they represent an inviting option for newspaper tablets at the turn of the century.

Usable tablets, however, will arrive long before then. At the August Siggraph show, Xerox demonstrated a 13-inch-diagonal liquid crystal display with a record 6.3 million pixels, delivering 279 dots per inch of resolution. The 279 dots per inch provide some three times more definition than the screen of a Sun workstation—the current desktop graphics workhorse—and negligibly short of the 300-dot resolution of a laser printer.

Beyond resolution, the key to the newspaper tablet is portability. Portability means low power. Active-matrix LCDs are inherently a high-power, low-transmissive medium. The crystals absorb light; the polarizer wastes half the light; the transistors at each pixel squander power. For high contrast, backlighting is essential. That sinks another 20 to 30 watts. The higher the resolution, the worse all these problems become.

FULL-MOTION IMAGES OR FULL-MOTION USERS?

According to the Fidler vision, the U.S. should stop emulating the Japanese, who boldly invested some $12 billion in manufacturing capacity for power-hungry liquid crystal displays used on notebook computers and flat-screen TVs. Urged by the Clinton administration, this U.S. industrial policy is based on a strategy of "catch up and copy," and it will fail. Rather than chase the Japanese by achieving high resolution at high power to compete with cathode ray tubes, the U.S. should target high resolution at low power to compete with paper.

As in semiconductor electronics, the winners will follow a strategy of low and slow. The law of the microcosm ordains exponential performance gains from slower and lower-powered transistors packed ever closer together on individual microchips. Throughout the history of semiconductors—from the first transistor to the latest microprocessor—the industry has succeeded by following this law: replacing faster and higher-powered components with smaller, slower and lower-powered devices. When you pack enough of the slow and low transistors close enough together, your system may end up operating faster than a supercomputer based on the highest-powered and fastest discrete transistors. And it will definitely be more efficient in MIPS per dollar.

The law of the microcosm has not been suspended for displays. The Japanese have been focusing on high-powered screens capable of reproducing the features of low-end CRTs: full-motion color video. Rather than favoring full-motion video, however, the U.S.

should foster full-motion readers through low-powered and slow components. It is the people rather than the pixels that should be able to move. Speed will come in due course.

Demonstrating the first prototype of such a system is Zvi Yaniv of Advanced Technology Incubator (ATI) of Farmington Hills, Mich. Long among the most inventive figures in America's eternally embryonic flat-panel industry, Yaniv was a founder of Optical Imaging Systems, currently the leading U.S.-based producer, with well under one-percent global market share.

For his tablet, Yaniv uses a material invented at Kent State University in Ohio called Polymer Stabilized Cholesteric Texture (PSCT). On it he inscribes pixels in the form of helical liquid crystal devices. The helices are chemically doped to give them a specific reflectivity: showing all wavelengths or colors of light that do not match the resonant wavelengths in the helix.

So far ATI has demonstrated images in black and white and in 16 levels of gray scale. Color, according to Yaniv, poses no theoretical problems. Based on current experimental successes, it will be achieved within the next two years. For the first newspanels, however, color is less important than the high-resolution text capability, which ATI delivers at a breakthrough price.

This technology offers four key advantages over the active-matrix LCD: no transistors, no polarizers, no color filters, no backlighting. Without these power-and space-hungry features, Yaniv's screens can achieve higher density of pixels at far lower energy use. This adds up to far higher resolution at milliwatts of power (rather than 20 watts) and at far higher manufacturing yields, and thus far lower cost. Yaniv predicts screens with laser-printer resolution and with contrast higher than paper, costing between $1 and $2 per square inch (compared with around $10 for current active-matrix devices). That means 8-1/2-by-11-inch tablets for $100 to $200 in manufacturing cost, well under Fidler's target price.

Still an R&D project in an intensely competitive industry, ATI may not have all the answers, but it points the way to a solution. Within the next three or four years, a portable tablet with laser-printer resolution and contrast and with hundreds of megabytes of solid-state or hard disk memory will be purchasable for an acceptable price. Fat Panel's tablet is not merely a toy; it is the token of a technology that will sweep the world.

NEWS ON THE NET

Meanwhile, precusor solutions are being rolled out on personal computers, Newtons, Zoomers and other personal digital assistants. Already collecting and transmitting copy in digital form, reporters and editors could just as well provide digital content to all the other platforms that are emerging in the 1990s, from tiny portable personal communications services to supercomputer knowledge bases.

Also empowering the newspaper industry will be the exploding new world of boundless bandwidth or communications power in both the atmosphere and the fiber-sphere (see *Forbes ASAP*, December 7, 1992, and March 29, 1993). One of the most difficult concepts for many business planners to grasp is the onset of bandwidth abundance: the idea that the electromagnetic spectrum is not scarce but nearly limitless. The text of a daily newspaper takes up about a megabyte; a hundred or so black-and-white photographs take up about 100 megabytes; 25 color photos could run another 100 megabytes, or even a gigabyte, depending on resolution. Video clips would take about 100 megabytes apiece. With just 500 megabytes, you could throw in the entire "MacNeil/Lehrer News Hour."

Summing it all up, the total bit-cost of a paper, including video-rich ads, might be comparable to that of a two-hour movie—perhaps two gigabytes with compression. Two gigabytes can be transmitted in a second down fiberoptic lines, in perhaps 10 seconds down a gigahertz cable connection, and in perhaps a matter of three or four minutes down a twisted-pair copper line equipped with Asymmetrical Digital Subscriber Loop (ADSL) technology, Amati Corp.'s amazing new phone-company access system. From Digital Equipment Corp. and Zenith to Hybrid Technologies and Continental Cablevision, several firms are demonstrating impressive ways to use cable lines for two-way digital data transmission at a rate of 10 megabits a second or more, which would fill up a two-gigabyte newspanel in just over three minutes. Electrical power companies also are laying fiber along with their power lines. All these pipes are little used for long hours of the night and could be employed to deliver newspapers.

Complementing this web of wires will be wireless methods of delivery. Cellular technology is moving toward a code division multiple access (CDMA) protocol that allows use of the entire spectrum every mile or so, and toward millimeter wave frequencies that offer gigahertz of capacity. Again, access to these systems might be expensive on a demand basis, but a newspaper can be sent whenever space or time is available. Delivery of the basic paper through wires and fiber and delivery of short updates and extras via the air would be optimal. Whatever electronic or photonic techniques are used, the laws of the microcosm and telecosm ordain that distribution of newspapers will become vastly cheaper, more efficient and more timely than their present methods: trucks and bicycles.

THE "DOMONETICS" OF THE WORD

The future of newspapers will not depend on technology alone, however. The ultimate strength of the "press" comes not from its machinery but from its "domonetics"—a word that describes an institution's cultural sources and effects.

Judeo-Christian scripture declares that in the beginning was the word. There is no mention of the image. Today in information technology, the word still widely prevails. In 1992, trade publications, newspapers and magazines alone generated some $73 billion in sales, compared with television revenues of $57 billion.

In general, images are valuable as an enhancement to words. As Robert Lucky of Bellcore has pointed out, images are not in themselves usually an efficient mode of communication. In his definitive work *Silicon Dreams*, just released in a new paperback edition, Lucky writes that after an evening of television, "we sink into bed, bloated with pictorial bits, starved for information."

People who gush that a picture is worth a thousand words usually fail to point out that it may well take a million computer "words" to send or store it. Written words are a form of compression that has evolved over thousands of years of civilization. In a multimedia encyclopedia, such as Microsoft's Encarta, some 10,000 images take up 90 percent of the bits, but supply perhaps one-100th of the information. With the pictures alone, the encyclopedia is nearly worthless; with the words alone, you still have a valuable encyclopedia. Most of the work and the worth are in the words. Supremely the masters of words, newspapers can add cosmetic pictures, sounds and video clips far more easily than TV or game machines can add reporting depth, expertise, research and cogent opinion.

More profoundly, the domonetics of the new technologies strongly favors text-based communications. Video is most effective in conveying shocks and sensations and appealing to prurient interests of large miscellaneous audiences. Images easily excel in blasting through to the glandular substrates of the human community; there's nothing like a body naked or bloody or both to arrest the eye and forestall the TV zapper.

TV news succeeds because of timeliness and vividness. Compared with TV imagery, news photos tend to be late and lame. Nonetheless, for all its power and influence, broadcast television news is a dead medium, awaiting early burial by newspapers using new technologies.

The TV news problem is summed up by the two-minute rule—the usual requirement that, short of earthquake or war, no story take more than two minutes to tell. This rule even applies to the epitome of broadcast news—CNN. It is entirely a negative rule. The reason for it is not that the audience desires no more than two minutes of coverage of stories of interest. On any matter deeply interesting to the viewer, two minutes is much too little.

The rationale for the two-minute rule is that the viewer will not tolerate more than two minutes of an unwanted story. Its only function is to forestall the zapper, but its effect is to frustrate any viewer with more than a superficial interest in a story. Increasingly it reduces TV news to a kaleidoscope of shocks and sensations, portents and propaganda, gossip and titillation.

The new technologies, however, put individual customers in command. Making their own first choices among scores of thousands of possibilities, individuals eschew the hair-trigger poise of the channel surfer. Narrowcasting allows appeal to the special interests and ambitions, the hobbies and curiosities, the career pursuits and learning needs of particular individuals. Thus, the new media open up domonetic vistas entirely missed by mass media.

At the domonetic elevation of newspapers, images are supplementary, not primary. The new technologies thus favor text over pure video because text—enhanced by graphics where needed—is by far the best (and digitally most efficient) way to convey most information and ideas. Where graphics are overwhelmingly more efficient than alphanumerics—as in visualization of huge bodies of data or statistics—the newspanel can supply true computer graphics and simulations. Interactivity, after all, is the computer's forte.

THE $700 MILLION INCENTIVE

As early as 1981, Fidler saw and predicted that computer technology using flat-panel screens would allow the newspaper business to eliminate much of its centralized manufacturing and printing plant and much of its distribution expenses, and deliver the product directly to the customer at half the cost. He saw that this process would jeopardize neither the branded identity nor the editing functions nor the essential character of the paper. The distribution of intelligence would simply permit the customer rather than the newspaper to supply the display and the printer. This microcosmic shift would drastically simplify and improve the accessibility and worth of the information, enhancing the value of newspaper archives and other resources. This step could theoretically save Fidler's employer, Knight-Ridder, some $700 million, or between half and two-thirds of its current costs.

Fidler's vision is just as promising for magazines. In effect, his concept allows newspapers to combine the best features of daily journalism with the best qualities of specialty magazines. The front pages and shallower levels of the system will still function like a streamlined newspaper, which readers can browse, search and explore as they do a conventional paper without thrashing about through the pages. The deeper levels will function like magazines, focusing on business, technology, lifestyles, sports, religion or art. Indeed, to exalt their offerings into an ever richer cornucopia, news systems will want to collaborate with magazines, just as they often distribute magazines today with their Sunday papers.

THE SOUL OF THE NEW MEDIUM

In addition, electronic magazines can excel newspapers in providing a sense of community through interaction with other readers and authors in new kinds of dynamic letters, bulletin boards and classified sections. In a sense, the news panel never ends. Beyond its offering of news, articles and archives, it opens into new dimensions of interactivity.

As Stephen Case puts it: "Everybody will become information providers as well as consumers. The challenge is to create electronic communities that marry information and communications—thereby creating an interactive, participatory medium. This community aspect is crucial—it is the soul of the new medium."

The most practical current vessel for this expansion of the press is Case's own company, America Online, a supplier of an icon-based interface and gateway to scores of "infobases" and bulletin boards in Vienna, Va., outside the District of Columbia. Ten percent owned by the Tribune Co. of Chicago, eight percent controlled by Apple, allied with Knight-Ridder and providing access to such journals as the *New Republic*, *National Geographic*, *Time* and *Macworld*, America Online has uniquely focused on the vital center of the new market: the point of convergence of newspapers, magazines and computers in new communities of interest and interaction.

Following this strategy, America Online has invested just $20 million (one-100th the capital of Prodigy) and devoted half the time, to achieve nearly one-third the customer base and generate strong profits, in contrast to huge estimated losses on the part of IBM and Sears. Prodigy is now paying AOL the high tribute of imitation, making deals with Cox Enterprises Inc. and its 17 newspapers, and with Times-Mirror. Perhaps most audacious in pursuing this vision, however, is Murdoch's News Corp. Ltd., which recently purchased Delphi Internet Services Corp., the only on-line service with full Internet access to home PC users. Delphi already offers an array of news programs and special-interest conferences, including a popular computer news show led by moderator Jerry Pournelle that provides interactive dialogs on everything from abstruse computer features to science fiction. Pournelle and some 300 other conference moderators can function like editors in cyberspace.

Internet is the global agglomeration of data networks that has emerged from the original Pentagon research network called ARPANET. Growing at some 15 percent a month for several years to a current level of 10 to 20 million users, Internet has bifurcated into linked commercial and research nonprofit divisions. As John Evans, president of News Corp.'s Electronic Data, puts it, explaining the Delphi purchase: "Internet is like a giant jellyfish. You can't step on it. You can't go around it. You've got to go through it." Delphi now plans to go through it using much quicker access systems, including cable.

Evans declares that these new collaborations between News Corp. and Internet will "put the 'me' back into media." His concept, also shared by Nicholas Negroponte's Media Lab and Apple Computer's Knowledge Navigator, is an automated news database ultimately supplying the customer with a personal paper filtered from floods of daily information by an agent programmed to pursue your own interests. In Fidler's view, however, these digital papers will succeed only to the extent that they transcend this vision of the Daily Me.

Fidler prefers the vision of a Daily Us, shaped by human editors rather than by electronic agents or filters. According to Fidler, the law of the microcosm will put so much intelligence and storage in the tablet that the individual can personalize the "paper" every day in a different way. If, as Case puts it, the soul of the new medium is community, the reader will want to begin in a particular context, a specially favored "place" in the world of information, a place with a brand name and identity: a newspaper.

THE COMPUTER IMPERATIVE

Above all, the key to the special advantage of newspapers in the new era is their great good fortune in being forced to focus on computers. It should be evident by now to everyone in the information business that the energy, the creativity, the drive, the gusto, the pulse, the catalyst of this industry is computers. The magic is in the microcosm of solid-state electronics (doubling the density of components on a chip every 18 months) and in the concentric circles of enterprise and invention that surge outward from this creative core: the some 5,000 software firms, the thousands of manufacturers of chips, peripherals, printed circuit boards and add-on cards; the double-digit annual expansion in the armies of computer scientists and software engineers; the ever growing millions of PC owners devoting their creative energies and passions to this intoxicating machine.

What the Model T was to the industrial era—the teenage training board, the tinkerer's love and laboratory, the technological epitome-the PC is to the Information Age. Just as people who rode the wave of automobile technology-from tiremakers to fast-food franchisers—prevailed in the industrial era, so the firms that prey on the passion and feed on the force of the computer community will predominate in the information era.

Why, then, are so many apparently ambitious and visionary executives shrinking from the central arena to play around on the fringes with TVs and game machines? Why are American computer executives standing silently aside while the so-called U.S. Grand Alliance for the Future of Advanced Television, so-called digital HDTV, adopts an interlaced screen technology that is fundamentally hostile to computers?

For images, the human eye cannot tell the difference between interlaced and progressively scanned displays. But interlace poses endless problems for text and multimedia. Apart from Zenith, the American leaders in the Grand Alliance are AT&T, General Instrument Corp., MIT, Sarnoff Laboratories and GE-NBC. All but MIT capitulated to pressure from foreign TV interests such as Sony, Thomson Corp. and Philips Electronics to betray the American computer and newspaper industries by adopting a display scheme unsuited for the multimedia and text programs central to the next computer revolution.

Without text and multimedia capabilities, high-resolution images can open virtually no markets not already served by current "digitally enhanced" improved-definition television displays. Limiting the teleconferencing market, for example, is not the resolution of the screens but the bandwidth of the network. Without computer capabilities, digital TV is likely to be a large disappointment.

Claiming to set a standard that can survive deep into the next century, the Grand Alliance is focusing on short-term economies for manufacturing TVs tomorrow. These executives are all missing the point and the promise of the era in which they live. The Information Age is not chiefly about kicks and thrills, offering games for kids and so-called dildonics for "adults." Markets for educational programs and on line information services are already growing much faster than game markets. In 1992 in the computer business, according to the Software Publishers Association, entertainment software revenues rose some 29 percent to a level of $342 million. Educational software for the home rose some 47 percent to $146 million. Meanwhile, sales of computers with modems are rising at about 1,000 percent a year, hugely faster than the sales of TVs. Online services like America Online and Prodigy have been growing almost 500 percent per year since 1988. According to current projections based on microprocessor CPU sales, some 50 million PCs may be sold over the next 12 months, and perhaps three-quarters of them will contain either on-board modems or networking systems.

The ultimate reason that the newspapers will prevail in the Information Age is that they are better than anyone else at collecting, editing, filtering and presenting real information, and they are allying with the computer juggernaut to do it. The newspapers are pursuing the fastest expanding current markets rather than rearview markets. They are targeting adults with real interests and ambitions that generate buying power rather than distracting children from more edifying pursuits. In the computer age, follow the microcosm and you will find the money, too.

6

Life After Television, Updated

In 1994, four years after I wrote the first edition of *Life After Television*, the cornucopian afterlife is indeed at hand. With microchips and fiber optics eroding the logic of centralized institutions, networks of personal computers are indeed overthrowing IBM and CBS, NTT and EEC. But as the great pyramids of the broadcast and industrial eras—the familiar masters of the American imagination—break apart, new fear and anxieties arise about the future. If the center cannot hold, what rough beast, shuffling its slow thighs, slouches toward Hollywood to be born again in gigabytes—and gigadollars—on the information superhighway?

Will life after television mean the dissolution of the American hearth into a pornucopia of 900-number videos, full-color cold calls from sultry sisters at Lehman Brothers and real-crime performances in multimedia by superstar serial killers? Or will the new technologies uplift the culture and empower the people, as *Life After Television* predicted?

A Hughes Aircraft Corp. rocket's red glare in French Guiana, bombs bursting in air on 500 channels, give proof through the night that something is going on out there: 150 choices of DirecTV broadcast satellite images; up to one billion hertz of cable TV bandwidth; star-spangled malls of infomercials; CD radio with fidelity beyond the ken of the human ear; high-resolution wrestlemania; 3,000 films on-demand; interactive personals and impulse pay-per-view playmates; Yellow Pages blooming into home-shopping bonanzas; and videogames galore on compact discs and cartridges. All zooming through the air, blasting through cable and pulsing through fiber at the speed of light. All to be captured, decrypted, decompressed, rendered and rolled out from the new set-top boxes, game players and supertheaters in millions of colors and living rooms.

In such a phantasmagoria, what could be missing? The same thing that is missing in much of the media coverage of the information superhighway: the personal computer. What is driving the "telefuture" is not any convergence of films and TVs, consumer electronics and publishing, computers and games. What is driving the change is the onrush of computer technology invading and conquering all these domains. The computer industry is converging with the television industry in the same sense that the automobile converged with the horse, the TV with the nickelodeon, the word processing program with the typewriter, the computer-aided design program with the drafting board and digital desktop publishing with the linotype machine and the letterpress.

The computer industry feeds on the explosive advance of semiconductor and networking electronics: 1) the law of the microcosm, which shows that microchip cost-effectiveness rises by the square of the number of transistors crammed on a single chip, and 2) the law of the telecosm, which shows that computer cost-effectiveness rises by the square of the number of computers connected to networks. According to the famous projection of Intel Corp. chairman Gordon Moore, the number of transistors on a single chip will double every 18 months. According to the record of the last five years, the number of computers attached to networks is rising too fast to measure. Only by comprehending the full force of the computer juggernaut can one anticipate the future of the Information Age.

Focusing on the technologies alone, however, is not enough, because the new technologies are often retrofit into failing industries and concepts. To grasp the telefuture, it is still necessary to see the domonetics of the technologies—their social and cultural effects and contexts.

The microcosm and telecosm have generated a rich business and domestic culture—a supporting social fabric of PCs and network users—that not only nurtures, sustains, applies and expands the technologies but also is enriched and empowered by them. In positive feedback loops, the customers of the PC culture are also its creators and protagonists. If you keep your eyes on this culture, you can anticipate the sources and vectors of growth. If you focus on the hype of old industries—television and telephony, Hollywood and electronic games, consumer appliances and other diversionary devices—you will miss the real action.

THE LOGIC OF TECHNOLOGY

Behind all the changes are the supply-side rhythms of creative destruction. Radical innovations sweep nearly unnoticed through the economy from obscure niches such as Woz's garage, Bill Gates' Basic, Bob Metcalfe's ether, Bolt Beranek & Newman's Internet, Carver Mead's laboratories and Bob Noyce's workbench. On the heels of these seminal tides come much expensive hype and hullabaloo from the established industry, which is trying to absorb, deflect or co-opt the threat. This rhythm of real enterprise and reactive public relations explains why the telefuture prophesied in *Life After Television* rushed in faster than expected, and why the key developments are often downplayed or misinterpreted today. The publicity is easier to see than the broad tides of change that have swept through society since 1989.

Take John Malone and Tele-Communications Inc., for example. They are important not for the new dealmaking spectacles but for decades of enterprise that have created a new broadband network unique in the world. With links to 63 percent of America's homes—coaxial lines with a capacity some 416,000 times the capacity of telephone twisted-pair wires and easily upgradeable to two-way communications—the cable industry commands a key resource for the telefuture.

In 1989, however, as Malone consummated his network, he and TCI were still discussed by the press chiefly in the idiom of organized crime. Mostly financed by junk bonds, cable TV was derided at telecommunications meetings as a conspiracy of political action committees—"PACs with coax"—foisting junk services on the American people. Malone and his colleagues appeared in the pages of the *Wall Street Journal* and the *New York Times* chiefly in exposés of corporate chicanery.

By 1993, though, the "cable czar" had reemerged as Dr. Malone, the reigning genius of America's broadband future. TCI loomed as the spearhead of a cable industry that had become a unique American resource, putting the US as much as a decade ahead of Japan and Europe on the information superhighway.

Even Malone could not keep up with the pell-mell pace of change. In the early summer of 1992, on a panel at a NewsCorp Conference, he told me, "There is no short-term need to accelerate the deployment of fiber optics" in the cable system. The winners would follow a strategy of "step-by-step, incremental change," he told the crowd of news executives and Twentieth Century Fox movie and broadcasting magnates.

But the logic of the technology soon engulfed him. Less than a year later, on April 12, 1993, Malone publicly committed his company to a $2 billion investment in fiber—to connect a non-incremental 90 percent of his customers over the following four years. On October 13, 1993, he sold out, probably at the top, to Raymond Smith's Bell Atlantic Corp., once a sleepy-time regional Bell, now an entrepreneurial dervish on the digital highway. "There's no time to waste in deploying this infrastructure," Malone then explained.

In 1989 the great information companies financed by Michael Milken's junk bonds were still seen as sleazy corpocracies teetering on towers of debt. By 1993 TCI, McCaw Cellular, MCI, Turner, NewsCorp, Viacom and Time Warner—collective beneficiaries of $10 billion of Milken funds—had emerged as the titans of the new information economy and ruled the business pages of the press for months on end. Scorned in 1989 as part of a Milken scam or "Ponzi scheme" by Benjamin Stein in *Barrons*, James B. Stewart in the *Wall Street Journal*, Connie Bruck in the *New Yorker* and other acclaimed reporters and analysts, TCI and McCaw together attained in 1993 a total market value of around $50 billion.

In 1989 the most weighty wisdom on the future of media was the "Negroponte switch"—the theory launched by Nicholas Negroponte of MIT's Media Lab that what currently goes by air—chiefly broadcast video—would soon switch to wires (fiber optic and coax), while what currently goes by wires—chiefly voice telephony—would massively move to the air.

In *Life After Television* I urgently touted the Negroponte switch. I still believe it brilliantly captures the key vectors of change. Shortly afterward, though, I began to have my doubts that the victory of fiber as a delivery system would be quite so total as I had imagined. After all, the spectrum of electromagnetic vibrations is essentially infinite, and several companies, led by Motorola, were offering wireless local area network (LAN) equipment operating at Ethernet or Token Ring data rates in the 18-gigahertz band—a frequency previously used chiefly in outer space. Moreover, BIIC, Photonics and other firms were offering LANs in the infrared bands of the spectrum—up in the terahertz and beyond—previously used in the air only by low-data-rate TV remotes (although infrared pulses were the medium of fiber optics).

By 1994 the vision of scarce spectrum behind the Negroponte switch was in a rout. Qualcomm Corp. of San Diego introduced a cellular technology that allowed use of the entire spectrum in every cell (rather than permitting frequency reuse only once every seven cells as in current cellular technology). By creating smaller cells in larger numbers, it would be possible to multiply spectrum almost without limit while drastically lowering handset power usage. Spectrum once too scarce to waste on video was becoming as cheap and abundant in the air as in wires, where fiber optics had already opened an era of potential bandwidth abundance. Andrew Grove, CEO of Intel, memorably declared: "You think computer prices are plummeting. Wait till you see what happens to bandwidth."

Still, there remained limits to the use of higher frequencies for communication. Higher frequencies, it was believed, created prohibitive problems of interference and power. Rain, for example, would drown out microwave communications. Pigeons would fry on the antennas. Then Cellular Vision of New York Inc. overthrew this conventional wisdom. It announced in the fall of 1992 that it was broadcasting 49 channels of studio-quality video in the 28-gigahertz band of the electromagnetic spectrum to 500 homes in the Borough of Queens. The total cost was some $300 per home. Months later, Gigahertz Equipment of Phoenix was seeking similar licenses in the West.

Although many observers scoffed at these microwave ventures, on August 4, 1993, Bell Atlantic signed up to market the system through the City of New York and in neighboring suburbs to the north. US West signed up with Gigahertz to supply service in its own region.

Shaking most of the certainties of 1980s conventional wisdom, such insurgencies all stemmed from the still deeper forces of the microcosm and telecosm—described in *Life After Television*—that are still gaining momentum in 1994 and will continue to cascade through the technoscapes of the coming decade.

THE AVALANCHE OF BITS

But with Milken banished from financial markets and Malone in harvest mode, who will ride the next avalanche of bits on the information superhighway—and who will be buried under it? Widely regarded as likely winners are Edward McCracken of Silicon Graphics Inc., the aspiring king of the set-top box and the video server, and Jim Clark, SGI founder and chairman until February 28 (when he will leave to start his own interactive TV software company). In the form of 3D graphics hardware and software, SGI's technology is central to the triumph of computers over television and games. Yet the company's present strategy is to retrofit these digital engines into the television set-top boxes and Nintendo game machines of the precomputer culture. Clark hopes to provide the content.

SGI offers compelling reasons for this strategy: production volumes and foundries for the Mips 4000 microprocessor family comparable to those of the Intel X86 standard; a siphon amid the possible floods of software revenues to be earned by Nintendo using the SGI architecture; and sales of SGI superservers to the television programming industry. But in harvesting these benefits over the next five years, SGI and Clark risk dissipating their energies by serving the industries of the past.

Is Mickey Schulhof of Sony Corp. going to countervail these trends? He is trying to converge and digitize all the technologies of the past into a piñata of new consumer appliances, musical hits, videogames and movies, making blockbuster turkeys such as *Last Action Hero* and selling everything but the feathers and the popcorn. Schulhof grandly plans to rule both ends of the information superhighway, with Hollywood video and musical content and a panoply of appliances to play them, from high-definition TV sets to minidiscs, CDs and videotapes, game players and walkmasters. But Sony may merely be supplying digital cosmetics to two dying industrial establishments: Hollywood and consumer electronics. Making an array of incompatible and incommunicable devices, Sony is defying both the law of the microcosm, which compels the distribution of intelligence, and the law of the telecosm, which asserts the exponential benefits of interconnection.

Lest the information superhighway clog up with wrecked hopes and misbegotten plans, let us look for the false assumptions behind some of the disappointments of today.

GTE's Cerritos, Calif., project—the first full test of interactive services, launched in the mid-1980s—rolled out its cornucopia of on-demand video, instant banking, shopping, games and other services to an indifferent marketplace. Although the results are still shrouded in secrecy, news reports suggested that people just didn't want to take the trouble. US West and TCI are said to have made similar discoveries in Denver. If the world lusts for interactivity, why does it spurn the leading interactive market tests?

The "killer app" for these new broadband systems is supposed to be pay-per-view television. But, says Frank Biondi, president of Viacom, "there has been no serious take-up for pay-per-view in 20 years. We are way behind revenue projections on motion picture pay-per-view." When Time Warner raised its pay-per-view movie bandwidth from five to 60 channels in the Borough of Queens, monthly revenue is reported to have risen by only some $4 per home. "If people really hated going down the block to pick up a movie, video stores would have a thriving delivery business today," commented Michael Noll of the University of Southern California in the software newsletter *Release 1.0*.

3DO's new super-Cd-ROM multiplayer and graphics processor may someday find a market outside Wall Street. But judging from the fall of the company's stock price, from a high of 48-1/4 when the machine was launched into stores last October to 26 in mid-January, sales have been disappointing. 3DO indicated that some 50,000 units had been shipped to retailers, compared with earlier company projections of "fewer than 100,000" and euphoric expectations of many more. Similarly, after investment of untold hundreds of millions of dollars, the Philips CD-I players still lag in the marketplace. If the world is rushing to multimedia, why is it so slow to embrace the leading new multimedia players?

"LIKE FEEDING VITAMINS TO A HORSE"

Games show magnate Jon Goodson of Mark Goodson Productions declares that people don't want to interact with game shows. "It changes the game—for the worse." A 1993 Dataquest study reported that people really don't want to interact with sports events. TV Answer, now Eon, and Interactive Networks both failed to break through with plans to supply interactivity to current-day televisions over special radio frequencies allocated for the purpose by the FCC. Hollywood has determined that audiences have no interest in shaping the outcomes of films; they want to be surprised. If people don't want to interact with video, how can the world move beyond television?

The new standard for digital HDTV, though far ahead of the old analog systems, will not be officially unveiled until 1995, according to Richard Wiley, chairman of the FCC's Advisory Committee on Advanced Television. The broadcast companies that are supposed to adopt it are mostly uninterested. "We see no way any of us will make money out of this thing," says John Swanson, vice-president, engineering, at Cox Broadcasting.

Most of the fiber-to-the-home and fiber-to-the-curb companies have been disappointments—Raynet and BroadBand Technologies have had difficulty selling their equipment. A superb passive optical technology has so far failed to save BroadBand's stock price. It tumbled from a high of 52 early in 1993, amid the uproar over the information superhighway, to a low in the mid-20s by the end of January 1994 as revenue projections were lowered by analysts. Raychem has pumped more than $100 million into Raynet without yet generating a profit. Meanwhile, the telephone companies have been dallying with a new system called Asymmetrical Digital Subscriber Line, which will let them send full-motion video down a conventional phone line at six megabits per second (near to the practical rate of an Ethernet computer network). Although Eli Noam of the Columbia University Telecommunications Center says ADSL is "like feeding vitamins to a horse rather than buying a truck," the phone companies feel that if they have to compete with TV, it is cheaper to supercharge the old copper nag for the last few hundred yards.

On the content side the picture is equally cloudy. At multimedia conventions, television executives declare that there is no way they can make money with the kind of stuff currently available on CD-ROMs and other such platforms. During intermissions they mutter off the record that the only way to jump-start this market is through virtual sex.

In the late 1980s the entire Japanese electronics industry was riding high with the harvest of profits from decades of investment in consumer electronics. Deciding that "content is king," Sony and Matsushita each bought major Hollywood studios. As these companies moved on toward HDTV, Western pundits prophesied that Japan would dominate all advanced electronic industries, from semiconductors to supercomputers. Instead, however, the Japanese electronics industry entered a period of prolonged decline, suffering heavy financial setbacks and even losing its lead in semiconductors to American firms.

STRATEGISTS FOCUSED ON WRONG INDUSTRY

From Cerritos to Denver and on to Orlando, Omaha and Castro Valley, from 3DO to CD-I and beyond, from BroadBand to Raynet, from Sony to NEC, the current and impending disappointments spring from one key mistake. With some notable exceptions, the leading strategists are focusing on the wrong industry. You can't get beyond television by collaborating with TV companies in their long slide to obsolescence. You can't create a new information infrastructure by propping up the old telephone networks with the right to provide TV-type services.

The new 3DO and Philips CD-I game machines, for example, both link to interlaced TV screens that display every other line and then fill in the gaps on a second sweep. Interlaced screens mean cumbersome text and limited graphics. Interlaced screens doom multimedia to a fringe videotext fuzz. Yet these new game players shun the personal computer and its installed base of 33 million home units in order to build up a new installed base from scratch, connecting to visually inadequate televisions.

Interactivity, almost by definition, is a computer function, not a television function. Making the boob tube into an interactive hive of theater, museum, classroom, banking system, shopping center, post office and communicator is contrary to the nature of the box.

Millions of Americans, however, are eager to turn their personal computers to these pursuits. Therefore, it is natural that nearly all the relevant activity is in the computer industry rather than in the television industry. The PC world provides an environment totally alien to the downside dirges of consumer electronics.

As Peter Drucker has said, an entrepreneur should always heed the upside surprises. Upside surprises distract business leaders from a deadening focus on problems and target them on their opportunities. In the information economy, the best opportunities stem from the exponential rise in the power of computers and computer networks, microcosm and telecosm. In the computer industry, all the surprises tend to come on the upside.

For example, early in 1993 the two leading experts in the field, Bill Gates of Microsoft and Andrew Grove of Intel, both boldly predicted total PC sales between 35 and 40 million, up from a stupendous 32 million in 1992. In an outcome first predicted in February by semiconductor analyst Daniel Klesken of Robertson Stephens, the actual number came in at nearly 50 million, between 25 and 40 percent above the forecasts—during what was widely reported as a down year for computer companies.

This drastic surprise engendered waves of similar upside surprises through the industry. Despite a chaos of competing architectures and aspiring standards that meant any particular CD-ROM would most likely not be playable on your machine, the sales of multimedia-ready computers rose from a few thousand high-end devices in 1989 to some three-and-a-half million in 1993, bringing in some $5 billion in revenues. Despite general disappointment in the quality of the titles, the sales of CD-ROMs soared from a few hundred thousand in 1989 to nearly five million in 1993. As a harbinger of the future, sales of encyclopedias in CD-ROM format surpassed those of book copies in 1993.

More important is the explosive rise in networks. Since 1989 the share of US computers attached to networks rose from less than 10 percent to more than 60 percent. Some 15 million are now attached to the network of networks—the Internet—up from a few score thousand in 1989. For several years the Internet grew at a pace of 15 percent per month.

The fatal flaw of Silicon Graphics, 3DO, AT&T, Raynet, Eon and QVC is that they are trying to solve the problems of the telephone, TV, videogame and consumer appliance companies. The problems of these separate industries are unsolvable in the face of the integrating sweep of the computer networking industry juggernaut. Television problem solving just distracts computer firms from their huge and hugely demanding opportunity to usurp phones, televisions and videogame players entirely with multimedia PCs and networks. The huge telecom and consumer firms must be enlisted in their true role: supplying networks, peripherals and programs for the computer industry.

Hollywood may still be full of glamour, but the surest sell sign for a technology company is still a star- struck CEO. It is not altogether reassuring to hear Terrence Garnett, Oracle's vice-president, multimedia, discussing his boss' place in the industry. After schmoozing at a party with Hollywood stars, Garnett confided to a reporter: "I would have a hard time picturing Lewis Platt [president of Hewlett Packard] sitting at that party. I mean, you look at Larry Ellison and you could see him in that environment. I couldn't see Jim Manzi [president of Lotus Development] or Philippe Kahn [president of Borland] there. They don't look good in Armani."

The most Hollywood-savvy executive of Silicon Valley is Jerry Sanders of Advanced Micro Services. Star-struck at age 20 and bent on becoming a star, he discovered shortly afterward that actors are mostly fungible functions and their glamour mostly meretricious. Rather than trying to get rich in Hollywood, he decided to enjoy Hollywood on his own terms after he got rich in Silicon Valley.

The irony is that technology companies actually hurt the movie business more than they help it. The central message of *Life After Television* for the film industry is that the new technologies are targeted directly *at* Hollywood. Today some 70 percent of the costs of a film go to distribution and advertising. In every industry—from retailing to insurance— the key impact of the computer networking revolution is to collapse the costs of distribution and remove the middlemen. The movie business is now mostly middlemen. In an information industry such as the movie business, distribution costs will predictably plummet if the movie business embraces networking.

TVS AND TELEPHONES: CHANGE OR CRASH

Anyone with access to the information superhighway will be able to distribute a film at a tiny fraction of current costs. Moreover, webs of glass and light will free the producer from the burden of creating a product that can attract miscellaneous audiences to theaters. Instead, producers will be able to reach equally large but more specialized audiences dispersed around the globe. Rather than making lowest- common-denominator appeals to the masses, film makers will be able to appeal to the special interests, ambitions and curiosities of individuals anywhere, anytime.

Limiting these opportunities at present are both the bottleneck of telephone nets and the runaway costs of film making. Personal computers will not only pulverize the costs of distribution, they will also drastically diminish the costs of actual film production. Today leading directors can still imagine that they alone command the capital to deploy the new digital production and editing tools. But any capability now costing a few hundred thousand dollars is sure to cost less than $20,000 in five years.

Just as digital desktop publishing equipment unleashed thousands of new text-publishing companies, so the new digital desktop video-publishing systems will unleash thousands of new filmmakers. The video business will increasingly resemble not the current film business, in which output is 100 or so movies a year, but the book business, in which some 55,000 new hardcover titles are published annually in the US alone. After all, scores of thousands of screenplays are already written every year. In the next decade thousands of screenwriters will be able to make and distribute their own films.

Hollywood, meanwhile, will move toward providing enhanced experiences through virtual reality and other expensive technologies. The current harbinger is Circus Circus' Luxor resort in Las Vegas, a gigantic pyramid that is briefly the world's largest hotel. Luxor is not just another Vegas casino: It serves chiefly as a dormitory for six ride-film theaters on the first floor. Luxor cost some $375 million to build. The largest expense was the $40 million invested in the ride-films at the heart of the project. The individual who made these films was Douglas Trumbull, formerly Hollywood's leading supplier of special effects and now an enemy of the Hollywood establishment. He is pioneering the new technologies of theatrical presentation—a field abandoned by Hollywood in the 1950s when antitrust laws were interpreted as barring film companies from owning theaters. Trumbull's first ride-film hit, the incandescent *Back to the Future, The Ride*, saved the Universal Theme Park in Orlando and set a new technical standard for the medium.

Life After Television did not merely predict a technical revolution; it predicted a cultural upheaval. Moving authority from elites and establishments to creators and customers, the new technologies drastically change the cultural balance of power. Shifting the optimal target of commercial art from vulgar taste and sensations to special interests, curiosities, hobbies, ambitions and artistic aspirations, digital multimedia machines will transform the marketplace and elevate the culture. Only by addressing the new opportunities will companies prosper and prevail.

Computer networks are the pivotal technology of the new era. They are the chief engine of the division of labor—the force of creativity and specialization that Adam Smith identified as the key driver of economic growth. And they are the reigning spearhead of the creative destruction that Joseph Schumpeter saw as the key to all economic progress. The domonetics of computer networks are active and dynamic rather than passive and diversionary. Unlike games and movies, computer networks endow people with new powers of self-improvement and wealth creation. They free individuals from the shackles of corporate bureaucracy and geography and allow them to collaborate and exchange ideas with the best colleagues anywhere in the world. Computer networks give every hacker the creative potential of a factory tycoon of the industrial era and the communications power of a TV magnate of the broadcasting era.

The accelerating spread of computer networks in the early 1990s explains the high sense of opportunity and possibility in an economy otherwise in the doldrums. To prevail all industries will have to adapt to network powers and constraints. This means telephone and TV companies will have to change or crash. It also means that to fulfill the promise of the Information Age, computer companies will have to adapt to the laws of the microcosm and telecosm. They will have to stop dallying with game machines and set-top boxes, stop their infatuation with Hollywood and embrace the empowering promise of their own machines.

Leading any list of companies that grasp this reality are Apple and Intel. Both have made large strides in the past year toward the overthrow of the establishments of consumer electronics, telephony and television.

Although Apple suffered sharp setbacks in 1993, the "teleputer" strategy launched by John Sculley in recent years began to bear fruit that same year in such pioneering products as the Quicktime multimedia operating system, the Macintosh TV and the Mac Quadra 840AV.

First came the Mac TV, which boldly subsumed a full cable-ready television set in a Macintosh computer, together with a stereo CD-ROM drive, all in one chassis. Connectable to a VCR, camcorder, laserdisc or videogame player, the Mac TV cost around $2,000 and signals a new epoch.

Moving still closer to the teleputer ideal of the multimedia production center is the Mac Quadra 840AV. Standing for audio-visual, the AV fulfills the ultimate promise of the teleputer as a device that can not only display digital video but also store, edit and transmit it. With input port for all TV standards—including the European PAL and the American NTSC and studio modes S-video and composite video—the Quadra AV can convert analog images to a digital bit stream to be stored, edited and then transmitted. The AV can also function as a phone and stereo and contains an advanced digital signal processor that imparts powers of speech recognition and synthesis. Rivaled as a multi-media machine only by the most costly and powerful Silicon Graphics Indy workstation, the Quadra AV is unique in its pattern-matching and voice-recognition features.

In early December 1993 in Tokyo, Apple introduced the latest version of Quicktime running Moving Picture Experts Group (MPEG standard) video at 30 frames per second on a Mac Quadra. Fujitsu Ltd.'s announcement that it was licensing the technology for its own line of video computers signified a growing awareness that Quicktime was becoming a worldwide multimedia standard even before the Kaleida multimedia system and the so-called Power PC emerged from an Apple-IBM partnership.

Fulfilling Sculley's promise of usurping both phone and television set, these new computers and their software represent the first generation of the multimedia era. Already an upside surprise, the Quadra 840AV moved quickly to the forefront among Apple best-sellers, showing that Apple can still do best in the marketplace through genuine innovations. These technologies do not ape the price points and form factors of consumer electronics; they do not hunker down or twist themselves into pretzels to fit in a set-top box. These products extend the PC imperium into new territory.

However, in a world with Intel chieftain Andy Grove aboard, Apple cannot rest on its teleputer laurels. Intel is still more fiercely focused on the prize. As Grove says: "The PC is it. That sums up Intel's business plan and rallying cry." Scorning the obsession with set-top boxes elsewhere in the industry, he explains: "The PC is already in 30 percent of the nation's homes. How long will it be before these new set-top boxes are in 30 percent of homes? And what will PCs be doing by then? The PC is not any one thing. It is a continuing phenomenon, and every couple years its definition changes. The Intel goal is to make sure that the living organism of the PC evolves in the right direction to continue as the dominant interactive appliance in both home and business. The PC is not a fixed product but a continuum. By contrast, the set-top box is a stationary machine. The set-top box won't have the volume, the installed base, the software or the adaptability of the PC. By the time they get all the necessary functions into the set-top box at the right price point, the PC will be controlling the TV as a mere peripheral." Grove's warning is exactly on target.

BANDWIDTH FREES COMPUTERS' TRUE POWER

Bruce Ryon, Dataquest's chief multimedia analyst, observes: "If you talk to the cable set-top box guys, they are all saying that they are not going to get to the price points they need until three to five years out." After three to five more years of Moore's Law, the PC will be a multimedia machine with some eight times the power and storage capacity at the same price that brought nearly 50 million unit sales in 1993 and, according to Robertson Stephens' Klesken, promises to bring some 55 million unit sales in 1994. At this pace, within four or five years, PC penetration into homes will pass 60 percent.

Virtually all these PCs will be connected to networks—most of them with 10 megabits per second or more of bandwidth—and most will run internal buses (linking processors to memory and display) at rates of close to a billion bits per second, ample for full-motion video.

These new PCs being prepared at Intel and Apple will merge with the new tools of the information superhighway. Technologies of fiber optics and wireless communications, glass and air, they are advancing as fast as the microchip technologies of sand. Together they will consummate the computer revolution and wreak a new revolution in telecom.

Until endowed with broadband connections, the computer is a cripple that devotes huge portions of its processing power merely to compressing, decompressing, coding and decoding its data for the telephone system bottleneck. It is because of this bottleneck that the true power of the PC remains obscure to many observers. It is because of this bottleneck that the TV and consumer electronics industries can imagine themselves a significant rivals to the PC. But once provided with broadband communications, the PC will come fully into its exponential harvest from microcosm to telecosm.

As Grove points out: "Infinite processing power will get you only so far with limited bandwidth. But the coming era of nearly free bandwidth will liberate the computer to fulfill its powers. Just as the 1980s saw the demolition of the vertical structure of the computer industry, so the 1990s will see the demolition of the vertical structure of the communications industry."

To accelerate the day, at the December 1993 Western Cable TV Show, Intel announced that it is developing a new computer on-ramp for the information superhighway. In league with General Instrument and Hybrid Technology, Intel demonstrated a modem to connect computers to cable TV coax at Ethernet speeds of 10 megabits per second. One of several firms preparing to release computer powers onto cable networks, Intel has the manufacturing clout and marketing power to make cable PC a widespread reality.

To prepare for this new era of broadband teleputing, Intel is introducing a new bus standard, PCI, that runs at video speeds—around a gigabit per second. With Apple's recent endorsement, PCI seems likely to become the prevailing system for personal computer internal communications. At the same time, Intel announced a full desktop tele-conferencing system. Doggedly pursuing the dual goal of integrating both voice and video with the computer, Intel is far more ready to exploit the new era than firms panting after Paramount and Nintendo.

Nonetheless, neither the Intel nor the Apple machines bring nirvana. As multimedia guru Eric Hoffert of Apple points out, the consummated teleputer requires 10 key advances. They include an asynchronous transfer mode (ATM) interface, fast real-time compression/decompression chips, a full 64-bit microprocessor, a real-time operating system that can schedule events for specific times, internal buses that run the gigabits-per-second of raw high-definition video flows, networked multimedia standard software to sustain new applications, and improved human interfaces for multimedia communication and access to media databases. Furthermore, the teleputer will demand huge storage devices for the many gigabytes of data in ambitious multimedia projects. Finally, it will entail new ways of encrypting and metering information so that the creators can be paid for each access rather than requiring customers to "buy the reservoir," as Wave Systems chief Peter Sprague puts it, "every time you want a drink of water."

Although these capabilities are available today, their cost remains in the scores of thousands of dollars. Without these features, even the AV and the Indy suffer nagging limits in storing, processing, editing and transmitting the full-motion, full-screen, high-resolution digital video of our dreams.

Indeed, if this were the television industry, such a machine would remain a dream for decades to come. But in the entrepreneurial crucible of the PC industry, all these dreams can come true at the remorseless pace of Moore's Law. Within the next five years, cheap desktop machines could not only show digital movies of full quality and resolution, but also create, edit and transmit them.

With this development at hand, all through Wall Street a warning is whispered: "The train is leaving the station." Content is scarce. If you don't get it now, you will be left behind with the nerds in polyester.

So why didn't Andy Grove join the race with Viacom's Sumner Redstone, QVC's Barry Diller and all the rest for the grand prize of Paramount? Couldn't someone at Intel find him an Armani suit? Paramount is worth $10 billion. Intel is worth around $25 billion. It could easily swallow up the movie giant and combine the Intel computer and communications tools with Paramount's creative treasures.

Even more significant, though, if the train is leaving the station, where is America's sometimes richest man, the world's leading digital software tycoon? Most of the prerequisites for the multimedia teleputer are software projects now under way at Microsoft. Why didn't Bill Gates join the Hollywood rush? He is famously pursuing content, digitizing famous works of art. Like Grove, Gates commands a company worth close to $25 billion. Gates could scoop up Paramount into his content venture, Continuum Productions, and become as famous and fashionable as he is rich.

But Gates is the epitome of PC domonetics. Gates doesn't even own a TV set. Without mentioning movies or games, he can spiel off dozens of detailed ideas for applications for the digital highway in the time it takes John Malone to list his market tests and caveats. Gates invested nearly 10 years of fatigue and futility, money and energy in the CD-ROM market as an alternative to TV. Today's triumph of the CD-ROM is a supreme vindication of Gates' PC strategy. Why should he abandon it now?

Train leaving the station? Gates told *Forbes ASAP*, "*That's a joke.*" Gates has always acted on the assumption that Microsoft—or, more generally, the PC—is the train and he is driving it. In 1985 he declared: "Television is passive entertainment. We're betting that people want to interact, choose different paths and get feedback from the machine about what they have really learned." Almost a decade later, in the January 10, 1994, *New Yorker*, he was still making the same point. Calling interactive TV "a really bad name for the in-home device connected to the information highway," he stated: "The bottom line is that two-way communication is a very different beast than one-way communication. . . . A phone that has an unbelievable directory [and] lets you talk or send messages to lots of people, and works with text and pictures is a better analogy than TV. . . . Because TV had very few channels, the value of TV time was very high so only things of very broad interest could be aired on those few channels. The information highway will be the opposite of this—more like the Library of Congress but with an easy way to find things." Exactly the message of *Life After Television*.

Gates did not hustle after Hollywood. Barry Diller and Michael Ovitz had to seek him out in Seattle. Bill Gates has fiercely focused Microsoft on the PC culture. In the NT operating system, he is pushing a system with multimedia interfaces, which thrusts Microsoft into the middle of the fray in computer multiprocessing and computer networking. That is the heart of the new era.

PC'S SUPERIOR DEMOGRAPHICS

The reason Gates and Grove are not interested in Paramount is no mystery. They don't need it. They already command a much larger, faster-growing, more creative and more promising vehicle for their capital. Selling nearly 50 million units in 1993, at an average price some four times higher than that of a TV, the PC is not only a bigger market than television and movies put together, it is also a better market in every way. In 1992 the US computer industry commanded total sales of $161 billion, compared with $104 billion in total revenues for TV and films. The revenues from computer hardware sales were more than six times the revenues from TV sales, and home computer sales were growing 10 times as fast. More important, the demographics of the PC industry are far superior. Television buyers are median American couch potatoes who pay some $400 for their machines. PC buyers mostly come from the upper income quintiles, usually have higher education and pay an average of some $1,500 for their machines and then put out another $1,500 or so for software and peripherals.

Most crucial of all is the difference in the use of the two devices. While TV watchers use their machines to lull themselves and their children into a stupor, PC users exploit their machines to become yet richer and smarter and more productive—and still better able to exploit future computer advances. The PC customer is also the creator of new applications and add-on devices. The TV is a consumption product. The PC is a supply-side investment in the coming restoration of the home to a central role in the productive dynamics of capitalism, and the transformation of capitalism into a healing force in the present crisis of home and family, culture and community.

How can this be when the computer is so often condemned as a divisive and polarizing force in American life, the tool of an elite of nerds, a weapon of dehumanizing bureaucracy? These charges were partly valid for the mainframe computers of old. But as the PC gains communications powers and evolves into a teleputer, its social, cultural and political impacts change completely. As it ushers in a life beyond TV, it becomes a powerful force for democracy, individuality, community and high culture.

The leading-edge computers always go first to the elites who can use them best and help develop them for others. All new technologies are first purchased by elites and mastered by them before they reach a larger public. The PC plays a role in contemporary culture resembling the role of the Model T automobile in 20th-century industrial culture.

Owners of the Model T could not simply jump in and drive the machine. They had to learn how to maintain and repair it. Many of them learned how to take it apart and put it back together. They became an industrial elite with the mechanical skills that won two world wars and propelled the US to the forefront of the world economy.

Similarly, the linked PCs of today and the teleputer networks of tomorrow seem formidable—difficult to get in and drive. At times they appear to be the tools of a new elite. But teleputers feed on the most rapid learning curves in the world economy, and in proportion to their powers are the cheapest technologies in history. Just as the TV, once an exotic tool of elites, became even more ubiquitous in America than the telephone or the automobile, the teleputer will end the decade not as a luxury but as an indispensable appliance.

It is companies that shun the PC of today in order to cater to the TV, consumer electronics and telephone industries that will end up in luxury backwaters. They will resemble the companies that catered to the mainframe trade early in this decade, or those that catered to the horse business early in this century. They may find exotic or intriguing niches. Yet just as the real action was not at Churchill Downs or the Peapack Hunt Club but in Detroit, the real action today—the source of wealth and power—is not at Nintendo or Sega, Hollywood or QVC. It is in the scores of thousands of computer and software companies that make up the industrial fabric of the Information Age—the exhilarating new life after television.

7

Auctioning the Airwaves

Imagine it is 1971 and you are chair of the new Federal Computer Commission. This commission has been established to regulate the natural monopoly of computer technology as summed up in the famous Grosch's Law. In 1956 IBM engineer Herbert Grosch proved that computer power rises by the square of its cost and thus necessarily gravitates to the most costly machines.

According to a famous IBM projection, the entire world could use some 55 mainframes, time-sharing from dumb terminals and keypunch machines. The owners of these machines would rule the world of information in an ascendant information age. By the Orwellian dawn of 1984, Big Bre'r IBM would establish a new digital tyranny, with a new elite of the data-rich dominating the data-poor.

As head of the computer commission, you launch a bold program to forestall this grim outcome. Under a congressional mandate to promote competition for IBM and ensure the principle of universal computer service, you ordain the creation of some 2,500 mainframe licenses to be auctioned to the highest bidders (with special licenses reserved for minorities, women and farmers). To ensure widespread competition across all of America, you establish seven licenses in each metropolitan Major Trading Area and seven in every rural Basic Trading Area as defined by Rand McNally. To guarantee universal service, you mandate the free distribution of keypunch machines to all businesses and households so that they can access the local computer centers.

In establishing this auction in 1971, you had no reason at all to notice that a tiny company in Mountain View, Calif., called Intel was about to announce three new technologies together with some hype about "a new era of integrated electronics." After all, these technologies—the microprocessor; erasable, programmable read-only memory (EPROM); and a one-kilobit dynamic random access memory (DRAM)—were far too primitive to even compare with IBM's massive machines.

The likely results of such a Federal Computer Commission policy are not merely matters of conjecture. France pretty much did it when it distributed free Minitel terminals to its citizens to provide them access to government mainframes. While the United States made personal computers nearly ubiquitous—buying perhaps 100 million since the launch of the Minitel in the late 1970s—the French chatted through central databases and ended up with one-quarter as many computers per capita as this country, and one-tenth the number of computer networks. Today, PC networks are leading the US economy to world dominance while Europe founders without a single major computer company, software firm or semiconductor manufacturer.

It is now 1994, and Reed Hundt, the new chairman of the Federal Communications Commission, is indeed about to hold an auction.

Rather than selling exclusive mainframe licenses, the current FCC is going to sell exclusive ten-year licenses to about 2,500 shards of the radio spectrum. Meanwhile, a tiny company called Steinbrecher Corp. of Burlington, Mass., is introducing the new microprocessor of the radio business.

In the world of radio waves ruled by the Federal Communications Commission, the Steinbrecher MiniCell is even more revolutionary than the microprocessor was in the world of computing. While Intel put an entire computer on a single chip, Steinbrecher has put an entire cellular base station—now requiring some 1,000 square feet and costing $1.5 million—in a box the size of a briefcase that costs $100,000 today. Based on a unique invention by Donald Steinbrecher and on the sweeping advance of computer technology, the MiniCell represents a far bigger leap forward beyond the current state of the art than the microprocessor did. What's more, this MiniCell is in fact much superior to existing cellular base stations. Unlike the 416 hard-wired radio transceivers (transmitter-receivers) in existing base stations, the MiniCell contains a single digital broadband radio and is fully programmable. It can accommodate scores of different kinds of cellular handsets.

Most important, the MiniCell benefits from the same technology as the microprocessor. Making possible the creation of this broadband digital radio is the tidal onrush of Moore's Law. In an antithesis of Grosch's Law, Gordon Moore of Intel showed that the cost-effectiveness of microchip technology doubles every 18 months. This insight suggested the Law of the Microcosm—that computing power gravitates not to the costliest but to the cheapest machines. Costing $100,000 today, the MiniCell will predictably cost some $10,000 before the turn of the century.

In time, these digital MiniCells will have an impact similar to that of the PC. They will drive the creation of a cornucopia of new mobile services—from plain old telephony to wireless video conferencing—based on ubiquitous client/server networks in the air. Endowing Americans with universal mobile access to information superhighways, these MiniCells can spearhead another generation of computer-led growth in the US economy. Eventually, the implications of Steinbrecher's machines and other major innovations in wireless will crash in on the legalistic scene of the FCC.

And that's only the beginning of the story.

Going on the block in May will be 160 megahertz (millions of cycles per second) of the radio frequency spectrum, divided into seven sections of between 10 and 30 megahertz in each of 543 areas of the country, and devoted to enhanced Personal Communications Services (PCS).

Existing cellular systems operate in a total spectrum space of 50 megahertz in two frequency bands near the 800 megahertz level. By contrast, PCS will take four times that space in a frequency band near two gigahertz (billions of cycles per second). Became higher frequencies allow use of lower-power radios with smaller antennas and longer-lasting batteries, PCS offers the possibility of a drastically improved wireless system. Unfortunately, the major obstacle to the promise of PCS is the auction.

Amid the spectrum fever aroused by the bidding, however, new radio technologies are emerging that devastate its most basic assumptions. At a time when the world is about to take to information superhighways in the sky—plied by low-powered, pollution-free computer phones—the FCC is in danger of building a legal infrastructure and protectionist program for information smokestacks and gas guzzlers.

Even the language used to describe the auction betrays its fallacies. With real estate imagery, analysts depict spectrum as "beachfront property" and the auction as a "land rash." They assume that radio frequencies are like analog telephone circuit: no two users can occupy the same spot of spectrum at the same time. Whether large 50-kilowatt broadcast stations booming Rush Limbaugh's voice across the nation or milliwatt cellular phones beaming love murmurs to a nearby base station, radio transmitters are assumed to be infectious, high-powered and blind. If one is on the highway, everyone else has to clear out. Both the prevailing wisdom and the entrenched technology dictate that every transmitter be quarantined in its own spectrum slot.

However, innovations from such companies as Steinbrecher and Qualcomm Inc. of San Diego overthrow this paradigm. Not only can numerous radios operate at non-interfering levels in the same frequency band, they can also see other users' signals and move to avoid them. In baseball jargon, the new radios can hit 'em where they ain't; in football idiom, they run for daylight. If appropriately handled, these technologies can render spectrum not scarce but abundant.

These developments make it retrograde to assign exclusive spectrum rights to anyone or to foster technologies that require exclusivity. Spectrum no longer shares any features of beachfront property. A wave would be a better analogy.

THE NEW RULES OF WAVES

In the early decades of this century, radio was king. Electronics hackers played in the waves with a variety of ham, citizens band and short-wave machines. Experimenting with crystal sets, they innocently entered the domain of solid-state devices and acquired some of the skills that fueled the electronic revolution in the United States and the radar revolution that won World War II. The first point-contact transistor, created by John Bardeen and Walter Brattain at Bell Labs in 1948, functioned like a crystal radio. The first major solid-state product was a 1954 Texas Instruments pocket radio with six germanium transistors.

Over the following decades, the radio became a mass commodity. There are now some 230 million radios in the United States alone, not even including more than 16 million cellular phones (which are in fact portable two-way radios). Radios roll off Asian assembly lines at a rate that might be meaningfully measured in hertz (cycles per second), and they come in sizes fit for pockets, belts, watches and ears. But the romance of radio has died and given way to the romance of computers.

Today it is PC technology that engages the youthful energies previously invested in radio technology. The press trumpets a coming convergence between computers and TVs and games and films. But no one talks much about radios. For many years, we have been taking radios for granted.

As the foundation of wireless communications, however, radio—no less than TV or films—will burst into a new technoscape as a result of a convergence with computers. The hackers of the '50s and '60s are joining forces with the hackers of the '80s and '90s to create a new industry. Moore's Law is about to overrun the world of radio.

You double anything every 18 months and pretty soon you find yourself with a monster. During the 1970s and 1980s, Moore's Law overturned the established order in the computer industry and spawned some 100 million personal computers that are as powerful as million-dollar mainframes were when the revolution began. In the current decade, Moore's Law is upending the telephone and television industries with interactive teleputers that will be able to send, receive, shape and store interactive full-motion video. And during the next five years, Moore's Law is going to transform exotic and costly radio equipment once consigned to the military and outer space into the basic communications access routes for the new world economy.

To understand this new world of radio, however, you must forget much of what you learned about the old world of radio. For example, these new radios differ radically from the radios of the past in the way they use spectrum, the way they interfere with one another and the way they are built.

For some 15 years, a hacker of the 1950s named Don Steinbrecher and a small group of students and associates have been making the world's most powerful and aerobatic radios. Steinbrecher radio gear can soar to spectrum altitudes as high as 94 gigahertz to provide radar "eyes" for smart bombs and planes, plunge down to the cellular band at 800 megahertz to listen in on phone calls or drop discretely to 30 megahertz—waves that bounce off the ionosphere—for remote over-the-horizon radar work identifying cocaine traffickers flying in low from Latin America. At the same time, some of these radios may soon command enough dynamic ranges of accurate broadband reception—rumored to be as high as 120 decibels (one trillion-to-one)—to detect a pin drop at a heavy-metal rock concert without missing a high-fidelity note or twang.

Like every radio transceiver, a Steinbrecher radio must have four key components: an antenna, a tuner, a modem and a mixer. The antenna part is easy; for many purposes, your metal shirt hanger will do the trick (backyard wire fences collect millions of frequencies). But without tuners, modems and mixers, nothing reaches its final destination—the human ear.

A tuner selects a desired carrier frequency, usually by exploiting the science of resonant circuits. A modem is a modulator-demodulator. In transmitting, it applies infor-mation to the carrier frequency by wiggling the waves in a pattern, called a modulation scheme, such as AM or FM. In receiving, the modem strips out (demodulates) the information from the carrier wave.

The key to Steinbrecher radios is the broadband mixer. It surmounts what was long seen as an impossible challenge: moving a large array of the relatively high carrier frequencies on the antenna down to a so-called baseband level where they can be used without losing any of the information or adding spurious information in the process. Compared to FM carrier frequencies of 100 megahertz or even PCS frequencies of two gigahertz, baseband audio frequencies run between 20 hertz and 20 kilohertz.

Mixers were the basic Steinbrecher product, and in 1978 and 1980, Steinbrecher acquired patents on a unique broadband mixer with high range and sensitivity called the Paramixer. Even to its expected military customers, the Paramixer was a hard sell because other radio components were unable to keep pace with its performance. Today, however, the Paramixer is the foundation of the Steinbrecher radio in the MiniCell.

In the old world of radio, transceivers integrated all of these components—antenna, tuner, modem and mixer—into one analog hardware system. Because the radio is analog and hard-wired, its functions must be standardized. Each radio can receive or transmit only a very limited set of frequencies bearing information coded in a specific modulation scheme and exclusively occupying a specific spectrum space at a particular power range. If you are in the radio business—whether as an equipment manufacturer such as Motorola or Ericsson, a provider of services, such as McCaw or Comsat, or a broadcaster, such as NBC or Turner—you care deeply about these hard-wired specifications, frequencies and modulation schemes.

Comprising the "air standard," these issues embroil businesses, politicians, standards bodies and regulators in constant warfare. For everything from High Definition Television to digital cellular and cordless telephony, standards bodies are wrangling over frequencies and modulation schemes.

HOW DIGITAL RADIOS CAN END THE SPECTRUM WARS

To the people at Steinbrecher Corp., all these wrangles seem utterly unnecessary. With antennas, tuners, modems and mixers, wideband digital radios perform all the same functions as ordinary radios. Only the antenna and mixer are in hardware, and these are generic; they don't care any more about air standards than your shirt hanger does.

In Steinbrecher radios, all of the frequency tuning, all of the modulating and demodulating, all of the channelization, all of the coding and decoding that so embroil the politicians are performed by programmable digital signal processors and can be changed at a base station in real time. Strictly speaking, the tuner and modem are not part of the base station radio at all. The broadband radio in a Steinbrecher base station can send or receive signals to or from any handset or mobile unit operating within its bandwidth (in current cellular systems the full 12.5 megahertz of the band; in PCS, still larger bands of as much as 30 megahertz).

All the processing of codes, frequencies, channels and modulations, as well as all special mobile services, can move onto computers attached to the network. Steinbrecher technology thus can open up the spectrum for open and programmable client/server systems like those that now dominate the computer industry. Moore's Law, in fact, is changing radios into portable digital computers. The most pervasive personal computer of the next decade will be a digital cellular phone operating at least 40 MIPS (millions of instructions per second).

Today the performance of analog-to-digital converters defines the limits of Steinbrecher radios. Even if the mixers are perfect, the system's performance can be no better than the accuracy of the A/D processors that transform the output of the mixers into a digital bit stream for the DSPs. Steinbrecher estimates that better broadband A/D converters—which can sample wave forms more accurately at high frequencies—could increase the performance of Steinbrecher systems by an amazing factor of 10. Pushed by demands and designs from Steinbrecher, Analog Devices and other suppliers are advancing converter technology nearly at a pace with Moore's Law, and Steinbrecher's broadband digital radios are rapidly approaching the ideal.

As Don Steinbrecher puts it, broadband A/D and DSP have changed wireless "from a radio business to a computer business." At first, the computer portion of a broadband radio was very expensive. Until the early 1980s, military customers performed advanced broadband analog-to-digital conversion and digital signal processing on million-dollar custom supercomputers. In 1986, an advanced DSP system for graphics at Bell Labs entailed the use of 82 AT&T DSP32 chips and supporting devices in a custom computer that cost some $130,000. Today, these same functions are performed on an Apple Quadra 840 AV using an AT&T 3210 running at 33 megaflops (million floating-point operations per second) and 17 MIPS for under $20 in volume. This rising tide of advances in digital technology, propelled by Moore's Law, is about to sweep Steinbrecher's recondite radio company into the midst of a mass market in cellular telephony.

And the entire cellular and PCS industries will be beating a path to Steinbrecher's door. Just as millions of people today have learned the meaning of *MIPS* and *megabytes*, millions of people around the world, believe it or not, are going to come to understand the meaning of "spurious-free dynamic range."

As a very rough analogy, imagine cranking the volume of your radio as high as possible without marring the desired signal with static and distortion. The spurious-free dynamic range of your radio would measure the distance between the lowest and the highest volumes with a clear signal. In more technical terms, spurious-free dynamic range is defined as the range of signal amplitudes that can simultaneously be processed without distortion or be resolved by a receiver without the emergence of spurious signals above the noise floor.

In building *broadband* radios with high dynamic range, however, Steinbrecher faced a fundamental technical problem. As a general rule, bandwidth is inversely proportional to dynamic range. You can have one or the other, but you can't have both. The broader the band, the more difficult it is to capture all of its contents with full accuracy and sensitivity or with full spurious-free dynamic range. An ordinary radio may command a high dynamic range of volumes because it is narrowband.

But Steinbrecher radio does not begin by tuning to one frequency alone; it grasps every frequency in a particular swath of spectrum. In some extreme Paramixer applications (94-gigahertz radar, for example), the bandwidth could be 10 gigahertz—larger than the entire range of spectrum commonly used in the air, from submarine communications at 60 hertz to C band satellite at 6 gigahertz.

In most Steinbrecher applications that require high dynamic range, however, the bandwidth runs between a few megahertz and hundreds of megahertz (compared to 30 kilohertz in a cellular phone). Unless all of the frequencies captured by the broadband radio are really present in the band rather than as artifacts of the equipment—in technical jargon, unless the signals are spurious-free—the radio user cannot tell what is going on, cannot distinguish between spurs and signals.

Steinbrecher has devoted much of his career to the grail of spurious-free dynamic range. Soon after he arrived at Massachusetts Institute of Technology in September 1961 to pursue work on device physics, he moved into the school's new Radio Astronomy Lab. The radio astronomers were using millimeter waves at 75 gigahertz to probe remote galaxies and pour through evidence of a big bang at the beginning of time. Because the return reflections from outer space were infinitesimal, the radio telescopes had to command a bandwidth of at least two gigahertz, a spurious-free dynamic range of more than 100 decibels (tens of billions-, or even trillions-to-one) and noise levels of less than 10 decibels (millionths of a watt).

The telescope signals turned out not to be spurious-free. More than 90 percent of the receiver noise—the spurious signals—originated in the frequency converter or mixer, which translated the 75-gigahertz millimeter waves in cascading analog stages of diodes and transistors, fed by tunable local oscillators, down to baseband levels that could be usefully analyzed. This impelled Steinbrecher's obsession with spurious-free dynamic range in mixers.

To achieve high dynamic range in broadband mixers, Steinbrecher discovered, was chiefly a problem of the basic physics of diodes. At the University of Florida, at ECI Corp. and at MIT, Steinbrecher had pursued studies in device physics focusing on the theory of P/N junctions—the positive-negative interfaces that create the active regions in diodes and transistors. How cleanly and abruptly they switch from on to off—how fully these switches avoid transitional effects—determines how well they can translate one frequency to another without spurs.

From this experience, Steinbrecher concluded in 1968 that receivers could be built with at least a thousand times more dynamic range than was currently believed possible. He assigned his student Robert Snyder to investigate the issue mathematically, integrating the possible performance of each component into the performance of a mixer. Snyder's results stunningly confirmed Steinbrecher's hypothesis. They predicted that in principle—with unlimited time and effort—the linearity and dynamic range of a radio could be improved to any arbitrary standard. In a key invention, Steinbrecher figured out how to create a diode circuit that could produce a perfect square wave, creating a diode with essentially zero switching time.

Steinbrecher then proceeded to put his theory into practice by developing the crucial diode and field-effect transistor arrays, mixers, amplifiers and other components necessary to build a working system of unparalleled dynamic range. Most of their advances required detailed knowledge of the behavior of P/N junctions. To this day, the performance of Steinbrecher's equipment depends on adjustment to unexpected nonlinearities and noise sources that were discovered as part of Robert Snyder's work but are still not integrated into the prevailing models of diode behavior.

Beyond radio astronomy, the people who were interested in analyzing signals of unknown frequencies, rather than tuning into preset frequencies, were in the field of military intelligence. Enemies did not normally announce in advance the frequencies they planned to use or how they would modulate them. Steinbrecher Corp.'s first major contract came in the early 1980s for remote over-the-horizon radar (ROTHR) systems used to detect planes carrying drugs from Latin America. Steinbrecher also won contracts to supply MILSTAR satellite transceivers and 94-gigahertz "eyes" for smart munitions and jet aircraft.

In 1986 these large potential businesses began to attract venture capitalists, including EG&G venture partners, The Venture Capital Fund of New England and Raytheon. As often happens, the venture capitalists sought professional management. They pushed Steinbrecher upstairs to chairman and summoned a Stanford EE graduate named Douglas Shute to manage the company's move from a manufacturer of hard-sell mixers into a producer of revolutionary digital radios.

Still, Steinbrecher Corp. long remained a tiny firm occupying a dingy one-story building in a Woburn, Mass., industrial park, where it rarely pulled in more than $5 million in revenues. Not until the early 1990s, when its technology converged with Moore's Law, did the company begin to escape its niche.

COLLISION WITH TEXAS INSTRUMENTS' DSP

Indeed, strictly speaking, even Moore's Law was not enough to make this Pentagon turkey fly. Crucial was Texas Instruments' mid-1980s campaign to remake the digital signal processor into a commodity device comparable to Intel's microprocessor. Creating development systems and software tools, TI transformed the DSP from an exotic and expensive printed circuit board full of integrated circuits into a single programmable microchip manufactured in volume on the same factory floor the company used to produce hundreds of millions of dynamic random access memories. The results exceeded all expectations. Outpacing Moore's Law by a factor of nearly four for some eight years so far, DSP cost-effectiveness began soaring tenfold every two years. Pricing the devices for digital radios, Douglas Shute saw that the wideband digital radio had "moved onto the map as a commercial product."

Also in 1989, a secret contractor asked the company if its radios could snoop on calls in the cellular band. After gigahertz explorations in radio astronomy and military projects, the 12.5 megahertz of the cellular bandwidth seemed a piece of cake. Although this national security application never came through, the idea galvanized the company. If it should need a commercial market, cellular telephony was a good bet.

The pull of opportunity, however, is usually less potent than the push of catastrophe—which is the key reason for socialism's failure. Insulating the economy from failure, it also removes a key spur for success. For all the bureaucratic rigmarole of military procurement, producers for the Pentagon live in a relatively comfortable socialist world of cost plus contracts.

In 1989, however, just before the fall of the Soviet Union, Steinbrecher began to get clear signals from Washington that the market for his products was about to collapse. MILSTAR remained an experimental program; the ROTHR system was halted after the creation of just four stations with 1,600 mixers, and suddenly the cellular opportunity was not merely an attractive option—it was crucial for survival.

When Shute and Steinbrecher viewed the cellular scene in the United States, however, they became increasingly disdainful. These radio companies had no more idea of what was possible in radio technology than had the MIT engineering lab when he arrived in 1961. Indeed, Steinbrecher Corp.'s first potential customer—a wireless colossus—refused even to meet with Shute: The chief technologist said he had investigated digital radios several years before and determined they were unable to achieve the requisite dynamic range. Moreover, at scores of thousands of dollars apiece, digital signal processors were far too expensive. Most cellular executives, along with their Washington regulators, seemed stuck in a 1970s time warp when analog still ruled and DSP was a supercomputer.

IMPORTING OBSOLESCENCE

As a result, the entire industry was convulsed by what Shute and Steinbrecher saw as a retrograde war over standards. Because Europe in general lagged far behind the United States in adopting analog cellular technology, the EEC had sponsored a multinational drive to leapfrog the United States by adopting a digital standard, which could then be exported to America. The standard they chose was called GSM (global services mobile), a time-division multiple-access (TDMA) scheme that exceeded analog capacity by breaking each channel into three digital time slots. Racing to catch up, the American industry adopted a similar TDMA approach that also increased the current system's capacity by a factor of three. With McCaw Cellular in the lead, American firms quickly committed themselves to deploy TDMA as soon as possible.

Then in 1991, Qualcomm unleashed a bombshell. Exploiting the increasing power of DSPs to process digital codes, the company demonstrated a spread-spectrum, code-division multiple-access (CDMA) modulation scheme that not only increased capacity some twentyfold over analog but also allowed use of the entire 12.5 megahertz of the cellular bandwidth in every cell. To prevent interference between adjoining cells, analog and TDMA systems could use a frequency in only one cell out of seven.

Much of the industry seemed paralyzed by fear of choosing the wrong system. To Shute and Steinbrecher, however, these fears seemed entirely reckless. Using wideband digital radios, companies could accommodate any array of frequencies and modulation schemes they desired—TDMA, CDMA, voice, data and eventually even video. Shute resolved to adapt Steinbrecher's advanced radio technology to these new markets. In mid-1992, Shute rushed ahead with a program to create a prototype cellular transceiver that could process all 12.5 megahertz of the cellular bandwidth and convert it to a digital bit stream.

The first major customer for the radios turned out to be ADC-Kentrox, a designer of analog cell extenders designed to overcome "dead zones" caused by large buildings in urban areas. This system was limited in reach to the few hundred meters the signals could be sent over analog wires without deterioration. By converting the signals to digital at the remote site, the Steinbrecher radio extended this distance from hundreds of meters to scores of kilometers and allowed the price of the product to remain at $100,000.

But these gains concealed the potential impact and meaning of the Steinbrecher technology. Once again, the Steinbrecher radios are being used to complement the existing system rather than overthrow it. In a similar way, McCaw plans to buy some $30 million worth of Steinbrecher machines to carry through its cellular digital packet data (CDPD) network. To be provided to 95 percent of McCaw's regions by the end of 1995, CDPD is a data overlay of the existing cellular system, which allows users of the current analog system to send digital data at a rate of 19.2 kilobits per second, compared to the 9.6-kilobit-per-second rate offered by most modems over twisted-pair wires.

The Steinbrecher radio can survey any existing swath of spectrum in real time and determine almost instantly which channels are in use and which are free. It is this capability that convinced McCaw to buy Steinbrecher data cells despite the commitment of McCaw's putative owner, AT&T, to sell narrowband units made by Cirrus Logics' subsidiary Pacific Communications Sciences Inc. (PCSI), which have to scan through channels one at a time. McCaw is using the Steinbrecher radios as sniffers that constantly survey the cellular band and direct data bursts to those channels that are not being used at a particular time.

Indeed, the immediate needs of the marketplace alone justify the adoption of Steinbrecher data cells. With modems and antennas increasingly available and even moving sometime next year to PCMCIA slots the size of a credit card, demand for wireless data is likely to soar.

PCSI is now shipping a quintuple-threat communicator that fits into the floppy bay of an advanced IBM ThinkPad notebook or an Apple PowerBook, enabling them to send and receive faxes, make wireless or wire-line phone calls, dispatch data files across the existing cellular network or send CDPD packets at 19.2 kilobits per second. Speech recognition capabilities from IBM and Dragon Systems will come next year to personal digital assistants, permitting them to read or receive E-mail by voice. Although the first Newtons and Zoomers have disappointed their sponsors, the market will ignite over the next two years as vendors adopt the essential form factor of a digital cellular phone with computer functions rather than providing a kluge computer with a vaporware phone.

Nonetheless, McCaw has more on its mind with Steinbrecher than merely gaining a second source for CDPD sniffers. By simultaneously purchasing some 10 percent of the company and putting chief technical officer Nicholas Kauser on the Steinbrecher board, McCaw is signaling not a tactical move but a major strategic thrust. The Steinbrecher rollout in fact represents McCaw's stealth deployment of broadband digital capability.

Today the rival CDPD equipment from PCSI, Hughes and AT&T all can be made to perform CDPD communications as an overlay to the existing cellular phone system. However, only the Steinbrecher systems can be upgraded to perform all of the functions of a base station and more, for voice, data and video. Only Steinbrecher allows the replacement of 416 radio transceivers, one for each channel, with one broadband radio and some digital signal processing chips. Only Steinbrecher can replace a $1.5 million, 1,000-square-foot cellular base station with a box the size of a briefcase costing some $100,000 but, thanks to Moore's Law, racing toward $10,000.

It remains to be seen only whether McCaw will have the guts to follow through on this initiative by completely rebuilding its network to accommodate the wideband radio being installed at its heart. Self-cannibalization is the rule of success in information technology. Intel and Microsoft, for example, lead the way in constantly attacking their own products. But this mode of life is deeply alien to the telephone business—even an entrepreneurial outfit like McCaw.

With new software and a simple upgrade to a MiniCell, the Steinbrecher DataCell will allow the McCaw system to handle all modulation schemes simultaneously—AMPS, TDMA, CDMA and future methods such as Orthogonal Frequency Division Multiple Access—obviating the need for hybrid phones. The multiprotocol and aerobatic capabilities of broadband digital radios could enable McCaw to roll out a cornucopia of PCS services—for everything from monitoring vending machines or remote power stations to tracking trucks and packages, and linking laptops and PDAs—while the rest of the industry is still paralyzed by wrangles over incumbent users, regulatory procedures, frequency access and radio standards.

Making channel sizes a variable rather than a fixed function of radios, Steinbrecher systems offer the possibility of bandwidth on demand. They could open up the entire spectrum as one gigantic broadband pipe into which we would be able to insert packets in any empty space—dark fiber in the air.

SO STOP THE AUCTION!

So what does this have to do with the impending spectrum auction? Almost everything. Strictly speaking, the FCC is leasing 10-year exclusive rights to radiate electromagnetic waves at certain frequencies to deliver PCS. This entire auction concept is tied to thousands of exclusive frequency licenses. It has no place for broadband radios that treat all frequencies alike and offer bandwidth on demand. It has no place for modulation schemes that do not need exclusive spectrum space. Continuing to use interference standards based on analog transmissions that are affected by every passing spray of radiation,

FCC rules fail to grasp the far more robust nature of digital on-off codes with error correction. By the time the FCC gets around to selling its 2,500 shards of air, the air will have been radically changed by new technology.

The FCC is fostering a real estate paradigm for the spectrum. You buy or lease spectrum as you would a spread of land. Once you have your license, you can use it any way you want as long as you don't unduly disturb the neighbors. You rent a stretch of beach and build a wall.

The Steinbrecher system, by contrast, suggests a model not of a beach but of an ocean. You can no more lease electromagnetic waves than you can lease ocean waves. Enabled by new technology, this new model is suitable for an information superhighway in the sky. You can use the spectrum as much as you want as long as you don't collide with anyone else or pollute it with high-powered noise or other nuisances.

In the Steinbrecher model, you employ the spectrum as you use any public right of way. You are responsible for keeping your eyes open and avoiding others. You cannot just buy a 10-year lease and then barge blindly all over the air in a high-powered vessel, depending on the government to keep everyone else off your territory and out of your way. The spectrum is no longer dark. The Steinbrecher broadband radio supplies you with lights as you travel the information superhighway. You can see other travelers and avoid them.

Even if Steinbrecher radios did not exist, however, the assumptions of the auction are collapsing in the face of innovations by Qualcomm and other spread-spectrum companies. Like Steinbrecher radios, CDMA modulation schemes allow you to use spectrum without interfering with others. To auditors without the code, calls seem indistinguishable from noise. But radios with the code can dig up signals from under the noise floor. Up to the point of traffic congestion where the quality of the signal begins to degrade gracefully, numerous users can employ the same frequencies at the same time.

This property of CDMA has been tested in Qualcomm's CDMA Omnitracs position locator and two-way communications system. Mainly used by trucking companies, it is now being extended to cars, boats, trains and other mobile equipment. Based on geosynchronous satellites, it operates all across the country, with some 60,000 units, under a "secondary license" that forbids Qualcomm to interfere with the primary license-holders of the same frequencies. Qualcomm's transceivers on the tops of trucks use a small antenna that issues a beam six to 10 degrees in width. Because satellites are just two degrees apart, the Qualcomm beam can blanket several satellites. Other users, however, are entirely unconscious of the presence of the CDMA signal. Omnitracs has operated for some six years and has not interfered with anyone yet.

NO MORE BLIND DRIVERS ON THE INFORMATION SUPERHIGHWAY

With an increasing array of low-interference technologies available, the FCC should not give exclusive rights to anyone. Instead, it should impose a heavy burden of proof on any service providers with blind or high-powered systems that maintain that they cannot operate without an exclusive license, that want to build on the beach and keep everyone else out of the surf. In particular, the FCC should make all the proponents of TDMA, whether in the American or European GSM systems, explain why the government should wall off spectrum. The wireless systems of the future will offer bandwidth on demand and send their packets wherever there is room.

At the same time that new technologies make hash of the need to auction off exclusive licenses, Qualcomm and Steinbrecher also radically attack the very notion of spectrum scarcity on which the auction is based. Steinbrecher's radio makes it possible to manufacture new spectrum nearly at will. By putting one of his MiniCells on every telephone pole and down every alley and in every elevator shaft, the cellular industry can exponentially multiply the total number of calls it can handle. At some $100,000 apiece and dropping in price, these MiniCells can operate at 900 megahertz or six gigahertz just as well as at the two-gigahertz range being auctioned by the government. It is as if Reed Hundt is auctioning off beachfront property, with a long list of codicils and regulations and restrictive covenants, while the tide pours in around him and creates new surf everywhere.

Still more important in view of the coming auction, the wideband capability of the Steinbrecher radio joins CDMA in allowing the use of huge spans of spectrum that are ostensibly occupied by other users. The Steinbrecher radio can survey the gigahertz reserves of the military and intelligence services, UHF television and microwave, and direct usage to the many fallow regions. For example, the prime territory between 225 megahertz and 400 megahertz, consisting of some 3,000 25-kilohertz channels, is entirely occupied by government and air force communications. But most of the channels are largely unused. A Steinbrecher radio could sit on those frequencies and direct calls to empty slots.

An ideal system would combine Steinbrecher broadband machines with Qualcomm's modulation schemes. Steinbrecher supplies the lights and eyes to find space in already-licensed spectrum bands; CDMA allows the noninvasive entry into spans of spectrum that are in active use.

Meanwhile, the Steinbrecher system changes the very nature of spectrum "ownership" or rental. Unrestricted to a single band or range of frequencies, Steinbrecher radios can reach from the kilohertz to the high gigahertz and go to any unoccupied territory. As Steinbrecher radios become the dominant technology, the notion of spectrum assignments allotted in 2,500 specific shards becomes a technological absurdity.

Wall Street is beginning to catch on. When Steinbrecher announced in January a private placement through Alex. Brown, the company wanted to raise some $20 million. The response was overwhelming, and hundreds of frustrated investors were left wringing their hands as the new radio left the station. The sole proprietorship of the mid-1980s with revenues of $5 million or less was moving into sleek new headquarters off Route 128 in Burlington. Steinbrecher Corp. was becoming yet another of the Moore's Law monsters.

Meanwhile, the issue for Washington emerges starkly. Do we want a strategy for MiniCells or for Minitels?

8

Washington's Bogeymen

Big Government and Mass Media always feed on fear of monsters. While politicians promise to protect the people from the dreaded private sector, leading newspapers such as the *Washington Post* and network shows such as "60 Minutes" chime in with continuing reports on the economy as seen from the shores of Loch Ness. Peering through the shifting, inscrutable murk of the marketplace, pundits both private and public can descry beneath every ripple of industrial change the spectral shape of some circling shark or serpent from which only a new bureaucracy or liberal constabulary can save us.

There are always many witnesses to the threat. In his campaigns of creative destruction, any great capitalist provokes enough panic in the establishment to fuel the beadles who would bring him down. Losing competitors, whether in oil or software, are always in the vanguard of the monster hunt, which is therefore usually launched in the name of "competition" and is designed to stop it in its tracks before anyone wins.

In the industrial era it was the so-called Robber Barons—creators of the great industries of oil, steel and finance—who greased the growth of government with their chimerical menace. Radically reducing the prices of their products, such leaders as Rockefeller, Carnegie and Morgan expanded the economy to serve middle- and lower-income customers and laid the foundation for the American industrial leadership that triumphed in two world wars. But at the same time, charged with predatory pricing, collusive marketing dumping and other competitive violations, Rockefeller, Carnegie and Morgan emerged as the monsters of monopoly who fueled the growth of government through the first 40 years of the century.

Now, with information technology driving private sector wealth and power, there is a need for new monsters to fuel new sieges of government and regulatory growth. This time the monsters bear the names of Milken, Gates and Malone—new trolls to terrify little children and cause competitors to cozen Washington and judges to reach for their RICO bludgeons and commissioners to salivate and shuffle subpoenas and senators to tremble and wreak new tomes of law and bureaucrats to sow the economy with minefields of abstruse new rules.

Of the three new monsters, big government managed to deliver us first from Michael Milken, depicted as a Banker Shark. But Milken's vision impregnably survives in the form of the industries and infrastructures he financed, chiefly cellular phones, fiber optics and cable television—the forces that laid the foundation for a new broadband economy.

With Milken laid low by cancer and the courts, Washington needed new monsters for the 1990s. After serious and continuing contemplation of Bill Gates as a possible MicroShark hidden amid the mazes of Windows and DOS, Washington recently has focused on the formidable visage of John Malone.

As the titan of cable and leader of Tele-Communications Inc., better known as TCI, he was a billion-dollar beneficiary of Milken's bonds. At a time when governments everywhere covet the huge, new wealth emerging from information superhighways, Malone has become the favored target of the Loch Ness news hounds and public-law pinstripes: an Abominable Snowman ranging down from the Rockies to raid and ruin rival companies, terrorize politicians and gouge his 21 million customers. Or, in the words of then Senator Albert Gore, Malone is Darth Vader himself.

This particular monster hunt, however, could not be more ill-timed. There is no way that this administration can demonize the cable industry and micromanage telecom without direly damaging all its hopes for an information superhighway and thus the best prospects for the future of the U.S. economy. Just as the automobile industry was the real heir to the triumphs of the "robber barons" in oil, steel and finance, so the computer industry—the core of U.S. world industrial leadership—will be the chief beneficiary of cable and telecom ventures in broadband networks.

The U.S. now commands global dominance in computer technology. But as Andrew Grove told *Forbes ASAP*, "infinite processing power will only get you so far with limited bandwidth." The next generation of computer progress depends upon the efficient use of cable bandwidth to homes and home offices, which comprise a fist-growing 60 percent of the current market for computers. Even if computer executives fail to see the threat, the monster hunt against cable thus jeopardizes the supreme achievement of the American economy over the last decade—its global lead in computers.

The U.S. government constantly reiterates its desire for information superhighways. The problem is that punctuating the call for broadband nets is an insistent mantra of "competition" that reverberates through the speeches of nearly all participants in the debate. As Ward White, vice-president of government affairs for the U.S. Telephone Association, points out, however, this mantra of competition "disguises a new scheme of market allocation run by the regulators."

In this competition no one can win or make any money. The $10 billion in profits claimed by the Baby Bells still under the Greene thumb are highly questionable. Most of their copper wires and narrowband switches—rapidly obsolescing by any objective standard—are being written off over decades. That means the real costs of the Bells should be much higher than their announced costs, which do not adequately reflect the fact that their $300 billion worth of plant and equipment is rapidly losing market value.

As TCI's sharp and salty young COO, Brendan Clouston, points out, telephone companies are used to pretending to make money under rate-of-return regulations when they are really losing it.

Cable companies, by contrast, are used to pretending to lose money when in fact they are raking it in. A standing joke around the offices of John Malone's cable empire, which comprises TCI and Liberty Media, asks what Malone will do if the firm ever reports a large profit. The answer: Fire the accountant. Indeed, TCI did not report even a cosmetic profit until the first quarter of 1993. Cable firms were financed with junk bonds and other debt that allows investors to be paid off with tax-deductible interest payments rather than double-taxed dividends and capital gains favored by the telcos.

Michael Milken, the financial father of the cable industry, channeled some $10 billion in high-yield securities to TCI, Time-Warner, Turner, Viacom and other cable firms at a time when they were struggling for survival. As a result, the cable companies are eight times more leveraged in their debt-equity ratios than telephone companies are. But driven by the demands of debt, the cable firms use their capital some two-and-a-half times more efficiently. Generating $20 billion in revenues, one-fourth as much as the telcos, cable firms use just one-tenth the capital.

The cable companies are leveraged at a rate of between seven- and ten-to-one on their cash flow. Moreover, some 60 percent of cable company assets are "good will." Included in the purchase price of new acquisitions, "good will" represents the intangible value of cash flows and synergies expected from new technologies and programming.

Built on vision and debt, such entrepreneurial companies cannot invest without the possibility of large returns. Attack the cable industry's cash flow and prospects, and you attack its lifeline. Attack the cable industry's cash flow and prospects, and you reduce its available investment by a factor of five or more. Bell Atlantic was originally willing to pay for TCI nearly 12 times its cash flow.

THE REAL MONSTER: GOVERNMENT

In this highly leveraged arena government itself is the real monster: an 800-pound gorilla. Where does the 800-pound gorilla sit? Wherever it wants. Early in April of this year it chose to sit on the cable industry. More specifically, it plumped down in the middle of Brendan Clouston's desk in the form of a 700-page FCC document reregulating the cable industry. It was full of detailed regulations on everything from how fast he must pick up his phones for customer complaints and what he should charge for each tier of service and for each component of cable gear, to how large, implicitly, his return on investment can be (about 11.5 percent). He faced the mandate to adjust nearly every price and policy in the company within six weeks and to justify each price by filling out 60 pages of forms. In a menacing note for the future portending new government plans for redistributionist pricing, he is required to report the median income in each of his service areas.

The FCC is not really to blame for this onslaught, since it resisted the new congressional power grab. In any case, this agency is only part of Clouston's problem. He also faces an aggressive new spirit at the Federal Trade Commission, at the Department of Justice and in Congress, which permits him to collaborate with any company as long as it is not a telephone firm with useful fiber networks and switching systems in TCI's own regions. Full of rhetoric inviting every industry from the telcos to the power companies into the cable trade, many of the legislative proposals, FTC policies and FCC ukases converging on Clouston's desk seem to be intended to transform cable from a galvanizing entrepreneurial force in the U.S. economy into a sleepy-time public utility run by lawyers. At stake is the future of the information superhighway and thus the future of the U.S. economy.

SUPERHIGHWAY HYPE IS UNDERSTATED

Information superhighways are one of those rare technologies that are actually far more powerful and promising than the hype surrounding them. The first fruits of this development are already evident, as the U.S. has led the world in deploying computer networks. Over the next five years broadband networks can transform the entire economy, projecting it onto a higher plane of growth and productivity.

For the last decade the performance of the economy has perplexed the economics profession. Throughout the 1980s most economists predicted that U.S. interest rates would soar as a result of world-lagging rates of personal savings. When interest rates instead dropped, economists pointed to a "dangerous dependence" on foreign sources of capital such as Japan, which were investing close to $100 billion annually in the U.S.

Today, adverse tax and regulatory policies in the U.S. have entirely reversed capital flows, with funds now leaving the U.S. for foreign markets at an annual rate of $80 billion. Meanwhile, as Federal Reserve Governor Lawrence Lindsey has warned, personal savings have plunged to all-time lows. By every rule of economics, interest rates should soar or growth should collapse.

Yet despite a slight upward drift in recent months, U.S. interest rates remain low by historic standards, and the U.S. continues to lead the major powers in economic growth and has extended its lead in productivity. As Michael Jensen of Harvard Business School has shown, a close analysis of the figures from U.S. corporations now reveals a historic acceleration of U.S. productivity growth during the 1980s. According to an analysis by Morgan Stanley, between 1987 and 1992 U.S. corporations captured some 47.7 percent of global profits and 37.4 percent of global sales. Continued slumps in Europe and Japan combined with reviving growth in the U.S. indicate that U.S. market share is still rising.

This record of supremacy is entirely baffling to the economics profession and its megaphones in the media. Focusing on the Loch Ness news, they have spent a decade in lamentations over the prospects of the U.S. economy, reaching a pitch of funereal keening during the 1992 election campaigns. But to analysts focused on the ever-growing U.S. lead in technology, these results are no mystery at all.

U.S. supremacy is focused on information tools and spearheaded by computer networks. U.S. companies command some two-thirds of the world's profits in information technology, hardware and software, and entirely dominate world markets in computer networks. Half the world's 110 million personal computers are in the U.S., and between 1989 and 1993 the share connected to networks rose from less than 10 percent to more than 60 percent.

The ultimate information industry is finance. During the last decade the U.S. employed information technology to transform its financial system. Spearheaded by Milken and a $200 billion junk bond market, the U.S. drastically reduced the role of banks and proliferated an array of more flexible and specialized financial agencies. While over the last 12 years banks' share of private credit for non-financial companies dropped from two-thirds to less than 20 percent, the U.S. surged into global leadership in applying information technology to the field of financial innovation.

In essence, the law of the microcosm shattered the financial system into silicon smithereens and vastly enhanced its productivity. As the late Warren Brookes has written, "If every bank is nothing more than an information system, then by definition every information system has the capacity to be a bank, and every owner of an information system, from a desktop computer to a mainframe terminal, can be a banker." What happened was that thousands of brokers, mathematicians, financial consultants, insurance salespeople, credit card merchants and bonds traders took this opportunity to break into the field of financial entrepreneurship.

As a result, the U.S. set an entirely new world standard for capital efficiency, generating far more economic growth per dollar of savings than any other country. As explained two centuries ago by Adam Smith, key to productivity growth is the refinement of the division of labor, the expansion of specialization, the breakdown of functions into subfunctions and niches. The key force fostering specialization in the U.S. is computer networks.

Over the next decade computer networks will expand their bandwidth by factors of thousands and reconstruct the entire U.S. economy in their image. TV will expire and transpire into a new cornucopia of choice and empowerment. Great cities will hollow out as the best and brightest in them retreat to rural redoubts and reach out to global markets and communities. The most deprived ghetto child in the most blighted project will gain educational opportunities exceeding those of today's suburban preppie. Small towns will become industrial centers in the new information economy. Hollywood and Wall Street will totter and diffuse to all points of the nation and the globe. Families will regroup around the evolving silicon hearths of a new cottage economy. Video culture will transcend its current mass-media doldrums, playing to lowest-common-denominator shocks and prurient interests, and will effloresce into a plethora of products suggestive of the book industry.

In essence, people will no longer settle for whatever or whoever is playing on the tube or down the street or in their local office or corporation. Instead, they will seek out and command their first choices in employment, culture, entertainment and religion. They will reach out across the country and around the world to find the best colleagues for every major project. Productivity and efficiency will inexorably rise. A culture of first choices will evince a bias toward excellence rather than a bias toward the mediocre, convenient or crude.

The entire centralizing force of the Industrial Revolution, which brought capital and labor together in vast pyramidal institutions and reduced workers to accessories of the machine and the tube, will give way to the explosive centrifuge of the microcosm and telecosm. Yielding single-chip supercomputers linked in global broadband networks, these technologies fling intelligence beyond the boundaries of every top-down institution and Machine Age social system.

The vision of information superhighways revitalizing the American economy and culture is far more true and compelling than even its advocates comprehend. People who underestimate the impact of bandwidth will miss the supreme investment opportunities of the epoch.

DECLINE AND RISE OF THE MALONE MODEL

Dominant in the industry are two essential models for fulfilling the promise of the superhighway. One scheme, long associated with John Malone and other cable executives, is the monster model: combining content and conduit in order to gain monopoly rents.

Because it reaches more than 20 percent of all cable customers, access to the TCI conduit can heavily influence the success or failure of any content venture. As Andrew Kessler, partner and multimedia guru at Unterberg Harris and *Forbes ASAP* columnist, puts it, "If you want to create a cable channel, you may have to send it through Malone's bottleneck—a satellite dish farm outside Denver. I suspect that could cost you some $4 million in cash, or, alternatively, you can give Malone 30 percent of your company."

This monster model is in essence the way Malone built up Liberty Media and the content side of TCI, which together own parts of TNT, the Discovery Channel, American Movie Classics, Black Entertainment TV, Court TV, Encore, Starz, Family Channel, Home Shopping Network, QVC, Video Jukebox and an array of regional sports networks. It has been widely reported that AT&T and financier Herbert Allen are creating a new classic sports network and will give a chunk of it to Liberty in exchange for access to Malone's conduit.

The other model is that of the common-carrier, upheld both by the telephone companies and by Internet. In this model you build an open conduit and exercise virtually no influence on content. Using the phone system or Internet, people can communicate anything they want as long as they observe the protocols of the public switched telephone network or of Internet's TCP/IP. Extended to images, this model suggests a "video dial tone." You can dial up any other machine connected to the network and download or upload any films, files, documents, pictures or multimedia programs that you wish. Although telephone companies or Internet providers may own content, they cannot privilege their own programming. Their content has to compete for customers freely with all other content available on the network.

The notoriety of the Malone model and the resentment it arouses far and wide explain much of the hostility toward the cable industry and John Malone. This may even explain the current rage to reregulate the industry. The great irony today is that Malone and the rest of the cable leaders were in the process of abandoning the Malone model at the very moment that many telephone executives seemed to adopt it.

It was Malone, after all, who was willing to sell his content to Bell Atlantic, and it was Raymond Smith, above all, who insisted on acquiring the assets of Liberty Media. It was Bell South that was willing to pitch in some $2 billion to QVC's bidding for Paramount when John Malone left Batty Diller high and dry. Ameritech, too, was reported to be preparing a pitch for Paramount.

Malone was right in his attempt to sell out at the top to Bell Atlantic. The idea of combining conduit and content was valid in a regime of bandwidth scarcity. In a regime of broadband information superhighways, however, content providers will want to put their programming on everyone's conduits, and conduit owners will want to carry everyone's content. In a world of bandwidth abundance Paramount will not want to restrict its films to Bell South's network any more than Bell South will exclude films from other sources.

The key condition for the success of the open model and the eclipse of the Malone model, however, is real bandwidth abundance. If the federal government prohibits the interconnection of conduits, then the Malone model gains a new lease on life. In a world of bandwidth scarcity the owner of the conduit not only can but must control access to it. Thus, the owner of the conduit also shapes the content. It does not matter whether the conduit company is headed by a scheming monopolist or by Mitch Kapor and the members of the Electronic Frontier Foundation. Bandwidth scarcity will require the managers of the network to determine the video programming on it.

In a world of information superhighways, however, the most open networks will dominate, and the proprietary networks will wither. Malone's understanding of this fact—that his own model would soon expire in an environment of bandwidth abundance—motivated his effort to merge with Bell Atlantic.

The law of the telecosm inexorably dictates mergers not between content and conduit, but between conduit and conduit. In particular, today it mandates the merger of the huge fiber resources of the telephone companies—which are nine times as extensive as cable industry fiber and are estimated to rise to 2.7 million lines by next year—with the huge asset of 57 million broadband links to homes commanded by the cable industry. Obstructing such mergers in the name of competition, or antitrust, or regulatory caprice, is wantonly destructive to the future of the economy.

THE SIREN CALL FROM FOREIGN SHORES

Most of the gains of the telecosm depend on government willingness to allow the creation of coherent broadband networks with no prohibitions against the convergence of cable and telco systems. For a while it appeared that the Clinton administration was willing to accommodate this development. Now it appears that it prefers to lead the U.S. government into a private-sector monster hunt. Rather than releasing America's cable and telco firms to build this redemptive infrastructure, Washington leaders seem chiefly concerned with assuring themselves that no one will make any money from it. As a result, with some $1 billion in annual funding from Wall Street, cable and telephone firms are increasingly moving abroad to fulfill the promise of information superhighways.

TCI and U.S. West, for example, are serving some quarter-million British citizens with combined telephone and cable functions over a hybrid network of coax and fiber. The current regulatory climate dooms the proposed merger of Southwestern Bell and Cox Cable and their plans to launch information highways in Phoenix and Atlanta. But these companies continue to expand their hybrid cable and phone networks In Liverpool and Birmingham in England. In the U.S. NYNEX has been one of the most sluggish Bells in information superhighway projects. But from Gibraltar to Bangkok, it is supplying an array of wireless and wireline services. In the U.K. NYNEX Cablecomm holds 17 cable franchises passing 2.5 million homes and plans some $2 billion in future investments. In the wake of the new regulations Bell Canada International (BCI) reduced its offer for Jones Intercable by five percent, but the two companies are barging ahead in East London, Leeds and Aylesbury. Time-Warner, Ameritech and other cable and telephone companies are also rushing to less regulated realms to lay information infrastructure everywhere from Scotland to New Zealand.

In the U.S. such collaborations of cable and telephone companies would be paralyzed by litigation and bureaucracy. It appears increasingly possible that despite the huge lead created by the U.S. cable industry, which, unique in the world, has extended broadband access to some 95 percent of American homes, broadband networks will first be built outside the U.S.

American politicians must face reality. With cable, the U.S. is far and away the world leader in broadband technology. With cable, the U.S. can have a national network reaching every American community by the year 2000. Without cable, however, the U.S. can forget the idea of building a national system of information superhighways in this decade. Without cable, the global race is even, and several European and Asian countries command a significant edge as a result of their integrated cable and telephone firms.

The U.S. panacea of "competition" without winners may work for commodity markets, which require low levels of incremental investment and offer returns commensurate with the rate of interest. Governing technological progress, though, is the very different regime of dynamic competition and creative destruction.

Impelling most technology investment is the pursuit of transitory positions of monopoly that may yield massive profits. That's why in the late 1970s and early 1980s Milken directed some $17 billion to the cable TV, fiberoptic telephony and cellular telephone industries, giving the U.S. a decisive lead in all these areas. That's why Intel Corp. has been investing $2 billion a year in new wafer fabrication capacity to secure its global edge in microprocessors. That's why Microsoft invests $1 billion a year or more (depending on definitions) in new software technology to integrate ever-new functions into its dominant operating systems. And that's why Bell Atlantic contemplated investing what amounted to some $33 billion in John Malone's company, TCI.

Until replaced by a better system, every innovation gives its owner a temporary monopoly. Otherwise it is not a true innovation. Today, whether anyone likes it or not, the cable industry has a temporary monopoly on broadband links to the home. By interconnecting these links to the fiber networks of the phone companies, the two industries together can create a national information superhighway some five or 10 years sooner than can Japan or Europe.

Some 79 percent of the costs of a network come in the final connections to homes: the distribution and drops that the cable industry has installed over the last 25 years. Joined with the telephone industry's fiber optics—nine times more extensive than the cable industry's fiber deployment—this hybrid cable-telco network would represent an authentic innovation and would trigger a flood of real competition supplying a huge array of powerful new broadband communications services. According to authoritative estimates cited by Vice-President Gore and the FCC, these innovations would increase U.S. productivity growth by 40 percent over the next decade. This immense undertaking would also yield huge profits for as long as a decade to some of the companies that master it.

The government might regard these profits as "obscene." But they will be indispensable both to pay for the transformation of American media and to attract the next generation of competitors into the business. These rivals are already on the way: Direct Broadcast Satellite (DBS), wireless cellular "cable" at 28 gigahertz, low-earth-orbiting satellites such as the Gates-McCaw Teledesic, all-fiber "Internets" and the array of passive fiber-to-the-home technology summed up as the fibersphere. Even broadcasters and utilities will enter the field. In a world where the government micromanages communications in the name of "competition," however, all these capital-hungry competitors will languish.

DYNAMIC COMPETITION OR STATIC COMPETITORS?

The dynamics of competition on the information superhighway repeats the previous dynamics of competition in computers. Preventing the dominance of successful technologies—sustaining an artificial diversity—is anticompetitive. If in the early 1980s the Department of Justice had ruled against the Microsoft and Intel standards, for example, and had required a variety of microprocessor instruction sets and operating systems, the result would have been less competition in computers, not more. Perhaps Pick, Quarterdeck, Digital Research and others would have gained share against Microsoft. But the applications software business, with its floods of real competition in new programs for everything from financial management to videogames, would have languished, along with the parallel markets in hardware peripherals.

The fact is that Microsoft faces antitrust pressure at the twilight of its dominance. Impelled by the new markets for multimedia and handheld communicators, the industry is on the cusp of an entirely new landscape of competition. In this new arena Microsoft's present market share and installed base are barriers to entry for Microsoft rather than for its rivals. If Microsoft is to prevail in these new areas, it must cannibalize its own systems and compete on an equal basis with everyone else.

The laws of dynamic competition apply just as forcefully to networks as to computers. Just as the time arrived when text editing and disk utilities would be integrated into operating systems—or floating point computations would be integrated into microprocessors—broadband cable services now must be integrated into the public switched telephone network (PSTN), not segregated from it. Despite the "competitive" access dreams of politicians and regulators, true competition requires that the "two-wire model" of home communications give way to a broadband, one-wire system.

The best and most cost-effective network practicable today is a combination of telco fiber and cable coax. Even the telephone industry agrees. U.S. West, Pacific Telesis and Bellcore all have resolved on the same hybrid system that TCI, Time-Warner and Cablelabs have pioneered. Without mergers with cable firms, the telcos in essence will try to rebuild cable networks.

Attempting to duplicate the connections to homes built by the cable industry over the last 25 years, however, the telephone industry would have to spend some $200 billion. It would have to sustain this level of new investment while maintaining its existing plant and expanding into long-distance and other services. It would have to summon large incremental capital in the face of continued competition from the cable industry's taking of many of the most profitable markets.

The telcos currently declare they are willing to make these investments. They tell Washington regulators and politicians that all will be fine as long as they are allowed to own programming and information services and build equipment. But the message from the markets is clear and to the contrary. At the very time that telco executives were intoning their bold plans, telephone and cable share prices were plunging toward new lows. Now Raymond Smith of Bell Atlantic is announcing a half-billion-dollar reduction in infrastructure outlays. Southwestern Bell is giving up its plans to buy Cox Cable. Under a similar "competitive" regime in cellular telephony, even AT&T and McCaw have found their merger in jeopardy.

Under rate-of-return regulations with prohibition of cross-subsidies from current cash flow, a "competitive" information superhighway simply cannot fly. An information superhighway cannot be built under a canopy of federal tariffs, price controls, mandates and allocated markets.

HIGHWAY IMPERATIVE: CABLE-PC

Politicians must recognize that what is at stake is not merely games, entertainment and a few educational frills but the very future of the U.S. economy. Cable is central not only to the next generation of television technology but also to the next generation of computer technology.

Again, many companies offer bold words in business plans for interconnecting homes with new networks. Indeed, the telcos can provide some intriguing computer services through their accelerating rollout of Integrated Services Digital Networks (ISDN), as was so eloquently urged by Mitch Kapor and others. Internet will continue to expand rapidly its cornucopia of mostly narrowband offerings. Bill Gates and Craig McCaw may even enlarge the bandwidth available to homes to a level of 2.4 megabits per second through their elegant and ambitious Teledesic. Direct broadcast satellite systems and public utilities and wireless cable operators will all enrich the flow of video to the nation's homes.

Except in the short run, though, these systems are not remotely competitive with cable. Available ISDN, for example, offers less than one-100th the bandwidth of one digital cable channel and less than one-1,000th the bandwidth of a cable coax line. The other rivals to cable, from direct broadcast satellite to Teledesic, are similarly far too little and too late. Even the advanced 28-gigahertz wireless cable projects, for all their promise as supplementary systems, cannot ultimately compete with the potential two-way bandwidth of fiber-coax systems in the ground.

All the current plans of the telephone companies and the government leave the huge U.S. endowment of home computers—the fastest-growing and most promising segment of the computer industry—stranded in a narrowband world. Only the cable industry's gigahertz links, passing into some 95 percent of American homes, can launch the American personal computer industry into a new level of two-way broadband digital connectivity.

For that reason the future of the American computer industry largely depends on the future of the cable industry. By linking America's computers to broadband networks and then to telco fiber systems, cable can be the great enabler of the next phase of development in America's digital economy.

In laying broadband systems the cable industry has already been forced to solve many of the key problems of an information superhighway. Although often depicted as an intrinsically one-way service, cable technology has, in fact, long provided two-way capabilities.

Every cable coax line, for example, offers potential bandwidth equivalent to six times the 160 megahertz of spectrum assigned by the FCC for personal communications services. Cable can accommodate as much as one gigahertz—a billion cycles per second—of communications power. This is some 250,000 times the capacity of a four-kilohertz telephone line to the home. Just one six-megahertz cable channel commands 1,500 times the bandwidth of a telephone line. In every coax connection the first four channels, between five and 30 megahertz, are reserved not for broadcast but for reverse communications to the headend. Widely used to transfer video programming among headends and satellite dishes and other programming sources, these channels alone already represent a potential information highway for home computers 2,500 times faster than a 9,600-baud modem to a phone line.

Even these possibilities, however, underestimate the potential of cable. The coax laid by the cable firms must carry analog video material without interference or distortion. This means cable equipment must track perfectly all the analog waveforms representing the shape and brightness of the image, and must detect tiny differences in the frequencies of FM signals bearing color and sound information. Because any deviation in an analog wave imparts a defect to the picture, cable TV has had to develop extremely low loss technologies. Although most current cable systems function at much lower signal-to-noise ratios, measured logarithmically, a cable TV plant can potentially function at nearly 50 decibels, or at a signal-to-noise power ratio of almost 100,000-to-one.

Necessary to transmit high-quality analog video, between 10,000- and 100,000-to-1 signal-to-noise ratios are vast overkill for the relatively crude on-off codes of digital communications, which can function at 17 decibels or less. Therefore, the one-gigahertz coax lines can carry many more than one bit per hertz. Craig Tanner, vice-president of advanced TV projects at Cablelabs, the industry's research arm in Louisville, Colo., estimates that by wiggling every wave in readable patterns using a modulation scheme called 256 QAM (quadrature amplitude modulation), cable systems can transmit as many as seven bits per hertz. This means that the one-gigahertz bandwidth of an existing cable line might potentially carry between six and eight gigabits per second, or more than three gigabits per second each way. These potential links to homes are more capacious than the current telephone fiber lines that accommodate tens of thousands of phone calls among telco central offices.

This bandwidth represents the real potential of cable coax. For the next decade much of the cable plant will still be devoted to analog TV broadcasts or to digital renditions of pay-per-view movies. Time-Warner's Orlando project, however, envisions devoting the top 350 megahertz of its system to two-way digital communications, including 100 megahertz for the personal communications services of wireless telephony and 150 megahertz for digital two-way data flows. At a very conservative estimate of two bits per hertz, Time-Warner projects a total of 300 megabits per second from these digital channels. At these levels a computer could download a full movie of two-and-a-half hours in about one minute.

CABLE'S REAL POTENTIAL IS NOT TV

Abandonment of the Malone model by Malone and the rest of the cable industry ultimately requires that cable TV magnates develop a new grasp of the dynamics of the microcosm: the exponential growth of computer power and connections. Accustomed to the role of propagating mass entertainment, cable leaders have long downplayed the potential market in computer communications.

Gradually growing throughout TCI, Time-Warner, Continental Cablevision, Jones Intercable and other cable firms, however, is a recognition that the real future of cable is in computers rather than TVs. As David Fellows of Continental declared in launching his pioneering new Internet access system in Boston in late February, "The market for computer communications is huge."

Indeed, during the next decade the cable companies are going to discover that the computer market for their services is far more important than the television market. The computer industry, hardware and software, is already some 60 percent larger than the television and movie industries put together and is growing six times as fast. On-line networked computer services, such as Prodigy, CompuServe, Delphi and America Online, are collectively growing at a pace of close to 100 percent per year. When on-line services can exchange video and audio files as readily as they transfer text today, these computer networks will be able to outperform any television system. Against all their expectations and plans, cable executives are going to find themselves a central part of the computer networking industry.

As Fellows explains, "Cable and computer network topologies go together perfectly. Both provide shared bandwidth. Ethernet over cable is a natural." In both networks all the data flow by every terminal. The receiver tunes into the desired channel. For computers, cable offers the dumb bandwidth that is increasingly needed as terminals gain near-supercomputer powers. In the past networks had to be smart in order to provide needed services to the dumb terminals on their periphery, whether phones, computers or TVs. Dumb terminals could tolerate narrowband connections. In the future, however, all terminals will command supercomputer powers.

When terminals are smart, the intelligence in networks flows to the fringes. When terminals are smart, networks must be broad and dumb. There is no way that an intelligent switching fabric can anticipate the constantly evolving technology emerging from a computer industry in a frenzied process of change. There is no way that John Malone's satellite farm outside Denver will be able to satisfy the demands for programming and communications of 100 million networked teleputers. While the telephone business struggles with the increasing problems of intelligent central switches with some 25 million lines of software code, the cable industry is creating dumb networks in tune with the explosive growth of supersmart machines in every home and office.

The movement of computer networks onto cable need not await the development of advanced broadband systems such as those planned by Time-Warner in Orlando. Already several companies are supplying moderns that allow computers to link directly to cable systems.

Zenith provided the first system, HomeWorks, operating at a rate of 500 kilobits per second. It is being used by Cox Cable to deliver Prodigy service in San Diego at a rate 52 times faster than existing 9,600-baud phone modems. Also using HomeWorks is Jones Intercable for Internet services in Alexandria, Va., Continental Cablevision and CompuServe in Exeter, N.H., and TCI for a distance learning test in Provo, Utah.

Zenith is adding a system called ChannelMizer that can offer full Ethernet capability of 10 megabits per second over a 15-mile radius. Intel, General Instrument and Hybrid Technologies have announced an asymmetrical system that runs upstream from the home at 256 kilobits per second and downstream at 10 megabits per second, the Ethernet rate run in most office networks.

Pioneering in the field for several years has been Digital Equipment Corp. under the leadership of James Albrycht. Adapting equipment developed by LANcity, DEC's ChannelWorks offers the functionality needed for true information highway on-ramps. Extending a two-way Ethernet transparently from the office to the home by a full 70 miles, the ChannelWorks frequency-agile modem allows the use of all 83 cable frequency channels. Cable managers can send digital information over any underused part of the coax bandwidth. Currently deployed chiefly by telecommuting Digital employees, the system is under evaluation by a variety of hospitals, libraries, schools and other institutions favored by Vice-President Gore.

Absolutely crucial to the development of the broadband superhighway, however, is not only the merger of the two networks but also access to the capital of the telephone industry. Creation of high-bandwidth cable connections to homes will be far cheaper than laying new coax. But they still will require expensive upgrades to existing cable plant.

The telcos already invest more money every year—some $24 billion—than the total revenues of the cable industry. But even the telcos will not be able to create information superhighways if they also have to duplicate the broadband connections to homes already offered by the cable industry. Similarly, the cable industry alone cannot attract sufficient funds to duplicate the broadband fiber networks already commanded by the telcos, while the telcos move in to skim off the best pay-per-view movie markets. Particularly in an adverse regulatory climate neither industry is capable of building broadband networks. With relatively narrowband networks, the Malone model necessarily thrives. In the name of fighting monsters the administration is in fact pursuing what amounts to a monster-protection policy.

If this policy continues, innovation once more will follow its course toward the least-regulated arenas. Cable and telco firms will install their best technologies overseas. In the U.S. the computer networking industry will build the information superhighways. To Gore's bitter regret, only business and the wealthy will be able to afford access. Until the early decades of the next century, much of the rest of the nation will be left to the mercies of the Malone model for video entertainment and other cable programming. Interactivity will tend to take the form of games and pay-per-view TV.

Nonetheless, with the increasing movement of activity from big cities, corporate headquarters, hospitals, schools and other centralized institutions to homes and small cities, the demand for broadband computer connections is sure to soar. Most current congressional legislation that imposes mandates on businesses relating to everything from health care reform to parental leave tends to drive work away from corporations to contractual outsources. The market for "interactive TV" is likely to grow far more slowly than the market for computer connections over cable.

Both political parties are far behind the public in comprehending these developments. But the reversal of the earlier forces of conurbation and centralized industry responds to the most profound laws of new technology. It is the most important movement in America today. If the administration continues to strangle new technology with new regulation and red tape, a new coalition of liberals and conservatives alike will rise up against it and grasp the future. Al Gore may eventually wish he had never heard of broadband networks.

9

Ethersphere

New low earth orbit satellites mark as decisive a break in the history of space-based communications as the PC represented in the history of computing. Pay attention to much-maligned Teledesic. Backed by Craig McCaw and Bill Gates, it is the only LEO fully focused on serving computers

"They'll be crowding the skies."

Thus Steven Dorfman, president of telecommunications and space operations for GM Hughes—the colossus of the satellite industry—warned the world of a new peril in the skies. Planning to launch 840 satellites in low earth orbits, at an altitude of some 435 miles, were a gang of cellular phone jocks and computer hackers from Seattle going under the name of Teledesic. Led by Craig McCaw and Bill Gates, they were barging onto his turf and threatening to ruin the neighborhood.

You get the image of the heavens darkening and a new Ice Age looming as more and more of this low-orbit junk—including a total of some 1,200 satellites from Motorola's Iridium, Loral-Qualcomm's Globalstar and Teledesic, among other LEO projects—accumulates in the skies. Ultimately, from this point of view, you might imagine the clutter of LEOs eclipsing the geostationary orbit itself, the so-called Clarke belt, some 21,000 miles farther out. Named after science-fiction guru Arthur C. Clarke, the geostationary orbit is the girdle and firmament of the Hughes empire.

In an article in *Wireless* magazine in 1945, Clarke first predicted that satellites in orbit 22,282 miles (35,860 kilometers) above the equator, where the period of revolution is 24 hours, could maintain a constant elevation and angle from any point on Earth. In such a fixed orbit, a device could remain for decades, receiving signals from a transmitter on the earth and radiating them back across continents.

The Clarke orbit also posed a problem, however—the inverse square law for signal power. Signals in space attenuate in proportion to the square of the distance they travel. This means that communications with satellites 22,000 miles away typically require large antenna dishes (as much as 10 meters wide) or megawatts of focused beam power.

Now, however, a new satellite industry is emerging, based on gains in computer and microchip technology. These advances allow the use of compact handsets with small smart antennas that can track low earth orbit satellites sweeping across the skies at a speed of 25,000 kilometers an hour at a variety of altitudes between 500 and 1,400 kilometers above the earth. Roughly 60 times nearer than geostationary satellites, LEOs find the inverse square law working in their favor, allowing them to offer far more capacity, cheaper and smaller antennas, or some combination of both. Breaking out of the Clarke orbit, these systems vastly expand the total available room for space-based communications gear.

It is indeed possible to "crowd" the Clarke belt—a relatively narrow swath at a single altitude directly above the equator. But even this swath does not become *physically* congested; collisions are no problem. The Clarke belt becomes crowded because the ability of antennas on the ground to discriminate among satellites is limited by the size of the antenna. Spaceway and Teledesic both plan to use the Ka band of frequencies, between 17 gigahertz and 30 gigahertz, or billions of cycles per second. In this band, reasonably sized antennas 66 centimeters wide can distinguish between geostationary satellites two degrees apart. That's some 800 miles in the Clarke belt. Thus no physical crowding. But it means that there are only a total of 180 Clarke slots for Ka band devices, including undesirable space over oceans.

LEOs, however, can be launched anywhere between the earth's atmosphere and a layer of intense radiation called the Van Allen Belt. The very concept of crowding becomes absurd in this 900 kilometer span of elevations for moving orbits that can be 500 meters apart or less. Thus the 21 proposed orbital planes of Teledesic occupy a total of 10 kilometers of altitude. At this rate, 70 or more Teledesic systems, comprising some 65,000 satellites, could comfortably fit in low earth orbits.

Nonetheless, it was clear that the LEOs, one way or another, were crowding Hughes. Hughes commands satellite systems or projects that compete with every one of the LEOs. Hughes responded to the threat of Teledesic by announcing the expansion of its Spaceway satellite system, then planned for North America alone, to cover the entire globe. Then, invoking the absolute priority currently granted geostationary systems, Hughes asked the Federal Communications Commission to block Teledesic entirely by assigning Spaceway the full five gigahertz of spectrum internationally available in the Ka band.

On May 27, Dorfman summoned the upstarts, Craig McCaw and Teledesic President Russell Daggatt, to Hughes headquarters in Los Angeles for a talk. Busy with Microsoft—the Redmond, Wash., company that in 1993 temporarily surpassed the market value of General Motors—Teledesic partner Bill Gates did not make the trip. But as the epitome of the personal computer industry, his presence haunted the scene.

Together with Spaceway chief Kevin McGrath, Dorfman set out to convince the Seattle venturers to give up their foolhardy scheme and instead join with Hughes in the nine satellites of Spaceway. Not only could Spaceway's nine satellites cover the entire globe with the same services that Teledesic's 840 satellites would provide, Spaceway could be expanded incrementally as demand emerged. Just loft another Hughes satellite. Indeed, Spaceway's ultimate system envisaged 17 satellites. With "every component proprietary to Hughes," as Dorfman said, the satellites only cost some $150 million apiece. By contrast, most of the $9 billion Teledesic system would have to be launched before global services could begin.

Nonetheless, the new LEOs marked as decisive a break in the history of space-based communications as the PC represented in the history of computing. Moreover, Teledesic would be the only LEO fully focused on serving computers—the first truly "global Internet," as McCaw's vice president Tom Alberg depicted it. It brings space communications at last into the age of ubiquitous microchip intelligence, and it brings the law of the microcosm into space communications.

If you enjoyed the New World of Wireless on the ground with its fierce battles between communications standards, technical geniuses, giant companies, impetuous entrepreneurs and industrial politicians on three continents—you will relish the reprise hundreds and even thousands of miles up. Launching Teledesic, McCaw and Gates were extending bandwidth abundance from earth into space. Observers, however, often did not like what they heard.

BAD PRESS FOR TWO BILLIONAIRES

Every so often, the media is taken by the notion of technology as a morality tale. In place of a gripping saga of unjustly obscure geniuses enriching the world by their heroic creativity in the teeth of uncomprehending bureaucrats and politicians, the media treat technology ventures as a school for scandal. We have mock exposés of computer hype, monopoly, vaporware, viruses, infoscams, netporn, securities "fraud" and deviously undocumented software calls. Pundits gabble endlessly about the gap yawning between the information rich and the information poor, thus consigning themselves undeniably, amid many yawns, to the latter category. While American market share climbs near 70% in computers, networks, software and leading-edge semiconductors, analysts furrow the brows of the *Atlantic Monthly* with tales of farseeing foreign teams, spearheaded by visionary government officials, capturing the markets of American cowboy capitalists. They spiel implausible yams of tough-minded trade warriors prying open the jaws of Japan for Toys "R" Us, closing down vicious Korean vendors of low-priced dynamic RAMs, or blasting through barriers to U.S. telecom gear in the Tokyo-Osaka corridor, saving the day for Motorola's soon-to-be cobwebbed factories for analog cellular phones.

One of these sagas began early this year with two Seattle billionaires, McCaw and Gates, allegedly boarding McCaw's sleek yacht and going on an ego trip. With McCaw pitching in an early nickel, and the boat, and Gates hoisting his name as a sail, the two tycoons seemed to sweep away from the shores of rationality, as the media told it, into a sea of microwaves and arsenic. Spinning out Teledesic to build an information super-highway in the sky, they proposed to strew the heavens with 840 satellites, plus 84 spares. All would whirl around the world at a height of 700 kilometers (435 miles), using what they told the FCC would be some 500 million gallium arsenide microchips to issue frequencies between 20 and 60 gigahertz from some 180,000 phased-array antennas. The entire project seemed suffused with gigahertz and gigabucks. "We're bandwidth bulls," says Teledesic President Daggatt.

In case the hype of the sponsors failed to keep the system radiant and aloft, fueling it also would be a total of 12,000 batteries fed by thin film solar collectors stretching out behind the satellite "birds" in some 130 square kilometers of gossamer wings. Working at 4% efficiency, these cells would collectively generate 10 megawatts of power, enough to light a small city, but, so the critics said, insufficient to reach Seattle at microwave frequencies in the rain. (The Teledesic frequencies are readily absorbed by water in the air). To manage the elaborate mesh of fast-packet communications among the satellites and ground terminals, the constellation would bear some 282,000 mips, or millions of instructions per second, of radiation-hard microprocessors and a trillion bytes or so of rad-hard RAM. In effect, Teledesic would be launching into space one of the world's largest and most expensive massively parallel computer systems.

At a mere $9 billion, to be put up by interested investors, Teledesic's lawyers told the FCC, the price would be a bargain for the U.S. and the world. (By contrast, current plans call for $15 billion just to lay fiber for interactive TV in California). But former Motorola, now Kodak, chief George Fisher—fresh from pondering numbers for the apparently similar Iridium projects—suggested that $40 billion for Teledesic would be more like it. (Teledesic had the improbable result of making Iridium's 66-satellite plan, greeted in 1990 with much of the scorn now lavished on Teledesic, seem modest). Just rocketing the 840 satellites into orbit was said to entail a successful launch every week for a year and a half at a time when hoisting satellites is still a precarious and sometime thing.

Even if Teledesic succeeded in getting the things up, so other scientists suggested, the satellites would then be impaled on some 7,000 pieces of space debris in the chosen orbits. In any case, so it was widely reported, 10% would fail every year, some tumbling out of orbit, others joining the whirl of litter, where they would fly ready to impale the remainder of the satellites and the remnants of the two billionaires' reputations.

Surely these sages know that by the year 2001, when the systems would be up and running, the world will be swimming in the bandwidth of "information superhighways." Why support this lavish launch of technology for a communications system that would be dwarfed by capabilities already demonstrated on the ground?

Summing up a near-consensus of critics, John Pike, director of the Federation of American Scientists' Space Policy Project, declared to the *Wall Street Journal*, "God save us. It's the stupidest thing I've ever heard of!" Provoking Pike may have been the origins of the multisatellite architecture in the Star Wars "brilliant pebbles" program. Teledesic's most amazing achievement to date has been to displace the Strategic Defense Initiative as Pike's peak example of stupidity.

While McCaw and Gates could be dismissed as tyros in the satellite field, Hughes is world champion. Since 1963, the company has put 107 communications satellites into orbit. With 19 in 1994, this year should be its biggest ever. In 1993, well before the Teledesic announcement, Dorfman announced the first version of Spaceway—a $660 million, two-satellite system offering voice, data and video services—as a contribution to "information superhighways."

In the midst of all the terrestrial uproar surrounding superhighwaymen Al Gore, John Malone of TCI, Raymond Smith of Bell Atlantic and scores of other telco and cable magnates, however, no one paid much attention to Hughes.

Then came Gates and McCaw with Teledesic and claims of 20 million potential subscribers, two million simultaneous connections, billion-bit-per-second "gigalinks," bandwidth on demand and an array of other features, all advertised at a cost for Spaceway-type services nearly three times lower per bit per second. Everyone noticed Teledesic.

At the end of July, though, Hughes raised the stakes. With successful launches under way in China, Brazil and French Guiana to provide exclamation points, Hughes made a new submission to the FCC, extending Spaceway into a nine-satellite global system costing $3.2 billion. McGrath plausibly claimed it could be in place long before Teledesic and offer nearly all its functionality at a third of the price.

Already planned to be in place by 1998, however, were several other LEO projects, led by Motorola's Iridium and Loral-Qualcomm's Globalstar. As mobile phone projects, these systems could not readily offer service at T-1 data rates. But their sponsors promised availability for simple E-mail, faxes and paging.

By mid-1994, Motorola seemed to command the financial momentum. The company succeeded in raising some $800 million in equity investments from companies around the globe, including Lockheed and Raytheon (which would build the satellites), Great Wall of China and Khrunichev Enterprises of Russia (which together would launch a third of them), the Mawarid Group of Saudi Arabia (which pitched in $120 million) and Kyocera, Mitsui and DDI, which together put up another $120 million (Kyocera will build the dual mode handsets for Japan and DDI will sell and service them). On August 10, an Indian consortium purchased a 5% stake and a seat on the board for $38 million. Motorola claimed its share of the equity was dropping to 28.5%, well on the way to the company's final target of 15%. Motorola estimates that much of the additional $2 billion in the plan could come from debt securities and loans.

Iridium's attractions are impressive. It provides ubiquitous global phone service at a premium price with little or no dependence on local terrestrial facilities. In times of disaster or political crisis, or in places with sparse or unreliable local service, the system can route calls among the 66 satellites in space bypassing all infrastructure on the ground. For an elite of government officials and corporate figures operating in remote areas, the availability of Iridium should be worth the money. A bold and visionary concept when it emerged in 1987 from a team in the company's satellite systems engineering group, it endows many regions of the earth with voice and limited data communications for the first time. For example, it actually focuses on polar domains, such as parts of Siberia, poorly served by other satellite systems. Kazuo Inamori, the venerable chairman of Kyocera, also believes that Iridium will be popular in the 60% of territorial Japan not currently covered by cellular.

"GIVE US SPECTRUM, LET OTHERS FIGHT"

Nonetheless, beyond the bold and ingenious concept (Daggatt calls Iridium "the real pioneer of LEOs"), the system suffers from technical flaws. Were it not for Globalstar, perhaps these flaws would not have become evident until alter the 66 birds were aloft. A far simpler and cheaper solution, Globalstar uses 48 satellites with no links between them. Each functions as a "bent pipe" transponder, receiving signals from a phone on the ground and passing them back to any gateway within the satellite's 1,500-mile-wide footprint, linked to locally available telephone networks. Because Globalstar uses local phone systems rather than bypassing them, the system has been able to raise a total of some $300 million in support from Alcatel, France Telecom, Vodafone (serving the United Kingdom, Australia and Hong Kong), Airtouch-U S West, Hyundai and DACOM in Korea, Deutsche Aerospace and Alenia.

This amount may seem small beside the billion raised by Iridium. But Globalstar has capital costs (at $1.8 billion) one-half Iridium's, circuit costs one-third Iridium's, and terminal costs (at $750 each) one-fourth Iridium's. With no intelligence in space, Globalstar relies entirely on the advance of intelligent phones and portable computer devices on the ground; it is the Ethernet of satellite architectures. Costing one-half as much as Iridium, it will handle nearly 20 times more calls.

The advantages of Globalstar stem only partly from its avoidance of complex intersatellite connections and use of infrastructure already in place on the ground. More important is its avoidance of exclusive spectrum assignments. Originating several years before spread-spectrum technology was thoroughly tested for cellular phones, Iridium employs time division multiple access, an obsolescent system that requires exclusive command of spectrum but offers far less capacity than code division multiple access.

Like conventional cellular or radio transmissions that differentiate signals by time slot or frequency, TDMA sharply restricts the reuse of spectrum in nearby cells. By contrast, CDMA is a form of spread-spectrum communications that differentiates signals by a spreading code and allows the use of the same frequencies all the time, everywhere. Just as you can reduplicate wireline spectrum merely by laying another fiber, you can now manufacture new spectrum in the air merely by breaking large cells into smaller ones.

Among some six companies seeking low earth orbit satellite approval from the FCC in 1993, only Iridium used TDMA, requiring national and international bodies to pick it as a winner from the outset and assign it exclusive spectrum. By contrast, in a majority report issued to the FCC on April 6, 1993, CDMA companies in the U.S., including TRW, Loral-

Qualcomm, Celsat and American Mobile Satellite, could all agree to share spectrum and let the market choose winners. A Motorola lawyer explained to *Space News*, "Give us the spectrum and let the others fight for whatever's left." In the face of alternatives with no need for exclusive spectrum allocations, Iridium could fly only if it offered radically superior performance or capacity. But TDMA dooms it to generally inferior performance and capacity.

Unlike TDMA systems, which can "see" only one satellite signal at a time, CDMA handsets have "path" diversity, using "rake receivers" that can combine a number of weak signals into an intelligible stream. Iridium and other TDMA systems compensate by using more power. But no practical amount of power can propel a satellite signal through a tin roof. And excess power means larger handsets or heavier satellites. Iridium satellites together use 80% more power than Globalstar's, yet employ antennas nearly twice as large and offer 18.2 times less capacity per unit area.

Teledesic also suffers from the use of TDMA. But Teledesic's T-1 capabilities would compensate with 100,000 times more bandwidth and with a bit error rate that can accommodate the new fiber standards such as SONET-ATM (synchronous optical network/asynchronous transfer mode), which send packets without retransmission. The issue is whether these features can justify the political, financial, and performance costs of using a modulation scheme—TDMA—that severely limits spectrum sharing and path diversity.

So what is this, another saga of hubris on the information super-highway—to go with the Raymond Smith-John Malone follies? Perhaps good new ideas are harder to come by as company revenues grow into the billions, and Gates and McCaw disinvest and diversify as fast as they can from their increasingly cumbrous vessels of wealth. Having recently passed the billion-dollar mark in his systematic process of disinvestment from Microsoft—he retains $8 billion or so—Gates at times seemed embarrassed by his link to this gigantic project. He told us it was too early to write about Teledesic.

No, the story is in fact more interesting. Impelled by the onrushing rise in the cost-effectiveness of individual chips compared to multichip systems, the Law of the Microcosm dictates decentralization of all information architectures. During the 1980s, this centrifuge struck the mainframe computer establishment of IBM. During the 1990s, the personal teleputer, summoning and shaping films and files of images from around the world, will collide with the centralized establishments of TV broadcasting. At the end of the century, Teledesic and the other LEOs will usher in the age of decentralization in space.

From this point of view, Gates' participation becomes more readily intelligible. Gates seems always to follow the microcosm wherever it leads. A vision of software for decentralized systems of personal computers informs everything Microsoft does.

In 1994, for example, Microsoft made an investment in Metricom, a wireless terrestrial system that supplies links of up to 56 kilobits per second to portable computers or personal digital assistants. Within cells, the devices can communicate directly with one another; outside the cell, Metricom routes its calls through an expandable mesh of nodes each the size of a shoebox and costing less than $1,000. Based on spread-spectrum technology, the system operates at power levels low enough to avoid the need for FCC licenses. Yet it can be expanded to metropolitan-area dimensions.

In many respects, Teledesic is Metricom in the sky. It is focused on computer communications. It routes packets by the most convenient path through a mesh of nodes. It is based on microprocessor technology. (Both Teledesic and Metricom plan to employ devices from Motorola's 68000 family). As Gates explains the system: "Some functions are most efficiently performed by large numbers of small processors working together, rather than a few large ones." The entire new generation of low earth orbit satellite systems relies on this centrifugal force of the microcosm.

It was not supposed to happen this way. Just as Grosch's Law of the computer industry implied that computer power rose by the square of the cost, there was a similar law of the satellite industry that held satellite efficiency to be proportional to size. In a popular text, "Communications Satellite Systems," published in 1978, James Martin cited an AT&T study showing that just six satellites could carry all the long-distance traffic from the American continent; no fiber optics would be necessary. "The next major thrust in the space segment should capitalize on the economies of scale which today's technology offers," wrote Martin, urging creation of "massive hardware" as heavy as several tons and "immensely powerful satellites with large antennas beaming as much information as we are capable of using to our rooftops." Many satellite advocates, led by Arthur C. Clarke, viewed with impatient scorn the expensive terrestrial systems that somehow forestalled the manifest destiny of big birds to rule the world of communications.

BRINGING THE MICROCOSM TO SPACE

In 1994, the big-bird dream still flourishes in Spaceway, the international consortium Inmarsat, and the new launch this summer of direct broadcast satellite technology by Hughes's DirecTV, Hubbard's USSB, TCI's Primestar, and Rupert Murdoch's imperial systems in Europe and Asia. Using centralized satellites in geosynchronous orbits, DBS is the ultimate broadcast medium, reaching billions of potential customers at the cost of reaching hundreds of thousands through cable-TV systems. But these geostationary satellite systems suffer from the same flaws as mainframes: sclerosis by centralization. At a time when customers want the choice, control, convenience and interactivity of computers, the big birds offer one-size-fits-all programming at specified times, with little ability to control the flow or interact with it.

The real showstopper in the long run, though, is a nagging half-second time delay for Clarke orbit signals. Bad enough for voice, a half-second is near eternity for computer communications; for the living-room and desktop supercomputers of 2001, a half-second delay would mean gigabytes of information to be stored in buffers. While companies across the country, from Intel to Digital Equipment, are rushing to market with cable modems to allow computer connections to CATV coax, geosatellites remain mostly computer-hostile. Even with the new digital cosmetics of DBS, geosynchronous satellites are a last vestige of centralization in a centrifugal world.

By contrast, Teledesic brings the microcosm to space. Rather than gaming economies of scale from using a few huge satellites, Teledesic gains economies of scale by launching as many small birds as possible. Based on Peter Huber's concept of a geodesic network—a mesh of peers equally spaced apart like the nodes in a geodesic dome—Teledesic is not a hierarchy but a heterarchy. Distributing the system responsibilities among 840 autonomous satellites diminishes the requirements, such as message throughput and power usage, for each one. Building redundancy into the entire constellation, rather than within each satellite, yields higher overall reliability, while reducing the complexity and price of each unit.

As Craig McCaw explains, "At a certain point, redundant systems create more complexity and weight than they are worth. Rather than having each satellite a 747 in the sky with triply redundant systems, we have hundreds of satellites that offer self-redundancy." Eschewing the Hughes philosophy of "every component proprietary to Hughes," Teledesic will manufacture and launch a large number of satellite peers, using off-the-shelf parts whenever possible. This approach also provides economies of scale that, according to a study by brilliant pebbles contractor Martin Marietta, could lower unit costs by a factor of one hundred or more.

Just as microcosmic technology uses infinitesimal low-powered transistors and puts them so close together that they work faster than large high-powered transistors, Teledesic satellites follow the rules of low and slow. Rather than one big powerful bird spraying signals across continents, Teledesic offers 840, programmably targetable at small localities. Just 435 miles out, the delay is measured in milliseconds rather than half-seconds.

The total computing power and wattage of the constellation seems large, as is needed to sustain a volume of some two million connections at a time, four times Spaceway's capacity. But with other link features equal, between 1,226 and 3,545 times more power is needed to communicate with a geostationary satellite than with a LEO.

Perhaps most important, unlike Iridium, TRW's Odyssey, and Globalstar, Teledesic from the outset has targeted the fastest-growing market of the future: communications for the world's 125 million PCs, now growing some 20% a year. And Teledesic has correctly chosen the technology needed to extend computer networks globally—broadband low earth orbit satellites. The real issue is not the future of Teledesic but the future of Iridium.

In the short run Iridium's voice services cannot compete with Globalstar's cheaper and more robust CDMA system. But in the long run Iridium could be trumped by Teledesic. Although Teledesic has no such plans, the incremental cost of incorporating an "L" band transceiver in Teledesic, to perform the Iridium functions for voice, would be just 10% of Teledesic's total outlays, or less than $1 billion (compared with the $3.4 billion initial capital costs of Iridium). But 840 linked satellites could offer far more cost-effective service than Iridium's 66.

Iridium's dilemma is that the complexities and costs of its ingenious mesh of intersatellite links and switches can be justified only by offering broadband computer services. Yet Iridium is a doggedly narrowband system focused on voice.

Iridium eventually will have to adopt Teledesic's broadband logic and architecture. To protect its global lead in wireless communications and equipment, Motorola should join with Teledesic now, rather than later. Working with Lockheed, Motorola is making impressive gains in satellite-manufacturing technology. Supplying both handsets and space gear for computer networks, Motorola could turn its huge investment of time, money and prestige in Iridium into a dramatic global coup in wireless computer services. As part of a broadband system, Iridium could still become a superb brand name for Motorola. But persisting in a narrowband strategy in the name of avoiding Teledesic's larger initial costs, Motorola's executives will end up inflicting serious strategic costs on the company.

Most of the famous objections to Teledesic are based on ignorance or misinformation. Launch anxieties spring chiefly from the GEO experience. LEOs are 60 times nearer and between a tenth and a third the weight. Teledesic satellites are designed to be hoisted in groups of eight or more. From the Great Wall in China to Khrunichev in Russia, companies around the world will soon be competing to supply low-cost launching facilities for the system. Orbital Sciences, an entrepreneurial dervish near Washington's Dulles Airport with some $190 million in revenues, has developed a low-cost method for lofting groups of LEOs from an adapted Lockheed 1011 Tristar.

Other fears are similarly fallacious. Teledesic will work fine in the rain because the high minimum vertical angle (40 degrees) of its satellite links from the ground reduces the portion of the path exposed to water to a manageable level. By contrast, geostationary satellites must operate at eight degrees, passing the signal through a long span of atmosphere. Made of tough new composite materials, Teledesic satellites will endure the kind of debris found in space mostly unscathed. The solar arrays can accept holes without significantly damaging overall performance. All in all, Teledesic's designers expect the birds to remain in orbit for an average of ten years. With most of its key technologies plummeting in price along with the rest of electronic components, the system may well cost even less and perform better than its business plan promises or George Fisher speculates.

Indeed, widely charged with reckless technological presumption, the designers of Teledesic in fact seem recklessly cautious in their assumptions about the rate of microchip progress. For example, their dismissal of CDMA assumes that the high speed of the spreading code functions—requiring digital signal processors that race at least 100 times the data rate—pushes cheap T-1 performance far into the future. Yet in early 1995, Texas Instruments will ship its multimedia video processor, a marvel that combines four 64-bit DSPs, a 32-bit RISC CPU, 50 kilobytes of on-chip memory, a floating-point unit and a 64bit direct memory access controller all on one chip. This device now performs two billion operations per second and, with an upgrade from 35 megahertz to 50 megahertz clock rate, soon will perform three billion. The estimated cost in 1995 is around $400, or a stunning $133 per bop (current Pentiums charge three times as much for 100 mips). Five years from now, when Teledesic gets serious, that kind of one-chip computing power can implement CDMA for broadband data without any cost penalty. Future generations of CDMA systems may be able to offer, at a dramatically lower price, the same broadband services in *mobile* applications that Teledesic now promises for fixed services only.

Assuming that Teledesic meets the CDMA challenge, the other fear is that terrestrial systems will capture enough of the market to render Teledesic unprofitable. This fear, however, can come true only if governments delay this supremely beneficial system well into the next century.

Unlike the competition, satellite systems can provide global coverage at once. Whether for $9 billion or $90 billion, no terrestrial system will cover the entire world, or even the entire U.S., within decades of Teledesic. As soon as it is deployed, it will profoundly change the geography and topography of the globe. Suddenly the most remote rural redoubt, beach, or mountain will command computer communications comparable to urban corporations today. The system can make teleconferencing, telecommuting, telemedicine, and teleschooling possible anywhere. Gone will be the differences among regions in access to cultural and information resources. People will be able to live and work where they want rather than where corporations locate them.

This change transforms the dimensions of the world as decisively as trains, planes, automobiles, phones and TVs changed them in previous eras. It will extend "universal service" more dramatically than any new law can.

Moreover, Teledesic can eliminate the need to cross-subsidize rural customers. Determining the cost of wire-line services are the parameters of population density and distance from the central office. Rural customers now cost between 10 and 30 times as much to serve with wires as urban customers do. Teledesic will bring near-broadband capabilities to everyone in the world at the same price.

Most important, this expansion of the communications frontier will foster the very economic development that will fuel the demand for the service. Today, it does not pay to bring telecommunications to poor countries that might benefit most. Teledesic and other satellite services break the bottleneck of development. Simultaneously opening the entire world, it enriches every nation with new capital exceeding the fruits of all the foreign aid programs of the era.

Teledesic is a venture worthy of McCaw and Gates. In its impact on the world, it may even rival the Herculean contributions of its sponsors in cellular and software. The issue is not the technology or the commitment of the principals. The issue is the readiness of the U.S. government to accommodate this venture. Before Teledesic can be approved internationally, it will have to attain a license from the FCC in the U.S. It has taken four years to approve Iridium. It took 30 years to approve cellular. How long will it take to approve Teledesic?

Currently Teledesic, Iridium and Globalstar face several political obstacles. The International Telecommunications Union's Radio Regulation 2613 gives GEOs absolute priority over LEOs. For Spaceway, Hughes is now demanding an exclusive license for the full five gigahertz available in the Ka-band worldwide, leaving no room for Teledesic or any other Ka-band LEO. Under current law, Hughes or other GEO systems could usurp any LEO that was launched.

LEOs are a major American innovation. The U.S. government should take the lead now in spearheading a change in the regulations to accommodate LEOs. This is no minor matter. As the dimensions and promise of Teledesic loom more starkly, the Japanese or

Europeans are certain to make similar proposals. "When they do," Craig McCaw predicts, "they will immediately have their government on board. They will be able to go to the ITU right away. My greatest fear is that we will have the technology all ready, and foreign companies will beat us out because they can get their governments in line."

The U.S. government was on board for Apollo 25 years ago and the U.S. won the first space race. This space race is just as important, but the government is treating it as some sleepy-time infrastructure project. In fact, it is the information superhighway going global and ubiquitous. It is the ultimate promise of the information age, says McCaw.

SUSTAINING THE U.S. LEAD IN TECHNOLOGY

McCaw explains: "It'll mean ecological disaster if China mimics what we did— building more and more urban towers and filling them up with people who queue up every day on turnpikes into the city, emitting fumes into the air, and then building new towers and new highways when you want to move the company, and then digging up the highways to install new wires."

McCaw waves toward the window, out at Lake Washington. "Look at that floating bridge. It took $1.5 billion to cross Lake Washington, then it got busted in a storm. Cross this lake, any lake, any ocean in the world with broadband wireless. That's the promise of Teledesic. All you do is to reconfigure the communications in software at zero incremental cost. No wires for the final connections. It's what we do in Hong Kong and Shanghai, where everyone uses a cellular phone."

President Clinton, Vice President Gore and other members of the administration continually ask what they can do for technology. One thing they can do is vastly streamline the process for approval of communications projects. At the moment, Congress is determined to retain bureaucratic dominance over the most dynamic enterprise and technology in the world economy—what they like to term the information superhighway. They see it as a possible source of congressional power, campaign finance, employment and pelf, like the Baby Bells today or like existing construction projects. Rather than turn telecom into a vast porkbellied poverty program, however, the administration should deregulate the field. Communications companies must be permitted to compete and collaborate wherever the technology leads.

Whether the administration knows it or not, these technologies are its greatest political asset. The high-tech industries unleashed in the 1980s by venture capital and junk bonds are now the prime fuel of the economy of the 1990s. Comprising perhaps 60% of incremental GDP and 48% of exports, the momentous upsurge of computers and commu-nications is even compensating for the mistakes of the Bush and Clinton regimes and making plausible Clinton's continuing claims of economic success. But now Clinton, Gore and FCC Chairman Reed Hundt must make a choice. If they want to maintain this redemptive U.S. lead in technology, they must be willing to forge new alliances in Congress to get the politicians and bureaucrats out of the way of the future. A good start would be to open the floodgates for the global onrush of low earth orbit satellites dedicated to computer communications. If they do, they can help make the world, as McCaw's Alberg puts it, "a truly global Internet in an ever-expanding ethersphere."

AND THE WINNER IS . . .

Globalstar is the easy winner for current offering of mobile phone services under a CDMA regime of spectrum sharing. But Teledesic can add phone services to its broadband computer system. Over time, Teledesic's 840 satellites will outperform Globalstar's 48. Big question: When will microchip technology advance enough to allow broadband applications over CDMA? When that happens, Globalstar has a shot at the grand prize.

Iridium is both too expensive to compete in mobile phones and too narrowband for data. Today's champ **Spaceway** is maturing. Big winner for the next decade is . . . **Teledesic**.

10

The Bandwidth Tidal Wave

"We'll have Infinite bandwidth in a decade's time."
— *Bill Gates, PC Magazine, Oct. 11, 1994.*

Andrew Grove, Titan of Intel, is widely known for his belief, born in the vortex of the Hungarian Revolution and honed in the trenches of Silicon Valley, that "only the paranoid survive." If so, the Intel chief may soon need to resharpen the edges of fear that have driven his company to the top. Looming on the horizons of the global computer industry that Grove now shapes and spearheads is a gathering crest of change that threatens to reduce the microprocessor's supremacy and reestablish the information economy on new foundations. Imparting a personal edge to the challenge are the restless energies of Microsoft's Bill Gates and Tele-Communications Inc.'s John Malone, providing catalytic capital and leadership for the new tides of the telecosm.

Grove's response is seemingly persuasive. "We have state-of-the-art silicon technology, state-of-the art microprocessor design skills and we have mass production volumes." These huge assets endow Intel as a global engine of growth with 55% margins and more than 80% market share in the single most important product in the world economy. Why indeed should Grove worry?

One word only may challenge him and with him much of the existing computer establishment. Let us paraphrase a 1988 speech by John Moussouris, chairman and chief executive of the amazing Silicon Valley startup MicroUnity, which gains a portentous heft from being financed heavily by Gates and Malone: If the leading sage of computer design, in his last deathbed gasp, wanted to impart in one word all of his accumulated wisdom about the coming era to a prodigal son rushing home to inherit the business, that one word would be "bandwidth." Andy Grove knows it well. Early this year he memorably declaimed: "If you are amazed by the fast drop in the cost of computing power over the last decade, just wait till you see what is happening to the cost of bandwidth."

Eric Schmidt, chief technical officer of Sun Microsystems, is one of the few men who have measured this coming tide and mastered some of its crucial implications. His key insight is that the onrush of bandwidth abundance overthrows Moore's Law as the driving force of computer progress. Until now progress in the computer industry has ridden the revelation in 1979 by Intel co-founder Gordon Moore that the density of transistors on chips, and thus the price-performance of computers, doubles every 18 months. Soon, however, Schmidt ordains, bandwidth will be king.

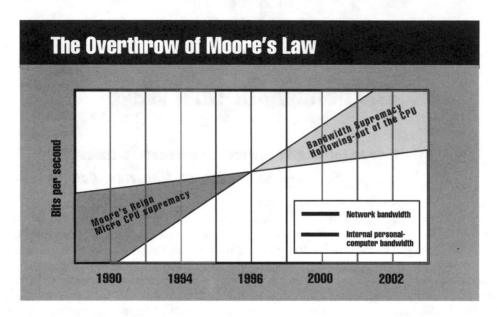

Bandwidth is communications power—the capacity of an information channel to transmit bits without error in the presence of noise. In fiber optics, in wireless communications, in new dumb switches, in digital signal processors, bandwidth will expand from five to 100 times as fast as the rise of microprocessor speeds. With the rapid spread of national networks of fiber and cable, the dribble of kilobits (thousands of bits) from twisted-pair telephone lines is about to become a firehose of gigabits (billions of bits). But the PC is not ready. Attach the firehose to the parallel port of your personal computer and the stream of bits becomes a blast of data smithereens.

TSUNAMI OF GIGABITS

The bandwidth bottleneck of telephone wires has long allowed the computer world to live in a strange and artificial isolation. In the computer world, Moore's Law has reigned.

At its awesome exponential pace, computer price-performance would increase some one hundredfold every 10 years. This means that for the price of a current 100 mips (millions of instructions per second) Pentium machine, you could buy a computer in 2004 running 10 billion instructions per second. Since today the fastest bit streams routinely linked to computers run 100 times slower, at 10 megabits per second on an Ethernet, 10 bips seems adequate as a 10-year target. All seems fine in computer land, where users rarely wonder what happens after the wire reaches the wall.

In the face of the 10 times faster increase in bandwidth, however, Moore's Law seems almost paltry. The rise in bandwidth does not follow the smooth incremental ascent that the heroic exertions, inventions and investments of Andy Grove and his followers have maintained in microchips. Bandwidth bumps and grinds and then volcanically erupts. The communications equivalent of those 10 bips that would take 10 years to reach according to the existing trend would be 10-gigabit-per-second connections to their corporate customers next year.

During the very period of apparent bandwidth doldrums during the 1980s, phone companies installed some 10 million kilometers of optical fiber. So far only an infinitesimal portion of its potential bandwidth has been delivered to customers. Moussouris estimates that the bandwidth of fiber has been exploited one million times less fully than the bandwidth of coax or twisted pair copper.

Nonetheless, the tide is now gathering toward a crest. This year, MCI offers its corporate customers access to a fiber connection at 2.4 gigabits per second. Next year that link will run at 10 gigabits per second for the same price. Two years after that it is scheduled to rise to 40 gigabits per second. Meanwhile, at Martlesham Heath in the United Kingdom, home of British Telecom's research laboratories, Peter Cochrane announced in early September that he could send some 700 separate wavelength streams in parallel down a single fiber-optic thread the width of a human hair. Peter Scovell of Northern Telecom's Bell Northern Research facility declares that by using "solitons"—an exotic method of keeping the bits intact at high speeds through a kind of surface tension counterbalancing dispersion in the fiber—it will be possible to carry 2.4 gigahertz (billions of cycles per second) on each wave length stream. That would add up to more than 1,700 gigahertz on every fiber thread.

Blocking such bandwidths until recently was what is called in the optics trade the "electronic bottleneck." The light signals had to be converted to electronic pulses every 35 kilometers in order to be amplified and regenerated. Thus fiber optics could not function any faster than these electronic amplifiers did, or between two and 10 gigahertz. In the late 1980s, however, a team led by David Payne of the University of Southampton pioneered the concept of doping a fiber with the rare earth element erbium, to create an all-optical broadband amplifier. Perfected at Bell Labs, NTT and elsewhere, this device overcomes the electronic bottleneck and allows communications entirely at the speed of light.

IBM's optical guru Paul Green prophesies that within the next decade or so it will be possible to send some 10,000 wavelength streams down a single fiber thread. Long prophesied by fiber optics pioneer Will Hicks, these developments remain mostly in the esoteric domains of optical laboratories. But IBM recently installed its first all-optical product—its MuxMaster—for a customer running 20 wavelengths on a fiber connecting offices in New York to a backup tape drive in New Jersey. Telephone companies from Italy to Canada are now deploying erbium-doped amplifiers. Long the frenzied pursuit of telecom laboratories from Japan to Dallas and government bodies from ARPA to NTT (now turning private), all-optical networks have become the object of entrepreneurial startups, such as Ciena and Erbium Networks.

Returning from the ethers of innovation to existing broadband technology connecting to people's homes, Craig Tanner of CableLabs in Louisville, Colo., maintains that a typical cable coax line can accommodate two-way streams of data totaling eight gigabits per second. In Cambridge and other eastern Massachusetts cities, Continental Cablevision is now taking the first steps toward delivering some of this bandwidth for Andy Grove's PC users. Today, using Digital Equipment's LANCity broadband two-way cable modems, David Fellows, Continental's chief technical officer, can offer 10 megabits per second Ethernet capability 70 miles from your office. That increases the current 9.6 kilobits per second speeds of most telephone modems by a factor of 1,000.

The most important short-term contributor to the tides of bandwidth is a new communications technology called asynchronous transfer mode. ATM is to telecommunications what containerization is to transport. It puts everything into same-sized boxes that can be readily handled by automated equipment. Just as containerization revolutionized the transport business, ATM is revolutionizing communications. In the case of ATM, the boxes are called cells and each one is 53 bytes long, including a five-byte address. The telephone industry chose 53 bytes as the largest possible container that could deliver real-time voice communications. But the computer industry embraced it because it allows fully silicon switching and routing. Free of complex software, small packets of a uniform 53 bytes can be switched at enormous speeds through an ATM network and dispatched to the end users on a fixed schedule that can accommodate voice, video and data, all at once.

Available at rates of 155 megabits per second and moving this year to 622 megabits and 2.4 gigabits, ATM switches from Fujitsu, IBM, AT&T, Fore Systems, Cisco Systems, SynOptics Communications and every other major manufacturer of hubs and routers will swamp the ports of personal computers over the next five years.

Why should all this bandwidth arouse the competitive fire of Andy Grove? The new explosions of bandwidth enable interactive multimedia and video, riding on radio frequencies, into every household—through the air from satellites and terrestrial wireless systems, through fiberoptic threads and cable TV and even phone-company coax.

If the personal computer cannot handle these streams, John Malone's set-top boxes, Sega or Nintendo game machines or Bill Gates's new communications technology will. A communications technology that can manage multimedia in full flood can also in time relegate one of Grove's CPUs to service as a minor peripheral. The huge promise of the PC industry, with its richness of productivity tools and cultural benefits, could give way to an incoherent babel of toys, videophones and 3D games.

Redeeming the new era for the general-purpose PC entails overcoming the technical culture and mindset of bandwidth scarcity. In today's world of bandwidth scarcity, arrays of special-purpose microprocessors constantly use their hard-wired computer cycles to compensate for the narrow bandwidth of existing channels and to make up for the small capacity of the fast, expensive memories where the data must be buffered or stored on the way. This is the world that Intel dominates today—a world of CPUs incapable of handling full multimedia and radio frequency demands, a world of narrowband four-kilohertz pipes to the home accessed by modems at 9.6 kilobits per second and a world of what Moussouris calls arrays of "twisty little processors," such as MPEG (Motion Picture Experts Group) decoders from C-Cube and IIT, graphics accelerators from Texas Instruments and an array of chips from Intel.

By fixing the necessary algorithms in hardware, these devices bypass the time-consuming tasks of retrieving software instructions and data from memory. Thus these chips can perform their functions at least 100 times faster than more general-purpose devices, such as Intel's Pentium, that use software. But all this speed comes at the cost of rigid specialization. An MPEG-1 processor cannot even decode MPEG-2. When the technology changes, you have to replace the chip. Such special-purpose devices now handle the broadband heavy lifting for video compression and decompression, digital radio processing, voice and sound synthesis, speech recognition, echo cancellation, graphics acceleration and other functions too demanding for the central processor.

By contrast, contemplate a world of bandwidth abundance. In a world of bandwidth abundance, specialized, hard-wired processing will be mostly unnecessary. In the extreme case, images can flow uncompressed through the network and onto the display. Bandwidth will have obviated thousands of mips of processing. The microprocessor instead can focus on managing documents on the screen, popping up needed information from databases, performing simulations or visualizations and otherwise enriching the conference. The arrival of bandwidth abundance transforms the computing environment.

Led by Grove's and Intel's bold investments in chip-making capability some $2.4 billion in 1994 alone—the entire information industry has waxed fat and happy on the bonanzas of Moore's Law. Now, however, some industry leaders are gasping for breath. Eckhard Pfeiffer of Compaq has denounced Intel's avid campaign to shift customers toward the leading-edge processors such as Pentium, embodying the latest Moore's Law advances. Gordon Moore himself has recently questioned whether the pace of microchip progress can continue in the face of wafer factory costs rising toward $2 billion for a typical "fab." He has pronounced a new Moore's Law: The costs of a wafer fab double for each new generation of microprocessor.

Sorry, but the new world of the telecosm offers no rest for weary microchip magnates or future-shocked PC producers. Driven by the new demands of video and multimedia, the pace of advance will now accelerate sharply rather than slow down.

FEEDING THE TIGER

Contemplate the advance of the Tiger, Microsoft's all-software scheme for video-on-demand based entirely on PCs. Although Tiger has been presented as merely another way to build a "movie central" for cable headends or telco central offices, its real promise is not to redeem the existing centralized structure of video but to allow any PC owner to create a headend in the kitchen for video-on-demand. Today, such capability would mean buying a supercomputer plus an array of expensive boards containing special-purpose processors. Tiger's consummation as a popular product therefore will require a new regime of semiconductor progress.

Driven by this imperative, a pioneering combine of Gates, Malone and Moussouris is making an audacious grab for supremacy in the telecosm. Just three miles from Intel and fueled by ideas from a 1984 defector from an Intel fabrication team, Moussouris's MicroUnity is a flagrantly ambitious Sunnyvale, Calif., startup launched in 1988. Fueled by some $15 million from Microsoft and $15 million from TCI, among several other rumored backers, it plans a transformation of chip-making for the age of the telecosm, optimized for communications rather than computations.

MicroUnity's goal is a general-purpose mediaprocessor, software programmable, that can run at no less than 400 billion bits per second—some hundreds of times faster than a Pentium—and perform all the functions currently done in special-purpose multimedia devices. Escaping the tyranny of fixed hardware standards, the mediaprocessor could receive decompression codes and other protocols, algorithms and services over the network with the video to be displayed in real time.

THE GREAT BANDWIDTH SWITCH

In launching Tiger and MicroUnity (see box), Gates and Malone are signaling a fundamental shift in the industry. Ruling the new era will be bandwidth or communications power, measured in billions of bits per second rather than in the millions of instructions per second of current computers. The telecosmic shift from mips to bandwidth, from storage-oriented computing to communications processing, will change the entire structure of information technology.

In the past, the industry has been driven by increases in computer power embodied in new generations of microprocessors—from the 8086 to the Pentium and on to the P-6 and new Reduced Instruction Set screamers such as the Power PC, Digital Equipment's Alpha and Silicon Graphics new R-1000 (the latest in the family from Moussouris's previous company Mips Computer, now owned by Silicon Graphics). External computer networks typically run much more slowly than internal networks, the backplane buses connecting microprocessors, memories, keyboards and screens. These buses race along at some 40 megabits per second, up to Intel's new gigabit-per-second PCI bus. Even when computers are linked in local area networks in particular buildings at 10 megabit-per-second Ethernet speeds, they face a communications cliff at LAN's end: the four-kilohertz wires of the telephone company. Under this regime, the processor is king and Moore's Law dictates the pace of change.

In the age of the telecosm, however, all these rules collapse. When the network increasingly runs faster than the processors and buses in the PC, the computer "hollows out," in the words of Eric Schmidt. The network becomes the bus and any set of interconnected processors and memories can become a computer regardless of their location. In this bandwidth-driven world, the key chips are communications processors, such as digital signal processors (DSPs) and MicroUnity's mediaprocessors, which must function at the pace of the network firehose rather than at the pace of the Pentium.

For the last five years, communications processors have indeed been improving their price/performance tenfold every two years—more than three times as fast as microprocessors. This kind of difference add up. Soaring DSP capabilities have already made possible the achievement of many new digital technologies previously unattainable. Among them are digital video compression, video teleconferencing, broadband digital radios pioneered by Steinbrecher (see *Forbes ASAP*, April 11, 1994), digital echo cancellation and spread-spectrum cellular systems that allow 100% frequency reuse in every cell. All these schemes require processing speeds far in excess of the bit rate of the information.

For example, in accord with the prevailing MPEG standards, digital video compression produces a bit stream running at between 1.5 and six megabits per second. But in order to produce this signal manageable by a 100 mips Pentium, a supercomputer or special-purpose machine must process raw video bit flowing 100 times as fast as the compressed format—uncompressed video at a pace of 150 to 600 megabits per second. The complex and exacting process of compressing this onrush of bits—compensating for motion, comparing blocks of pixels for redundancy, smoothing out the flow of data— entails computer operations running 1,000 times as fast as the raw video bits. That is, the video compression algorithm requires a processing speed of between 150 and 600 gigabits per second—hundred of times faster than the Pentium.

Similarly, just to digitize radio signals requires a sampling rate twice as fast as the radio frequency—at a time when new wireless personal communications systems are moving to the two gigahertz bands and wireless cable is moving to 28 gigahertz. A broadband digital radio must handle some large multiple of the highest frequency it will process. Code division multiple access (CDMA) cellular systems depend on a spreading code at least 100 times faster than the bit rate of the message.

In order to feed the Tiger and other such bandwidth-hungry systems, communications processors will have to continue this breathtaking binge of progress beyond the bounds of the microcosm. Grove does not believe this possible. He contends that the surge in DSP will dwindle and converge with Moore's Law, allowing the central processor to suck in functions currently performed in digital signal processors and other communications chips. DSP is nice, Grove observes, "but it is not free"—unless, that is, it is performed in the Intel CPU, obviating the need to buy a DSP chip at all.

But in an era when the network advances faster than the CPU, it is more likely that communications processors will gradually "suck in" and "hollow out" the functions of the CPU, rather than the other way around. Echoing Sun's perennial slogan, Schmidt predicts that the network will become the computer. In this era, Moore's Law and the law of the microcosm are no longer the driving force of progress in information technology. Bandwidth is king.

As the great pioneer of communications theory Claude Shannon wrote in 1948, bandwidth is a replacement for switching. Since ultimately a microprocessor is a set of millions of transistor switches inscribed on a chip, bandwidth can even serve as a substitute for mips. With sufficient bandwidth, engineers can duplicate any computer network topology they want. As the network becomes the computer, they thus redefine the optimal architectures of computing. As an example, take the problem of video-on-demand now being confronted by every major company in the industry from IBM to Microsoft.

In 1992, Microsoft assigned this problem to Craig Mundie, a veteran of Data General in Massachusetts, who had gone on to found Alliant Computer, one of the more successful of the massively parallel computer firms. As a supercomputer man, Mundie initially explored a hardware solution, hiring a team of computer designers from Supercomputer Systems Inc. SSI was Steve Chen's effort to follow up on his successes at Cray Research with a machine for IBM. Although IBM ultimately closed SSI down, Chen commanded some of the best talent in supercomputers. Mundie hired George Spix and a team from SSI.

LOOKING TO SOFTWARE

On the surface, video-on-demand seems a super-computer task. It entails taking tens of thousands of streams of digital images, smoothing them into real-time flows, and switching them to the customers requesting them. Essentially huge hierarchies of storage devices, including fast silicon memories, connected through a specialized switching fabric to arrays of fast processors, supercomputers seem perfectly adapted to video-on-demand, which as Bill Gates explains, is "essentially a switching problem." This is the solution chosen by Oracle Systems, using its nCube supercomputer, and by Silicon Graphics, employing its PowerChallenge server.

According to Mundie, the SSI team developed an impressive video server design. But they soon discovered they were in the wrong company. As Gates told *Forbes ASAP*, "Microsoft looks for a software solution to all problems. IBM looks for a mainframe hardware solution. Larry Ellison owned a supercomputer company so he looked for that solution. Fortunately for us, software solutions are the most scaleable, flexible, fault-tolerant and low cost."

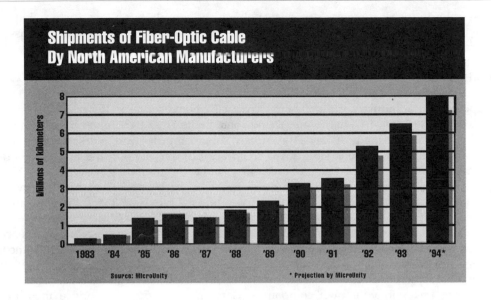

Enter Rick Rashid, a professor from Carnegie Mellon and designer of the Mach kernel adopted by Next, IBM and the Open Software Foundation and incorporated in part in Microsoft's Windows NT operating system. Rashid joined Microsoft in September 1991 and began to focus on video-on-demand in 1992. Like most other people confronting this challenge, he first assumed that the huge bit streams involved would require specialized hardware—RAID (redundant arrays of inexpensive disk) storage, fast buffer memories and supercomputer-style switches. Soon, however, he came to the conclusion that progress in the personal computer industry would enable an entirely software solution.

For example, the memory problem illustrates a tradeoff between bandwidth and processing speed. Expensive hierarchies of RAID drives and semiconductor buffer memories managed by complex controller logic can speed the bit streams to the switch at the necessary pace. But Rashid and Mundie saw that bandwidth offered a cheaper solution. Through clever software, you could "stripe" the film bits across large arrays of conventional disk drives and gain speed through bandwidth. Rather than using one fast memory, plus fast processors, and hard-wired fault tolerance to send the movie reliably to a customer, you spread the images across arrays of cheap, slow disk drives—Seagate Barracudas—which, working in parallel, offer bandwidth and redundancy limited only the number of devices. Having dispensed with the idea of contriving expensive hardware solutions for the memory problem, Rashid recognized that with Windows NT he commanded an operating system with real-time scheduling guarantees that laid the foundation for a software solution. On it, he could proceed to build Tiger as a continuous digital stream operating system.

Liberated from special-purpose hardware, the team could revel in all the advantages of using off-the-shelf personal computer components. Mundie explains: "The personal computer industry commands intrinsic volume and a multi-supplier structure that takes anything in its path and drives its costs to ground." A burly entrepreneur of massively parallel supercomputers, Mundie became a fervent convert to the manifest destiny of the PC to dominate all other technologies in the race to multimedia services, grinding all costs and functions into the ground of microprocessor silicon.

Video-on-demand has been heralded as the salvation of the television industry, the supercomputer industry, the game industry, the high-end server industry. It has been seen as Microsoft's move into hardware. Yet nowhere in the Tiger Laboratory in Building Nine is there any device made by any TV company, supercomputer firm, workstation company, or Microsoft itself. On one side of the room are 12 monitors. On the other side are 12 Compaq computers piled on top of each other, said to be simulating set-top boxes. Next to these are a pile of Seagate Barracuda disk drives, each capable of holding the nine gigabytes of video in three high-resolution compressed movies. Next to them are another pile of Compaq computers functioning as video servers.

All this gear works together to extend Microsoft's long mastery of the science of leverage, getting most of the world to drive costs to ground—or grind costs into silicon—while the grim reapers of Redmond collect tolls on the software. Exploiting another of Sun Microsystems co-founder Bill Joy's famous laws—"The smartest people in every field are never in your own company"—Gates has contrived to induce most of the personal computer industry, from Bangalore to Taiwan, to work for Microsoft without joining the payroll.

In the new world of bandwidth abundance, however, it is no longer sufficient to leverage the PC industry alone. Gates is now reaching out to leverage the telephone and network equipment manufacturing industries as well. Transforming all this PC hardware into a "Tiger" that can consume the TV industry is an ATM switch. In the Tiger application, once one ATM switch has correctly sequenced the movie bits streaming from the tower of Seagate disks, another ATM switch in a metropolitan public network will dispatch the now ordered code to the appropriate display. Microsoft's Tiger and its client "cubs" all march in asynchronous transfer mode.

THE MASTERS OF LEVERAGE

Why is this a brilliant coup? It positions Microsoft to harvest the fruits of the single most massive and far-reaching project in all electronics today. Some 600 companies are now active in the ATM forum, with collective investments approaching $10 billion and rising every year. Not only are ATM switches produced by a competitive swarm of companies resembling the PC industry, ATM also turns networks of small computers into scaleable supercomputers. It combines with fiber-optic links to provide a far simpler, more modular and more scaleable solution than the complex copper backplane buses that perform the same functions in large computers. ATM and fiber prevail by using band-width as a substitute for complex protocols and computations.

Fiber Miles (Millions) Deployed in U.S. as of 1993	
Local Exchange Carriers	7.28
Inter-Exchange Carriers	2.50
Competitive Access Providers	0.24
Total	10.02

Source: MicroUnity

Microsoft Technical Director Nathan Myhrvold points to the Silicon Graphics Power-Challenge superserver as a contrast. "They have a bus that can handle 2.4 gigabytes per second and which is electrically balanced to take a bunch of add-in cards (for processor and memory)." The complexities of this solution yield an expensive machine, costing more than $100,000, with specialized DRAM boards, for example, that cost 10 times as much per megabyte as DRAM in a PC.

This problem is not specific to Silicon Graphics. All supercomputers with multiple microprocessors linked with fast buses face the same remorseless economics and complexities. By contrast, the $30,000 Fore systems ATM switch being used in Tiger proto-types—together with the PCI buses in the PCs on the network—supply the same 2.4 gigabytes per second of bandwidth that the PowerChallenge does. And, as Myhrvold points out, "ATM prices are dropping like a stone."

The Microsoft sage explains: ATM switches linked by fiber optic lines are far more efficient at high bandwidth than copper buses on a backplane. ATM allows "fault tolerance and other issues to be handled in software by treating machines (or disks, or even the ATM switch itself) as being replaceable and redundant, with hot spares standing by."

As Gates told *ASAP*, video-on-demand is essentially a switching problem. You can create an expensive, proprietary, and unscaleable switch using copper lines and complex protocols on the backplane of a supercomputer, or you can use the bandwidth of fiber optics and ATM as a substitute for these complexities. You can put the ATM switches wherever you need them to create a system optimized for any application, allowing any group of PCs using Windows NT and PCI buses to function as video clients or servers as desired. As Microsoft leverages the world, it won't object if the world chooses to lift NT into the forefront of operating systems in unit sales.

Mundie and his assistant Redd Becker earnestly explain the virtues of this scheme and demonstrate its robustness and fault tolerance by disabling several of the disk drives, cubs and servers without perceptibly affecting the 12 images on the screen. They offer it as a system to function as a movie central server resembling the Oracle nCube system adopted by Bell Atlantic, or the Silicon Graphics system used by Time Warner in its heralded Orlando project. But the Tiger is fundamentally different from these systems in that it is completely scaleable and reconfigurable, functioning with full VCR interactivity for a single citizen or for a city. It epitomizes the future of computing in the age of ATM, a system that will soon operate at up to 2.4 gigabits per second. Two point four gigabits per second is more than twice as fast as the Intel PCI bus that links the internal components of a Pentium-based personal computer.

Thus, ATM technology can largely eclipse the difference between an internal hard drive and an external Barracuda, between a video client and a video server. To the CPU, a local area network or even a wide area network running ATM can function as a mother-board backplane. With NT and Tiger software, PCs will be able to tap databases and libraries across the world as readily as they can reach their own hard disks or CD-ROM drives. Presented as an application-specific system for multimedia or movie distribution in real time, it is in fact a new operating system for client-server computing in the new age of image processing.

Gordon Bell, now on Microsoft's technical advisory board, sums up the future of computing in an ATM world: "We can imagine a network with a range of PC-sized nodes costing between $500 and $5,000 that provide person-to-person communication, television and when used together (including in parallel), an arbitrarily large computer. Clearly, because of standards, ubiquity of service and software market size, this architecture will drive out most other computer structures such as massively parallel computers, low-priced workstations and all but a few special-purpose processors. This doomsday for hardware manufacturers will arrive before the next two generations of computer hardware play out at the end of the decade. But it will be ideal for users." And for Microsoft.

For manufacturers of equipment that feeds the Tiger, however, what Bell calls "doomsday for hardware manufacturers" may well be as profitable as the current rage of "Doom," the new computer game infectiously spreading from the Internet into computer stores. The new Tiger model provides huge opportunities for manufacturers of new ATM switches on every scale, for PCs equipped with fast video buses such as PCI, for vendors of network hardware and software, and perhaps most of all for the producers of the new communications processors.

For all the elegance of the Tiger system, however, Gates understands that it cannot achieve its goals within the constraints of Moore's Law in the semiconductor industry. The vision of "any high school dropout buying PCs and entering the interactive TV business" cannot prevail if it takes a supercomputer to compress the images and an array of special-purpose processors to decode, decrypt and decompress them. Facing an ATM stream of 622 megabits per second—perhaps uncompressed video, 3-D or multimedia images—Eric Schmidt points out, a 100 mips Pentium machine would have to process

1.47 million 53-byte cells a second. That means well under 100 instruction cycles to read, store, display and analyze a packet. Since most computers use many cycles for hidden background tasks, the Pentium could not begin to do the job. Gate's adoption of Tiger, his alliance with TCI, his investments in Teledesic, Metricom, and MicroUnity, all bring home face-to-face with the limits of current computer technology in confronting the telecosm. With MicroUnity, however, he may have arrived at a solution just in time.

MicroUnity seems like a throwback to the early years of Silicon Valley, when all things seemed possible—when Robert Widlar could invent a new product for National Semiconductor on the beach in Puerto Vallarta, and develop a new process to build it with David Talbert and his wife Dolores over beers on a bench at the Wagon Wheel. It was an era when scores of semiconductor companies were racing down the learning curve to enhance the speed and functions of electronic devices. Most of all, the MicroUnity project is a climactic episode in the long saga of the industry's struggle between two strategies for accelerating the switching speeds in computers.

A NEW MOORE'S LAW?

Intel Chairman Gordon Moore recently promulgated a new Moore's Law, supposedly deflecting the course of the old Moore's Law, which ordains that chip densities double every 18 months. The new law is that the costs of a chip factory double with each generation of microprocessor. Moore speculated that these capital burdens might deter or suppress the necessary investment to continue the pace of advance in the industry.

Gerhard ("Gerry") Parker, Intel's chief technical officer, however, presents contrary evidence. The cost for each new structure may be approximately doubling as Moore says. But the cost per transistor—and thus the cost per computer function—continues to drop by a factor of between three and four every three years. Not only does the number of transistors on a chip rise by a factor of four, but the number of chips sold doubles with every generation of microprocessor, as the personal computer market doubles every three years. Thus there will be some eight times more transistors sold by Intel from a Pentium fab that from a 486 fab. At merely twice the cost, the new fab seems a bargain.

Of course, Intel gets paid not for transistors but for computer functions. To realize the benefits of the new fabs, therefore, Intel must deliver new computer functions that successfully adapt to the era of bandwidth abundance.

Moreover, it is worth noting that measured in telecosmic terms of useful terabits per second of bandwidth, a MicroUnity fab ultimately costing some $150 million might generate more added value than a $2 billion megafab of Intel.

RETURN TO LOW AND SLOW

Since as a general rule, the more the power, the faster the switch, you can get speed by using high-powered or exotic individual components. It is an approach that worked well for years at Cray, IBM, NEC and other supercomputer vendors. Wire together superfast switches and you will get a superfast machine.

The other choice for speed is to use low-powered, slow switches. You make them so small and jam them so close together, the signals get to their destinations nearly as fast as the high-powered signals. This approach works well in the microprocessor industry and in the human brain.

Despite occasional deviations at Cray and IBM, low and slow has been the secret of all success in semiconductors from the outset. Inventor William Shockley substituted slow, low-powered transistors for faster, high-powered vacuum tubes. Gordon Teal at Texas Instruments replaced fast germanium with slower silicon. Jean Hoerni at Fairchild spurned the fast track of mountainous Mesa transistors to adopt a flat "planar" technology in which devices were implanted below the surface of the chip. Jack Kilby and Robert Noyce then substituted slow resistors and capacitors as well as slow transistors on integrated circuits for faster, high-powered devices on modules and printed circuit boards. Federico Faggin made possible the microprocessor by replacing fast metal gates on transistors with slow gates made of polysilicon. Frank Wanlass and others replaced faster NMOS and PMOS technologies with the 1,000 times slower and 10 times lower-power Complementary Metal Oxide Semiconductors (CMOS) that now rule the industry.

Low and slow finds its roots in the very physics of solid state, separating the microcosm from the macrocosm. Chips consist of complex patterns of wires and switches. In the macrocosm of electromechanics, wires were simple, fast, cool, reliable and virtually free; switches were vacuum tubes, complex, fragile, hot and expensive. In the macrocosm, the rule was economize on switches, squander on wires. But in the microcosm, all these rules of electromechanics collapsed.

In the microcosm, switches are almost free—a few millionths of a cent. Wires are the problem. However fast they may be, longer wires laid down on the chip and more wires connected to it translated directly into greater resistance and capacitance and more needed power and resulting heat. These problems become exponentially more acute as wire diameters drop. On the other hand, the shorter the wires the purer the signal and the smaller the resistance, capacitance and heat.

This fact of physics is the heart of microelectronics. As electron movements approach their mean free path—the distance they can travel "ballistically" without bouncing off the internal atomic structure of the silicon—they get faster, cheaper and cooler.

At the quantum level, noise plummets and bandwidth explodes. Tunneling electrons, the fastest of all, emit virtually no heat at all. It was a new quantum paradox; the smaller the space the more the room, the narrower the switches the broader the bandwidth, the faster the transport the lower the noise. As transistors are jammed more closely together, the power delay product—the crucial index of semiconductor performance combining switching delays with heat emission—improves as the square of the number of transistors on a single chip.

Since the breakthrough to CMOS in the early 1980s, however, the industry has been slipping away from the low and slow regime. Falling for the electromechanical temptation, they are substituting fast metals for slow polysilicon. For better performance, companies are increasingly turning to gallium arsenide and silicon germanium technologies. Semiconductor engineers are increasingly crowding the surface of CMOS with as many as four layers of fast aluminum wires, with tungsten now in fashion among the speed freaks of the industry. The planar chips that built Silicon Valley have given way to high sierras of metal, interlarded with uneven spreads of silicon dioxide and other insulators. Meanwhile, the power used on each chip is rising rapidly, since the increasing number of transistors and layers of metal nullify a belated move to three-volt operation from the five volts adopted with Transistor Transistor Logic in 1971. And as the industry loses touch with its early inspiration of low and slow, the costs of wafer fabrication continue to rise—to an extent that even demoralizes Gordon Moore.

In radically transforming the methods of semiconductor fabrication, John Moussouris and James ("Al") Matthews, MicroUnity's director of technology, seem to many observers to be embarking on a reckless and self-defeating course. But MicroUnity is betting on the redemptive paradoxes of the microcosm. Returning to low and slow, Moussouris and Matthews promise to increase peak clock speeds by a factor of five in the next two years and chip performance by factors of several hundred, launching communications chips in 1995 that function at 1.2 gigahertz and perform as many as 400 gigabits per second.

MATTHEWS AND MEAD

In pursuing this renewal of wafer fabrication at MicroUnity, Matthews has applied for some 70 patents and won about 20 to date. A veteran of Hewlett-Packard's bipolar process labs who moved to Intel in the early 1980s and spearheaded Intel's switch to CMOS for the 386 microprocessor, Matthews has also worked as an engineer at HP-Avantek's gallium arsenide fabs for microwave chips. Commanding experience in diverse fab cultures, Matthews thus escapes the cognitive trap of seeing the established regime as a given, rather than a choice.

At Avantek, Matthews plunged toward the microcosm and prepared the way for his MicroUnity process after reading an early paper by Carver Mead, the inventor of the gallium arsenide MESFET transistor. Mead had prophesied that the behavior of these transistors would deteriorate drastically if the feature sizes were pushed below two-tenths of a micron at particular doping levels (technically impossible at the time). In the mid-1980s, though, Matthews noticed that these feature sizes were then feasible. Testing the Mead thesis, he was startled to discover that far from deteriorating below the Mead threshold, these transistors instead showed "startlingly anomalous levels of good behavior," marked by high gain and plummeting noise.

Based on this discovery, he created a low-noise, gigahertz-frequency amplifier for satellite dishes being sold in the European market. Matthews's process reduced the cost so drastically that Sony officials were said to be contemplating claims of dumping. Avantek was charging a few dollars for microwave frequency chips that cost Sony perhaps some hundreds of dollars to make.

Having discovered the "anomalous good behavior" of gallium arsenide devices pushed beyond the theoretical limits, Matthews at MicroUnity decided to experiment with bipolar devices. Bipolar devices are usually used at high power levels with so-called emitter coupled logic to achieve high speeds in supercomputers and other advanced machines. Inspired by his breakthrough with gallium arsenide, Matthews believed that biopolar performance also might be radically different at extremely low power—under half a volt and at gate lengths approaching the so-called Debye limit, near one-tenth of a micron.

Once again, Matthews was startled by "anomalous good behavior" as processes approached the quantum mechanical threshold. It turned out that at high frequencies biopolar transistors use far less power even than CMOS transistors, famous for their low-power characteristics. At these radio-frequency speeds, however, he discovered that the transistors could not operate with aluminum wires insulated by oxide. Therefore, he introduced a technique he had used with fast bipolar and gallium arsenide devices: gold wires insulated by air. Replacing oxide insulators with "air bridges" drastically reduces the capacitance of the wires and allows the transistor to operate at speeds impossible with conventional device structures.

With these adventures in the microcosm behind him, Matthews was ready to develop a new process and technology for MicroUnity. Based on combining the best features of biopolar and CMOS at radically small geometries, the new technology uses bipolar logic functioning at gigahertz clock speeds, with CMOS retained chiefly for memory cells and with gold air bridges for the metalization layers. Perhaps it is a portent that the gold wires across the top of the chip repeat the most controversial feature of Jack Kilby's original integrated circuit. (Matthews is also seeking patents for methods of using optical communications on the top of a silicon chip).

In essence, Matthews is returning to low and slow. He is shearing off the sierras of metal and oxides and restoring the planar surfaces of Jean Hoerni. Because the surface is flat to a tolerance of one-tenth of a micron, photolithography gear can function at higher resolution despite a narrow depth of field. Elimination of the aluminum sierras also removes a major source of parasitic currents and transistors and allows smaller poly-silicon devices to be implanted closer together. A major gain from these innovations is a drastic move to lower power transistors. Rather than using the usual three volts or five volts, the MicroUnity devices operate at 0.3 volts to 0.5 volts (300 to 500 millivolts). In the microcosm, smaller devices closer together at lower power is the secret of speed.

Although MicroUnity will not divulge the details of future products, *ASAP* calculates on the basis of information from other sources that the MicroUnity chip can hold more than 10 million transistors in a space half the size of a Pentium with three million transistors. With lower power transistors set closer together, the MicroUnity chip can operate with a clock rate as much as 10 times faster than most current microprocessors and at an overall data rate more than 100 times faster. Low and slow results in blazing speed.

For ordinary microprocessor applications, an ultrafast clock is superfluous. Since ordinary memory technology is falling ever farther behind processor speeds, fast clocks mean complex arrangements of cache on cache of fast static RAM and specialized video memory chips. By using the MicroUnity technology at the relatively slow clock rates of a Pentium, MicroUnity might be able to produce Pentiums that use from five to 10 times less power—enabling new generations of portable equipment.

MicroUnity, however, is not building a CPU but a communications processor. In the communications world, the fast clock rate gives the "mediaprocessor" the ability to couple to broadband pipes using high radio frequencies. Most crucially, the mediaprocessor can connect to the radio frequency transmissions over cable coax.

Along with Bill Gates, one of the leading enthusiasts of MicroUnity is John Malone, who for the last year has been celebrating its potential to create a "Cray on a tray" for his set-top boxes and cable modems. For the rest of this decade, most Americans will be able to connect to broadband networks only over cable coax. Thus the link of TCI to MicroUnity and to Tiger offers the best promise of an information infrastructure over the next five years, affording a potential increase in bandwidth of 250,000-fold over the current four-kilohertz telephone wires.

The Regional Bell Operating Companies and the cable companies agree that cable coax is the optimal broadband conduit to homes and that fiber optics is the best technology for connecting central switches or headends to neighborhoods. Looping through communities, with a short drop at each home—rather than running a separate wire from the central office to every household—hybrid fiber-coax networks, according to a Pacific Bell study can reduce the cost of setup and maintenance of connections by some 75% and cut back the need for wire by a factor of 600.

In order to bring broadband video to homes, companies must collaborate with the cable TV industry. Collaborating with TCI, Microsoft once again has chosen the correct technology to leverage. With Digital Equipment, Zenith and Intel all engaged in alliances for the creation of cable modems—and several other companies announcing cable modem projects—Gates may well be leading the pack in transforming his company from a computer company into a communications concern, from the microcosm into the telecosm.

DRIVING FORCE OF PROGRESS

All the bandwidth in the world, however, will get you nowhere if your transceiver cannot process it. By returning to the inspiration of the original Silicon Valley, MicroUnity offers a promising route to the communications infrastructure of the next century, overthrowing Moore's Law and issuing the first fundamental challenge to Moore's company. As Al Matthews puts it: "Bob Noyce [the late Intel founder with Gordon Moore] is my hero. But there is a new generation at hand in Silicon Valley today, and this generation is doing things that Bob Noyce never dreamed of."

Moussouris promises to deliver 10,000 mediaprocessors for set-top boxes in 1995. As everyone agrees, this is a high-risk project (although Bill Gates favorably compares MicroUnity's risk to his other gamble, Teledesic). Even if it takes years for MicroUnity to reach its telecosmic millennium, the advance of communications processors continues to accelerate. Already available today, for example, is Texas Instruments' MVP system—the first full-fledged mediaprocessor on one chip. It will function at a mere 30 to 50 megahertz but performs between two and three billion signal processing steps per second or roughly between 1,000 and 1,500 DSP mips. Rather than revving up the clock to gigahertz frenzies, TI gained its performance through a Multiple Instruction, Multiple Data approach associated with the massively parallel supercomputer industry. The MVP combines four 64-bit digital signal processors with a 32-bit RISC CPU, a floating point unit, two video controllers, 64 kilobytes of static RAM cache and a 64-bit direct memory access controller—all on one sliver of silicon, costing some $232 per thousand mips in 1995, when Pentiums will give you a hundred mips for perhaps twice as much.

This does not favor the notion that microprocessors will soon "suck in" DSPs. DSP mips and computer mips are different animals. As DSP guru Will Strauss points out, "As a rule of thumb, a microprocessor mips rating must be divided by about five to get a DSP mips rating." To equal an MVP for DSP operations, a microprocessor would have to achieve some 5,000 mips.

Designed with the aid of teleconferencing company VTEL and Sony, the MVP chip can simultaneously encode or decode video using any favored compression scheme, process audio, faxes or input from a scanner and perform speech recognition or other pattern-matching algorithms. While Intel and Hewlett-Packard have been winning most of the headlines for their new RISC processing alliance, the key development in the microprocessor domain is the emergence of this new class of one-chip multimedia communications systems.

One thing is certain. Over the next decade, computer speeds will rise about a hundredfold, while bandwidth increases a thousandfold or more. Under these circumstances, the winners will be the companies that learn to use bandwidth as a substitute for computer processing and switching. The winners will be the companies that most truly embrace the Sun slogan: "The network is the computer." As Schmidt predicts, over the next few years "the value-added of the network will so exceed the value-added of the CPU that your future computer will be rated not in mips but in gigabits per second. Bragging rights will go not to the person with the fastest CPU but to the person with the fastest network—and associated database lookup, browsing and information retrieval engines."

The law of the telecosm will eclipse the law of the microcosm as the driving force of progress. Springing from the exponential improvement in the power delay product as transistors are made smaller, the law of the microcosm holds that if you take any number (N) transistors and put them on a single sliver of silicon you will get N squared performance and value. Conceived by Robert Metcalfe, inventor of the Ethernet, the law of the telecosm holds that if you take any number (*n*) computers and link them in networks, you get *n* squared performance and value. Thus the telecosm builds on and compounds the microcosmic law. The power of Tiger, MicroUnity and TCI comes from fusing the two laws into a gathering tide of bandwidth.

With network technology advancing 10 times as fast as central processors, the network and its nodes will become increasingly central while CPUs become increasingly peripheral. Faced with a CPU bottleneck, multimedia systems will simply bypass the CPU on broadband pipes. Circumventing Amdahl's Law, system designers will adapt their architectures to exploit the high bandwidth components, such as mediaprocessors, ATM switches and fiber links. In time the microprocessor will become a vestigial link to the legacy systems such as word processing and spreadsheets that once defined the machine. All of this means that while the last two decades have been the epoch of the computer industry, the next two decades will belong to the suppliers of digital networks.

The chief beneficiaries of all this invention, however, will be the people of the world, ascending to new pinnacles of prosperity in an Information Age. Although many observers fear that these new tools will chiefly aid the existing rich   or the educated and smart—these technologies have already brought prosperity to a billion Asians, from India and Malaysia to Indonesia and China, previously mired in penury.

Communications bandwidth is not only the secret of electronic progress. It is also the heart of economic growth, stretching the webs of interconnection that extend the reach of markets and the realms of opportunity. Lavishing the exponential gains of networks, endowing old jobs with newly productive tools and unleashing creativity with increasingly fertile and targeted capital, the advance of the telecosm offers unprecedented hope to the masses of people whom the industrial revolution passed by.

11

Gilder Meets His Critics

ASAP contributing editor George Gilder ran into a buzz saw over recent bandwidth and big-bird articles.

BILL GATES
Chairman and CEO,
Microsoft, Redmond, WA

George Gilder's piece on bandwidth was good. But I don't understand how Intel gets hurt unless it stops delivering the best price/performance microprocessors. The more network connectivity the more we need MIPS. Andy Grove is right that DSPs are just a complex way of getting more MIPS. Just because bandwidth reduces some of the need for compression doesn't mean bandwidth reduces demand for cycles.

In any case Gilder is very stimulating even when I disagree with him, and most of·the time I agree with him.

NICHOLAS NEGROPONTE
Director, MIT Media Laboratory,
Boston, MA

Debunking Bandwidth:

When our world is fibered, the planet is like a desktop. Earth is but a backplane for a single computer. True. But as mere humans, the bandwidth we're really interested in is the one that exists between us and computers, be they the size of a cuff link or a country. That bandwidth is often one we want to be smaller, not bigger. Most of us, most of the time, want less bits, not more bits. Sure we want gigabits, but only for a few millionths of a second at a time.

Remember the early days of computing when stacks of fanfolded output were dropped on an executive's desk? People caught on quickly; that was data, not information. Today, for some reason, we have forgotten some simple concepts about what constitutes meaning and understanding and where they come from. You. So while it is real easy to ship vast amounts of data and high-resolution images back and forth between computers and while it is suddenly possible to ignore geographic constraints, let's not forget that in many cases "less is more" when it comes to bandwidth."

Narrow channels force us to be smarter. Yes, bandwidth will be free, but so will computing. The future will not be driven by either MIPS or BPS, but information and entertainment content. Andy Grove does not need to worry about John Malone or Bill Gates. He has to worry about Michael Ovitz.

MARK STAHLMAN
President, New Media
Associates, New York, NY

Bandwidth to Burn: Now What Do We Do?

Gilder has made a case for vastly expanded bandwidth overwhelming the influence of the steady march of computing power. [But] what new need will drive businesses to translate the inventions Gilder describes into significant new media opportunities?

Apparently, it's the need for video-on-demand. [But] if this were a plausible mass market, the streets of New York would be filled with bicycle messengers delivering Tom Cruise with bags of Chinese food. No, during the next five to 10 years, bandwidth will certainly be consumed in much greater quantities—but for completely different reasons. We will dramatically extend ourselves and our social relationships with video-telephones. We will consume substantial bandwidth by substituting bandwidth for gasoline—through telecommuting. We will network to multimedia databases (such as the current Internet-based World Wide Web) and dramatically expand our range of social contacts—across borders, cultures and tribes.

Unfortunately for Gilder's bandwidth braggarts, these enormous markets will be built using a telecommunications technology which began deployment over 10 years ago—ISDN—and in which none of them has any important financial stake today. Unglamorous, ungainly, even downright ugly, ISDN (integrated services digital network) will be supplied by old-time telephone companies (not cable companies) and it will be driven by the steady progress of personal computers—themselves now a 15- to 20-year-old industry. As has been widely noted, we tend to overestimate (sometimes dramatically) the near-term impact of new technologies and underestimate the long-range effects.

In this age, new technology hype has become an epidemic. Reality itself, as it turns out, is far more interesting.

MICHAEL SLATER

President, MicroDesign Resources, and Editorial Director,
Microprocessor Report, Sebastopol, CA

Increasing bandwidth will provide computers with more information to process, and this will increase, not decrease, the computational requirements. Having high bandwidth makes it possible for the interface nodes to be less intelligent, but this is not necessarily desirable. Furthermore, the time frame must be considered; high-bandwidth WAN (wide area network) connections are not going to be widely available for years, and in the meantime, computational power will continue to be critical as a way to mitigate bandwidth limitations.

No matter how much bandwidth is available, it is still very desirable to have high-performance computational ability in desktop systems. Rendering of three-dimensional images from mathematical representations, for example, is something that has widespread application not only in games, but in other consumer applications (like home and garden design programs). Orders of magnitude more performance will result in direct improvements in such applications, and bandwidth is no substitute here.

Finally, with regard to the inclusion of signal-processing capabilities in general-purpose microprocessors, I disagree with Gilder's conclusion that this will not occur. Minor extensions to general-purpose architectures, such as the ability to perform four 8-bit additions in parallel using the same hardware that normally performs a single 32-bit addition, will provide a significant boost for applications such as video decompression. The cost of adding these features is small, and the benefit is great. Sun and HP have already made such additions to their processors, and I expect Intel and other x86 vendors will do so in the future. Dedicated DSPs will always be able to provide higher performance, but the incremental cost/performance of adding functions to the host CPU is superior.

MICHAEL E. TREACY

President, Treacy & Co., Cambridge, MA
[Treacy is co-author of *The Discipline of Market Leaders*]

[Gilder's] view is rounded on the narrow philosophy of technological determinism. It is a peculiar and persistent form of myopia based on the wobbly assertion that the best technology will win in the marketplace. He who rides the best technological wave will ascend to glory. Oh, if it were only so! If technology determined success, there would be no Microsoft today. By any reasonable standards, MS-DOS, the foundation of Mr. Gate's empire, was an average technology when it was brought to market more than a decade ago. But Microsoft had all the other elements that created a compelling value proposition for its customer.

Value is what customers want. Intel has got what it takes and has been a value leader for many years. Andy Grove has already begun to direct Intel's development portfolio toward communications opportunities. He has read the signals and made the call, just as he did several years ago when he vacated the memory-chip business, in advance of grinding competition and shrinking margins. With constant vigilance and change, Intel's success can continue for years to come.

HOWARD ANDERSON
Managing Director, The Yankee Group, and General Partner,
Battery Ventures, Boston, MA

George Gilder's analysis of the changes in the computing and communications tradeoff is brilliant, concise, analytical—and flawed. His portrait of the rapid changes in communications and relative disadvantage of the old-line computer industry (Intel, etc.) does not overestimate the movement. It underestimates how the next 10 years will be the decade of Bandwidth on Demand. Consider this:

From 1995–2005, the cost of bandwidth will drop faster than the cost of computing.
From 1995–2005, the cost of switching will drop faster than the cost of bandwidth.

Historical examples: The cost of a T1 line (1.54 megabits) coast to coast in 1985 was $40,000/month. Today? Under $2,000/month, a drop of 95%.

Assume the following: by 2000, computing is free, and bandwidth is free. Now—design the future!

The amount of money spent on ATM Research and Development (Source: Yankee Group ATM Planning Service):

1993: $335 million
1994: $550 million
1995: $950 million

So Gilder is right on about the impact of ATM. In fact, Fore Systems, where our sister company Battery Ventures is the second-largest outside stockholder, carries a market capitalization of $900 million—on a $60 million sales base demonstrating that the ATM value is well known within the industry.

This past year, the Yankee Group trained 5,000 end-users on the use of ATM technology and the most frequently asked question was, "How in the world am I going to use all that bandwidth?" But it was only 10 years ago that users thought they would fall off the end of the earth if they went faster than 2.4 kilobits!

Which leads to some immutable laws about networks, which Gilder alludes to:

Networks always grow.
Networks always become more complex.
Networks find applications that double the bandwidth needed every three years.
The cost of bandwidth is artificially high.

Andy Grove is right: "Only the paranoid survive."

G. A. KEYWORTH, II

The Progress and Freedom Foundation,
Washington, D.C.

George Gilder's article goes yet another step in establishing him as the forefront "signal-to-noise processor" of information technology. Yet, I confess to being somewhat confused by it.

My dilemma resides in what I will call the "30-30 rule"—that we humans can take in information at only about 30 megahertz through our eyes or, even slower, at 30 kilohertz through our ears. The kind of bandwidth that Gilder projects are important to machine-to-machine communications, i.e., to networks, but it is the computer (in some form, whether PC, PDA, digital-phone or digital-TV) that will continue to determine the "match" between bandwidth and the inherent limitation of the 30-30 rule.

Bandwidth is important, because it will make the connection a richer one, but the fact remains that we humans lack broadband input channel to access all that bandwidth directly. And it is the computer that must bridge that gap, keeping it in the driver's seat as we enter the realm of ubiquitous, connected computing.

Gilder's article makes an additional point, and one that falls too often on deaf ears in Washington. That is that bandwidth scarcity, the basis for much of our telecommunications regulation, is an outdated concept. Only major revamping of the government's role in telecommunications will permit the natural competition between computing and communications to play out.

ERIC SCHMIDT

Chief Technical Officer,
Sun Microsystems, Mountain View, CA

Gilder's article does a wonderful job showing the potential impact of the bandwidth revolution. Let me give you two examples of approaches in computer systems to exploit enormous bandwidth increases:

The speed of light is not doubling every 18 months. There is a revolution in system design for small, fast machines just as significant as the one for broadband networks in your article. What we call today "large servers" will in fact have to become physically very small. We are now approaching "design for light speed" in computer systems, and we have to keep our handy ruler, measured in nanoseconds, ready for each new board design. Light travels about four inches in a nanosecond in today's wires, so that, in a 500-megahertz (two nanosecond) computer design, we have less than eight inches of room for our signals to travel in a synchronous processor design (as most are). This means that the fastest computers in our future will also have to be the smallest!

The backplanes of these machines have to be physically very short. The limit of a single backplane makes it hard to keep up with the improvements in processor speeds, using traditional backplane designs.

Switching becomes a core strategy for computer systems. Two approaches that merge switching and architecture are now popular. One, called Distributed Shared Memory, uses a switching network to link cache-coherent memories together. In DSM computers, the power of shared memory designs can be extended over very high-speed switched memory networks. The other, called clustering, has been around for at least 15 years, and uses a switching network to link computer systems. In this approach, applications are modified to share common disks, peripherals and software.

Small size and switching are the future of high-performance computing. Both are based on networking as their core. As the switched networks get faster these architectures will come to dominate computing. The fastest improving technology, in this case networking, always drives the architecture. The hollowing out of the computer occurs when high-performance computers truly span networks. ATM asynchronous transfer model, now in its infancy, is the likely network for us to bet on.

STEVEN DORFMAN
President,
Hughes Telecommunications and Space Co.
GM Hughes, Los Angeles, CA

In "Ethersphere" (Oct. 10) Gilder offers the view that high-powered geostationary satellites—the mainstay, high-capacity platforms of our past, current and future service offerings—are already antiques, and soon will be displaced entirely by thousands of low earth orbiting satellites. That these highly touted systems are nonexistent, unlaunched and unproven [and require major technical breakthroughs] are details that conveniently escape Gilder's scathing assault on geostationary systems.

Gilder should recognize that new technology products are designed and brought to market based on a host of considerations in addition to pure technical feasibility. Tradeoffs are—must be—made. But to Gilder, "tradeoff" would appear to be synonymous with "sellout."

In the corporate world, this is business naiveté. In deciding what form Hughes's new Spaceway and DirecTV services, for example, should take, our goal was to deploy systems that: maximized technology insertion, thereby minimizing risk; provided a low-cost service for which there was demonstrated consumer demand; and faced minimal regulatory, technology-development, or financing delays, thereby expediting service introduction.

A Ka-band GEO system, evolved from U.S. defense communication satellite applications, Spaceway is the logical extension of Hughes's universe of 120,000 very small aperture terminal antennas worldwide, used for private network, two-way voice, data and video. Our me-satellite regional approach provides global coverage at a cost of $3 billion. Because service can be rolled out incrementally, revenues can be generated before full system deployment. (By contrast, virtually all 840 Teledesic satellites must be operational—at a $9 billion system cost—before service can begin.)

Our comparatively low investment cost and highly efficient spot beam architecture, whereby we cost-effectively target our capacity to the world's most populated regions, yield significant savings and low user costs . . . critical because developing nations with limited communications infrastructure are a key market.

For voice, we expect that developing regions without access to low-cost terrestrial voice service will embrace Spaceway despite the fractional time delay—at least until terrestrial infrastructure is available. This is a significant, revenue-generating window of opportunity for us. As for data applications, our VSAT experience has shown that custom developed protocols provide totally acceptable throughput efficiency and seamless inter-activity. In short, we believe "the delay issue" has been overstated. There is a different delay issue, however, that cannot be overstated. Gilder is, I believe, overly optimistic about how soon Teledesic's technology will be ready—and hence, how soon service revenues can be generated.

I believe Spaceway is the best technological solution for this market at this time. But if tomorrow the technology and market are in place so that the LEO system makes sense, rest assured that Hughes will introduce an innovative LEO product of our own.

Gilder attaches far too little import and value (in the form of operating profits) to today's technology. Nowhere is this more clear than in his assessment of satellite direct-to-home television programming. Gilder calls DBS "one-size-fits-all programming," stressing its lack of sufficient consumer choice and absence of Interactivity. But in holding out for a fiber solution, Gilder is making a poor business decision.

Today, Hughes's two DirecTV GEO satellites are filled with 150 program channels. We are adding 3,000 subscribers a day, and will break even (three million) by mid-1996. With 10 million subscribers projected by 2000, DirecTV will be a $3 billion a year business, with $1 billion in operating profit.

Waiting for the future, Gilder, carries a price tag most CEOs can't afford, and are not prepared to pay.

GEORGE GILDER REPLIES

I want to thank my correspondents for their alternately poetic, ironic, trenchant and pithy responses. So many of them, though, share the notion that I predicted dire straits for Intel that I must assume a lack of clarity in my treatment of the issue. I predicted that new and larger opportunities would arise in the field of communications processors and systems that central processing units would bear a declining share of total processing not that they would in themselves decline in any absolute sense. Indeed, CPUs should continue to improve their cost-effectiveness apace with Moore's Law, plus an increment for architectural advances in parallelism. Such advances, however, will fail to keep pace with the onrushing expansion of bandwidth, as further detailed by Howard Anderson's intriguing letter. Bandwidth gains will be fed on the demand side, as Mark Stahlman incisively observes, more by the needs of teleconferencing and telecommuting than by the need for one-way video-on-demand.

Thus I agree with Bill Gates that Intel can continue to thrive as long as it continues to produce the most cost-effective microprocessors. I did raise the possibility, foreshadowed by Microunity's new semiconductor lab process, that Intel's existing technology might face rivals that could produce more MIPs or gigabits per second per watt. Power efficiency will be a crucial index in a time of seething CPUs and increasing demands for power-saving designs from producers of mobile appliances, such as the digital cellular communicators which will be the most common PCs of the next decade.

Focusing on gigabits per second as a prime spec, these devices may well eclipse CPUs in raw processing pace and find a wide range of applications in digital radio, real-time compression and decompression, pattern recognition, echo-cancellation and other digital signal processing uses. The demands of these applications have already impelled an array of processing and architectural advances at Microunity, Texas Instruments and elsewhere in the pullulating field of DSP. Unconstrained by proprietary legacies and immense installed bases, perhaps other manufacturers will also find ways to excel the Moore's Law pace of Intel's majestic progress down the learning curve of three-volt CMOS technology.

Jay Keyworth and Nicholas Negroponte both eloquently point to the central paradox of the information age. While production systems of the industrial age use scarce resources, such as land, labor, and capital, to create abundance, production systems of the information age use abundant resources, such as bits and bandwidth, to create knowledge scarce enough to fit the bandwidth of humans. This distillation function—delivering correct and useful data to human beings with their Keyworth window of roughly 30 kilohertz cochlea and 30 megahertz retinas—requires processing speeds orders of magnitude above the human rates, just to sample, quantize and codify the flow. To scan, select, recognize, correct, decompress, echo-cancel, visualize or otherwise manipulate the data entails still further accelerations of processing power.

Communications processors may well emerge as most efficient for many of these tasks. The idea that all such functions will be sucked into the CPU has a long history, but motherboards and their buses remain as crowded as ever. I suspect that the bandwidth explosion will offer many opportunities for processors specializing in communications.

Steven Dorfman of Hughes, I predict, will do better both for his company and his two-way communications from space by moving quickly rather than slowly to low earth orbits. I fully share his admiration for the point-to multipoint-powers of DBS and I have long cited them as a prime reason for the obsolescence of cable TV regulations based on the assumption of monopoly. Indeed, I predict far more than 10 million users by 2000 if Hughes and its suppliers can meet the demand. But satellite and cable TV vendors will prosper best by providing two-way channels for the 110 million personal computers in the land. I expect that these channels—particularly CATV, not ISDN—will provide the dominant access channel for computers over the next decade.

Above all, I hope that whoever Andy Grove fears most, it is not Michael Ovitz. Grove goes Hollywood and we'll all be in trouble.

12

Mike Milken and the Two Trillion Dollar Opportunity

It's time to deregulate America's telecom infrastructure. And let the creative destroyers go to work.

Michael Milken is back! Back, so the story goes, from the orgies of '80s greed, back from the best-selling den of thieves, back from his preening at the predators' ball, back from soft time at Pleasanton pen, back from prostate cancer and plagues of litigation, back to tell his own book to William Novak and to buy his redemption with the spoils of his crimes. Yes, so they say, Milken is back, while thousands of plundered companies and communities labor to regain their standard of living and jobs, long lost in the shuffle of his dismal deals and loaded down with his "high yields."

Yes, Milken is back. Back from the gutters of Ponzi finance, the rot of junk and S&L sleaze, angling to launder his weaseled wealth with educational hype and charity hustles. Back, aiming now at history and posterity rather than at new opportunity, but hitting it big instead with Michael Jackson, Doonesbury laughs and Clifton compassion photo ops. Meanwhile, even the ascendant Republicans in Washington try to steer clear of "eighties excesses" of debt and deficits and supply-side economics.

Or so it looks to media observers of the Milken saga. And yet slowly and arduously, there is emerging from the carrels of the Harvard Business School and other institutions a distinctly different tale.

Under the leadership of Michael Jensen, a small group of Harvard Business School scholars has been scrutinizing all the statistics of corporate behavior during the 1980s. They have laboriously appraised the results of all the leveraged buyouts, junk bond issues, venture capital, and other tools of corporate making and remaking. They have arrived at unexpected conclusions and have developed a new body of theory to explain them. From this perspective, the events of the 1980s—and Milken's role—assume a wholly new meaning.

Jensen puts the Milken episode in the context of another form of wretched excess for which Milken was the remedy: namely, the excesses of corporate waste and conglomeration by empire-building managers with scarcely any ownership stake in their companies. Amid the sieges of deregulation and tax rate reduction, amid the obvious tumult in the markets for oil, tires, tobacco, real estate, gold and commodities, many industries needed profound restructuring. But their entrenched managements were set to expand their domains through acquisition and investment in new capacity. Meanwhile, a thousandfold rise in the cost-effectiveness of microchips, governed by the centrifugal law of the microcosm, rendered obsolete the dominant architecture of information technology.

Most conspicuously, between 1977 and 1987 the percentage of total computer power commanded by centralized systems dropped from nearly 100% to under 1%. Less obviously, but no less profoundly, the equally centralized structures of television and telephony were also falling before the distributive force of the microcosm. Ordaining that the price performance of microchips rises by the square of the increase in the number of transistors on a single chip, the law of the microcosm exalts single chip systems, led by the PC. Pushed into obsolescence were all monopolies and hierarchies, pyramids and power grids of the old information structure, epitomized by the mainframe computer, the broadcast network and the central telephone switch.

The old establishment of AT&T, the big three TV networks and some 1,400 over-the-air broadcast stations was breaking down into a new formation of cable and wireless schemes. Affecting virtually every company in the economy and threatening most existing management plans and practices, these trends created huge opportunities for wealth creation and disruption.

Beginning with his move to Century City in Los Angeles in July of 1978, Milken aggressively rode the microcosm—inside and outside of Drexel. Inside, he concentrated on what Jensen describes as a key role of information technology: "taking the specific knowledge previously scattered through a firm and making it into general knowledge usable by all." In this case, it was a matter of turning Milken's command of the details of hundreds and then thousands of high-yield issues into the foundation for a company that could make these bonds the prime venture capital in the U.S. economy. From the beginning, crucial to this goal was computer technology.

A specialist in finance, information systems and operational research at Wharton, he had begun his career at Drexel in 1970 with a computerized move to speed up the delivery of securities to its customers, thus saving the company some $500,000 in interest charges and setting a new standard in the industry.

In Los Angeles, he created an advanced system for trading based on what was then a state-of-the-art Prime 550 Model 2. Through the RS-232 9600-baud serial ports of up to 250 Televideo terminals, the Prime computer time-shared a Fortran database containing the trading history of all Drexel customers, some 1,700 high-yield securities and some 8,000 securities in the public market.

With a quick query, a member of Milken's team could determine the customer's history, the amount of his potential profits or losses, his investment philosophy and ability to buy new issues. Thus the team could link the buyers and sellers of securities in a uniquely targeted and opportunistic way and could command the detailed knowledge needed to counteract the strong prejudice and ratings stigma against high-yield securities.

Under William Haloc, a former systems analyst for Prime who joined Drexel, the team also developed real-time analytics to allow instant calculation of pricing for these intricate securities. These functions allowed salespeople to view the name, issue and ratings of a security and to compute complex yields and cash flows involving call features, sinking funds, refund schedules, puts, warrants and prices, all instantly calculable on line. Meanwhile, at rival firms, many dealers still fumbled with the levers on $3,000 Monroe calculators.

The entire system was monitored by Drexel Burnham's New York headquarters and linked indirectly to the floors of the exchanges by Quotron, Reuters and 10 other on-line services, each with a separate Rich monitor, switchable from a keyboard. These arrays of small black monitors spread across the desk collectively functioned like a present-day Windows display.

Most of the features of Milken's system are common today. But in 1980 they were novel. This customized $2 million computer scheme, with five times that amount for programming and maintenance, gave the Drexel team a mastery of 5 the high-yield market that sometimes seemed positively sinister to outside observers and competitors. But it was not magic or malfeasance; it was the microcosm of the new technology joined with the knowledge and investment genius of Michael Milken.

More famously, Milken's grasp of the information age extended well beyond Drexel's IS department. Focusing on emergent information companies responding to the tectonic and regulatory turmoil unleashed by the microchip in TV and telephony, Milken channeled a total of some $26 billion into MCI, McCaw, Viacom, TCI, Time-Warner, Turner, Cablevision Systems, News Corp. and other cable, telecom, wireless, publishing and entertainment companies. At the time, virtually none of these firms commanded substantial collateral acceptable to a bank, and thus they could have raised these billions nowhere else. Now, these companies are collectively worth some $224 billion and comprise the foundations of a national information infrastructure unrivaled in the world.

With an eventual $2.5 billion from Drexel, MCI built the first national single-mode fiberoptic network and spurred AT&T and Sprint into action to give the U.S. a global lead in the technology. With another $1.2 billion, McCaw launched the first national wireless telephone system. And with $8 billion, TCI, Viacom, Time-Warner, Cablevision Systems and Turner, followed by many other Drexel high-yield issuers, made U.S. cable television a unique national asset, with unequaled programming and broadband links. Redeemed in the process were troubled companies providing equipment and services. One of them was Corning, which supplied 62, 112 miles of state-of-the-art fiber to MCI's pioneering network at a time when Corning had no other customers for this crucial technology developed over the previous 17 years.

Milken's influence reached well beyond his actual transactions. A once-lame Disney was restructured with Milken's guidance and takeover pressure in some three years of 5 a.m. meetings with Roy Disney, Frank Wells and Stanley Gold. Then worth $ 1.8 billion, Disney emerged as a revamped Hollywood colossus worth $30 billion 11 years later in 1995.

Comprising more than half of all high-yield bond issues, Milken's activities also embraced thousands of companies beyond the telecom, cable TV and entertainment field—for example, building Hasbro into the world's leading toy company and Barnes & Noble into the leading independent bookseller. His example helped inspire many rivals, including Kohlberg Kravis Roberts, Forstmann Little, and Morgan Stanley, who also made heroic contributions to this campaign of corporate renewal. In particular, Morgan Stanley channeled crucial billions in high-yield funds to the computer, semiconductor and hard-disk drive industries during extreme industry crises in the mid—and late 1980s as Drexel was leaving the scene.

Between 1976 and 1993, Jensen calculates that in these campaigns of corporate restructuring, American corporations conducted 42,621 merger and acquisition deals worth a total of $3.1 trillion. In these transactions, selling firms won premiums of some 41%, generating $899 billion in constant dollar gains to the shareholders. Since buying firms also gained on average, by increments that increased over the years, Jensen's estimate represents a lower bound on the yields of the restructuring movement.

No substantial evidence supports the speculations by Larry Summers (now Treasury Undersecretary) and others that these gains disguise large wealth transfers from bond-holders, workers, suppliers and communities. Indeed, the evidence assembled by Jensen, Steven Kaplan of the University of Chicago, Harvard economist Andre Schleifer and Jensen colleague Karen Wruck, among others, shows that capital expenditures, employment, and research and development all rose in the aftermath of these transactions.

As Jensen now sums it up: "These are lower-bound estimates because they do not include gains that came about later or voluntary gains that were achieved as a result of hostile offers. I don't know any way to add up all these benefits. But it is clear that the impact was dramatic and it left us much more competitive as a country. Today the Japanese and the Europeans are suffering from their delay of restructuring and the U.S. is much leaner and more efficient."

Both Jensen and Milken agree that the opportunities today exceed even the gains of the 1980s. Impelled by the restructuring campaign, the real value of the equity of public firms more than doubled between 1981 and 1990, rising by $1.6 trillion, or from $1.4 trillion to $3 trillion. Since then the pace of technical change has accelerated and the possibilities for a deregulatory breakthrough have soared with the election of a new Congress. *Forbes ASAP* projects possible stock market gains for the rest of this decade of another $2 trillion.

The heightened pace of change, however, creates a desperate need for restructuring. This $2 trillion opportunity depends on emancipating into the markets the resources currently trapped in obsolete structures by capital gains taxes near 40%, compounded by inflation, and by new antitakeover rules and outdated telecom regulations. Flowing again into a new communications infrastructure, into venture funds and into restructuring campaigns, freed capital can endow entrepreneurs with the power to align their companies with the most potent force in the history of technology.

But first, America needs a new Milken.

THE ONRUSH OF THE TELECOSM

With chip densities still doubling every 18 months and chip sales up nearly 30% each of the last two years, with computer MIPS (millions of instructions per second) per dollar doubling every year and computer sales up over 25% in each of the last two years, with hard-disk cost-effectiveness doubling every nine months, and fiber-optics bandwidth exploding a thousandfold while fiber deployment spreads at a pace of 1,300 miles a day— the onrush of technology is now accelerating well beyond the pace of the 1980s.

In essence, the law of the microcosm is now potentially converging with the law of the telecosm. This law ordains that the value and performance of a network rise apace with the square of the increase in the number and power of computers linked on it. As these forces fuse, the world of computers and communications can ride an exponential rocket.

The 50 million new computers sold into America's homes and offices over the last two years guarantee a huge market for broadband networks. Half of the PCs sold in December bore Pentium microprocessors, and 60% of the PCs went into homes. These computers process data at a pace rapidly approaching 100 MIPS. Early in the next century, just five years from now, most American households will command multimedia teleputers processing data in billions of instructions per second and pouring it out at gigabit-per-second rates—or as much as a million times the current digital dribble of 9.6-kilobit modems.

But not today. This computer-rich, bandwidth-poor situation means a crippling and unnecessary mismatch between microcosm and telecosm, between the power of PCs and the bandwidth of the networks that serve them—between PC instructions per second on single-chip silicon and telco bits per second on twisted-pair copper wires. Tens of millions of PC owners are demanding electronic commerce, distance learning, full-motion videoconferencing, and ready access to the graphics and hypertext of the Internet. World Wide Web.

Yet phone and cable executives dawdle with market surveys and experiments with interactive TV that amazingly manage to prove that people don't even want full-motion movies. Meanwhile, the values and sales of their companies languish. In the last 12 months, for example, the 24 leading telecom and cable companies, led by the Regional Bell Operating Companies, lost an average of 12.8% of their market value. Facing a world of shining broadband opportunities in their own businesses, narrowband executives grope for glamour in Hollywood and grasp for growth overseas.

American industry is still cowed by overreaching regulators obsessed with corporate power. In a world of exploding competition in the telecosm—galvanized by new wireless and wireline technologies emerging every week—the administration, the FCC and

Congress have long been paralyzed by nightmares of John Malone of TCI and a possible single-wire stranglehold in St. Louis or of a blight of disinvestment in phone service for South Dakota or Alaska.

If current fears of monopoly result in a contrived two-wire mandate on America's communications infrastructure, however, all the hopes for an integrated broadband two-way net will die until well into the next century. With oceans of bandwidth languishing just out of reach, the tremendous resource of broadband home computers will waste away, gasping on the beach for two-way channels for teleconferencing, telecommuting, telemedicine and telecommerce, while the telephone and cable companies "compete" with rival offerings of mostly one-way floods of movies, shopping and the Sega Channel for TVs. By betraying its precious world-leading endowment of PCs in order to save its existing telcos and TV companies, the U.S. still could make a literal $2 trillion mistake.

THE AMAZING VINDICATION OF JUNK

To grasp the size of possible opportunity and the possible mistake, let us return to Milken and his achievement of the 1980s, which set the stage for the current drama. Never in history has a convicted white-collar felon been so luminously vindicated by the passage of time. His six alleged felonies dwindled to a series of debatable violations, devoid of insider trading and essentially costing their victims nothing (or a total of $318,082, according to a dubious estimate by the court that forced him into a plea through RICO threats against him, his family and Drexel). Returning to the volumes of the 1980s peak, his supposed Ponzi scheme of junk finance became the most profitable class of domestic fixed-income securities of the early 1990s.

Indeed, if the few Savings & Loans that held a substantial portfolio of junk had been permitted to keep it, they would have survived, prospered and paid millions of dollars of taxes rather than collapsed into the hands of the FDIC. For example, the shareholders of Columbia Savings & Loan may have suffered from Thomas Spiegel's undue extravagance in company jets and bullet-proof bathrooms. But the government crackdown cost them $700 million and cost the taxpayers $1 billion, though the bank was on track to profit massively from falling interest rates on its deposits and thriving high-yield securities.

Entrepreneurs such as ex-Drexel luminary Leon Black, who purchased the bonds from the government at bargain-basement rates, became billionaires on the proceeds and were charged with gulling the regulators. Meanwhile, the companies that Milken financed with these securities now form the foundations of a new information economy.

A minor triumph came at the end of 1994 when *Vanity Fair* magazine, avid vessel of many a lurid exposed of Milken and his team, published a lavishly photographed story on "America's New Establishment." Among the 19 names were Ted Turner, Craig McCaw, Sumner Redstone, Gerald Levin, John Malone, Rupert Murdoch, Barry Diller, Michael Eisner, Ronald Perelman and Bill Gates. Although Milken was never mentioned, all these high fliers—with the exception of Gates—rose to prominence largely or partly on a cresting tide of Milken's junk.

Why does junk work! Primarily because it frees capital from corporate bureaucracy and gets it into the hands of entrepreneurs. During the 1980s, lower taxes and new technologies had transformed the economic environment. What was precious in the 1970s—metals, minerals, real estate and collectibles, all mashed together in diversified conglomerates and tax shelters-became disposable junk in the 1980s. What was junk in the 1970s and early 1980s—Milken's array of leveraged cable, fiber, wireless and content schemes—became the precious foundations of a new information infrastructure.

How could this be so? How could one man with a poorly named venture-debt financing vehicle contribute so hugely to the U.S. economy while, according to Jensen's analysis, the nation's 500 largest corporations, led by a $100 billion opportunity loss at General Motors in 11 years, incurred negative returns with their free cash flow (cash flow beyond the amount needed to fund all internal investments with a positive net present value)?

Did not Franco Modigliani and Merton Miller win a Nobel prize for their so-called M&M theorems showing that the performance of corporations is independent of their capital structure? Have not scores of economists pursuing the Efficient Market Hypothesis demonstrated that in general the capital exchanges are fully efficient, that company prices reflect all of the available information and no individual investor can systematically outwit the tape without illegal manipulation or insider trading?

In his presidential address to the American Finance Association in 1993, however, Jensen answered all these arguments. On the basis of new research on the experience of the 1980s, he declared that the M&M theorems, "while logically sound, are empirically incorrect."

The central problem of the corporation, according to Jensen, is the "agency" dilemma—the divergence between the interests of the managers and the owners of large businesses. This problem is inherent in all cooperative human endeavor: the interests of the individuals always deviate at the margin from the goals of the group. But in times of rapid technological and political transformation, as Jensen argues, the agency gap becomes a gulf. The structure of the corporation, the training of its engineers, the skills of its executives, the costs of its processes all become misaligned with the realities of a new technological base, a rapidly changing state of the art, and a political environment in upheaval.

General Motors was the worst example, investing $121.8 billion during the 1980s in R&D and capital equipment while the value of the company dropped to $22.9 billion. IBM invested $101 billion while its value was dropping to $64.6 billion by the end of 1990 (on the way to further collapse to $41 billion in early 1995). Collectively, the 500 largest U.S. corporations wasted hundreds of billions of dollars of free cash flow. What was needed, according to Jensen, was a total overhaul of most of these companies, their strategic redirection, and the replacement or redeployment of roughly half of the existing managers. What occurred was a prodigal waste of resources in defense of the obsolete structures and practices of the incumbent management.

Creating most of the new value during the 1980s were companies funded or restructured by corporate raiders, venture capitalists and even—in the case of a $75 billion gain from the AT&T breakup—the courts (disbanding a monopoly previously created by government). Using equity, venture capitalists overcome the agency gulf by playing an active controlling role on company boards and managements and by insisting that executives are compensated chiefly through stock and options. Using venture debt and an array of complex securities, Michael Milken overcame the agency gulf by similarly active intervention.

Millken channeled billions of dollars into companies such as McCaw or MCI largely owned by the management, to compete with industry leviathans. For companies not owned by their executives, he funded leveraged buyouts that transformed nonowner managers feeding on free cash flow into heavy owners of equity with virtually no liquid resources. Contracted to divert all their free cash flow to the holders of high-yield debt, the new owner-managers were forced to please the capital markets in order to fund any new projects.

THE PRODUCTIVITY BOOM

With the agency problem solved, these companies became lean and mean leaders of the global economy. Contrary to the claims of many economists, from Alan Blinder to Lester Thurow, productivity soared. Mired in the murky data on service-sector productivity—which was stultified by the practice of measuring most outputs by the cost of the inputs—economists tended to miss the prodigious real growth of the 1980s. For example, in the brokerage and finance arenas, productivity stagnated in the data, but between 1973 and 1987 the number of shares traded daily grew from 5.7 million to 63.8 million, while employment only doubled in the industry.

Manufacturing productivity numbers, though more accurate, also suffer from severe miscalculations. In a world of creative destruction, they tend to assume that products, such as computers, that decline in price are dropping in value. And while registering every new steel ingot, automobile or chocolate bar, they assume that novel products represent no productivity gain at all. These are not trivial mistakes. During the past 20 years, the cost of computers has dropped approximately one millionfold. Yet the Bureau of Labor Statistics shows merely an annual drop varying between 14.9% in 1992 and 6.7% in 1994. The government has finally recognized the flaws in this statistical series, and is moving ever so slowly to correct it. But the problem is fundamental.

Using the criteria applied to productivity in the auto industry, the statisticians would have to multiply the improvement in computing cost-effectiveness by the increase in the number of computers sold. Thus, with the explosion of sales of billions of microcomputers of all kinds, from desktop systems to embedded devices, a consistent BLS would find that the contribution of computers to gross domestic product was close to a billion times larger than the entire GDP of 1970. Of course, such an exercise would be preposterous. But hardly more preposterous than mostly ignoring the productivity gains in these industries of rapid advance, plummeting prices and cornucopian innovation.

Even using existing data, total factor productivity in the U.S. manufacturing sector more than doubled during the 1980s from the level during the previous 30 years. From 1950 to 1980, this productivity index rose an average of 1.4% per year; between 1981 and 1990, it rose at a rate of 3.3%. Labor productivity rose from 1.4% per year in the earlier period to 3.8% in the 80s. Contrary to the usual claims, wages rose at least 10%, according to Social Security system data, while the number of jobs rose by 18 million.

But the most striking productivity surge came in the growth of the productivity of capital. In essence, Milken, Kohlberg Kravis Roberts, Forstmann Little and others took the vast incarcerated capital resources trapped in old-line businesses and put it back into the markets. Not only was the productivity of the capital left behind hugely enhanced by the disciplines of restructuring, but the freed capital flowed into venture funds and high-yield markets where it fueled what Jensen calls "a Third Industrial Revolution."

The results were dramatic. In decline for 30 years, at an annual rate of minus 1.03%, the capital productivity index has long been beloved by Marxists as a portent of the collapse of capitalism. During the 1980s, however, this decline was decisively reversed. The productivity of capital as measured in the data rose by 2.03% annually as computerized information systems transformed the technology of finance.

Decisively reversed as well was a long decline of U.S. market share in the global economy. By the period between 1987 and 1992, U.S. corporations were generating 47.7% of all the profits in the industrial world on 37.5% of the revenues. Spearheading the U.S. economy were information firms, with some 70% of global profits.

Thus was overthrown by the restructuring of the 1980s all the indifference theorems, Efficient Market Hypotheses, corporate optimality concepts, macroeconomic monothe ories wielded in business schools and economics departments to explain away the power and "wash" away the paramount worth of individual entrepreneurs and investors. Indeed, the giant corporation, with managers largely free of ownership claims, gained its preeminence as a way of diffusing risk among millions of stockholders with diverse portfolios. But with the securitization of venture debt by Michael Milken and others, these behemoths emerge as marketplace survivors largely because of their prowess at politics, litigation and media management—core competencies that in the course of a decade succeeded both in derailing the Milken threat and enacting laws and regulations to forestall any followers.

Perhaps because of a bias in favor of the capitalists, Jensen's course vies with Michael Porter's similarly entrepreneurial class as the most popular in the last 15 years with students at Harvard Business School—a fact which bodes well for the future of the economy.

Jensen and Milken agree that today's economy faces technological transformations, agency misalignments and restructuring chances even greater than the economy of the late 1970s and early 1980s. "The opportunity is truly huge," says Jensen. *ASAP* estimates that in this 40% larger economy, there should be a chance for Milkenesque investors to raise stock market value by more than 67%, implying both a revitalized U.S. economy, a Dow level over 6500, a Standard & Poor's Index exceeding 700, and a Nasdaq over 1400.

The question remains, however, how to realize these gains. Because of the incredible continuing grip of obsolete regulations and the huge mismatch between microcosm and telecosm, the fabulous new fiber and wireless technologies have yet to force a corresponding industrial restructuring. The same old players are still on the field protected by the same government rules, administered still by Judge Harold Greene in the Modified Final Judgment breaking up AT&T 11 years ago, and regulated still by the FCC, the Federal Trade Commission, the Justice Department and 50 state Public Utilities Commissions as if history had stood still. Forty million computers with multimedia powers remain stranded in homes with four-kilohertz copper connections to the world while communications companies still ponder the perplexities of interactive TV and regulators ruminate about how to prevent monopoly and preserve universal service.

CABLE TV'S IMPENDING DEATH

Capsizing this entire teetering apparatus of petty fears and pettifoggery will be this year's ascent of new wireless technologies. The basic problem of universal service is that with current wireline telephony and cable TV, it costs 10 to 30 times as much to serve rural customers as urban customers. By nature, the U.S. Senate is dominated by rural customers. Many are Republicans. Therefore, universal service has posed a paralyzing problem for programs of deregulation. But new wireless digital technologies have utterly banished this problem.

At a time when all voice telephony is rapidly moving to wireless, new digital cellular systems will soon lower the price of wireless telephony tenfold and totally close the gap in costs between rural and urban customers. At the same time, with supreme universality across the entire continent, Direct Broadcast Satellite already delivers service superior to cable. Already in the sky, DBS is a big bang that will ultimately transform the entire corporate landscape of U.S. communications with a cascade of imperious new realities.

In digital DBS, GM Hughes, Hubbard Broadcasting and Thomson's RCA have delivered a knockout new conduit for delivering one-way video. In image resolution, in audio quality, in number of channels and in raw reach and efficiency of point-to-multi-point transmission, DirecTV not only decisively outpaces even the studio offerings at cable company headends but also vastly and instantly excelled them in coverage.

Currently the only weakness of DBS is a lack of certain critical content such as local and broadcast network programming. The lack will be addressed, with the help of Michael Milken, by major new restructuring this year.

Absolutely devastating to broadcast cable TV, a still more powerful DBS will send reverberations throughout the broadcast industry and profoundly affect computers, government regulators and telephone companies as well. As Milken explains, "Everything in the information economy is connected to everything else."

As government regulators will be the last to notice, DBS utterly overthrows the prime premise of cable regulation: the view that cable commands some kind of monopoly in delivering one-way video programming. Far from a monopoly, one-way cable TV is essentially dead. In response to DBS, cable has no choice but to change its business radically to two-way computer services.

The market opportunity is obvious and immense. The Internet boasted five million host computers and over 30 million estimated users in January, and growth of 26% in the last quarter of 1994. The largest spurt of expansion in recent history, this surge came despite acute frustration at the narrow bandwidth of available phone connections.

At present, only the cable TV industry commands conduits to homes capable of accommodating these multimedia teleputers. One-gigahertz cable TV coax can accommodate some eight billion bits per second of two-way data or some 5,000 channels of the kind of MPEG1 video now offered in one direction by DBS. Such bandwidth could accommodate ubiquitous videoconferencing and commerce. By contrast, your phone line modem labors to transmit 14.4 thousand bits per second, or enough to send one MPEG movie in two weeks.

Reaching 63% of U.S. households, including at least 92% of homes with PCs, cable supplies the obvious conduit for the exploding computer business. Intel, General Instrument, Digital Equipment, Hybrid and Com21, among other companies, are supplying cable modems and software for high-speed bidirectional traffic over the existing cable plant. But consummation of the network will entail large investments in fiber and switching at a time when cable is just emerging from its regulatory shadows into the deadly Ku-band radiance of DBS.

The most obvious source of capital is the RBOCs, the local telephone companies (though Milken stresses that the public utilities are a major alternative). The Bells already command nine times as much fiber as cable TV does and invest every year more money than the total $23 billion of cable revenues. What they lack is bandwidth for broadband access to homes.

The key to access to these huge new computer markets, therefore, is forthcoming congressional action to permit collaboration between the RBOCs and the cable companies within their own regions. If necessary, the telephone companies must be allowed to buy cable companies and merge their systems. The coming ascent of DBS should relieve the fears of monopoly that have long deterred action. If it does, the cascade of change spurred by DBS will lead to a flood of new commerce and communication on the networks of America.

The endowment of DBS with new programming clout, however, will prove to be the last triumph of conduit-content convergence. The restructuring paladins of the broadband era will devote much of their efforts to dismantling the content-conduit conglomerates that currently dominate the cable industry and that are now in formation by the telephone companies.

In a broadband era, content-conduit combines no longer make sense. Consider that you are Warner Entertainment, a content company. You do not want to restrict your movies to one conduit. You want to sell them through everyone's conduit. Consider that you are Warner Communications, a cable firm. With eight gigabits per second—enough for 5,000 movie channels—you want to sell everyone's movies, not restrict yourself to Warner's.

Efforts to mix content and conduit—artists and engineers—produce misaligned companies that need restructuring. Content follies crowd into the agency gulf. Nynex, Bell Atlantic and Pacific Telesis gave superagent Michael Ovitz $14 million to pursue more "content" while Ameritech, BellSouth and Southwestern Bell (SBC) romanced Disney.

What would a new restructuring king do in the face of such ham-handed diversification? Bring on the raiders. Sic some junkyard Doberman on the succulent bells and whistles acquired by cable and telephone firms. Let him spin off their recent acquisitions and interactive TV experiments and game channels and refocus these companies on the computer networking business where they belong, and where they can harvest the bonanza of a global economy rapidly uploading onto the Net.

THE TWO-WIRE DELUSION

Washington has to make a choice. Is it going to allow a freedom model that permits telephone companies and cable companies to combine as common carriers to build a true broadband infrastructure, in which millions of entrepreneurs can cavort and compete in content and context? Or will regulators impose a spurious competitive model, with two or more wires to every home, all imitating the current cable strategy of wannabe content-conduit monopolies.

As venture capitalist Roger McNamee warned in the Feb. 27 issue of *ASAP*: "There is an unspoken assumption in government circles that we can move local loop communications to a fiercely competitive business model and build an information superhighway at the same time . . . an implicit assumption that the regional Bell operating companies and the cable companies are a bunch of knuckle-dragging dimwits who will build the superhighway no matter what . . . [But] telecom businesses are characterized by high fixed costs. There is no such thing as limited competition . . . As you infuse competition . . . the value model of the industry collapses. And when it does, the effect will be exactly the same as stepping on a large cow pie in your hiking boots."

Congressman Jack Fields, new Republican chairman of the House Telecom Subcommittee, disagrees: "I am convinced that the [industry] people we talked with will respond to telecom reform. They have tens of billions of dollars parked on the side of the information superhighway waiting for us to pass a piece of legislation to give definition and certainty to the scene." But the people he consulted—chiefly the leaders and the lobbyists of the RBOCs and cable companies—are not the ones who will decide whether the highway is built.

Making that decision will be the same capital markets that punished Bell Atlantic and TCI for their broadband plans and thwarted the merger between them. As soon as it became clear—through the passage of the cable re-regulation act of 1992 and related policies of the FCC—that the regulators would permit collaboration only in regions where the two companies had no competitive advantage, the case for the combine collapsed. Under a regulatory system in which the government can sweep down and confiscate profits and channel them into quixotic schemes of universal service in three dimensions for the homeless or require irrational competitive behavior in a two-wire multisubsidiary world, a true broadband two-way network makes no business sense. What will emerge instead is an array of dueling brands of 500-channel TV, claiming to be interactive for the benefit of Congress and the press.

Capital markets will avoid cow-pie competition at all costs. Under these circumstances, a true broadband system will not be completed until 2020 in the U.S. But the competitive model is fundamentally misconceived.

To the Washington regulators and their elected allies, competition has always meant rivalry between the existing competitors—long distance, broadcast, Baby Bells and Cable TV—and the regulation succeeds as long as all the teams stay on the field. But all technological competition—all innovation—consists of the pursuit of fugitive positions of monopoly. Current legislative proposals from the administration and its congressional allies resemble a broad national effort in 1981 to defend the mainframe BUNCH (Burroughs, Univac, NCR, Control Data, and Honeywell) from imperial IBM. Just as the IBM "monopoly" was about to fall before the microcosm, led by Intel and Microsoft, so the RBOC and broadcasting "monopolies" are about to fall before the telecosm of broadband digital computer networks, which will also sorely challenge Intel and Microsoft.

The new information infrastructure will bring a cornucopia of new services from a variety of new sources that cannot even be defined as yet. All we know is that none of the existing rivals is likely to survive in recognizable form. Only a true freedom model that allows a complete reconstruction of the world of communications—with anyone collaborating or competing, merging or metamorphing with anyone rise—can allow this new era to come to fruition. Only a freedom model can release the $2 trillion of new asset value that the scholars of restructuring promise for the U.S. economy of the 1990s and beyond.

This result the Republicans on Capitol Hill command the unique and precious and passing opportunity to achieve. So open the floodgates of capital for new corporate raiders and remakers, venturers and reinventors. Rejoice in the return of Milken and pray that he be joined by scores of rivals, including those allowed to use the securities markets. Virtually all the cable and telephone companies, from MCI to TCI to SBC, should be up for grabs, by each other and from outside firms. Sitting on $10 billion of cash, IBM could fruitfully enter the fray, or be frayed itself. IBM could combine its global ATM network with cable access to homes. For many of these companies, capital is far less scarce than vision.

Milken cites MCI. "Twelve years ago, they had a cash shortage with billions of dollars of capital expenditures to make. They had a clear understanding of what their business was. We supplied them with billions of dollars of capital and that fueled the spread of fiberoptics throughout the country during the 1980s. Today their situation is far less clear. They have $3 billion in cash, they could borrow $6 billion more; they've got a strategic worldwide partnership with British Telecom. Today the challenge is not capital. It is vision. It is, what should MCI's future be?"

With MCI's current resources, it could buy cable facilities across the country, join them with its fiber network, complement them with wireless personal communications services and Internet connections, and outwit AT&T as brilliantly as it did in the 1980s. But it has to be willing to bet the company again. The question is whether the current management, with Bill McGowan in his grave, can escape the agency trap, shun the cushions of large corporate life, and become a real competitor again rather than a protected player in a continued government sham of "competition."

When a visitor at one of the Capitol Hill offices in charge of telecom policy points to the benefits of real competition and restructuring, the politician will usually respond: "The companies do not tell us that." The dirty little secret of all too many telephone and cable companies is that they prefer government-regulated "competition" to real entrepreneurial risks and rewards. As long as telco and cable lobbyists fail to urge true competition, these companies deserve much of the blame for the Third World regulations that still limit the horizons of their industry.

Amazingly, however, the situation is changing from an unexpected source. While much of industry still lags, the politicians seem ready at last to seize the day with a new freedom model. Now the congealed glaciers of telecom can begin to break up under the blows of a reinvigorated market for corporate control.

Perhaps, the best solution will be again to deregulate Milken.

POSTSCRIPT: THE RETURN OF MIKE MILKEN

One morning, in his office on a quiet street in Los Angeles near Bel Air, Milken is probing some of the outward edges of the new regime, delving into a business plan for ridefilms. Ridefilms are a brand new industry of convergence that blends features of theatrical films, theme-park rides and arcade games. Giving the viewer the sensation of plummeting motion and soaring flight on platforms that move in sync with motion on the screen, these systems are virtual reality that really works.

Presenting the project of the day is Whitmore Kelley of Berkshire Motion Pictures, the firm that created the pioneering "Back to the Future: The Ride" for Universal Theme Parks. He is proposing Ridetime, a low-cost system of theater capsules for children between the ages of four and 10.

These turnkey theaters could bring ridefilms to malls, shopping centers, toy stores, theme parks, resorts, restaurants and family entertainment centers at a toll of $1.50 per child, eight children at a time. Offering four-minute musical adventures with engaging plots and educational themes, these systems would be the first to shun the "testosterone market" of the arcades and focus on young children.

Milken had heard enough. He confessed he had only been able to read five sections of the business plan during the two or three minutes that had elapsed. But with a quizzical

Columbo look, he said he had some questions. He had recently seen similar systems in Norway and Sweden. Small groups of parents and kids together paid the equivalent of $4 apiece to plummet down an Olympic Alpine downhill or bobsledding course. No, they weren't real ridefilms, with synchronized physical movement, but they were cheap to produce and offered a similar experience and there would be a lot more where those came from. How would Berkshire compete with these? Let's say he owned space in an arcade. Teenagers pump in money all day long and deep into the night. Why would he give space to a children's ride that takes up twice as much room and closes down at bedtime? Interactivity? Watch out for that. Kids today get real interactivity on their computers and Nintendo machines at home. Any effort to provide interactive features for eight kids at once might well turn them off. Where would the parents be? They would see the show for nothing, standing behind the kids, without the motion that makes it interesting. That's a downer. A four-year-old will demand that the parents sit with him. The parents are your customers. Make them pay and let them ride.

Commenting that Kelley had described other ridefilm companies as the competition, Milken demurred. The computer software industry would be the competition. He grilled Kelley on the size of the capsule, its cost per square foot, its yield to the owner of the space in a mall, the quality of the images, the nature of the liquid crystal projection technology.

As Kelley described it, "Milken is so mentally aggressive and determined I was astonished. I came in and he began playing the flute and several other instruments at once, and I had to figure out what the dance was and start moving and shaking in time. Teaching, learning and testing at the same time . . . he was amazing." At the end of the presentation, Milken announced that he was impressed and would go visit a prototype of the new system nearby in the L.A. suburbs.

Or watch him on President's Day in a paneled room in Atlanta's Occidental Grand Hotel. He is contemplating a new learning network as a climax to some 25 years and $250 million of Milken family ventures in the field of education. Milken has assembled leading experts on education, film and finance to consult with the CEO of the new project, Hamilton Jordan, recently of Whittle Communications.

Milken began with the crucial rule that the educational network "go first to the home, later to the schools," rather than the other way around (which was Whittle's mistake). "The teachers themselves will bring any good material into the schools," he said. He ended by suggesting that the group had radically underestimated the size of their potential market. He pointed to his earlier investment in Interface Group, the sponsor of Comdex, recently sold to Japanese entrepreneur Masayoshi Son of Softbank Corporation for $800 million. Virtual conferences and teleconferences for training and education and lifelong learning could become a leading vehicle of convergence, joining software, computers, consumer electronics, telephones and even public utilities.

As he summed up, he declared that the size of the educational market, appropriately defined today to include corporate training, was not $400 billion as Jordan had said, but more than $1 trillion. Visionary and trenchant as ever, lifting the horizons of all around him, Milken was clearly back.

13

From Wires to Waves

As wireless telephony goes digital,
it gets very cheap very fast.

U.S. Sen. Ted Stevens of Alaska wants to know.

With deregulation of telecommunications, who will bring connections to Unalakleet, to Aleknagik and to Sleetmute? Who will bring 500 channels up the Yukon with the salmon to the people in Beaver? What will happen to the Yupik, the Inupiat and the Inuit? Will we leave them stranded in the snow while the world zooms off to new riches on an information superhighway?

A senior Republican on the Senate Commerce Subcommittee on Communications, Stevens is a key figure in the telecom deregulation debate on Capitol Hill. As he contemplates the issues of restructuring communications law, he has reason to be suspicious of the grand claims of an information age. He knows that universal service—the magic of available dial tone in your own home—has hardly reached rural Alaska at all. As George Calhoun points out in his definitive book, *Wireless Access*, twisted-pair copper wire connections (of the sort invented by Alexander Graham Bell in 1881 and now extended to some 95% of American households) are simply not feasible, either technically or economically, in many remote regions.

In Beaver, for example, there is one telephone in a hut linked to a nine-foot satellite dish. Permafrost and cold economic reality make it impossible to extend dial tone to the several hundred households of this town, even though its average household income, mostly from salmon fishing, is some $120,000.

Ted Stevens is right to be concerned. Portentiously sharing his concern are other powerful Republicans from rural states, including Larry Pressler of South Dakota, the chairman of the subcommittee. Extended now from phone service to broadband digital superhighways, their concerns could pose a deadly obstacle to true deregulation of

171

communications and thus to continued American leadership in these central technologies of the age. At stake is some $2 trillion of potential value to the U.S. economy (see *Forbes ASAP*, April 10). The problems of universal service in Alaska disguise the more profound paradox of telephone service in most of the world.

The fact is that the universality of telephones is crucial to their usefulness; yet universal service using current technology is totally uneconomical and impractical. Snow and ice are the least of it. The basic problem is the architecture of the system, with a separate pair of lines, on average two miles long, devoted exclusively to each user. It simply does not pay to lay, entrench, string, protect, test and maintain miles of copper wire pairs, each dedicated to one household that uses them on average some 15 or 20 minutes a day.

Connections in cities are one thing. Urban access systems comprise a bramble of millions of wire loops, each linking a home or business telephone to a nearby central office switch. Under a half mile in length, these lines still represent some 80% of the cost of the system. But because the lines are short and often bundled together, city telephony benefits from economies of scale and convenience. In rural areas, however, the copper lines cost between 10 and 30 times as much per customer as they do in cities.

Moreover, Calhoun reports that in general, phone companies cannot supply ISDN (integrated services digital network) and other digital services over twisted-pair wire more than 18,000 feet (some 3.5 miles) from the central office. Perhaps a third of all the nation's phones are more than 3.5 miles from a central office.

What saves us is socialism. Closing the huge differential between the costs of serving rural and urban customers is a Byzantine web of cross-subsidies, whereby inner-city and business callers in urban areas subsidize the worthy citizens of Kirby, Vt.; Vail, Colo.; Mendocino, Calif.; Round Rock, Texas, and Tyringham, Mass., among other bucolic locales, to the tune of billions of dollars. Overall, subsidies from business and urban customers to rural and other expensive residential users total some $20 billion a year. In case the cross-subsidies do not suffice to guarantee universality, Congress has established a $700 million "Universal Service Fund." For all that, some 5% of homes still lack telephone service (compared with 2% unreached by TV, which faces no universal service requirement).

Lending huge physical authority to this Sisyphean socialist scheme are some 65,049,600 tons of copper wire rooted deep in the rights of way, depreciation schedules, balance sheets, mental processes and corporate cultures of the regional Bell operating companies and other so-called local-exchange carriers. The minimum replacement cost of these lines deployed over the last 50 years or more—and still being installed through the mid-1990s at a rate of at least five million lines a year—is some $300 billion. By comparison, Calhoun estimates, the telcos could replace every telephone switch for one-tenth that amount while radically upgrading the system.

In this cage of twisted copper wires writhe not only the executives of the telephone companies, but also the addled armies of telecommunications regulators, from the Federal Communications Commission and other Washington bodies to 50 state public utilities commissions and the towering hives of lawyers in the communications bar. The coils of copper also subtly penetrate the thought processes of MIT Media Lab gurus, libertarian lobbyists from the Electronic Frontier Foundation and myriad political analysts who see this massive metal millstone as a fell weapon of monopoly power. The copper colossus even intimidates scores of staunch Republicans who have arrived in Washington determined to extirpate every government excess, but who bow before the totem of universal service in their districts.

Like any socialist system, the copper colossus will die hard. But die it must.

Some 20 years ago, AT&T's long-distance lines comprised a similarly imperious cage of copper wires, installed over the previous 50 years and similarly impossible for rivals to duplicate. Then too, analysts termed telephony a natural monopoly because the system could handle additional calls for essentially zero incremental cost and because network externalities ensured that the larger the number of customers, the more valuable the system. These assumptions had led to government endorsement of the Bell monopoly as a common carrier committed to universal service.

Regulators, politicians and litigators always imagine that they can control the future of telecom, awarding monopoly privileges in exchange for various high-minded goals, such as universal or enriched services. But their actual role, as Peter Huber and his associates show in their new text, *Federal Broadband Law,* is mostly to promote monopoly at the expense of such values as universality, which ultimately depend not on law but on innovation. As a form of tax, regulations reduce the supply of the taxed output. It is technological and entrepreneurial progress, impelled by low tax rates and deregulation, that brings once-rare products into the reach of the poor, always the world's largest untapped market.

In this case, the decline and fall of the long-distance monopoly was not chiefly an effect of politics or litigation but of technology. Effectively dissolving the copper cage of long distance were the millimeter waves of microwave radio. Over the years, it turned out you could set up microwave towers anywhere and duplicate long-distance services at radically lower cost without installing any new wires at all. But this realization came woefully slowly to the regulators.

In the "above-890-megahertz" decision of 1959, made possible by new Klystron tubes and other devices that opened up higher frequencies to communications, the FCC permitted creation of private microwave networks. On the surface, it was a narrow decision affecting a few large corporations. But as AT&T planners noted at the time, it represented a clear break from the previous principles of common carriage, cross-subsidy and nationwide price averaging in the telephone network.

Sure enough, over the next two decades a cascade of further decisions climaxed with the authorization of MCI to emerge as a direct competitor to AT&T. Within less than a decade, MCI added to its panoply of aerial microwaves the yet more advanced technology of single-mode glass fibers. Issuing some $3 billion of junk bonds over a four-year period, MCI built the first nationwide network of advanced fiber optics. GTE made comparable investments in Sprint, and AT&T rushed to excel its new rivals. Combining microwave with fiber, long-distance telephony became a technologically aggressive and openly competitive arena; AT&T's monopoly was a thing of the past.

Today, the remaining monopolies in local phone service face a threat from radio technology still more devastating than the microwave threat to AT&T in long distance. As with microwaves, the government—in the name of preventing monopoly—dallied for decades before acting to allow elimination of the monopolies it had earlier established. After the invention of cellular at Bell Labs in 1947, some 34 years passed before the FCC finally began granting licenses for cellular telephony. By the 1980s, the FCC and Judge Harold Greene, managing the Modified Final Judgment breaking up AT&T, permitted limited competition in wireless telephony. However, the FCC allocated half the metropolitan licenses to existing RBOCs, which had no interest in using wireless to attack the local loop monopoly. The other licenses it assigned by lottery to gamblers and financiers with no ability to create an alternative local loop. The process of buying out the spectrum speculators required leading wireless carriers to hobble themselves with huge amounts of junk-bond debt. Although McCaw Cellular Communications created a robust national system, its financial structure prevented aggressive price competition with wireline service.

As a result, the idea persists that wireless telephony is an expensive supplement to the existing copper colossus rather than a deadly rival of it. The installed base of twisted-pair wire still appears to many to be a barrier to entry for new competitors in the local loop, rather than a barrier to RBOC entry into modern communications markets. The conventional wisdom sees the electromagnetic spectrum as a scarce resource. Few believe that it will soon emerge as a cheaper and better alternative to the local loop, in the same way that microwave emerged as a cheaper and better substitute for copper long-distance wires.

MAKING WAVES

At the foundation of the information economy, from computers to telephony, is the microcosm of semiconductor electronics. It reaches out in a fractal filigree of wires and switches that repeat their network patterns at every level from the half-adder in a calculator chip or the SLIC in a telephone handset to the coaxial trees and branches of a cable TV system or the mazes of switched and routed lines in the global Internet. In computers, engineers lay out the wires and switches across the tiny silicon substrates of microchips. In telecommunications, engineers lay out the wires and switches across the mostly silicon substrates of continents and seabeds. But it is essentially the same technology, governed by quantum science and electrical circuit theory.

Semiconductor engineers may still spend more of their time with circuit theory, contemplating the operations of resistors, inductors and capacitors on currents and voltages in the device. But quantum theory is most fundamental, because it allows humans for the first time to manipulate matter from the inside—to control the conduction bands and energy-band gaps of the internal atomic structure of silicon and other elements, and to make electrons, holes and photons leap and lase at the behest of the designer. It is quantum theory that allows chip engineers to control with exquisite precision, gauged in tenths of microns and trillionths of seconds, the movements of electrons at the heart of electronics.

At the heart of quantum theory, however, is a perplexing duality. Most of contemporary physics seems to deal with particles—electrons, quarks, leptons, neutrons, protons. In 1994, for example, scientists at Fermilabs in Chicago announced "discovery" of the "top quark," which they described as the "last building block of matter." Yet these entities manifest themselves only in the midst of explosions in which their wave signatures can be identified. So-called quantum particle theory is unintelligible without quantum wave theory.

The elements of quantum physics intrinsically combine the characteristics of particles—definite specks of mass—with the characteristics of waves—an infinite radiance of fields and forces. Entirely unlike particles, waves merge, mingle and mesh in vectors and tensors propagating boundlessly through space.

It is this paradoxical combination of the definite with the infinite that gives the microcosm its promise as a medium, not only for computation in one place, but for communications everywhere. Spectrum unfolds in a global ethersphere of interpenetrating waves that reach in a self-similar fractal pattern from the plasmas of semiconductor lasers through the ethers of the planet.

Today, the telecosm of modern communications brings decisively to the fore the wave side of the quantum duality. Wires may seem more solid and reliable than air. But the distinction is largely spurious. In proportion to the size of its nucleus, an atom in a copper wire is as empty as the solar system is in proportion to the size of the sun. The atmosphere and wires are alternative media, and to the electron or photon are only arbitrarily distinguishable. Whether insulated by air or by plastic, both offer resistance, capacitance, inductance, noise and interference. In thinking about communications, the concept of solidity is mostly a distraction. The essence of new devices emerges more and more as manifestations of waves.

Whether in the air or in a wire, the electrons or photons do not travel; they wiggle their charges, causing oscillations that pass through the medium at close to the speed of light. As in waves of water, the wave moves, but the molecules of water stay in the same place. Thus belied is the analogy of particles or even bullets favored by physics teachers who give primacy to the mass rather than to the wave. Since the age of carrier pigeons and catapults, communications systems have transmitted masses only in the postal services.

Today, even in entirely stationary electronic systems, the wave action is increasingly dominant. The microchip itself—a Pentium processor, say—now runs at 120 megahertz, a rate in cycles per second that puts it in the middle of the FM radio band. New computers must pass the FCC requirements for radio emissions. Texas Instruments now advertises its 486 SXL-66 microprocessors as selling for under 50 cents per megahertz. Increasingly in the world of computers, people speak of bandwidth and cycles, reserving the discussion of mass chiefly for the batteries. The world of the telecosm is subtly shifting from electronics, with its implicit primacy of electrons, to what might be termed spectronics, seeing the particle as an expression of the wave rather than the other way around—moving from Bohr's atom and Heisenberg's electronic uncertainty to Maxwell's rainbow and Schrodinger's wave equation.

In a global marketplace increasingly unified by telecommunications at the speed of light, the vision of waves as fundamental affords not only a better image of physics, but also a better purchase on economic reality than a spurious search for solid states, physical resources, national economies and commodity products.

Conceived as some irreducible essence, the particle of mass, whether in the form of a top quark or Higgs boson, wire conduit or central switch, pushes our thinking about the world toward a vision of ultimately discrete and confinable entities, with electrons moving through the p-n junctions of microchips like so many steel ingots crossing a national border. Conceived, by contrast, as a continuous span of waves and frequencies, tossing and cresting, reflecting, diffusing, superposing and interfering, the telecosmic vision accords with the ever-rising global commerce in information services—ubiquitous, simultaneous, convergent, emergent.

To grasp the next phases of the information economy, one begins not with the atom or any other discrete entity, but with the wave. In 1865, in a visionary coup that the late Richard Feynman said would leave the American Civil War of the same decade as a mere "parochial footnote" by comparison, Scotch physicist James Clerk Maxwell discovered the electromagnetic spectrum. This spread of frequencies usable for communications is both the practical resource and the most profound metaphor for the global information economy.

Is it a domain of limits, to be husbanded by governments and appropriately allocated by auctions at a price of billions of dollars for a tiny span of wiggle rates? Is it beachfront property to be coveted as a finite and unrenewable resource? Is it a constricted domain to be exploited under the iron laws of diminishing returns? Is it a zero-sum game to erupt in Star Wars and street fights as satellite magnates and personal communications entrepreneurs crowd into a feudal fray of frequencies? At the heart of the gathering abundance of the information economy, would it sustain a new economics of scarcity?

So one might imagine from today's conventional wisdom. Contemplating these limits, diminishing returns and zero-sum economics at Richard Shaffer's Mobile Forum in March was industry guru Carl Robert Aron. He sees the world of wireless entering a "new ice age," like the recent ordeal of the tire industry in the face of radials. He predicts that customers, capital and revenues will become increasingly scarce and many species of company will become extinct. Offering a similarly grim vision, BellSouth Vice President of Corporate Development Mark Feidler declares that the price elasticity of demand for telephony is negative—you lower the price and revenues will sink. On the same panel, AT&T-McCaw executive Rod Nelson asserted that he could see no threat from personal communications services, because McCaw was already offering "a low-priced, high-quality service." Even Martin Cooper of ArrayComm saw spectrum as a limited resource sure to grow more valuable over time.

What would Maxwell say? As he discovered it, the spectrum is infinite, ubiquitous, instantaneous and cornucopian. Infinite wave action, not the movement of masses, is the foundation of all physics. It ushers in an age of boundless bandwidth beyond the dreams of most communications prophets. As industry guru Ira Brodsky concludes in his authoritative new book, *Wireless: The Revolution in Personal Communications*, "We are quickly moving from the era of spectrum shortage to the age of spectrum glut." This expanding wavescape is the most fertile frontier of the information economy. In its actions are the essential character of the coming economics of abundance and increasing returns.

In contemporary networks, as Nicholas Negroponte stresses in his best-selling book, *Being Digital*, all bits are fungible. In spectronics, all spectrum is fungible. In particular, the distinction between wireline and wireless service dissolves. A wire is just a means of spectrum reuse. Down adjacent wires, appropriately twisted or insulated, you can transmit the same frequencies without fear of interference or noise.

Using new digital radio technologies, such as code division multiple access or smart and directional antenna systems, you can similarly beam the same frequencies through the atmosphere, insulated by air. The chief difference is that the wire system costs far more to install and inhibits mobility.

The only wire technology commanding a decisive edge over wireless for critical applications is fiber optics. The intrinsic bandwidth of a fiber thread is nearly 1,000 times larger than the bandwidth of all the "air" currently used for terrestrial radio communications. In both media, capacity is largely governed by the need to avoid the water molecules that absorb many frequencies of electromagnetic waves—in air, from humidity or precipitation; in fiber, from the unremovable residue of water in the structure of the glass.

Compared with perhaps 30 gigahertz of currently accessible frequencies in the air, every fiber thread can potentially bear 25,000 gigahertz. This huge bandwidth derives from the possibility of using infrared light frequencies for long-distance communications rather than radio or microwave frequencies. When you are dealing in terahertz (infrared light encompasses some 50 trillion hertz worth of frequencies between 7.5×10^{11} and 3.5×10^{14}), there is a lot of room for sending messages.

One fiber thread the width of a human hair can potentially use about 25 trillion of those hertz for communications (the rest tend to be fraught with moisture). This span is enough to carry all the phone calls in America on the peak moment of Mother's Day, or to bear three million six-megahertz high-definition television channels—all down one fiber thread the width of a human hair. As Paul Green sums it up, fiber commands 10 orders of magnitude greater bandwidth than copper telephone lines and 10 orders of magnitude lower bit-error rates. Optical engineers have packed as many as a million such threads in one bundle with a cross-section a centimeter square. Such feats plausibly support the assertion that, as a practical matter, spectrum is infinite.

The capacity of fiber is so large that the best way to think of it is as a radio system in glass—a fibersphere that can potentially accommodate as many as 10,000 separate wavelength bitstreams. Under a system called wavelength division multiplexing, users will tune in to a chosen frequency band in the same way they currently time in to a chosen radio or television channel, whether in the air or in a coaxial cable. Indeed, engineers can take the same infrared frequencies used in fiber and move them to the air for shorter distance applications such as local-area networks, point-to-point connections between buildings, links between handheld computers and desktop hosts, and even television remote controls. As tunable laser transmitters and photodiodes, along with other optoelectronic gear, become more sensitive and efficient, airborne infrared will become more robust and useful. Experiments by the Israelis with ultraviolet frequencies suggest that even these superhigh frequencies above visible light might someday be used for communications through the atmosphere (offering tens of thousands of TV channels, for example).

Now the FCC has auctioned off 120 megahertz of frequencies for personal communications services. The most prominent winning bidders were consortia led by Sprint, TCI, Comcast and Cox (a long-distance carrier and three cable companies going under the name Wireless Co.); by AT&T; and by AirTouch, Bell Atlantic, NYNEX and U S West as PCS PrimeCo. Most analysis has focused on what is called the wireless market and has assumed the major competitor to PCS to be the current cellular companies. Aron's ice-age ruminations stemmed from contemplation of this radical increase in competition for a limited number of cellular customers who currently cost some $540 each to sign up (counting handset subsidies) and whose per-capita revenues are declining at a pace of some 8% per year. Remember BellSouth's Feidler's vision of a negative elasticity of phone markets, meaning that lower prices bring lower revenues?

From a spectronic perspective, all this analysis is deeply misleading. Whether channeled down wires or through the air, spectrum is spectrum. Digital wireless is a cheaper and better way of delivering service. The market for PCS is not the cellular customer, but the one billion wireline customers in rich countries and the several billions of potential phone and teleputer customers around the globe. In pursuing these customers, the price elasticities will be dramatically positive, with various price points reachable with new wireless technologies releasing torrents of new demand and new revenues. What Aron calls an ice age will in fact prove to be a gigantic global warming, unleashing huge new growth in telephony, using spectrum in all its various forms (except perhaps the twisted-pair copper wires that currently dominate the installed base of the industry).

The winning bidders from AT&T and Sprint did not put up their $3.7 billion in order to join a zero-sum straggle for new cellular customers. These bidders are dominated by long-distance businesses that can use PCS to reduce their some $30 billion in access charges to the local exchange carriers by creating an alternative local loop. Similarly, MCI, though avoiding the auction, created a subsidiary called MCI Metro that may seek to manage service for spectrum winners in 17 cities, again harvesting the benefits of obviated access charges. Then all these companies can use their PCS technologies to pursue customers around the world without any thought of wire.

A chart created by industry analyst Herschel Shosteck illustrates the opportunity. The Shosteck chart is a bell curve relating the incomes of the world's households to telephone penetration rates. He shows that telephony has so far penetrated only to countries representing the top tail of the curve, where national wealth suffices to reduce the cost of telephony to a threshold of between 4% and 5% of incomes. As incomes rise around the globe, more and more people cross the telecom threshold. A chart of GDP in real dollars per capita versus telephone penetration shows that a 40% rise in incomes could bring a 1,600% increase in potential customers.

Compounding the surge in incomes, however, will be the plummeting cost of wireless telephony. Shosteck estimates that between 1985 and 1994 the price per customer dropped 80%, from $5,000 to $1,000. Combining these two trends, he calculates that there will be between 400 million and 800 million new wireless subscribers by the end of the year 2000. These numbers represent an awesome upsurge from the world's current level of some 60 million cellular customers. Any further acceleration in income growth or decline in telephone prices will increase these numbers. A 50% further drop in telephone prices combined with a 50% rise in incomes would quickly thrust the vast bulk of the world's population above the Shosteck threshold. Far from the negative elasticities that U.S. phone executives see in their saturated wireline voice business, the world-wide communications market will be a financial trampoline.

JUST CHIPS AND ANTENNAS

In an ordinary industry, a 50% drop in price seems a major obstacle. But telephony is becoming a branch of the computer industry, which doubles its cost effectiveness every 18 months. The wireless convergence of digital electronics and spectronics will allow the industry to escape its copper cage and achieve at least a tenfold drop in the real price of telephony in the next seven years.

Sen. Stevens should meet Martin Cooper, a former research chief at Motorola and now CEO of ArrayComm. Located in San Jose, ArrayComm is devoted to drastically reducing the cost of telephone access over the next two years while entirely obviating the problems of twisted-pair wiring that afflict Alaska.

The current pitch of ice-age cellular providers is "pay more and get less . . . and don't even think about universal service." Although they claim penetration rates in industrial countries of nearly 10%, most cellular users make most of their calls on wireline systems. The real market share of cellular is in fact under 1% in the industrial world. The cellular companies' formula for success is to exploit the public hunger for mobility by charging more money for worse service—extracting premium prices for calls with acoustics and reliability far inferior to wireline telephony. Followed by both sides of the cellular duopoly—by Bells, McCaws and other suppliers—this pay-more-for-less-and-worse formula has concealed from much of the industry the basic technological fact that wireless will soon be acoustically better than wireline and drastically cheaper as well. As the CD example shows, after all, digital sound systems are superior to analog. And without wires, phones finesse the largest capital and labor costs of conventional telephony.

In economic terms, the intrinsic cost advantage of wireless is concealed by the colossal installed base of copper. Already mostly paid for and largely written off, the 154 million twisted-pair access lines will allow the Bells to compete in price for some time with wireless rivals that have lower real costs.

Nonetheless, technical reality will prevail in the end. Spectronics offers technologies in four dimensions for dividing and conquering spectrum: Frequency division, time division, code division and space division. All address in various ways the issue of frequency rouse—how many times in a system particular frequencies can be roused without causing interference in other calls using the same frequencies. Of the four techniques, so far only frequency division has been widely exploited. As these other methods come on line, the cost of telephony will go over the same kind of digital cliff long familiar in computers.

Surveying all these proposed schemes and their promised upgrades, it is safe to project between a 60% and 90% drop in the cost of wireless telephony over the next five years, depending mostly on the progress of CDMA. Qualcomm's CDMA could reduce costs tenfold, compared with the threefold gains from current global services mobile (GSM) technology, which contemplates an upgrade path chiefly through downgrading the voice quality with a half-rate vocoder.

All these gains in wireless efficiency from dividing by time, code or frequency are compounded by dividing spectrum by space. Mathematically, every 50% reduction in the cell radius yields a 400% increase in the number of customers who can be served in a given area with a given technology. Huge theoretical gains accrue from cell-splitting—reducing the physical extent of cells and multiplying their numbery—converting current macrocells as large as 35 miles in diameter into microcells a mile or so in width, and into picocells measured in hundreds of yards in buildings, shopping centers or congested urban streets.

All these gains, however, could be nullified by the expense and difficulty of implanting base stations all over cities and neighborhoods. The key to the gains of space division, therefore, is creation of base stations drastically cheaper, smaller, more discreet and more functional than the current cell sites, costing between $500,000 and $1 million, occupying 1,000 square feet and containing between 55 and 416 radios, depending on the frequency reuse factor. The most notable breakthrough in base stations is the Steinbrecher MiniCell, to be demonstrated in July and launched at the end of the year.

Putting a base station into a briefcase, Steinbrecher uses a single broadband digital radio to perform the functions of between 55 and 416 analog transceivers. The key breakthrough is a proprietary mixer that can flawlessly down-convert all the waveforms in the entire cellular spectrum into a stream of baseband digital bits without losing any information or introducing spurious signals. Containing all the electromagnetic contents of the cell, this digital bitstream is broken into channels by a 0.4- micron technology application-specific integrated circuit and is interpreted by digital signal processors. Governed by the learning curves of semiconductors, the MiniCell promises to reduce the cost of a cell site by an initial factor of 10 and by an eventual factor governed chiefly by the Moore's Law exponentials manifested in the PC industry.

In an important article in the April issue of IEEE *Personal Communications*, Donald Cox, former Bellcore wireless leader who is now at Stanford, calculated that such digital base station technologies soon could lower capital costs per wireless customer to $14, compared with a current cellular cost of $5,555 (assuming, in both cases, 180 channels per unit).

Using leading-edge silicon technology, the broadband digital radio can transform the entire landscape of wireless. It takes the channeling, tuning, filtering, modulation, demodulation, coding, decoding and other processing out of the analog radio domain, where a different radio system is needed for each frequency band or modulation scheme.

Moved into a digital signal processor or ASIC, these functions yield to the huge efficiencies of the computer.

The ultimate in space division, for example, is devoting the entire available spectrum to every caller. Using broadband digital radios fed by arrays of smart antennas, Cooper's ArrayComm is approaching this ultimate. "We believe that over the next few years, everyone will be using broadband radios," Cooper says, pointing to Watkins- Johnson and Airnet joining Steinbrecher in this business (though with far narrower bandwidths).

All base stations, one way or another, have to find all the callers in a cell and link them to callers outside. Broadband digital radios move the search function from an array of radios to a single computer. Cooper contrasts the technology with radar. As he puts it, traditional radar systems use active beams to scan a location and find a targeted object; ArrayComm uses a passive array of antennas and a digital radio to provide a broadband snapshot of a cell 20 times a second, and employs computers to locate the targeted object, in this case a handset.

Like the Craig McCaw-Bill Gates low-earth-orbit satellite scheme called Teledesic, the ArrayComm IntelliCell originated with work done for the Strategic Defense Initiative program. Inventor Richard Roy developed algorithms for rapidly calculating the source and trajectory of missiles from their electromagnetic emissions as detected by satellite antennas scanning the surface of the earth. Now he is using similar algorithms to identify the position, direction, distance and amplitude of electromagnetic emissions from handsets in a wireless cell, as collected by arrays of smart antennas at a base station. Once the information is digitized, Roy's algorithms can sort out all the calls by their location in the cell, excavating signals otherwise buried in neighboring noise or shrouded in cross-talk, and conducting several calls at once on the same frequencies.

Cooper gives the analogy of human hearing. "You close your eyes and I walk around talking, and you can point to me at any moment. Add another voice and you can still listen to me, or shift to the other voice. You can hear the voice you want to hear twice as loudly as the voice you want to suppress. You null out the interference. This is not a physical process. You don't move your ears. Your brain calculates and correlates the different sounds or signals. That's what Dick Roy's algorithms do in our smart base stations."

Roy explains further: "That works if you have a variety of frequencies. Suppose, though, you were faced with a chorus of monks all chanting in monotone in the same frequencies. This is more like the cellular telephone or PCS situation in the presence of interference or cross-talk. This is what prevents frequency reuse in adjacent cells. Amid the drone of the monks, you could not isolate the sound of one monk. What you need is more ears. Then you could resolve the source of a particular sound by its location. That is what we do with antenna arrays."

Adding a spatial dimension to the frequencies, time slots or codes tracked by ordinary cell sites, an ArrayComm system can distinguish signals entirely unintelligible to other systems. For example, an array with eight antennas can effectively magnify the signal by a factor of eight. There is no theoretical limit to the number of antennas, but as a practical matter, the size of the array becomes a problem in urban cells. By moving up spectrum from 900 megahertz 15 centimeters to 1,800 megahertz, PCS reduces the size of the antenna array from two meters across to one meter across (antenna size drops in proportion to the decline in wavelength at higher frequencies).

As a result of the effective magnification of signals, an eight-antenna array could double the range of a base station, quadruple the area covered, reduce to one-third or one-fourth the number of cell sites, and raise frequency reuse to 100%, without CDMA. Because CDMA doesn't define channels by frequency at all, but by codes, its limit is the number of codes that can be differentiated in the cell. Thus, Roy believes that among all the competing technologies, CDMA can benefit most from using the spatial dimension. Spatial processing can help differentiate the calls in a cell as the noise of call codes accumulates toward the limit where further traffic is impossible. As Qualcomm leader Andrew Viterbi declared in a paper released on Jan. 13: "Spatial processing remains as the most promising, if not the last frontier, in the evolution of multiple access systems."

ArrayComm is part of what Don Steinbrecher calls "the transformation of wireless from a radio business to a computer business." As a computer business, wireless will share in the gains of Moore's Law. It will double cost effectiveness every 18 months, rather than continuing on the stagnant price curves of wireline telephony in its cage of copper, dominated by the costs of rolling out trucks, digging trenches, laying wire and climbing poles.

Cooper predicts that over the next five years, the combination of broadband digital radios, ArrayComm smart antennas and a stream of other advances in wireless telephony will reduce the cost per minute of wireless phone calls to a penny a minute, one-quarter the average wireline level and one-twelfth the current cellular price. This price collapse will ignite huge positive elasticities in demand, reaching for the first time billions of new customers in India, China and Latin America who are now untouched by telephony.

ArrayComm's first customers are Alcatel in Europe, which is creating a system for GSM, and DDI Tokyo Pocket Telephone. The fastest growing company on the Tokyo stock exchange for the last five years, DDI is often termed the MCI of Japan. Using transceiver chipsets from Cirrus Logic's PCSI subsidiary, DDI is already the world leader in low-cost wireless telephony. The ArrayComm technology should lower its costs to the point where these pocket telephones can break through as a wireless local loop throughout the huge new markets of Asia and elsewhere. Earlier this year, the DDI technology, called Personal Handy Phone, was combined with a Bellcore-Motorola proposal as a new low-end wireless standard under the name Personal Access Communications Systems.

By transforming the technical landscape of communications, spectronics are also transforming the lawscape. Indeed, by entirely closing the gap between the costs of serving rural and urban customers, digital wireless phones will obliterate the need for cross-subsidies that underlie the entire regulatory edifice. In the new world of bandwidth abundance, the only group that will need cross-subsidies and emergency aid is the communications bar.

As a guide to the era ahead, telephone executives, regulators and Washington politicians should contemplate the computer industry. The market share of centralized time-shared computer systems dropped from 100% in 1977 to less than 1% in 1987. International Business Machines and Digital Equipment Corp. lost nearly $100 billion in market cap in five years.

Or, for a more recent example of the power of wireless technology in the digital age, the telcos, regulators and politicians should consider the video distribution industry. Last year, Washington was so obsessed with the cable industry and its apparent monopoly power that Congress enacted a reregulation bill that ultimately imposed 700 pages of new rules on the distribution of video news and entertainment. Politicians and pundits let forth a stream of lamentations about the future access of the poor and the rural to the new services of digital television and proposed a series of new requirements for universal service.

A year later, however, the very survival of the cable industry as a distributor of point-multipoint video is in doubt. Before Congress could enact broadband universal service rules, Direct Broadcast Satellites were propagating 150 channels of digital video with supreme universality over the entire expanse of the continental United States. Attaching 18-inch dishes to the tops of their igloos, the Inuits might acquire television images of a variety and resolution far excelling any offering of cable television in the midst of the nation's capital. With a software upgrade to MPEG-2 video planned later this year, the number of channels will rise to some 200.

Privately dubbed "deathstar" by cable industry executives, digital DBS became the fastest growing product in the history of consumer electronics. Just seven months after its introduction, it had already surpassed the combined first-year sales of VCRs, CD players and big-screen TVs.

Today, in the name of deregulation, politicians are preparing to impose a series of new competitive requirements upon the Bell operating companies, on the assumption that they still wield monopoly power. Pundits still seem to believe that the copper cage protects local telephone companies from outside competition. But in fact, the cage incarcerates them in copper wires, while the world prepares to pass them by.

The digital future is not wired or wireless. It is spectronic and spectacular. To participate in this explosive market, all telephone companies will have to escape from their copper cages into the infinite reaches of the spectrum.

14

The Coming Software Shift

"I was trying to conceive of how one could approach it in a way that would be fundamental . . . like being at the center of a sphere, where there were opportunities—and problems, of course!—in all directions."

—Patrick Haggerty of Texas Instruments, explaining his decision to license the transistor from Bell Laboratories in 1952.

What will it take to launch a new Bill Gates—an Archimedean man who sharply shifts the center of the sphere, alters the axes of technology and economy, and builds a new business empire on new foundations? Who can inherit the imperial throne in the microcosm and telecosm currently held by the Redmond Rockefeller?

I will open the envelope in a minute. But first I want to tell you about a new software program called Netscape Navigator Personal Edition. I brought it back from Silicon Valley in late June and put the package next to my PC. The PC was proudly running a beta version of Windows 95. I had presented Windows 95 with great fanfare to my 11-year-old son Richard as his route to the most thrilling new frontiers of the computer world. Multitasking, 32-bit operation, flat memory! Object linking and embedding! "Information at your fingertips!" But, all in all, he preferred his Mac Quadra 840AV or even Windows 3.1. They don't crash so often, he explained.

I live out in the boondocks of western Massachusetts where there are no convenient full-service connections to the Internet. So I was much less excited about Netscape than I was about Windows 95. I hoped Windows 95 would put me on line through the Microsoft Network system. Some 10 minutes later, though, Richard wanted to know my credit card number so I could choose an Internet service provider. A couple of minutes after that, linked through internetMCI's 800 number, Richard was on the World Wide Web, using the InfoSeek service to examine my chapters from *Telecosm* on line, searching the secrets of Sim City 2000 at Maxis, exchanging messages with Microsoft Flight Simulator buffs, and exploring Disney. As far as I know, he is still there.

The next thing I knew, my brother Walter came by. He worked for a computer company, New World Technologies in Ashland, Mass., that builds customized Pentium machines and delivers them to value-added resellers within 48 hours. Walter wanted the Netscape program. He took it back to my parents' farm down the road and booted it up on a four-megabyte 386SX Dynatech previously used to map the pedigrees of a flock of Romney sheep. Soon he was on the Web scouting out the competition from Dell and Micron and showing off the Gilder Web page. This intrigued my 77-year-old mother, who had scarcely even noticed a computer before. I don't know how it happened, but before the night was out, she too was on the Web, exploring catalogs of British colleges for her namesake granddaughter who was soon to leave for London.

Now let me tell you about my introduction to Java, a new programming language that menaces Microsoft's software supremacy. I encountered Java in early June at a Sun Micro-systems conference at the Westin St. Francis Hotel in downtown San Francisco. For a speech I was to give, I had planned to use a multimedia presentation, complete with Macro-Mind Director images and QuickTime video that I had contrived with an expensive professional some months earlier. The complexities of Director prompted me to convert the program to Astound. However, it required an external disk drive and ran erratically with the eight megabytes of RAM on my PowerBook. I decided to speak nakedly from notes on the coming technologies of sand and glass and air.

Following me immediately to the stage was Sun's amiable chief scientist, John Gage. He decided to illustrate his speech entirely from the World Wide Web. He began with a handsome page, contrived minutes before, giving an account of my speech, headlined: "Gilder Addresses Sun, Tells of Technologies of Opaque Silicon and Transparent Silicon." Then he moved to the Gilder Telecosm archives run by Gordon Jacobson of Portman Communications at a Web site of the University of Pennsylvania's engineering school. Gage illustrated his talk with real-time reports on traffic conditions in San Diego (where I was about to go), weather conditions in Florida as a hurricane loomed, and developments on Wall Street as IBM bid for Lotus. He showed the Nasdaq ticker running across the screen. He showed animations of relevant charts, cute little Java gymnasts cartwheeling across the screen, three-dimensional interactive molecular models and an overflowing coffee cup, entitled "HotJava."

None of his information and images used a desktop presentation program, whether from MacroMind or from Microsoft. None of them used a database engine, whether SQL or Oracular. Indeed, except for the Gilder speech report, none were created beforehand. Incurring no memory or disk drive problems, Gage summoned all the illustrations to his PowerBook directly from the Internet. The animations employed a new computer language, Java, written for the Web by the venerable Sun programmer James Gosling. Java allows transmission of executable programs to any computer connected to the Net to be interpreted and played safely and securely in real time.

Clifford Stoll, calls it "Silicon snake oil." But I call it a fundamental break in the history of technology. It is the software complement of the hollowing out of the computer described in Forbes ASAP ("The Bandwidth Tidal Wave," December 5, 1994). Almost over-night, the CPU and its software have become peripheral; the network, central. I had spent weeks working on a presentation on my desktop computer, using an array of presentation software. But Gage improvised a more impressive and animated presentation without using any desktop presentation programs at all. The World Wide Web and the Java language were enough. Restricted to the files of my computer, I struggled with storage problems and incompatible research formats, while he used the storage capacity and information resources of more than five million host computers on the Net.

Similarly for my family, the limitations of my parents' barnyard four-megabyte 386SX didn't matter. The operating system also didn't matter. What was crucial was the network gear and software. My brother Walter had installed a modem that linked to the Web at an average of 24.6 kilobits per second. With the Netscape Navigator, that was enough. Actually 14.4 would have been enough. Enough to launch a new Bill Gates.

Admit it, the legacy version, once so luminous, is beginning to lose its shine. You thrill no longer at his vaporware $50 million house, fenestrated with $40 billion Windows, offering misty views of Daytona, Memphis, Cairo, and other far-off places you no longer really care to go, even if—OLE—they are swimming with GML 3D screensavers from London's National Gallery endlessly hurdling the 640K barrier as if it were flat as a Mac.

At the most essential level, Bill Joy of Sun illuminated Gates's dilemma at Esther Dyson's *PC Forum* conference in 1990. Known as one of the great minds in software, yet losing share inexorably to Microsoft, Joy seemed to be moving into the role of conference crank. Year after year, he lamented the prolix inelegance of the triumphant waves of Microsoft programs sweeping through the industry: "As we add more and more of these features to older systems," he said, "the complexity gets multiplicative. I have 10 different packages that interact in 10-to-the-10th different ways. I get all sorts of surprises, and yet because these things don't play together well the power is only additive. I get this feature and that feature but the combinations don't work. What I'd really like to see is a system where the complexity goes up in a linear way but the power goes up exponentially."

In software, complexity has long been rising exponentially, while power has been rising additively. In response, Niklaus Wirth, the inventor of Pascal and other programming languages, has propounded two new Parkinson's Laws for software: "Software expands to fill the available memory," and "Software is getting slower more rapidly than hardware gets faster." Indeed, newer programs seem to run more slowly on most systems than their previous releases. Compare Word 6.0 for the Mac, for example, with Word 5.0, or WordPerfect 6.0 for Windows with WordPerfect for DOS.

But none of this matters. Gates has moved from triumph to triumph by shrewdly exploiting the advances of microcosmic hardware. With Moore's Law and the Law of the Microcosm, the number of transistors on a chip doubles every 18 months, and cost/performance rises as the square of the number of transistors. The complexity sinks into the microcosm and power rises exponentially on the chip to absorb all the complexity grenades rolling down from Redmond.

Gates travels in the slipstream behind Moore's Law, following a key rule of the microcosm: Waste transistors. As Nicholas Negroponte puts it, "Every time Andy [Grove] makes a faster chip, Bill uses all of it." Wasting transistors is the law of thrift in the microcosm, and Gates has been its most brilliant and resourceful exponent.

Meanwhile, in the face of Gates's ascendancy, Bill Joy seemed to grow curls and shed influence, as Sun played rope-a-dope with Hewlett-Packard and other workstation rivals. In 1990, he retreated to a sylvan aerie in Aspen, Colo., to pursue "advanced research" for Sun. But his talk of small programs and handheld consumer appliances seemed irrelevant to the company.

Nonetheless, in early 1990, showing up late—in a Hawaiian shirt—to address a formal dinner in Silicon Valley, Bill Joy had a great prophetic moment. He cited the Moore's Law trends as grounds for granting the first five years of the 1990s to Bill Gates. "It's pretty much determined," he said. Indeed, in the late 1980s, Joy had personally made a separate peace with Microsoft by selling a large portion of his Sun holdings and buying Microsoft shares, thus becoming the second richest of Sun's four founders. (The richest, Andy Bechtolsheim, jumped even deeper into Microsoft.) But then, around 1995, predicted Joy, everything would change. There would be a "breakthrough that we cannot imagine today." He even acknowledged that the breakthrough would not come from Sun, but "from people and companies we cannot know today."

The key to software innovation, he said, was smart programmers. Smart programmers are hundreds of times more productive than ordinary programmers. And "let's be truthful," said the sage of Sun, propounding what has become known as Joy's Law, "most of the bright people don't work for you—no matter who you are. You need a strategy that allows for innovation occurring elsewhere." To the Justice Department, Microsoft's overwhelming OS market share and its teeming armies of programmers seem a barrier to entry for other software competitors. To Joy, Microsoft's size and dominance could become a barrier to entry for Microsoft, blocking it from the key new markets of the late 1990s.

It is now clear that Joy was on target. The breakthrough is here in force, invading and occupying all the commanding heights of the information economy, from the media to the universities. It is the World Wide Web and its powerful browsers, servers, languages and programming tools. Software on individual machines still bogs down in the macrocosmic swamps of complexity. But in the telecosm, yields rise exponentially almost without limit in proportion to the number and power of the machines on the network. No matter how much memory and other storage is created on the desktop, no matter what information resources are assembled on CD-ROMs, no matter how powerful are the database tools created for the LAN, the desktop imperium will pale and wither before the telecosmic amplitudes of the Internet.

For the last five years, the number of machines on the network has been rising between five and 10 times faster than the number of transistors on a chip. With 1,300 miles of fiber-optic lines being laid every day in the U.S., bandwidth is sure to rise even faster than the number of networked computers (see *Forbes ASAP*, "The Bankwidth Tidal Wave," December 5, 1994). This awesome transition presents a supreme chance for new leadership in developing software focused less on wasting transistors than on wasting bandwidth.

A computer on every desktop and in every home? Information at your fingertips? SQL Server 6.0? My son Richard yawns. Let's face it, Bill, that stuff is yesterday. In the new era, Microsoft can continue to feed on the microcosm. But the leading-edge companies will move to the frontiers of the telecosm, where collectively they will grow far faster than Microsoft.

So, open the envelope. Let's find a new Bill Gates.

Start by adding 100 pounds of extra heft, half a foot of height and two further years of schooling, then make him $12.9 billion hungrier. Give him a gargantuan appetite for pizza and Oreos, Bach, newsprint, algorithms, ideas, John Barth, Nabokov, images, Unix code, bandwidth. Give him a nearly unspellable Scandinavian name—Marc Andreessen.

Put him to work for $6.85 per hour at Illinois's National Center for Supercomputing Applications (NCSA) writing 3D visualization code on a Silicon Graphics Indy for a Thinking Machine C-5 or a Cray YMP16. Surround him on all sides by the most advanced computers and software in the world, under the leadership of cybernetic visionary Larry Smarr. What will happen next? "Boredom," Andreessen replies. Supercomputers, already at the end of their tether, turned out to be "underwhelming Unix machines."

Then, for a further image of the end of the world, take him in the fall of 1990 off to Austin, Tex., for two semesters at IBM. "They were going to take over the 3D graphics market, they were going to win the Malcolm Baldridge Award, they were going to blow Silicon Graphics [the regnant Silicon Valley 3D workstation company] off the map, all in six months." Andreessen began by doing performance analysis and moved on to work on the operating system kernel. In mid-1991, after constant delays, the company was finally ready to ship a world-beating 3D engine. But the new IBM machine turned out to be four times slower at seven times the price of the equivalent Silicon Graphics hardware that IBM had bundled a year and a half earlier with its RS6000 RISC (reduced instruction set computing) workstation. Austin IBM returned to the drawing board and Andreessen returned to Illinois to get his degree.

In both commercial and academic settings, Andreessen thus had the good fortune of working at the very heart of the old order of computing in its climactic phase. As Andreessen saw it, little of long-term interest was going on at either establishment. But both did command one huge and felicitous resource, vastly underused, and that was the Internet. "Designed for all the wrong reasons—to link some 2,000 scientists to a tiny number of supercomputers," it had exploded into a global ganglion thronged by millions of people and machines.

Many people saw the Internet as throbbing with hype and seething with problems— Clifford Stoll's book, *Silicon Snake Oil*, catalogs many: the lack of security, substance, reliability, bandwidth, easy access; the presence of porn, fraud, frivolity and freaks guarantees, so he says, that no serious business can depend on it for critical functions. But to Andreessen the problems of the Internet are only the other side of its incredible virtues.

"By usual standards," says Andreessen, "the Internet was far from perfect. But the Internet finds its own perfection—in the millions of people that are able to use it and the hundreds of thousands who can provide services for it." To Andreessen, all the problems signaled that he was at the center of the sphere, gazing in wild surmise at "a giant hole in the middle of the world"—the supreme opportunity of the age.

Andreessen saw that, for all its potential, there was a monstrous incongruity at the heart of the Internet. Its access software was at least 10 years behind. "PC Windows had penetrated all the desktops, the Mac was a huge success, and point-and-click interfaces had become part of everyday life. But to use the Net you still had to understand Unix. You had to type FTP [file transfer protocol] commands by hand and you had to be able to do addressmapping in your head between IP addresses and host names and you had to know where all the FTP archives were; you had to understand IRC [Internet relay chat] protocols, you had to know how to use this particular news reader and that particular Unix shell prompt, and you pretty much had to know Unix itself to get anything done. And the current users had little interest in making it easier. In fact, there was a definite element of not wanting to make it easier, of actually wanting to keep the riffraff out."

The almost miraculous key to opening up the Internet was the concept of hypertext, invented by Theodor Holm Nelson, the famously fractious prophet of the "Xanadu" network, and son of Celeste Holm, the actress. A hypnotic speaker, with a gaunt countenance and flowing golden hair, Nelson seems an Old Testament Jeremiah from Central Casting as he rails against the flaws and foibles of current-day computing.

Hypertext is simply text embedded with pointers to other text, instantly and fully available by a point and click. For the source of the concept, Nelson quotes an essay by Vannevar Bush written in 1945 and read to him by his father as a boy: "The human mind . . . operates by association. With one item in its grasp, it snaps instantly to the next that is suggested by the association of thoughts, in accordance with some intricate web of trails carried by the cells of the brain." Projecting this idea from a single human brain to a global ganglion, Nelson sowed the conceptual seeds of the World Wide Web.

Andreessen can explain both the power of hypertext and its slow emergence in commercial products: "Xanadu was just a tremendous idea. But hypertext depends on the network. If the network is there, hypertext is incredibly useful. It is the key mechanism. But if the network is not there, hypertext does not give you any of the richness." Hence, Apple's HyperCard and similar schemes failed to ignite. The link is not hyper if it is restricted to your hard drive or CD-ROM. Connected to millions of computers around the globe, it becomes exponentially hyper.

"The other thing about hypertext," says Andreessen, "is that, even on networks, traditionally it had been developed by theoreticians and people very deep in the computer science community, and they tended to worry very deeply about problems like, 'Well, what happens if the information moves?'" As Gates put it in 1992: "The idea of locating things that move by their properties and dealing with the security and efficiency issues, including using replication to do this stuff well, is a very tough problem. That's what Windows's Cairo is all about. Three or four Ph.D. theses talk about this, but a commercial system has never done it."

Andreessen brings the issue down to earth: "You've got a pointer at a piece of information on the network, but Joe, who's running that information, moves it somewhere else. Computer scientists would take a look at the problem and say, 'Oh, the system doesn't work.' On the Internet, we look at that problem and say, 'Oh well, here's another 20,000 pointers that do work.' And maybe we can send e-mail to Joe and he'll put his information back." In other words, you don't wait for Cairo or Xanadu to try to solve every problem. You go with the fabulous flow of opportunities.

Nelson's idea led to what Gary Wolf, a contributing writer of *Wired*, calls "one of the most powerful designs of the 20th century"—a universal library, a global information index and a computerized royalty system. But Nelson's quest for perfection led to a 20-year adventure in futility. "The opinion of the Xanadu people to this day is that the Web and the Internet are much too simple. They don't solve the problems. For instance, the links aren't fully bidirectional. You don't know exactly who's pointing to your page, and there's two ways to look at that. The way that Ted Nelson looks at it is 'That's bad!' The way that I look at it is 'That's great!' All of a sudden anyone can point to your page without permission. The Net can grow at its own rate. You get the network effect, you get Metcalfe's Law, it spirals completely out of control. Isn't that fantastic?"

In 1988, Xanadu found funding from John Walker, the charismatic recluse, taxpatriate in Switzerland, and founder of Autodesk, the desktop computer-aided design (CAD) company. As Walker prophetically declared in 1988: "In 1964, Xanadu was a dream in a single mind. In 1980, it was the shared goal of a small group of brilliant technologists. By 1989, it will be a product. And by 1995, it will begin to change the world." All truer than Walker could have imagined, but it would not happen, alas, at Autodesk. Haunted by dreams of perfection and hobbled by hyperventilation at the helm, Xanadu misted over. Autodesk sustained the effort until it was mercifully terminated by the new CEO, Carol Bartz, in 1993 at the very moment that a real Xanadu, deemed hopelessly imperfect and inadequate by Nelson, was about to burst forth efflorescently on the Internet.

The demiurgic step came from Tim Berners-Lee at CERN in Switzerland, creating the World Wide Web based on a universal hypertext function. He launched the initial HTTP (hypertext transfer protocol) governing transport on the Web. He developed URLs (uniform resource locators) as a common addressing system that joined most of the existing Internet search and linkage technologies. He conceived the HTML (hypertext markup language), a kind of PostScript for the Web. He made the system ignore failures (Joe's moving data could not crash your machine). Thus, invoking a browser (i.e., a hypertext reader), the user could point and click to information anywhere on the Net, unconscious of whether it was in the form of a file transfer, an e-mail, a Gopher search or a news posting, or whether it was in the next room or in Tasmania.

Berners-Lee addressed a basic problem of the Internet from the point of view of an academic researcher. But the real opportunity was to open the Internet to the world and the world to the Internet, and that would require more than a facility for cruising through textual materials. After all, the bulk of human bandwidth is in a person's eyes and ears. For absorbing text, as Robert Lucky, author of *Silicon Dreams*, has pointed out, the speed limit is only some 55 bits per second.

To burst open the Internet would require reaching out to the riffraff who travel through pictures and sounds at megahertz speeds. To critics of a more vulgar Net, such as Stoll, more riffraff sending a callipygian naked-lady bitmaps and voluminous digital ululations from the Grateful Dead and QuickTime first-step baby videos traipsing down the lines and wriggling through the routers would soon cause a gigantic crash. Even some of Andreessen's main allies at the NCSA shared some of these fears. At CERN, Berners-Lee opposed images and video on these grounds. The technologists all held a narrowband view of the world, imagining bandwidth as an essentially scarce resource to be carefully husbanded by responsible citizens of the cybersphere.

So Tim Berners-Lee alone could not burst open the Internet piñata and give it to the world. As Richard Wiggins, author of *Internet for Everyone: A Guide for Users and Providers*, observes, "During 1992 and early 1993, graphical Gopher clients for the Macintosh and Windows evolved, and it appeared that Gopher would outstrip the fledgling Web." It was the ultimate broadband booster, Marc Andreessen, working with NCSA colleague Eric Bina, who ignited the Web rocket. One late December night in 1992 at the Espresso Royale cafe in Champaign-Urbana, Andreessen looked his friend Eric Bina in the eye and said: "Let's go for it."

Every Gates has to have his Paul Allen (or Jobs, his Steve Wozniak). Andreessen's is Bina—short and wiry where Andreessen is ursine, cautious where he is cosmic, focused where he is expansive, apprehensive where he is evangelical, bitwise where he is prodigal with bandwidth, ready to stay home and write the code where Andreessen is moving on to conquer the globe. Wildly contrasting but completely trusting and complementary, these two—in an inspired siege of marathon code-wreaking between January and March 1993—made Mosaic happen. A rich image-based program for accessing the World Wide Web and other parts of the Internet, Mosaic requires no more knowledge of its internal mechanics than is needed by the user of the steering wheel of a car. With a mere 9,000 lines of code (compared to Windows 95's 11 million lines, including 3 million lines of MSN code), Mosaic would become the most rapidly propagated software program ever written.

Andreessen could defy all the fears of an Internet image crash because he lived in a world of bandwidth abundance and fiber galore. He fully grasped the law of the telecosm. Every new host computer added to the Net would not only use the Net; it would also be a new resource for it, providing a new route for the bits and new room to store them. Every new flood of megabyte bitmaps would make the Net more interesting, useful and attractive, and increase the pressure for backbones running at gigabits per second and above. The Internet must be adapted to people with eyes and ears. They won't abuse it, he assured Bina without a smile. After all, he knew he would have to rely on Bina for much of the graphics coding.

"I was right," Bina says now. "People abused it horribly. People would scan in a page of PostScript text in a bitmap, taking over a megabyte to display a page that would take maybe 1,000 bytes of text. But Marc was also right. As a result of the glitz and glitter, thousands of people wasted time to put in pretty pictures and valuable information on the Web, and millions of people use it."

Working night and day at the NCSA, wrangling over issues, arts and letters, music and Unix code at the Espresso Royale down the street, the two programmers achieved a rare synergy. "We each did the job that most appealed to us," says Bina, "so each of us thinks the other did the hard stuff." Bina wrote most of the new code—in particular, the graphics, modifying HTML to handle images, adding a GIF (graphics interchange format) decoder, incorporating color management tools. Andreessen took the existing library of communications code from CERN and tore it apart and rewrote it so it would run more quickly and efficiently on the network.

As time passed, they brought in other young programmers from the NCSA—among them Chris Wilson, Jon Mittelhauser, Chris Houck and Aleks Totic—to port the system to Windows and Mac machines. With help from them, they designed dynamic forms with type-in fields, check boxes, toggle buttons and other ordered ways of entering simple text for searches and other functions, beyond simple hypertext pointing at a URL. For example, a dynamic form is now used by Pizza Hut for ordering a pizza on line. Finally, because every change in the browser required complementary changes in the servers at CERN—where the physicists tended to be busy and glitz-averse—Bina and Andreessen decided to do their own servers. The NCSA's Rob McCool took charge of this crucial project.

In the end, they had created an entirely new interface for the Internet and new communications software to render it crisply accessible—a look and feel that almost immediately struck everyone who used it as an amazing breakthrough. In February 1995, Bob Metcalfe wrote a column in *InfoWorld* predicting that Web browsers would become, in effect, the dominant operating system for the next era.

Browsers are now ubiquitous. Every major company and many minor ones are building them. Some eight million people use them. IBM, AT&T, Novell, Microsoft, NetCom, Sun, Silicon Graphics, America Online, Net-Manage, Quarterdeck, Quadralay, Apple, SPRY-CompuServe, Frontier Technologies, Delphi, MCI, Wollongong, even the Spyglass spinoff from the NCSA—you name it—all these companies are building, licensing, enhancing or bundling a browser. Many of these ventures, led by Quarterdeck's smart hotlists and "drag-and-drop" ease of use, have outpaced Mosaic and prompted a leapfrogging contest of can-you-top-this.

That is what happens when an entrepreneur performs a truly revolutionary act, supplies the smallest missing factor, as Peter Drucker puts it, that can transform a jumble of elements into a working system—the minimal mutation that provokes a new paradigm. In 1977, the relevant jumble was small computers, microprocessors and assembly language programming. Bill Gates and Paul Allen supplied the key increment: software tools and the Basic language for the embryonic personal computer. In 1993, Andreessen and Bina set out to supply the minimal increment to convert the entire Net, with its then one to two million linked computers (today it's an estimated seven million computers) and immense information resources, into a domain as readily accessible to an 11-year-old as a hard drive or CD-ROM on a Mac or Windows PC.

As a result, the same forces of exploding bandwidth, the same laws of the telecosm that are wreaking revolution in hardware, hollowing out the computer—rendering the CPU peripheral and the network central—are also transforming software. All forms of desktop software—operating systems, applications and utilities—are becoming similarly peripheral. The ever-growing gigapedal resources of the Internet will always dwarf any powers and functions that can be distilled on a desktop or mobilized on the backplane of a supercomputer.

Last year, for example, four researchers at MIT, Iowa State, Bellcore and Oxford (U.K.) triumphantly claimed a $100 reward for solving a grand challenge problem. They announced that they had broken an RSA encryption code of 129 digits that one of RSA's inventors, R.L. Rivest, when offering the $100 prize in 1977, calculated would take four quadrillion years for a supercomputer to crack. They did not accomplish their feat on a single machine (none yet exists that can perform these computations) but on a virtual machine consisting of 1,600 mostly modest workstations scattered around the Internet. Similarly, Gordon Bell in 1992 for the first time granted his achievement award for price and performance in the application of supercomputers, not to a single machine, but to a distributed Internet virtual system.

The success of the Internet model even in these high-powered processing applications portends and symbolizes a definitive reality, which gathers increasing force as network bandwidth begins to exceed the internal bandwidth on computer backplanes. From now on, the relevant computer is the network and the ascendant software is Internet software.

Giving the program away on the Net, Andreessen released Mosaic in binary form, already compiled for any popular computer platform, and helped bring more than a million newcomers to the Web in six months. In that time, such an upheaval would even reach the notice of the management of the NCSA. At the National Science Foundation in Washington, D.C., a friend eagerly showed Mosaic to Larry Smarr, who was visiting from Illinois. He was startled to see that this new marvel was a creation of his own shop at the NCSA. Perhaps he should look into it. Perhaps there was more to sell to Washington than Fiber Channels between scientists and Crays. From that moment on, pushing Mosaic became the chief "grand challenge problem" of the University of Illinois Supercomputing Center.

After Andreessen's college graduation in December 1993, Joseph Hardin, head of the NCSA, asked him to stay on at the center. But he added one condition, namely, that the young programmer leave the Mosaic project. "Some 40 people had a role in creating Mosaic," he said. "Don't you think it's time to give someone else a chance to share the glory?" Reasoning that they would have a still better chance in his absence, Andreessen left for Silicon Valley.

After a few months doing Internet security functions at a company called EIT, Andreessen attracted the attention of the legendary Jim Clark, founder of Silicon Graphics Inc. and inventor of the Geometry Engine, capable of 3D graphics, that impelled SGI's growth. At loose ends, like most of the industry's venturers, Clark was looking for opportunity in all the wrong places—3D games, interactive TV, Hollywood. He found himself increasingly entranced with the Mosaic browser. Hearing that the author of Mosaic had arrived in Silicon Valley, he sent Andreessen an e-mail in early February 1994.

The rest is history, in the accelerated form familiar in the Valley. Jim Clark met with Andreessen and signed him up as the first employee of a new company. "What has happened to the other NCSA programmers?" he wanted to know. Hearing that Chris Wilson, who had helped port the system to the PC, had left the center to join SPRY, Clark decided to act fast. He invited Bina to come to Silicon Valley and meet with him on his yacht. Avoiding temptation (Bina's wife is a tenured professor of database technology at Champaign-Urbana and is wary of snake oil), Bina spurned the invitation. Andreessen wrote him a glum e-mail: "Sorry. It would have been nice to have had you here."

The next thing Bina knew, Andreessen called him to announce that he and Clark were flying to Champaign-Urbana and wanted to meet with Bina and the rest of the key programmers the next day at the local University Inn. "When I got off the elevator at the hotel," Bina recalls, "this blond guy who reminded me of my dad stepped back, looked me slowly up and down, and spoke: 'Marc said you could walk on water. I have never seen anyone who could do that before.'" Clark soon assured him he could stay in Illinois.

According to Bina, Clark spread a contagion of entrepreneurial excitement. Then one by one he made seven of them offers. All signed up. By the first week of April, Mosaic software was on the way and Jim Clark forgot about interactive TV.

Greeting this bold new company, however, were rumblings about a possible intellectual property suit from the NCSA. This surprise banished any idea of using Mosaic in any form. That was fine with them. They knew Mosaic was a quickly written hack designed for T1 and T3 lines running at up to 45 megabits a second at the NCSA. "We knew that everyone had Mosaic," says Bina. "We were glad to start from scratch again." Moving into a small office in Mountain View at a cost of less than $1 per square foot, they set to work.

In the new company, then called Mosaic Communications, Andreessen ascended to management. Bina, working in Illinois for all but one frenzied week a month, immersed himself in creating the new code. They revised it to work over a 14.4 modem. They focused on making it the only system that is fully secure. They added new supports for more elegant layouts and richer documents. Giving the program away on the Net, within a few months Netscape won 70% of the Web browser market, which it still holds.

Most important for the future of the company, they developed a stream of new server products, which they sold to most of the existing and aspiring on-line services and Internet service providers, from internetMCI and marketplaceMCI to IBM's Prodigy and Murdoch's Delphi. Altogether, they had released a total of 11 new products by midsummer of this year, from $50,000 secure server applications to the $39 Netscape Navigator Personal Edition complete with TCP/IP stack for full connection to the Internet in 10 minutes anywhere in the country.

As Wall Street began pouring money on any rival company with an Internet product, the stock market became a Netscape imperative. This posed a problem for Clark. There would be no difficulty attracting a frenzy of interest. The question was, Where would they hide Andreessen during the road show? Introducing him to John Doerr of Kleiner Perkins Caufield & Byers and other Silicon Valley clout, however, Clark instead resolved to teach the young bear how to chew with his mouth closed, tie a tie and get to work earlier than 8:30 . . . p.m. Then he prepared to place him in the nose cone of an Initial Public Orbiting that would value the gang at hundreds of millions of dollars, point Andreessen toward the Millennium and, with luck and the right characterological chemistry, have a new Bill Gates for the late 1990s.

Here he is, well after 8 p.m., roaring down El Camino Real in his '94 red Mustang, filled with pizza rinds, empty cans of Sprite, a mostly shredded copy of the *San Jose Mercury News* and a bulging issue of *MicroTimes* smeared in popcorn butter, talking with both hands to a writer from *Forbes ASAP* hunched amid the clutter and stealthily searching for a seat belt.

Amazingly free of the NIH (not invented here) syndrome afflicting many of his elders—his browser combines products from some 17 sources—Andreessen was discoursing on the virtues of Java, a language he says portends a telecosmic advance even more profound and enduring than the browser and related servers themselves.

For creating innovative stuff on the Web, Andreessen explains, "The alternative languages are grim, Perl is limited to text strings. Telescript from General Magic doesn't pass because it's proprietary. Tickle [Tcl] lacks power and features. Scheme and LISP are dead. Visual Basic lacks expressiveness and it is too much controlled by Microsoft. Dylan is still an Apple research project. None of them are truly suited to the Web environment. Java is as revolutionary as the Web itself." Tying Netscape to Java assures the company a central role in a coming efflorescence of the Web more significant in its implications than even the current manifestation. In the process, it will invert the entire world of software in a way that may permanently displace Microsoft from the center of the sphere.

Behind this development is not some 24-year-old geek from a supercomputer center, but the industry's most venerable leader after Bill Gates, not only Microsoft's most persistent critic and nemesis, but also its most eminent defeated rival: Bill Joy of Sun. In engineering Mosaic and Netscape Navigator, streamlining the communications functions and putting it all on the Net, Andreessen was following in the codesteps of Joy.

Joy was not only a founder of Sun Microsystems, he was also the primary champion of the Berkeley brand of Unix—BSD (Berkeley Software Distribution) Unix—that he husbanded as a student at the university. BSD Unix was not only Sun's essential software technology, but also the reference code for TCP/IP (Transmission Control Protocol/ Internet Protocol), the basic protocol stack of the Arpanet in its evolution toward the current Internet).

By upgrading the TCP/IP protocol to run on an ethernet rather than only on 50-kilobit-per-second Arpanet lines and then giving away the code, Bill Joy made the Internet possible. When Sun declared in 1988 that the network is the computer, the network it had in mind was run by Bill Joy's Network File System (NFS), and it incorporated TCP/IP. Says Eric Schmidt—Bill Joy's Berkeley colleague, now chief technical officer of Sun and leading prophet of the coming software inversion—"Sun was selling the Internet before the Internet was there."

Indeed, because Sun computers running BSD Unix were the most robust vessels for TCP/IP, the lion's share of all host computers on the Web are still Sun's, and Sun is experiencing an unexpected surge of earnings in the wake of the Web. Now the computer world is wielding Marc Andreessen's browser to rush toward the Net, wrenching the sphere from its moorings in Redmond, and allowing it to oscillate toward a new center in Silicon Valley. Even Bill Gates, the last holdout against Joy's network standard, is now bundling TCP/IP with Windows 95. Joy must feel that the industry is coming home at last.

Just as Gates ignited the personal computer market by writing Basic for the PC, Joy is launching a new era on the Net by supplying a suitable software language, Java. Joy foreshadowed Java at the 1990 *PC Forum* conference when he said, "Large programs are embarrassing because they have a fixed set of ideas and so much code that it's very difficult to change them. And they all tend to reflect existing metaphors, not the new metaphors. Everybody's using C++. That's a 'crufty' language. It's very hard to understand.

"I'm starting a small group to try to do something small—Sun Aspen Smallworks. I believe it's possible to do small systems of a few hundred thousand lines of code that live in this world of persistent distributed objects with open protocols [and] make an incredible difference—much more than an extra 100,000 lines on a 10-million-line system. So I'm looking for a few great hackers."

The one he found was redoubtable Sun engineer James Gosling. Called by John Doerr of Kleiner Perkins "perhaps the world's greatest living programmer," Gosling is a bearded man with shaggy blondish hair. He displays a subtly wounded look that is possibly the effect of a career that, to that point, had consisted mostly of brilliant failures. But, like Joy, Gosling was eager to do something small; to bring Sun into the world of consumer electronics where a large program used no more than a few thousand lines. In 1992, the company spun out a subsidiary named FirstPerson Inc. to pursue this market.

The goal was to conceive a way to take news, images, animations and other real-time functions in cell sites and base stations and download them to handheld devices such as digital cellular phones. But with the Newton fiasco, personal digital assistants began to fall from favor and Sun and the rest of the lemmings decided to pursue the suddenly seductive siren of interactive TV. Again, they would use the Java (at the time called "Oak") programming language, this time running not on cellular phones, but in set-top boxes. Here, too, the programs would have to be elegant and compact to use the sparse memories affordable for a consumer appliance. However, like Jim Clark—and everyone else—Sun would soon discover that interactivity merely offers cosmetics for the corpse of a dying television industry.

At this point, the project was in turmoil and former Apple designer Wayne Rosing, its first manager, was on his way out. In May of last year, Sun technical chief Eric Schmidt entered the breach, collapsed the set-top project into a joint venture with Thomson Consumer Electronics, which had bought RCA, and summoned Joy from Aspen. Joy returned and spent the entire summer last year in Palo Alto working with Schmidt and Gosling to figure out a strategy for Java. As the work proceeded, it became clear that the characteristics of a language suitable for PDAs not only gratified Joy's Laws of software, but also fit almost perfectly the needs of the Web.

Like many technology projects that seem to spring full-blown from the brow of a genius, Java is in fact the fruit of a near-lifelong quest. Gosling's career began at age 14 in Calgary when, during a high school tour, he memorized the code to the locks on the doors of the computer center at the University of Calgary. He then regularly admitted himself to read computer texts and use the DEC PDP-8s. He became so proficient that he was hired a year later by Digital Equipment to write machine code to be used for analyses of data on the aurora borealis from Isis satellites.

Going on to Carnegie Mellon University to study under the eminent Robert Sproull and Raj Reddy, he wrote a text editor called EMACS, a Pascal compiler and a thesis entailing the creation of a program to do drawings of levers and strings in visual, interactive models. After graduation in 1981, he joined an IBM lab in Pittsburgh, where he developed the Andrew Windows system. The first major program that could control a window on a computer remotely across a network, it never found a home. But it launched Gosling on a 15-year struggle with the challenge of how to send programs across a network that could be executed on other computers.

Gosling had a breakthrough in 1983 at a Sun Microsystems conference at the Red Lion in San Jose. There, Joy observed Gosling's Andrew Windows System dramatically outperforming a workstation running Sun View, and began a concerted effort to recruit him. Soon after, Gosling came to Sun to develop a remote windows system called NeWS (Networked Extensible Windows System). Initially received with great critical acclaim in the industry, it was eventually blocked by the X-Windows consortium despite performing far more efficiently over a network. Long a student of object-oriented programming beginning with the Simula language, Gosling followed his NeWS project with a compound document architecture, joining text and images. It, too, garnered much praise and paltry use.

Then came Sun's ill-fated pursuit of consumer electronic products. Gosling set out to develop appropriate programs in C++. But it soon became clear to him that this language failed on nearly all the crucial criteria. In particular, it was neither reliable nor secure, which, funnily enough, turned out to be two sides of the same coin. "The gun you shoot the burglar with can also shoot you in the foot." That was C++. It had pointer code that allowed rogue programs to invade and corrupt a target operating system.

So Gosling began revising C++ code into something that has been termed "C++ minus minus." Returning to the inspiration of Andrew and NeWS, he adapted the language to enable real-time operations across a network. In order to run a variety of different programs on a variety of linked devices, from set-top boxes to palmtop remotes, he made it inherently platform-neutral and nomadic. It would have to be a language at home on a network.

The project ended with Java, an efficient programming language that is safe, simple, reliable and real-time, yet familiar to anyone who has used C or C++. Designed for PDAs on infrared networks, it turned out to be perfectly adapted for the Internet. Many of Java's virtues are made possible by the fact that it is interpreted rather than compiled—that means that it is translated line by line in real time in the user's computer rather than converted to machine language in batch mode by the software vendor.

Most languages are written in two stages. The first is source code, couched at a level of abstraction that rarely reveals its purposes or algorithmic procedures. Normally, source code is proprietary and not revealed to the user.

The second stage is compilation. The compiler translates the abstractions of the source code into "binaries"—the machine language of a particular computer, locked into the set of instructions that its central processing unit can perform.

Java, by contrast, is compiled not to an instruction set peculiar to a particular microprocessor but to a virtual machine or generic computer. Putting the language into an intermediate binary form allows creation of programs that are not locked into any particular hardware platform, but that can still be adapted to run fast. The intermediate code is translated line by line by a software program called an interpreter located in the target computer.

Java's interpreters take up a parsimonious 45 kilobytes of memory. Sun already has Java interpreters in the works for Microsoft Windows 95, the Mac, Windows NIT and several flavors of Unix. Netscape will include the appropriate interpreter in future versions of the Netscape browser. This means that any program written in Java will be portable to any common computer platform.

On the surface, this portability does not seem remarkable. All programs written in C, C++ or other compiled languages can be ported to any target platform simply by running the source code through the appropriate compiler, just as Mosaic was compiled for various platforms at the NCSA. The difference is that Java can be "compiled" line by line in real time. That is, it is interpreted in byte-level code in the client machine. This makes all the difference.

It means that programs no longer have to reside in the machine where they are used, or be written for that machine in order to be executed by it. Potentially, a Java program can reside anywhere on the entire Internet and be executed by any computer attached to the Internet. The little interpreters—sure to become cheap and ubiquitous as they are distributed by Netscape and by other suppliers of browsers—make Java programs "dynamically portable" in real time.

Dynamically portable programs are suitable for a nomadic existence on the Net, rather than a mere settled life on the desktop. Java thus emancipates software from computer architecture. It offers a software paradigm radically different from the Microsoft model, which is based not only on static compilation, but on often-concealed, proprietary source code.

Suddenly, the entire world of new software is potentially available to every computer owner. Rather than being restricted to the set of programs you own, you can use any program on the Net, just as now you can tap any information on the Net. You not only have data at your fingertips, you have programs at your fingertips. This means "executable content," as Joy describes it and as John Gage demonstrated in his speech at the West St. in Francis Hotel this June. Whether a film, a graph, an animation, a real-time bit stream on the Nasdaq ticker or the Reuters wire, a virtual reality visualization, or a game, it can be downloaded to your machine with its program in tow.

Owning the operating system and associated tool libraries becomes irrelevant to selling applications. Owning the application or channel becomes irrelevant to selling the content. To the extent that Java or a similar language prevails, software becomes truly open for the first time. The Microsoft desktop becomes a commodity; the Intel microprocessor becomes peripheral—the key "microprocessor" is the software code in the Java interpreter.

Interpreted or not, however, nomadic programs will not be permitted to range the Net unless they are also secure programs. By several judicious alterations of C++ procedures, Gosling made Java above all a secure language. Many viruses depend on taking an integer in the program and using it to "point" to a low address in the memory where operating code resides. Java removes this pointer conversion function. In addition, incorporated into the Java interpreter is a code verifier. As soon as an application shows up in a machine, the interpreter does an instant virus scan. Finally, when Java binary arrives at a machine, it will bear an RSA data signature that verifies the source of the code and guarantees that it has not been altered or corrupted.

These security provisions make Java programs the first certifiable citizens of the Net. As Java interpreters become ubiquitous, any application program that is anchored on a particular platform and desktop will eventually become a cripple, like a pro athlete who fears to fly.

The computer hollows out, and you no longer are concerned with its idiosyncrasies, its operating system, its instruction set, even its resident applications. Instead, you can focus on content—on the world rather than on the desktop architecture. If you want to run a helicopter model on your screen, you don't have to worry about whether you have AutoCAD on your hard drive. You can run a video of the helicopter without owning the right decoder, whether Indeo (Intel's standard) or MPEG-4 (designed for portable appliances) or dynamic JPEG. The helicopter flies over the Net with its own executable code. The network is no longer a threatening place. If you want to use a program from Finland, you don't have to worry that it will introduce a malignant virus to your machine.

Your computer will never be the same. No longer will the features of the desktop decide the features of the machine. No longer will the size of your hard drive or the database in your LAN server determine the reach of your information processing. No longer will the programs in your machine determine the functions you can perform. The network is the computer. The computer becomes a peripheral to the Internet and the Web.

Since the release of Java and a demonstration Web browser called HotJava, written in the language on the Sun home page, Gosling has experienced the kind of sudden Internet celebrity undergone by Andreessen and Bina. Unlike Andreessen, he seems somewhat baffled by it all. But in the long run, his contribution may be greater. Browsers and servers may come and go, but successful new languages are extremely rare. Java, or something like it, is the key to a truly interactive Internet and a fully hollowed-out computer.

Recently, Bill Joy made a presentation to the Sun board, outlining an upgrade path for the future of the language. Joy is resolved that Java will not go the way of Andrew and NeWS. Like Jim Clark, he has even turned to the troubled supercomputer arena to find a treasure trove of new hackers. Sun hired some 20 new programmers from the recently defunct but boldly pioneering Thinking Machines and Kendall Square Research. Presumably, they can learn to think small.

Gosling shakes his head at all the uproar. He now finds himself falling thousands of messages behind in his e-mail. Linked to the Net by a mere T1 line, even Sun's Java server broke down under the overload. But Gosling himself seems to be holding up better. His speaking schedule has multiplied to a rate of three talks a week. Scores of people tell him they are using the language as a replacement for C, for IR (information resource) tools and for other general-purpose applications. Giant Japanese companies such as Sony and Sega besiege him. Finally, late in June, even Berners-Lee gave Java his imprimatur as "one of the most exciting things happening on the Web right now."

A movie buff, Gosling sees Java, Netscape and similar programs changing the image of the cypersphere from an alien and menacing dystopia, as depicted famously in *Blade Runner*, into a realm resembling *Star Trek*, where computers are trusted tools. Perhaps this transformation will favor the emergence of the amiable and gregarious young Marc Andreessen as the paladin of cyberspace, replacing the fiercely brilliant but widely feared Bill Gates.

But as Andreessen admits, a more likely outcome is a massive move by Microsoft onto the Net where the two will enter battle with scores of contenders. This month, Microsoft announced an array of Internet services, under the rubric Blackbird, with many interesting features. But it works only with Microsoft Network Services, which will not become truly widespread for another year. Beginning with virtually no market share and a year or so behind, Gates will become an underdog at last. Perhaps even the Justice Department will notice. In the age of the hollowed-out computer, the king of the desktop rules an emigrating empire.

15

George Gilder and His Critics—II

Every now and then, timing is all. Take George Gilder's Aug. 28 Forbes ASAP *piece, "The Coming Software Shift." Lucky* Forbes *readers got their copies in mid-August, smack between the year's two biggest technology events—Netscape's record-hot IPO and the release of Windows 95.*

Gilder used the timing to explain why creative energy and profits in desk-top software would soon migrate from Microsoft to the Internet and toward companies like Netscape. Needless to say, Gilder's point is controversial, drawing fire and praise from a host of computerdom's biggest names

NATHAN MYHRVOLD
Group Vice-President,
Applications and Content Group, Microsoft

As usual, George Gilder's diagnosis is dead-on. The software industry functions by turning its fuel-cheap processing power, as described by Moore's Law—into value for consumers. In turn, software soon soaks up CPU power, fueling market demand, which sustains Moore's Law. The software-hardware twosome is about to become a ménage à trois, with the addition of communications. The three-way cycle will drive growth and value creation in each area at an even faster rate than we've seen so far.

I begin to differ when George frames the computer industry in lurid terms of battle. In reality, computer industry shifts are quite dull affairs. The multidecade decline of the mainframe has been a lot like watching a glacier melt. A leading company fails to invest in new technology and ultimately finds its product obsolete. New entrants might capitalize on this, but most—including Netscape and HotJava—blaze new trails instead. When an established leader does fall, the proximate cause is almost always slow suicide or atrophy through internal mismanagement; not the wounds of combat.

The Internet means opportunity for all software developers—new and old. Mosaic and its commercial descendants are currently at the center of the cyclones, but their day in the sun will pass just as surely as it did for previous Internet standards like Gopher or FTP. The instant rise of Mosaic and Netscape foreshadows what George might dub another Law of the Telecosm: In a world with easy electronic distribution, it is very hard to hang onto your position—easy come, easy go.

A particular weakness of HTML is that it is a data format no different in spirit from the protocols of 1970s-vintage mainframe terminals. Next-generation Internet software will use programmability at both ends of the pipe. Java is noteworthy and may play a role, but its hype falls into a very old trap. Every new programming language is heralded as a breakthrough. Fortran was going to computerize science and engineering, Cobol would revolutionize business, and Lisp (and later, Prolog) would deliver us to the promised land of AI. The reality is quite different—new languages offer some modest benefits, but all of the real value resides in the programs created with them.

Finally, I must comment on the obsession with finding the next Gates. Bill has been my friend and colleague for nearly 10 years, so the topic is familiar. Writing great software and founding a company is a first step, but that only matches Bill Gates circa 1976. The secret that made the Bill Gates of 1995 is to have the technical and business skills to develop new product lines repeatedly. Microsoft is unique in this accomplishment. Our competition is invariably single-product companies, or ex post facto assemblages of them. I don't doubt that the next Gates will eventually appear, and the Internet may fuel her rise, but it's one hell of a tough act to follow.

SCOTT MCNEALY
Chief Executive Officer,
Sun Microsystems

I'd like to compliment George Gilder for so eloquently articulating Sun's nearly decade-old credo: "The network is the computer."

I believe in Gilder's thesis that we are, indeed, at the onset of the age of network-accessed, disposable software. Desktop operating systems, utilities and applications will soon be relegated to peripheral status. The network will be the operating system, and, as Gilder points out, this change is being brought about the almost incomprehensible momentum of the Internet. The ultimate change agent, Gilder suggests, may in fact be Java, yet another technology that Sun has offered to the industry in an open and barrier-free way.

Java is a programming language that creates the first true network operating system for the globe, because it is safe, secure, robust, fault tolerant and, among many other attributes, platform-independent. Here's how we see it playing out. Three computer science students from Berkeley hacking code late at night will create a Java word processing program. Let's call it "NetWord."

They put it on their Web server at http://www.netword.com. It will be free because these kids want fame first, knowing that will lead to fortune as with their hero, Marc Andreessen. It will be 100,000 lines of code versus 1.5 million for WordPerfect, because NetWord isn't bogged down with all the APIs [applications programming interfaces] and other extraneous baggage of typical applications that must interoperate with a specific operating system, or have become overfeatured.

So you're shopping for a new word processing program. You've seen the ads offering Word on sale for $249. Of course, you know that means you get the privilege of upgrading in a year for another $89. Your buddy sends an e-mail and says check out NetWord. You take a test drive. It works! Cool! You are not alone. A few million others have heard about NetWord. Now the makers have a following and in a few months they start a company and offer NetWord 2.0 for a mere $2 per copy.

You and 10 million other avid followers have no qualms about paying the nominal fee. It sure beats the competition. In fact, at that price, you'll be checking the NetWord home page monthly to download the latest copy. As of the three college kids, they are now millionaires.

Suddenly the OS that controls the CPU on your desktop is a legally of an old paradigm, relegated to a secondary tier in the software food chain. This means that Microsoft is now a severely overpriced personal productivity tools applications vendor with an OS business that is no longer able to "captivate" the end user by being the only platform to run desired applications. Keeping API's secret won't work anymore. Controlling the interfaces won't work anymore. The wall is down and there's no turning back.

So where will that leave Microsoft? Scrambling to explain to investors why the company's market cap is 10 times revenues, scrambling to explain how they can survive in the world of disposable, run anywhere Internet software. Of course, the marketing muscle up in the Northwest will try to figure out a way to play in this space. But playing now means playing on a level field. The rules are the same for everyone. They're spelled TCP/IP, Mosaic, WWW, HTTP, HTML and now Java—all the open protocols and languages that make up the Internet.

It's barrier-free computing. It's consumer choice. It's a free-market economy in the information age, finally. From there, just about anything is possible.

LARRY TESLER

Vice President and Chief Scientist,
Apple Computer

To report technology history accurately is a difficult task requiring percipience, perspiration and perspective. Gilder has done it. He has combed through the attics of computing and assembled for the family a gripping album of the events and circumstances that created the phenomenon we call the Web.

If the past is buried in clutter, however, the future is still more difficult to perceive, especially before the dazzle of Netscape and Java. In my view, the Web is a catalyst, but it is not all that matters about the Internet. The browser is to the Internet what the spread-sheet was to the desktop computer.

Mosaic is the new VisiCalc, Netscape Navigator the new Lotus 1-2-3. Microsoft would like to make Explorer the new Excel. Wall Street is as enamored with Netscape today as it was with Lotus when that company went public. Netscape is a winner, but is the winner? With the aid of its ally, the Sun King, will it inherit the throne? Not necessarily.

Where is the proprietary operating system that runs not merely the equivalent of spreadsheets, but thousands of applications? Where is the PI that some megalomaniac weaves into, well, a web, to attract, ensnare and ultimately consume hapless applications developers and most of the profits they worked so hard to earn?

I hope that the nameless idealists who create the Internet on a daily basis succeed in their resistance to central control more successfully than did their computer club counter-parts a decade ago. If they do, there may be no single successor to Bill Gates. If they don't then it's anyone's guess who will maneuver into that role. The drama promises to remain gripping.

HOWARD ANDERSON
Founder, Yankee Group

George, George, George—what took you so long?

What is so surprising is that you were so surprised that the Netscape revolution may supersede the Microsoft revolution.

Think back! Fifteen years ago, the office automation hype was about word processing, but the real revolution was electronic mail. Today 36 million Americans get their mail elec-tronically and no one really gives a damn about new word processing packages.

Your beatification of Marc Andreessen is a little premature, don't you think? There are many visionaries, but few company builders. We in the venture community intuitively know that there is little likelihood that the visionaries will turn into the operating managers new industries need. Other than Gates, who? What you have proposed (correctly) is that the peripheral becomes the major focus. Five years ago, the thought that IBM and the clone industry would become "value-added resellers" for Intel and Microsoft would have been heresy. Now you are suggesting that the Internet will become the major focus—and Intel and Microsoft will be relegated to that "value-added" focus. You are right. Nonetheless, quite frankly, the Internet needs three years to be ready for prime time. Meanwhile, we will go through a sine curve of hype, backlash, then reality. Just when the naysayers sound and seem logical, the Internet will begin to fulfill its destiny, and that destiny is to become the most potent force in technology. And George, invite your mother to dinner for me. Of your technobabble family, she seems the most interesting!

JOHN PERRY BARLOW
Rancher, Writer, Web Guru,
Grateful Dead Lyricist

I am enormously encouraged by George Gilder's discovery of the World Wide Web. I'm tempted to stoop to catty remarks about how long it took him. Lately, he's seemed almost alone among intelligent commentators in continuing to credit the myth of the information superhighway—a belief that you can sustain only if you don't know about the Web or if your perceptions have been profoundly altered by the reality-distortion fields generated within large content conglomerates, telcos or cable companies, or the vast cluelessness that is Washington, D.C.

In fact, anyone using the phrase *information superhighway* is almost certainly in the thrall of some large and doomed institution, or is a complete nimrod who knows only what he hears on television. Which is, for obvious reasons, filled with people who believe in it. They're not going to be roadkill on it, by golly. They're going to find that on-ramp . . . hey, they're going to be the on-ramp!

No way, San Jose! The future of the Industrial Era media megaliths, whether Disney, Time-Warner or, more to the point, Microsoft, will arrive over the Web, not the mythical infobahn. The Web will be the end of them. We are up against a discontinuous leap as we hit the next layer of interactive complexity, both in software and in thought. It has now reached a point where about the only way to develop all the scripts, scraps and code objects from which the next World Wide Operating System (WWOS) will assemble itself is to grow them in the distributed, massively parallel amalgam of minds and processes that make up the Net.

The Web is alive, and filled with life, nearly as mysterious, complex and, well, natural as a primordial swamp. Microsoft is a factory. You can't manufacture life in a factory. You have to grow it in nature. This is not so new, really. Bell Labs' proprietary claims notwithstanding, I take the first WWOS, Unix, as proof that if enough graduate students type into enough terminals long enough, they will eventually produce an operating system. And given enough graduate students, you can be sure that somewhere among them will be a Bill Joy or a Marc Andreessen. In accordance with Joy's Law, they won't be working at Microsoft.

Furthermore, the Web and most browsers give them a way to crib from one another, lavishly and easily. All that's necessary to see the code that generated what's on your screen is to click: "View source." All that's necessary to get your page employing some of the same innovations is to copy and paste. This creates an environment of dense autocollaboration. To see how productive it's already been in less than two years of existence, get on the Web now. This will make the micromputer revolution look like a good start.

Gilder's article is a fine thing. I've been talking about the End of Microsoft for a couple of years and have felt like a madman parading a ragged sign. When it starts coming from such impeccable seersuckers as George Gilder, it may be time to short a little of that Microsoft stock.

BERT C. ROBERTS, JR.
Chairman & CEO, MCI Communications

Gilder is dead-on right that hardware and operating systems will become subordinate to the network; that the network will, in effect, become subordinate to the network; that the network will, in effect, become everything and the only thing. And he's right, too, about the evolution and impact of the Internet and the resultant focus on content.

Gilder's allusions to Gates and Microsoft, however, yield a very real question: Can they deal with the coming transformation? Doing so will require a new vision of the future and a new understanding of merging industries, evolving ways of computing, and some hard new facts. Here's a key one: Companies that don't address and act on the need for collaborative work from a widening universe will fall hard—and fast.

Confronting any rival with the market dominance of Microsoft will be very difficult. But trying to run in place could be even harder. The challenge is not only to understand, as Gilder writes, "that your computer will never be the same"—but also that it's your company that will never be the same.

DAN LYNCH
Founder, Interop Chairman, Cybercash

Gilder has got it figured out. His article is dead-on about how the Internet is the architecture of the future for information dissemination. Want proof?

Pouring huge resources into its Microsoft Network and Microsoft Navigator offerings, Microsoft admits that it does not really know the business model for how to make money in this new arena, but it is determined to get on the playing field in a big way. Meanwhile, Sun is too hooked on hardware profits to make a new fortune on this round. No doubt that Java is the right technology for making the Net be the center of the universe. Sun should simply spin that group out as a new company unfettered by dragging along hardware.

The only fault I find with Gilder's article is his picking Marc Andreessen as the next Bill Gates. Marc only has a few percent of Netscape stock; Bill has tons of Microsoft stock. Marc will make a lot of others much richer and he surely won't suffer, but he will not become a feared/loved mogul because of Netscape. Maybe he and Bill Joy should bolt and start their own company? Marc is still younger than Gates was when Microsoft got its plum from IBM.

I asked Marc one question when I met him during his brief stint at EIT in Menlo Park. What was the central design assumption for Mosaic? He said 45 megabits per second! I asked why. He said that it makes it easy to program because you do not have to develop hairy mechanisms to mask out the slowness of the network. Then commercial reality set in when he and Jim Clark got together and they recentered their Netscape Navigator for the 14.4 kilobit world, thus giving us the MS-DOS of the Internet. It is a good start, but

Marc was right about 45 megabits—only it is not just to make the programmer's life easy, it is to make the consumer's life joyful.

NICHOLAS NEGROPONTE
Director, MIT Media Lab Author,
Being Digital

Once again, George Gilder's got it right. His guide to the past and future of the Net is on the digital dime and, as best I hear from my colleagues at the MIT Media Lab, Java is really hot. We're betting our house on it.

The Net, however, is no place for kings. It is a collective intelligence that will work in spite of government and any attempts to control it. No Carnegies, Rockefellers or Harrimans this time. The white envelope, George, is empty. When Larry Roberts invented the Internet in 1969, his decentralist approach made the idea interesting for the military, because it was fail-safe. More than 25 years later, after the Vietnam and Cold wars, the Net is also safe from dominance of any kind. Supercomputer émigrés, Unix hackers and Media Lab alumni have moved it forward (not Windows or Mac users), because they are made of the right stuff. This is serious media and computer science, not the world of Windows applications.

Here is where George is wrong. The next Bill Gates is not Marc Andreessen. Yes, Marc will do very well. However, if you were a sucker to pay $75 per share for Netscape at the opening on Aug. 9, keep it to yourself (if I hadn't been traveling between Rio and Buenos Aires that day, I would have sold short and made 25 points in a few minutes). There will be many browsers, hundreds of them. Today, I'll bet on Niki Grauso's, which will come out in 37 languages. Browsers are the surface of a much deeper phenomenon.

Sun Microsystems has it right: Java. Why? Because Java is a language and many smart people will express themselves and invent new applications in that language. Netscape is but one awning on the Virtual Boulevard of Digital Cafes. Java is the coffee.

ANDY GROVE
President and CEO, Intel

George, George, George—you haven't met a new technology you didn't like, and conversely you haven't met an older one that you don't think is ready to be toppled by the new.

Do you remember when you wrote that "specialized computers-to-a-chip will become the prevailing product category"? Well, it didn't happen. Not that silicon compilers were back, not that ASICs are insignificant, but the general-purpose computer that you pooh-poohed has become the prevailing paradigm of the subsequent six years since the publication of *Microsm*. Now you predict that the PC will become a peripheral attached to an all-knowing, all-powerful Internet. I don't think so, George. Not that the Internet won't be important; I look at it as one of the most important applications that will be used on my PC in the future. And that is the difference between us. What matters to me is my computer. I use my computer. I am using a word processor to write this response; I use e-mail to communicate with hundreds of coworkers from my desk and from my home; I use CompuServe to get updated industry news; I use ProShare conferencing to do business with partners across the world in real time. And I use Netscape to check out a new home page that I have hears about.

A couple of years from now, I may spend more time in the Net-based applications than in some of the others, just as today I spend my time differently among my applications than I did five years ago. My computer will evolve and adapt (as PCs have been so good at doing) to the ever-changing mix of applications with which I work.

You are wrong in another area. Implicit in so much of your writing is a fantasy: the notion of high-bandwidth communications reaching every PC. Today my computer is connected with ISDN to other computers; it is also connected to LANs and to an ordinary phone line. Five years from now, my computer will still be connected to an ordinary phone line and to ISDN, but also to broadband networks via a cable modem and to an ATM network to reach other luck computer users; and probably to do some kind of wireless connection. Ten years from now, it will be another set of communications transport media. But it will never be a single superconnection, because goodness doesn't arrive in a sing step. It comes a little at a time.

To be sure, if God erased all computers and networks and forced us to start from scratch, we would certainly come a lot closer to your utopian view of broadband to the computer, with intelligence cleverly distributed between network and computers. But then, if God erased New York City, it would not be rebuilt the way it is today. In real life, both cities and computer networks evolve, increment by valuable increment.

The bottom line is this: The magic of the PC business is that there is a computer that I can look at, put my hands on and say, "This computer is mine, and it opens the universe of tens of millions of computers to me through its screen and keyboard—and whatever connection scheme is available to me." Don't bury this magic; cherish it.

ANDY KESSLER

Partner, Unterberg Harris

Once again, my colleague and trend-tender, George Gilder, has eloquently set forth the next wave of innovation. But in the process, the PC or client device will not be hollowed out. Rather than living with fast servers and PCs acting as relatively dumb terminals, which is the architecture of Mosaic and the Web and even Java so far, the endgame is instead a network where every device is a server, even your own lousy PC. This means terribly intelligent and "fat" clients, enabling rather than just hanging off the network.

Moreover, it is much too early to be handing out crowns to the new kings of the network. George's trends are dead-on, but the kings are coronated by natural selection, not by just showing up and claiming the throne.

STEPHEN MANES

Columnist, *New York Times*, Author of *Gates*

Slow down, George! Sake's alive! Ma missed signs four and five!

What sprang to mind upon reading Gilder's latest panegyric was not the rosey technology future, but a Burma Shave ditty from my youth. I don't know Colombian beans about Java, but I've been watching this industry too long not to reach for my methane detector when somebody announces in the language of corporate propaganda that "your computer will never be the same." This particular locution almost always signifies too much time spent amid the rarefied gases that hove around chairmen and CEOs.

A particularly toxic dose is to be suspected when the proclaimed agent in change is an interpreted language. Interpreted languages have a long line of champions, not the least of whom is that great Basic patron, William Henry Gates III (who seems less "Archimdean" than Charles Foster Kancan). But their magic has its limits, as Gates himself found out when Microsoft developed its Multiplan spreadsheet on the interpreted runs-on-everything (but kinda slow) model and watched the compiled runs-on-DOS-only (but really fast) Lotus 1-2-3 force some massive recalculations at Microsoft headquarters. Wasn't it only a few months ago that the press went gaga over General Magic's interpreted Telescript, which now reportedly has, uh, some problems?

The runs-everywhere promise of interpreted languages generally manages to get broken when it hits some Least Common Denominator—say, another LCD, the liquid crystal display. If you want to run Gilder's helicopter model on your crappy little Personal Digital Assistant, you may not have to worry about having AutoCAD on your hard drive, but you probably will have to worry about having a hard drive, not to mention a screen with enough detail and contrast to make the thing look vaguely like the original. The IBM PC version of Multiplan was no prize, but it looked and felt great compared with the on that ran on the toy Commodore 64. Software is never truly independent of the hardware it runs on, interpreting programs tend to run with all the speed of a tricycle, and bandwidth is still a long, long way from being free.

JESSE BERST

Editor, *Windows Watcher*

Mr. Gilder's article on the coming software shift is 10% fact and 90% wishful thinking. Fact: Windows's dominance will come to an end when it is rendered irrelevant by a new platform. Wishful thinking: hoping the new platform will be owned by somebody other than Microsoft.

Gilder's fantasy of a Microsoft-free computer industry might come to pass if Bill Gates spent his time in his vault counting his money. He doesn't. He obsessively watches the horizon for threats to his hegemony. When he spots a danger, he works feverishly to use his current monopolies to leverage his way into the new arena. He spotted the Internet danger about two years ago and has already spent more than $100 million to make sure that Microsoft isn't left out.

Yes, George, we will all eventually emigrate from the Windows desktop empire. But when we get to the new promised land, we're likely to find that Bill Gates has already acquired the prime real estate.

SCOTT COOK
Chairman, Intuit

Gilder chronicles invention like no other. He finds the history in the most recent events. He finds the significance in invention before that significance is real or realized. But Paul Saffo of the Institute for the Future tells how the innovations that reshape our lives follow their enabling inventions by years or decades.

Gutenberg invented movable type. It took another 40 years for an entrepreneur named Aldus to assemble what created book publishing as we know it. Marconi invented radio exactly 100 years ago. It took another 25 years for entrepreneurs in Pittsburgh and New York to create broadcasting. It was through broadcasting that radio reshaped our lives.

None of us expect it will taken 25 years for this chapter of the Internet story. But I hope Gilder will tackle the next question: How will these inventions change our lives?

GORDON BELL
Research Fellow, Microsoft,
Inventor of Digital VAX computer

Telecosm, like microcosm, is another interesting Gilder story. Like transistors that follow Moore's Law, bandwidth increases at 60% per year. The Gilder Fallacy is that transistors and bandwidth will also be cheap. This may be true in the very long run, and I hope to live long enough to see it. Meanwhile, the memory cartel has kept prices constant at $50 per megabyte and the telephone cartel has metered out bits in 64 kilobit POTS [plain old telephone service] = chunks for decades. For example, full ISDN lines (two voice lines) cost at least twice POTS. ISDN is also very inelegant since it makes poor use of the precious last mile, and is not adequate or scaleable. Only modems, created by a new datacom industry, have gotten faster.

My version of the Internet story is at http://www.uvc.com. It is called "Internet 1.0 (Arpanet), 2.0 (today), and 3.0 (what we need)," subtitled: "It's bandwidth and Symmetry, Stupid." In 1987, I chaired the cross-agency federal task force that proposed NREN [National Research and Education Network], aka NII [National Information Infrastructure], aka GII [Global Information Infrastructure]. Our recommendation was "that an advanced network be designed and developed to interconnect academic, industrial and government research facilities in the U.S.," with the plan for a factor of a ten thousandfold increase in bandwidth by 2002.

Things have gone according to our "vision" to maintain constant doubling for the last 25 years. Thank goodness Berners-Lee created the http://www network, aka the Web, so that Andreessen could build Mosaic and its viewers; that's the serendipity part. Public funding of research (this time at Illinois' National Center for Supercomputing Applications) "saved" us again.

Intermixed in Gilder's piece is another story about a new Sun programming language, Java, which when combined with the Web, will render Microsoft ineffective. If that's the case, then Sun needn't support the anti-Microsoft legal consortium and should concentrate on toppling it with their products. However, as a newly hired Microsoft researcher, anxious to work his way down the corporate hierarchy to programmer, I hope that he's wrong about our undoing.

Microsoft is its own greatest enemy if it fails to make every product embrace the Internet. In an organization that has to keep with chaotic hardware platform evolution, having an external standard and threat is the best thing that could happen. Of the 50-plus million Word and PowerPoint users, however, perhaps 10,000 will see Java as an Internet development tool. More likely it's a tool for developing Internet tools. Word already produced HTML pages and PowerPoint should have the goal of being the most used Internet content editor. I'll bet that Windows NT (created by Dave Cutler, who also happens to be the world's greatest programmer) will become the "standard" server platform, just as the Wintel platform, like the Gilders use, runs nearly all the viewers. As for staying in the center of the sphere——Gilder's right: Andreessen's there, but I wouldn't count Gates out . . . yet.

CHARLES MANN

Contributing Editor, *Atlantic Monthly*

The vision Mr. Gilder proposes is wonderfully attractive—who could not like the idea of a future in which nobody has to struggle with the maddening limitations and incompatibilities of the PC? But the idea of plugging everyone into the Net for their work and play poses problems of its own, pride of place perhaps going to security. The number of Internet crackers and wannabe crackers is rising; worse, the very speed and ubiquity of the Net means that each new break-in technique becomes instantly available to all of them, as the spread of Root Kit an its analogues attests. Putting the whole world online will increase the opportunity for mischief enormously.

At present, we have two basic means for fending off these guys—firewalls and encryption. Put crudely, firewalls are small computers that stand between you and the Net, scanning for unwanted incoming bits. (CheckPoint Software Technologies in Israel, makes one of the more interesting examples). In one way or another, firewalls intercept and read parts of every Internet packet that comes your way. If everyone's software is based somewhere "out there" on the web, the computing power and bandwidth required to filter every screen dump and rewrite through the firewall is interesting to contemplate. A worse problem comes when the information is encrypted—how is the firewall to read it without decoding it? And if it does decode it, aren't you decoding information outside the intended recipient network? It's a problem.

For this reason, most Net aficionados argue that some form of public-key encryption is the answer. Leaving aside the extraordinary reserves of computing power that will be required to encrypt every bit of info going in and out of every system in the world—and the even more vexing question of who will pay for it, a subject on which I am not nearly as sanguine as Mr. Gilder—one has to worry about the possibilities of breakthroughs such as those reported recently in *Science*, where researchers took advantage of the vagaries of quantum mechanics to reduce the time required to factor large numbers enormously. Because encryption in its present form depends on the huge amount of time it now takes to factor such numbers, these advances have dismaying implications.

We could face a future in which advances in encryption and decoding race each other, Red Queen-style—hardly a situation favoring the confident use of a global network. Until these problems are resolved, they will be a big damper on the kind of bustling, productive, interconnected future that Mr. Gilder and I both hope is just around the corner.

BOB METCALFE
Ethernet Inventor and 3Corm Founder,
InfoWorld Columnist

To refind Gilder's model for how Gates gets dethroned, I'll briefly explain how Gates made his billions. Gates came of age just as Grosch's Law about the scale economies of bigger computers was giving way to Moore's Law about the volume economies of smaller computers. Gates saw early and clearly the profit potential in controlling standards, like the horizontal protocol standards for communicating back and forth among computers, and like the vertical interface standards for communicating up and down between applications software and underlying computer operating systems software.

I went with horizontal protocol standards, namely Ethernet, which I advanced by giving it away to all other comers. Gates went with vertical interface standards, namely IBM's PC-DOS, which he advanced more shrewdly by giving it away to IBM but selling it to all comers. To build the value of PC-DOS, Gates gathered a huge flock of application software developers and got them committed to his interface standards. Then by controlling changes to DOS's interfaces, upgrading them step-by-step all the way up to Windows 95, Gates was also able to sell them over and over again in upgraded forms.

With that money, he could exploit inside knowledge of his own interface changes to pick off one after another of the larger application developers, like those in word processing, spreadsheets, presentations and, now, electronic mail and databases. His only major failure to date has been in networking, where he's failed so far to kill Novell. That failure involved control of Novell's protocol standards rather than interface standards where Microsoft is king.

Gilder says that Moore's Law is giving way to Metcalfe's Law, which projects the runaway value of numerous internetworked computers. According to Gilder's point of view, this exponential effect shifts importance from the vertical programming interface standards upon which the Redmond Rockefeller's fortune is built to horizontal communication protocol standards which the likes of Marc Andreessen might be expected to dethrone Gates, perhaps becoming the Microsoft of the Internet.

But Gates, of course, aims to be the Microsoft of the Internet. And he need only broaden his tried-and-true interface strategy to include the protocols from the World Wide Web, now threatening his standards dominance. Gates has the advantage of his current Windows monopoly, which he is now trying to leverage into control of the Web—let's hope our antitrust sheepdogs eventually arrive on the scene. Andreessen and company have the disadvantage of coming from the virtuously open but fractious Unix world. Unless they can keep their Web standards act together, they will lose the Web to the Windows Microsoft Network in the same way they lost Unix to DOS.

MSN and Netscape will likely shape up to be the major opponents in the coming Web Wars. MSN is making its play to replace Berners-Lee's Web standards with its own under Blackbird. Microsoft is now giving away MSN browsers like Netscape and can be expected at some point to sell MSN servers and tools directly opposite Netscape's servers. Netscape, on the other hand, with its very busy Web pages is looking more and more like an on-line service in competition with MSN, advertising and all. I must say that this battle is one that my InfoWorld readers will enjoy, as the fierce competition will drive the Web toward its full potential. Gates doesn't need it, and certainly doesn't expect it from me, but I do have to defend him. Andreessen and company have not yet made their billions, and they now look innocently charming, gregarious and eager, attractive compared with the shrewd and intense Mr. Gates. But, I've seen close up what even $1 million can do to people, and frankly Gates handles his billions about as well as it is reasonable to expect.

STEPHEN S. ROACH

Chief Economist, Morgan Stanley & Co.

Gilder's gushing hype has finally come full circle. He has come to the key recognition that there's more to the information age than the alluring power of Moore's Law. This time-worn mantra of a vendor-driven rhetoric extols the miracles of performance of payback—the productivity paradox whereby startling advances in computational speed fail to deliver the value-added solutions that truly matter for society as a whole. But now

Gilder heralds a new "killer app" in user-friendly browsers and new "minimalist" programming languages such as Java.

But don't count on it—at least not yet. In the fast-track 1990s, technology must still come to grips with a profound upheaval in American lifestyles. For the first time ever, white-collar workers—fully two-thirds of the U.S. workforce—are being asked to up the ante of their own productivity contributions through longer and harder work, squeezing family and leisure time as never before in the last 50 years.

Surfing the Net in a quest for the "best" application—and learning how to use each of the new tools—takes considerable time. And that's the rub: Time-intensive surfing is in direct conflict with the harsh realities of a time-constrained era.

In the end, it all boils down to return. The average U.S. worker who has toiled under the burden of stagnant real wages for more than a decade will insist on measurable improvements in personal productivity before squandering ever-greater amounts of leisure and family time on an open-ended journey on the telecosm. However alluring the latest breakthroughs in electronic shopping, banking, and video selection may seem to be, my guess is that they don't meet the hurdle rate for the average American.

That's the crux of the dilemma that Gilder still doesn't get: The promises of the telecosm will ring hollow until new means of income generation and wealth creation for society as a whole are created. At best, a flexible software paradigm is merely another means to automate existing tasks. The big steps come with applications that truly change the functions of work and leisure. And they have yet to be taken.

LARRY ELLISON
Founder, CEO and Chairman,
Oracle Systems Corp.

I believe George has it half right.

The center of gravity is indeed shifting away from the personal computer and toward the network—specifically toward the Internet's World Wide Web.

Despite the Clinton administration's most determined regulatory efforts, networks are getting faster and cheaper. Various telecommunication bills pending in Congress will decrease regulation, increase competition and accelerate this trend. Cost and ease-of-use improvements, plus video capability, will make the World Wide Web as popular as the familiar TV and telephone networks for communication and commerce, as well as for information and entertainment. Bandwidth will expand exponentially and so will the quality and quantity of information on the Net. The information age will move from dawn to full daylight. And our world will be changed.

But probably not by Netscape: Wall Street and Mr. Gilder are greatly charmed by he most exciting startup since 3DO, but it is important to remember that Netscape's improbably $2.4 billion valuation comes without earnings or any quick hope thereof. In the absence of any commercial competition, Netscape was able to achieve a 70% ="market share" by distributing its browser for free via the Internet. When a clearly superior

Browser becomes available, people will replace their Netscape browser just the way they got it—with the touch of a button. The most important new feature announced for a future version of the Netscape browser is Sun's hot new Java programming language, which Sun is trying to make an open standard. We're all for it, but you don't get to be the next Microsoft by distributing Sun software and helping create open standards. You get to be Microsoft by creating your own proprietary standard, while convincing everybody it's actually an open standard. Fortunately, this trick usually works only once, so there will be no new Microsoft. One is quite enough, thank you.

Marc Andreessen is not Bill Gates. It's probably possible to be great without being Bill. But it takes a lot of work. Gates is the chairman of Microsoft, the CEO, its founder and the man who makes every key hiring decision. Andreessen is neither chairman (that's Jim Clark), nor CEO (that's Jim Barksdale), but a hired gun. Hired, in fact, by Jim Clark. History generally shows us only one Rockefeller per industry—the first one tends to get rid of future rivals. If a cosmic shift causes King Bill to lose his throne, it will not be filled by Andreessen or anybody else. There is no next Bill Gates—in software—at least.

STEVE CASE
President and CEO, America Online

I have a simple request: Let's not forget about the customer. A "reality gap" exists between technologists (breathlessly enchanted with the latest and greatest revolutionary developments) and the mass consumer market (inevitably preferring evolutionary incrementalism). Invariably, developers have powerful workstations, superfast networks, and a certain affinity for complexity. Meanwhile, tens of millions of people out there struggle with memory-deprived 386s, painfully slow modems (in the real world 14.4 kbps is considered pretty fast, and 28.8 kbps is the promised land), and a tremendous thirst for simplicity.

Yes, telephone companies are getting more aggressive with ISDN pricing and marketing, and developers are reaching for plug-and-play solutions, but it's still too hard and still too expensive. Yes, cable companies are testing cable modems, but the tests are going slowly and broad deployment is likely to take many years.

Switching gears to software, Gilder embraces the commonly held notion that Netscape's browser is the standard, commanding a dominant ("70%") market share. But all of the commercial on-line services now provide Web access, and they have overnight become the dominant force in the consumer Web. Neither of the two largest existing players (AOL and CompuServe), nor the most significant entrant (Microsoft), are Netscape's licensees, so Netscape's market share is therefore zero in this emerging segment. The already fragmented Web market is likely to get even more fragmented, creating havoc for publishers and confusion for consumers. Ultimately, the services with the largest audiences will drive standardization.

So when I read about the "dynamically portable" Java, linked with the Netscape browser "standard" and coupled with a "bandwidth tidal wave," leading a "telecosmic advance" towards a world chock-full of custom applets filled with tasty morsels of "executable content." Exciting, but I wonder how—and when—it will all come together into a mass market for interactive services.

People don't buy browsers. They don't buy objects. They don't buy bandwidth. They buy services. They want access to a broad range of content, packaged and presented in a friendly, useful, engaging manner, priced simply and affordably, with a strong underlying sense of community. At AOL, our aim is to reach tens of millions of people and help shape this new medium. We will continue to leverage technology to do—but we'll also remind ourselves that although technologists believe the journey is the reward, for everybody else, the destination is what really counts.

GEORGE GILDER REPLIES

When the responses to an article exceed the original in pith and pertinence, the writer may be tempted merely to step back, point and applaud. However, at the risk of revealing *Forbes ASAP* trade secrets, I will correct the impression that I am some kind of sappy seersucker who gets his information from doting CEOs, perhaps in the telephone and TV industries. In fact, much to the irritation of the PR firms surrounding large companies, I invariably rely mostly on engineers, programmers and other technologists and consult the imperial suits chiefly en route to the illuminati in the nether reaches of their companies.

As Stephen Roach of Morgan Stanley has noticed with some impatience, I also give short shrift to the kind of macrovisions, strategies and statistics that float up to the top of economic models. These data are too light on the technical details in which reside the angels and devils of industrial destiny. For example, Roach remains perplexed by the "productivity paradox," the lack of evident payoff of information tools, the failures of the industry to surmount the hurdle rates of humbler households, all in the face of some 60 million worldwide prospective PC sales in 1995, exceeding TV unit sales in the U.S., with e-mail passing the U.S. Postal Service in message units. Meanwhile, U.S. companies are capturing some 50% of all the profits of the industrial world and maintaining market share between 60% and 90% in most leading-edge products, while deploying three times as much computer power per capita as either Europe or Japan.

Roach trusts government productivity data and wage levels more than the demonstrable achievements of U.S. companies and calls the conflict a portentous paradox. I say that both the wage and productivity data are largely bunkum, based on silly deflators that mostly fail to capture the plummeting prices in the industry, while U.S. leadership in PCs, peripherals, networks and software is the real payoff. PC companies alone have generated some $250 billion in market caps over the last decade; Internet companies will generate trillions. These bonanzas answer all the questions on hurdle rates and social yields (though if you want to see some real high-speed hurdling in homes, wait until cable modems proliferate next year). The payoff of information technology is the global leadership of the U.S. economy despite appalling policy mistakes from the Bush and Clinton administrations.

Like me, Andy Grove likes to wrangle and I hesitate to deny him his pugilistic jollies. Among the new technologies I did not like from the outset are HDTV, interactive TV, TV chopping, game machines, Japanese fifth-generation computers, NMOS, videophones, flash memories, serial Crays, Thinking Machines, 3DO and pencentric PDAs. But perhaps we can make a deal. I will concede to him and Andy Kessler that the use of the term "hollowing out of the computer," borrowed from the estimable Eric Schmidt of Sun, is hyperbolic, even misleading in an absolute sense. But they should acknowledge that in relative terms, the balance between desktop and network is shifting sharply. After all, in five out of the six PC uses Grove cites, most of the value originates on the network. Nonetheless, I do cherish the PC; indeed, using the Internet, I believe it will displace both the telephone and television over the next five years or so.

16

Angst and Awe on the Internet

In 1995, Internet stories trumped even O.J.
The Net will have a far happier ending.

Well, it had to happen. As the Internet emerges as the central nervous system of global capitalism, the Luddite left is bursting into "flames" against the microcosm and telecosm, against interlinked computers and the global radiance of electromagnetic communications.

This rising resistance resonates with the press coverage that has long lavished attention on the excesses of the Net. Richard Shaffer of the *Computer Letter* counts 39,158 Internet stories during the first three quarters of 1995, beating O. J. by some 15,000 citations. Much of the coverage has been lurid. For psychedelic visions of virtual reality, the media have exalted Jaron Lanier in dreadlocks and bankruptcy above Bob Metcalfe, creator of Ethernet, or Gordon Moore, inventor of IC processing, or Charles Kao, father of fiberoptics, all of whom reshaped the boundaries of human possibility. Computer viruses and Net porn win headlines and magazine covers that elude the creators of vast new computer powers, such as RSA encryption or the World Wide Web or new tools of chip fabrication at the quarter-micron level. Last August, Windows 95, a modest advance in operating systems, exploded across the press and the airwaves as if the entire media had been preempted for a Microsoft infomercial. No wonder befuddled academics, politicians and book publishers gain a grotesquely distorted view of the industry.

In Tom Peters's first *Forbes ASAP* interview (March 29, 1993), he predicted that the '90s would see a fabulous unfolding of new technology, accompanied with increasing outbreaks of technophobia, Luddism and Marxism. Alvin Toffler greeted the initial readers of *Wired* with a similar dual prophecy of networked marvels, foiled by a multi-front war against the Third Wave. Once again, Peters and Toffler may well be right, as from Hollywood to Harvard, America's brainlords rebel against computer technology.

In his pungent new book *War of the Worlds*, Mark Slouka joins the rising chorus of resistance. Slouka finds it all a "kind of lie." Like a "speech of Ronald Reagan" or a spiritual vision from the "religious right," the virtual world is increasingly usurping reality and identity itself. "Rather than doing away with the couch potato, the telecomputer has actually created a new, more tenacious variety of tuber: the individual who swivels from the television screen to computer monitor without missing a beat. . . . "

Today, Sandra Bullock writhes in anguish in the sinister clutches of *The Net*, with a blond, predatory, arachnoid Bill Gates (using "Gateway" software) masterminding the Web. Similar chimeras recur in antitech crusades. Bathed in the ultraviolet frequencies of sunlight, humans throughout the history of the species have raced through a planetary magnetic field of half a gauss in power on a terrestrial sphere charged by worldwide lightning strikes a hundred times a second to a capacitive level of 100 volts per meter of height. Yet Paul Brodeur and other electrophobes panic at power lines, power plants, cathode-ray tubes, microprocessors, cellular antennas and other high-tech oscillators with an impact on humans measurable only in millionths of a gauss. They defy the fact that around the world use of electricity correlates almost perfectly with greater longevity.

Meanwhile, despite the higher longevity and the globally spreading jobs and riches springing from high technology, pseudoeconomists prattle endlessly about the growing gap between the "information rich" and the "information poor." Publishers sign up other disgruntled nerds to write hymns to noble savagery and gardening. And from the fever swamps, a Marxist *enrage* posts bombs through the mail and addled editors detonate them in the pages of the *Washington Post*.

Such fears and fantasies have always afflicted the course of human innovation and progress. With life expectancies rising eight years in the developed countries and 22 years in the Third World since 1950, people have more time to lash out at industrial benefactors who gain wealth and create it from sources hard to comprehend.

Misconceptions about the Internet, however, also abound in more savvy circles. From Stewart Alsop's Agenda conference to the Internet Society, serious critics are emerging to predict that the network itself will bog down and degrade, jammed by traffic and trivia. Often unconsciously, these critics feed upon a spurious vision of capitalist ecology. Constantly recycling Garrett Hardin's "The Tragedy of the Commons" as a theory of the Internet, writers such as Clifford Stoll in *Silicon Snake Oil*, and others from publications such as the *New York Times* to the *National Review* and the *Atlantic*, predict that the Web, as a public good, will be overgrazed, like the commonly owned fields of feudal Britain. Each herdsman or entrepreneur gains from adding to his herd or bandwidth, beating rivals to the remaining grass or spectrum, until congestion ruins the common space.

As the epitome of a capitalist commons, the Internet, according to the critics' predictions, will collapse under the impact of this law, clogged with traffic and polluted with porn and violence. As a precursor, the same writers cite citizens band radio, an earlier fad that rose meteorically and collapsed ignominiously when, as they see it, millions of middle- and lower-class hoi polloi rushed in and polluted the bandwidth without renewing it.

Overall, the resistance converges many streams of reaction. In general, the "humanist" opponents mistake the Internet for a continuation of television technology. Thus they ascribe to the Internet the very flaws that they find in TV—crudeness, violence, porn, entertainment for "diverting ourselves to death"—and extend to the computer the old and mostly valid arguments of Neil Postman and Jerry Mander against the idiot box. Some of the other critics of the Internet benefit from TV and fear the Web will replace their familiar tube. The executives of media companies are mostly baffled by the new technology. Paralyzed by market research, as Jim Barksdale, CEO of Netscape puts it, "They are trying to build bridges by counting the swimmers." A Washington lobbyist for a long-distance carrier wonders poignantly if "America is ready for all this bandwidth." Baby Bells spurn the Internet to fund Hollywood films and TV.

Blinded by the robber-baron image assigned in U.S. history courses to the heroic builders of American capitalism, many critics see Bill Gates as a menacing monopolist. They mistake for greed the gargantuan tenacity of Microsoft as it struggles to assure the compatibility of its standard with tens of thousands of applications and peripherals over generations of dynamically changing technology (avoiding the dialectical babel of the more open Unix, for example). They see the Internet as another arena likely to be dominated by Microsoft and a few giant media companies, increasing the wealth of Wall Street at the expense of the stultified masses of consumers and opening an ever-greater gap between the "information rich" and the "information poor."

Focused on the summits of the industry—CEO séances among media conglomerates and software kings—all the critics can foster the impression that the Internet is a questionable, unpromising venue, vulnerable to monopoly and trash, thereby vindicating the Luddites and the Cassandras. From the beginning of its civilian eruption, however (see *Forbes ASAP*, "The Issaquah Miracle," June 7, 1993), the Net has risen from the bottom up rather than from the top down; by nature, it is a heterarchy rather than a hierarchy.

To get a view of the future of the Net, let us turn aside from Herb Allen's golfing groves and Bill Gates's mansion and Louis Gerstner's "net-centric" revelation, and visit some of the fertile bottomlands where the Web is growing fastest. Here no robber barons or monopolists come into view and there are no signs at all of an impending slide toward tragedy and decline. Here the negative externalities of the degraded commons fall before the huge positive externalities of Moore's Law and Metcalfe's Law, the microcosm and the telecosm, where smaller transistors yield exponentially more efficient machines and the value of networks rises by the square of the power of all the computers attached to them. Governing the positive externalities of the Internet is the convergence of these forces, compounded by the creativity of entrepreneurs.

Perhaps such a combinatorial explosion explains the mind of Avi Freedman of Net Access. Among the vanguard of the armies of the Internet, Freedman is a classic American entrepreneur, entirely alien to the megalithic visions of the critics. As an Internet service provider (ISP), Freedman supplies the Philadelphia area with access to the goods and services of this global ganglion of networks at a flat rate of between $12.50 and $20 per month, depending on the services chosen.

Net Access still operates chiefly out of his cellar in a marginally middle-class suburb of Wyndmoor. The street bristles with wires, transformer nodes, terminal boxes and power lines, many of them converging on the duplex red-brick bungalow where Freedman lives with his wife in an apartment above a basement crammed floor-to-ceiling with multiplying racks of electromagnetic conversion and processing gear for computers and telecom. These technologies are all oscillating and radiating like crazy in the spirit of their hyperkinetic owner, who is multiplexing Internet insights between his cellular phone and an attentive audience of aspiring ISPs from western Pennsylvania and geek students visiting from the University of Pennsylvania, gathered at his door next to the power-line link.

Is this an entrepreneurial dream, or a carcinogenic nightmare out of the muddled pages of Paul Brodeur? Avi is too busy to give the issue much thought. Extending business service to New York City, Washington, D.C., and Chicago, overflowing his basement, he is now moving his operations to a collocation cage at the Philadelphia central office of MFS (Metropolitan Fiber Systems) where he has just turned up a T-3 fiber circuit (45 megabits per second) direct to MAE East, the major East Coast Internet exchange point. From Seattle to San Jose, top companies are besieging him with multi-million-dollar buyout offers, but looking to the future and its promise, Freedman calculates that he can't afford to sell.

With only 4,000 customers, however, Net Access hardly seems to pose a threat to such local colossi as Bell Atlantic and Comcast, now searching the world for "content" opportunities and looming ever larger on Rodeo Drive. Yet Ray Smith and Brian Roberts should pay attention to what is going on in Freedman's teeming mind and basement. Millions of PC owners may well become part-time Internet service providers in the future—as their home and small-business PCs supply content for others, perhaps beginning with teleconferencing and telecommuting activities that will soon dwarf Hollywood in volume.

One of the students hanging on Freedman's words, for example, is Meng-Weng Wong, whose personal Web page at Penn attracts some 35,000 hits a week with its restaurant reviews, film criticisms, Philadelphia maps, technology insights and other delectations. Drawing wide media attention, from *Forbes ASAP* to Scandinavian TV (a crew is visiting this very day from the Netherlands), Wong has now established a server at Net Access, pobox.com, which supplies his clients with a permanent Internet address wherever they may go, and he is developing a Web-page design business.

Responding to the onrush of innovative customers like Wong, the configuration of Freedman's bottom-up operations offers clues to the future shape of the industry. A portly, perspiring, blond, balding geek-genius bursting with monologic humor and street smarts—hardly full-duplex (scant signs of upstream flow)—Freedman has just hustled past his 26th birthday. He has been deep in computers since age eight, when a prescient uncle gave him a book on the Basic programming language at a Seder. Within months he was entrenched among the information rich, opening an unbridgeable gap in computer savvy between himself and nearly all of the other five billion inhabitants of the planet. If you think you are going to catch up, forget it. By the age of 12, in 1982, he was an active user of e-mail and Usenet news and familiar with the abstruse command codes of the

Unix operating system that ran on his father's DEC PDP-11. Freedman senior, a pulmonary physician, inherited the machine indirectly from Bell Labs, where it had been employed as a Usenet news hub until displaced by a VAX.

In 1986, still a teenager, Freedman began exploring the uses of Unix machines for commercial databases and discovered to his surprise that serious businessmen would give him gouts of money to get help with their computers. Eventually, he was earning "lawyers' rates" (his mother is a Philadelphia tax attorney) for work he found "amazingly routine" and "even fun." Nonetheless, after high school, his parents sent him off to college in Massachusetts, where his computer skills were underappreciated. He returned after a few weeks to get a job at the National Software Testing Labs in the Philadelphia suburb of Conshohocken before enlisting at nearby Temple University, which he chose because it offered more freedom for computer experiments and consulting work than the more prestigious Penn a few miles away.

After arriving, he discovered that Temple's computer lab also commanded a superb resource: bandwidth, in the form of a nearly empty T-1 line linking to the Internet at 1.544 megabits per second. Already computer rich, he was becoming communications rich as well. In Avi Freedman, Temple's department of computer science got rather more than it bargained for. Realizing that the available PCs were network hostile and the lab's MicroVAXes ran VMS rather than Unix, Freedman used his savings to buy five secondhand Sun 3 workstations for $600 apiece.

In short order, Freedman began his career as an Internet service provider and "professional geek," albeit unpaid. Soon he had some 100 students as users, mostly cavorting through games of Multiuser Dungeons (MUD). Temple's address, supplied by Freedman—bigboy.cis.temple.edu—became known far and wide as a hive of MUD activity. Temple's computer science professors began to rebel at this untoward distinction, particularly when they found that lost in the crypts and catacombs of the Net, their charges were virtually unreachable for assignments in higher-level languages. Freedman was forced to close down local access to the game portions of the server during daytime hours.

Freedman has given some thought to the problem of "how to civilize young, intelligent teenage males." He concludes, "You have got to get them interested." He says the students playing MUD at least were learning Unix commands, "a better way to get a job than mastering the Pascal programming language," which was then being taught in the regular classes.

As a student, working with Prof. Yuan Shi and other Temple professors, Freedman developed a toolkit for distributed processing on Suns and presented a paper in London in 1989 at a conference on computer-aided software engineering. As his time at Temple drew to a close, he began contemplating graduate school. "Everyone was very surprised that anyone who could do anything on the outside was going to graduate school," he says, "but Stony Brook on Long Island offered me a nice job as a research assistant in the lab and I went up there."

After graduating from Temple, Freedman also encountered the harsh facts of life in the world beyond college computer laboratories. With their local-area networks and T-1 links to the Internet, universities offered a revel for budding cybernauts. Marc Andreessen of Netscape discovered a similar disjunction between college lab and residential communications. At LAN's end was a communications cliff and a bandwidth scandal. Most homes and offices connected to the world only through twisted-pair, four-kilohertz, copper telephone wires.

In October of 1992, Freedman became an ISP chiefly to continue his college revels by chasing bandwidth. Twenty-three at the time and engaged, he could still recall his days in high school and remembered how much he had learned from the Internet through his father's PDP-11. He began to fill up his basement with second-hand Sun machines, mostly at prices well below new Pentium levels, all using Berkeley Unix, equipped by Bill Joy with fast TCP/IP (Transmission Control Protocol/Internet Protocol) for Internet access.

Beginning with 40 customers from local bulletin board systems, Freedman provided access through the serial ports of a single SPARCstation IPC with a 200-megabyte hard drive and 12 megabytes of memory that he purchased secondhand for $1,500. The serial ports ran up to 38.4 kilobits per second, linked to 14.4-kilobit-per-second Zoom and Supra modems connected to POTS (plain old telephone service) outside lines running from the phone company's central office. Costing a total of some $4,000, the system worked well enough until his clientele began to multiply and the modems balked at continual resetting. In April 1992, he bought a 16-port Iolan terminal server that answered the phones and connected subscribers to the Sun servers, which supplied e-mail, Usenet news, Gopher searches, Telnet and file-transfer services in a Unix environment.

In June of 1992 emerged the menace of competition. A local entrepreneur launched Voicenet by simply linking a 386 PC with a modem to each phone line through a terminal server. Charging fees several times higher than Net Access's, Voicenet thrived through the device of hiring two full-time people to scan in pictures from porno magazines for what Freedman describes as the "sticky keyboard set." Eventually the "adult" bulletin board service enlisted some 5,000 members paying $4 per hour to peruse images. Nonetheless, Voicenet protested what it called Net Access's predatory low pricing, a $12.50 to $20 flat rate per month with no full-time employees to pay.

In the early years of the Net's development, the late '80s, the Internet business outside campuses and corporations was a small-time and sometimes tacky trade. In 1992, the entire Net comprised a million linked computers, many of them in university and government labs. It wasn't until November 1993 that Net Access acquired a dedicated 56-kilobit line for direct connection to an official network access point. Costing $400 per month, it multiplexed 22 dial-up modems among 250 users. With the Mosaic World Wide Web browser yet to catch on outside the universities, Net Access did not even have to supply SLIP (serial line interface protocol) or PPP (point-to-point protocol) accounts, which shield the user from the details of Unix.

Freedman, however, saw the need for new technology to link people to the full resources of the Net without having to know abstruse Unix commands. "As a professional geek, writing code is my true calling," he says, adding that he threw himself into this work. Although the program was eclipsed by Mosaic, Lynx and other approaches, he still believes that his software provided easier access to the Internet, complete with the ability to trace routes and "ping" remote machines. Enabling users to log in to the program in 1992, he put Net Access on the technological forefront of ISPs.

The largest challenge for an ISP, then and now, is managing the floods of bits engulfing a Usenet news server at a rate of some 500 megabytes per day, five news articles per second, each with a unique identification that has to be scanned to assure that the news is fresh and not duplicated. The heart of the Internet until the arrival of the World Wide Web—and still cherished more than the Web by many Internet veterans—Usenet is the huge collection of textual bulletin boards and other information troves and exchanges from which the communities of the Net exfoliate. As Steve Willens of Livingston Enterprises puts it: "This is the real source of the Internet as we know it and the challenge that forced the development of technology specialized for the Net"—notably Livingston communications servers that linked modems to the Net through fast comports functioning with compression at 115.2 kilobits per second.

In 1994, Freedman recognized he had a major business on his hands. He decided to lease a T-1 line from PREP-NET (Pennsylvania Research and Economic Partnership Network), which required a prepayment of $1,000 per month. With 50 phone lines and modems and 500 users, he broke all ties with Stony Brook and began hiring people to handle a rising tide of traffic and a surging demand for technical support.

That summer, he had three full-time people: "Myself, my wife, Gail, and my 20-year-old brother, Noam. Working with him made me realize why people pay me so much money as a consultant [up to $150 an hour]. He served as a kind of Avi echo, intuitively knowing what I wanted and when." A student in computer science at the University of Chicago, Noam is in the process of extending the business to that city, while Avi has established points of presence in New York and Washington, D.C. He has hired five Net Access customers, none with college degrees, to provide technical support full time as the number of users has climbed at a pace of some 15% per month since the end of 1994.

For links to other cities, Freedman relied on advice from telecommunications consultant Gordon Jacobson, a Penn alumnus who maintains close links to the Penn school of engineering, where his father graduated. With Jacobson's help, Freedman is ending 1995 with a fiber circuit connecting him to MAE East at 45 megabits a second, a 10-megabit-per-second link to Sprint's network-access point, and more than half a dozen point-to-point T-1 lines, all for well under half of the normally tariffed prices for these services. With increasing broadband connectivity, Net Access commands more than half as much bandwidth at the nerve centers of the Net as Netcom, which has 50 times more customers.

Though indispensable, technology alone cannot sustain a successful ISP. It is people that make the vital difference. If Freedman had originally hired people to perform the work that he did himself part-time—"keeping the machines running, maintaining software, recovering from disasters, installing and tuning equipment and circuits"—he would have incurred expenses of some $100,000 per year and his financial model would have collapsed. The reason many corporations are so slow to develop Internet programs is not the lack of equipment but the dearth of personnel. The large companies pursuing Net Access did not care about Freedman's rooms full of gear. They were after Freedman himself.

Freedman's entrepreneurship and technology ride on a tide of other enterprise by the suppliers of Internet gear. These, too, are not huge telephone company equipment manufacturers or rising software monopolists but mostly small or medium-size companies, led by young entrepreneurs, fighting to survive in the most intensely competitive arena of the world economy.

An Internet service provider must begin by supplying modems through which the outside world can connect to his offerings. With millions of home customers who dwarf the ISP modem volumes, U.S. Robotics is currently ascendant in most ISPs, but Freedman spurns them for cheaper devices from Multi-Tech. These modems connect to a Xylogics terminal server that authenticates the name and password combination entered by the user and validates the caller as legitimate. Then the customer enters Net Access's local-area network linking a set of Sun Microsystems servers that supply World Wide Web, Gopher, Usenet, e-mail, file transfer, Telnet and other Internet services.

Net Access is unusual for an ISP, since few use Xylogics equipment. Recently bought out by Bay Networks, Xylogics supplied nearly all the terminal servers for the university market, and it still shies away from the tumultuous world of ISPs. These customers mostly use Livingston products that run a security protocol named Radius (remote authentication dial-in user services). Channeling the bits around the ISP's internal net and on to other networks are banks of routers, also often built by Cisco or Livingston (although Freedman originally chose Morningstar because it was cheaper). Linking a particular ISP to other ISPs and network access points are T-1 cables running at 1.544 megabits per second through multiplexing and demultiplexing and conditioning equipment. These functions are performed by DSU-CSUs (data service units-channel service units) made by such companies as TxPort, Adtran, General DataComm and ADC Kentrox.

Freedman insists on the Law of the Microcosm in choosing all his equipment and in making all his projects for expansion. Since his study of distributed computing at Temple, he has everywhere cherished duplication and redundancy and cheap components over centralization and scale economies. He at first bought a nine-gigabyte drive from Micropolis. Now he regrets the decision and is replacing it with five two-gigabyte drives (more I/O [input/output], redundancy and reliability). "The more spindles the better," he says. He buys lots of cheap secondhand Suns rather than one powerful server. He criticizes some of the larger ISPs, such as Netcom, for centralizing their servers and technical support. It causes bottlenecks and delays, he says, and opens the system to crashes if any of the communication lines go down.

Freedman's rule is to provide service as locally as possible. He believes ISPs with fully equipped local network sites, rather than mere communications nodes like Netcom's, will prevail. Like most small ISPs, Freedman is wedded to flat-rate pricing, though his accounts of altercations with customers who want to resell or overgraze his commons may undermine confidence that this pricing regime can survive into the future. But managing flat-rate prices is a core competence of the ISPs. Believing that bits will flee toward flat rates, Freedman says MCI will fail in its plans to transform Internet pricing models by adding some as yet unannounced scale of measured usage based on time, packets or both.

Is Freedman's model scalable, or is it doomed as he grows? Could Freedman be displaced by MCI or Sprint-Comcast or Bell Atlantic or Microsoft-UUNet or AT&T in a siege of merger-monopolization? He believes that up until a threshold of some 25,000 to 50,000 customers, meaning revenues of between $5 million and $10 million net of more lucrative business clients, his economic and technical model can trump all comers. At that point, he will face the usual entrepreneurial crisis of transition: Freedman will need business partners, routinized technology management schemes and expensive accounting to maintain operations as Net Access spreads across the country.

But he does not fear competition. His problems, he says, are servicing the flood of new customers and anticipating the depredations of "Congresscritters" who want to make him liable for any vagrant flasher who strays onto one of his hard drives.

Still a small force in the global matrix of telecommunications, Freedman now dreams of exploiting available resources of fiber, dark and lit, to acquire major new bandwidth, linking cities up and down the East Coast and across the U.S. Helping Freedman move this project toward reality is his telecom guru Jacobson, an entrepreneurial dervish from Portman Communications. With financiers on the line to supply some $5 million in startup capital, Jacobson is planning to launch a national IRamp network. The service will ultimately open fully staffed Internet access facilities in 30 cities nationwide, linked everywhere by fiber, at a cost of some $1 million per site.

Such investment looms large compared to the rock-bottom base of Freedman's operation, and easily eclipses a national ISP's point-of-presence facility that can cost upwards of $70,000. But David Farber, gigabit-testbed guru, recently told a New York audience at the Penn Club that, spurred by business needs, the marketplace is seeking higher-end, stable-broadband ISP services that can handle millions of hits a day at a Web site with no access delays or congestion and that provide local access and custom software configuration. For these high-end customers, the SPARC 20 servers and T-1 and 56-kilobit links of the many small ISPs will no longer suffice.

Pioneering the kind of broadband channels that will eventually become ubiquitous on the Net, IRamp's planned facilities will command OC-3 fiber (155 megabits per second) links to a national network of both dark and lit fiber, available from utilities, pipelines and other unusual sources. Such bypass strategies will become increasingly common in coming years. The 10 million miles of fiber currently installed in the U.S., after all, is exploited to approximately one-millionth of its potential capacity—and much of it is unused "dark fiber."

For key ISP server and security functions, Jacobson plans to use fully fault-tolerant Tandem S4000 servers running the new ServerNet multibus scheme. It was conceived by venerable Tandem designer Robert Horst as a new-generation architecture explicitly optimized to substitute bandwidth for switching speeds. Fully scalable, ServerNet was licensed in October by Compaq, yet it commands a theoretical throughput limit of an unprecedented petabit per second (a million billion bits). For graphics-intensive applications, Jacobson envisages Silicon Graphics WebForce Challenge S servers using Irix software. Even with as few as 5,000 subscribers per site paying a competitive nonusage-based rate, Jacobson projects a high rate of return.

Meanwhile, at Netcom, the nation's largest ISP, David Garrison, the CEO, is undergoing the stresses that Freedman foresees for himself as he expands his business. During his previous stint at the helm of the meteoric paging company, SkyTel, Garrison, a rangy dark-haired entrepreneur with a slight uneasiness in his ready smile of prosperity, thought he had approached the ultimate in entrepreneurial excitement. But nothing in his career in the wireless industry prepared him for his first nine months as head of Netcom. Here is a company that during the last three quarters grew from 400 to 1,200 employees, from 58 to 201 points of presence, from 72,000 to more than 200,000 customers, and from revenues of $12.4 million in 1994 to a $50 million run rate in 1995 and to a market cap of some $400 million, while the traffic in bits grows at an even faster pace—impelled by the graphic demands of the World Wide Web, itself expanding at the rate of more than 1,000 new servers per week.

Netcom pares down its points of presence to simple communications nodes and handles all the technical support and Internet services for them at the company's headquarters. This operation fills up a high-rise in San Jose. Some floors teem with desks manned by earnest engineers in jeans, many of them Asian, working the phones. Other floors are replete with row upon row of racks filled wall-to-wall with Cisco routers, Sun servers, Livingston PortMasters, Ascend ISDN pipelines, Cascade edge switches and U.S. Robotics modems. Walking through these ever-expanding mazes of machinery, Garrison's entrepreneurial smile at times moves from the ready to the giddy.

In this environment of riotous growth, the telcos move their slow thighs like trolls under the bridges and routers of the Internet. Currently commanding perhaps 2% of the traffic, AT&T, for example, has declared its ambition to capture 60% of the Internet business over the next two years. But Garrison demurs: "From the Olympian perspective of a McKinsey & Co. consultant, AT&T could take over any business. They have one of the greatest brand names in the world, they've got more money than God, a billing relationship with some 40 million people, a global network and alliances and consortia, Internet pioneer Bolt, Beranek & Newman in their fold, and they have perhaps the world's largest internal World Wide Web on their own Unix servers among their 300,000 employees."

But like most of the telcos, AT&T lacks focus. As Netcom marketing chief John Zeisler explains: "Phone companies have their 700 numbers, 800 numbers, corporate customers, their Hollywood links, their leased lines, their frame relay, their ADSL (asymmetric digital subscriber line), their cable aspirations, their huge wireless opportunities, their bureaucracy, their regulatory tariffs, their pricing confusions. Should voice be priced as data or should data be priced as voice? They are great at laying fiber and wire, connecting it to switches and bringing signals to the central office and to the curb. But the Internet is a second thought, just another business to them."

As in the PC industry, focus and agility are crucial. In an arena where the technologies ride a remorseless onrush of exponential changes, no prolonged bureaucratic process can succeed. Even the maps and schematics of rapid convergence among media industries miss the point. Dominating this arena is the computer industry—with its millions of piranha processors and entrepreneurs—and it doesn't converge with anything; it eats everything in its path.

Now ascendant is the Internet computer industry. Most of these new companies, from Livingston to Netscape, focus on the Internet. Using personal computer components to reduce the price of ISP infrastructure far below the price of telco installations, these companies endow the ISPs with a further advantage in a dynamic industry.

Livingston Enterprises epitomizes the success of the new companies creating this new industry. Secreted in Pleasanton, Calif., and financed by corporate cash flow, Livingston has grown up with the Internet at a pace not far in the wake of its more illustrious rival, Cisco Systems. Livingston PortMasters crowd Netcom's headquarters, as they do most of the other ISPs.

Launched in 1989 under the leadership of Steven Sillens, then a manager of multipro cessors at Sun Microsystems, Livingston's networking drive began by creating a cheap router and communications server based on a new operating system, ComOS, specifically developed to help ISPs meet their Usenet burdens. Livingston quickly became a dominant force in Internet terminal servers and routers, and grew at a pace of more than 50% per year until engulfed by an explosion of demand in 1995. In August of this year, Livingston launched cheap low-end routers to serve both ends of an Internet connection: a $1,395 two-port PortMaster to link small offices to the Net at up to 230.4 kilobits per second and a sleek space-saving $3,495 PortMaster with 24 ports for ISPs. In October, Livingston announced a series of ISDN remote-access machines that will compete with the currently dominant Ascend ISDN pipeline system, if ISDN becomes the preferred mode of Internet access.

Now everywhere in the Internet industry companies are resigning themselves to ISDN as the next "modem" (though, in fact it just brings into home and office the 64Kbps digital channels long used by the telcos between central offices). The scandal of U.S. telecom, however, is that the telcos could just as easily be bringing video capable T-1 service (1.544 megabits per second of bandwidth, equivalent to CD-ROMs) to homes if regulations permitted a reasonable tariff structure.

Moreover, new access technologies are emerging, such as cable modems and AT&T's new SDSL (symmetrical digital subscriber loop). Available this year and under test by Bell Atlantic, SDSL modems promise to bring T-1-Line capability to homes on twisted-pair copper wires for about $10 a month. SDSL follows many such copper prosthetics announced over the years (notably HDSL) [high bit rate digital subscriber line] from Level One, PairGain, Brooktree and others), all largely spurned by the telcos on pricing grounds, but capable of transforming the entire world of Internet access before ISDN's niggardly pipes catch on with the public.

While Internet hardware rushes ahead, Netscape, Sun and other providers of Internet software make the ISP a fast and elusively moving target for the telcos that wish to compete. With eight million browsers in the field, all upgradeable to the new 2.0 system—with the Java interpreter and Java multimedia programming language and toolkit—Netscape expects to attract some 100,000 software developers to its platform over the next year. There are already some 400 Java applications available, including word processors, spreadsheets and games that can play on any machine with a browser running a Java interpreter, regardless of operating system or microprocessor instruction set.

Netscape's expected army of 100,000 developers compares with some 10,000 developers for Apple's Macintosh and perhaps 3,000 for Microsoft's network, MSN. Emerging from a company that did not even exist two years ago, such a juggernaut will further empower the ISPs in their competition with the large invaders of the territory—not only the telcos but also the on-line services such as American Online and MSN.

The ISPs, however, are not usually in direct competition with the large phone companies. ISPs bring them new customers and new business users, and the ISPs also depend on them for home connections and for potential fiber-trunking services. The American telcos are currently laying some 1,300 miles of fiber-optic line every day. Moreover, beginning with TCI's and Kleiner Perkins' @home system, which functions with cable modems and new software from Netscape, the ISPs also may end up using cable plant. As cable modems become available, cable companies will likely turn to the ISPs to supply Internet services, local content, technical support and point-of-presence technology.

In the midst of these whitewater torrents of change, the some 4,000 ISPs and their increasing armies of supporters represent a serious threat to many of the established empires of telecom. Not only can they move much faster and more resourcefully, but they also have the key advantage of having bet exclusively on the PC and the Internet as the platforms of the future. However smart and powerful, Ray Smith, Mike Ovits of Disney, Gerland Levin and Ted Turner, Sumner Redstone and other aspiring Kings of the Road still entertain crippling visions of set-top boxes and interactive TV sets.

Andrew Grove of Intel had the last word for these efforts when he told *Forbes ASAP* last year: "By the time the set-top people reach the price points and form factors of consumer electronics and penetrate 30% of homes, the personal computer will be everywhere, controlling the TV like a minor peripheral." Bill Joy elaborated on this point in the October issue of *Red Herring*: "By the time [they] bring digital TV to the home, you will be able to take your Super Netscape version 4.0 Web browser with Super-Ultra-HotJava-Burners, and that will be your animated user interface. [The TV people tried, but] it's like the Internet happened in the meantime. Right?"

Distracting most of the large companies (seen by the Internet's critics as impending monopolists), the pursuit of the set-top not only misses the point and begs the question but it also blows the key new hardware opportunity of the epoch. Although the PC will not be dislodged for most office applications, there is a real and rare chance today to create a new home architecture and software optimized for the bandwidth rather than for installed base. Together with the Java language, the Web browser breakthrough allows creation of new network PC and software architectures at price points that take advantage of the "hollowing out of the computer" caused by the impact of the Internet. Sun, Apple, Oracle and Jean-Louis Gassée's BeBox are all focusing on this target today. All are trying to take advantage of the elusive opportunity of creating cheap machines optimized for bandwidth and graphics rather than for legacy software baggage (the storage can be supplied on the Net). That opportunity follows the PC and Internet model—the microcosm and the telecosm—into the cornucopian digital future of the information age, with the old analog TV and telephone left far behind.

Amid all these torrents of futuristic technology and prophecies of a tragic denouement in a wasted commons, it is comforting to return to the man who began it all, Vinton Cerf of MCI. Coinventor of the Internet protocol TCP/IP, developer of the once-pioneering MCI Mail service, and both a poet and a philosopher of the Net, he is now in charge of MCI's data network, which includes MCI's Internet backbone network. A rare combination of technical grit and visionary enthusiasm, he faces resistance from forces within the company that still lust for the glamour of Hollywood and see the Internet as the CB radio of the 1990s. Nonetheless, Cerf at 52 is leading MCI toward a new Internet-centric strategy that is more likely than the MCI lobbyists to save the company from the grave perils of long-distance deregulation. The company is already creating a new backbone for the National Science Foundation part of the Internet, connecting supercomputer centers and other high-bandwidth applications at speeds of up to 622 megabits per second. MCI also is a major supplier of Internet bandwidth. Its network connects to all six NAPs (national access points) through which the ISPs link to one another.

Cerf observes that the national phone network grew at a similar pace through much of its history and regularly met ever challenge. The telcos, for instance, surmounted the predicted crisis of the NAPs early this year, when—following the withdrawal of government funds—the network was expected to collapse under galloping increases in traffic. But the NAPs, despite unsuccessful struggles with the remaining instabilities of ATM (asynchronous transfer mode), ultimately rose to the challenge, saving the Net by using fiber optics and digitization, as well as transparent silicon and opaque silicon.

Today, new entrepreneurs are rising up to shape the future of broadband networks and possibly seize the market from the incumbent backbone suppliers. Silicon, both see-through and solid, remains at the heart of the solution. One of the ways MCI is meeting the challenge of the future is by purchasing eight "gigarouters" from NetStar, a startup in Minneapolis that is exploiting Moore's Law to bring IP (Internet Protocol) switching and router technology into the microcosm.

Launched five years ago by a group of veterans of the Minneapolis supercomputer scene—Lee Data, Cray and other companies—NetStar went public this fall at a $83 million valuation. It is pioneering an elegant routing architecture that gets eight times the throughput of a Cisco 7500 at a 20% lower price. While existing routers run bits down shared backplane buses, NetStar's IP router reserves a full one gigabit per each of up to 16 media cards attached to a single-chip TriQuint 16 gigabit-cross-bar switch.

Ubiquitous on the Internet, Cisco remains an imperial force. But as the microcosm advances, it too faces threats. Not only can it not compete with NetStar at the top of the line but it also faces Livingston, Ascend and possibly even Compaq at the bottom.

Critics of the Internet have long predicted that as ever-more-turbulent floods of broadband data and Web images crowd the commons, the Net will no longer be able to bear the load. The routers in the NAPs and other critical paths will jam up and crash. But the microcosm enables a constant stream of exponentially more powerful new architectures as functions that were once spread out across entire boards collapse into single chips and multichip modules.

For 1995 and beyond, MCI has bet on NetStar's feats of microchip integration to countervail every population explosion across the network commons. Following the laws of the telecosm rather than the megalithic visions of the critics, the fast new networks are becoming constantly dumber and more entrepreneurial. Ciena Corp., a small, venture-funded vendor of optical networks, is now supplying the next generation of back-bone gear, a system that can carry 16 separate bitstreams on every fiber thread. The first application of the new all-optical technology in public networks, Ciena's innovation is a precursor of the terabit (trillion-bit throughput) networks that will be filled with video teleconferencing, video on demand, virtual reality, and other bit-thronging and polygon-shuffling applications of the future.

Only one competitor, Northern Telecom, might challenge NetStar and the others providing the new superswitches dumb enough to prevail at the top of the line. In early October, Northern's BNR lab exhibited a terabit-switch architecture at the Telecom 95 show in Geneva. This machine, once again, illustrates the triumph of dumb networks. The dumb terminals of the past, whether POTS phones or mainframe 3270 panels, required smart networks, with central-office switches from Northern and AT&T containing no fewer than 26 million lines of software code. But the new Northern terabit uses passive optical components and virtually no software at all. It points to the evolution of a fiber-shpere for broadband wire traffic that will function like the atmosphere for wireless traffic. (See *Forbes ASAP*, "Into the Fibersphere," December 7, 1992).

While the critics of the new technology fix on the foibles of television and the monolithic aggregations of old media, the Internet is emerging as an entrepreneurial efflorescence. Comparing the Net to the decline of CB radio and the tragedy of the commons misses the providential convergence of the laws espoused by Moore and Metcalfe, with thousands of entrepreneurs in tow, exponentially expanding the commons with streams of new invention in a creative spiral of growth and opportunity. In seeing the technology as a killer of jobs and family life and a polarizer of opportunities between rich and poor, they miss the most radically egalitarian force in the history of the world economy.

The critics seem oblivious to the most basic realities of the U.S. job miracle. While the U.S. deployed three times as much computer power per capita as any other industrial region, this country created some 45 million jobs in 25 years at rising, real incomes. Not only was the U.S. a world leader in the proportion of its working-age population with jobs, but it also created employment for some 12 million immigrants, while its corporations endowed new work for people around the globe.

At the same time, a billion people, mostly Third World Asians, used the technology to leap into Third Wave riches without ever having to endure a heavy industrial phase. Gaps between the rich and the poor collapsed everywhere that the networks reached, as former peasants around the world—from Bangalore to Los Angeles—gained new freedom and opportunity from the information economy.

The Internet creates jobs by making workers more productive, and thus more employable, regardless of where they live. By engendering more investable wealth, it endows new work, providing the key remedy for the job displacement entailed by all human progress. By aggregating distant markets, the Internet enables more specialization, and more productivity and excellence. It will help all people, but most particularly the poor, who always comprise the largest untapped market for enterprise. And the Internet will continue to grow, transforming the global economy with its power and building a new industry even larger than the PC's.

Fueling the transformation are the laws of the telecosm. They begin with Metcalfe's Law: The power of computers on a network rises with the square of the total power of computers attached to it. Every new computer, therefore, both use the Net as a resource and adds resources to the Net in a spiral of increasing value and choice. This means that any limited, exclusive or proprietary network will tend to lose business to a more open, accessible and widely connected network. Metcalfe's Law dooms all the dreams of the Time Warners of the world to create exclusive and proprietary combinations of content and conduit.

As a further rule, networks prevail to the extent that they feed on the invention and creativity of their users, since the power of the computers on the edge of the network will increasingly dwarf the intelligence of the network fabric itself. For example, a 5ESS central-office switch from AT&T, commanding some 10 MIPS (millions of instructions per second) and linking some 110,000 lines, once represented the most powerful computer in a local phone network. Today those 10 MIPS are infinitesimal compared to the collective computer power of the tens of thousands of personal computers, each commanding 20 to 100 MIPS, linked by modems to the switch.

Lacking an entrepreneurial environment of inventive users, the government-run PTTs (Post Telegraph and Telephone) of Europe have been rapidly losing ground to the U.S.'s more rivalrous RBOCs (regional Bell operating companies) and long-distance carriers, and all have been losing ground to the explosion of interconnected private nets. The U.S. has some 700,000 private networks compared to just 14,000 in Europe and some 75,000 in Japan. Private nets that feed on the creativity of their users will always tend to prevail over public nets, such as France's Minitel or American's interactive TV projects, that try to supply their entire system from a central office.

Eric Schmidt of Sun offers a true parable of the Net. Back when the Internet was the Arpanet, two routers were added to the system, but the routers' hopping ratio (the number of hops to any destination) got struck at zero. Because traffic always seeks out the optimal path, most of the traffic on the Net rushed to these two machines, since they promised instant transmission. Until the settings were corrected, the system was swamped.

On the Net, traffic will always gravitate to the most efficient broadband channels. If the telcos and software monopolists attempt to gouge customers in a badly designed and costly "top-down" network, traffic will migrate rapidly toward the freedom and band-width of a bottom-up solution. In the emerging global Internet, these channels could emerge among bypass suppliers using dark fiber; among low-earth-orbit satellite systems, such as Teledesic and GlobalStar; among cable companies and renegade long-distance suppliers; or among companies as yet unknown.

Guided by the valuations of the market, capital follows a similar rule: It is routed rapidly to the channels where it can be used more productively. At present, afflicted by perverse regulations that bar phone and cable companies from collaborating in the same region, valuations of these companies are low. Meanwhile, analysis complain of the excessive valuations for ISPs, such as Netcom, and their suppliers, such as Cisco, 3Com and Netscape. Not only traffic but also investment flows to the least regulated and most enterpreneurial arena.

A further law of the telecosm ordains that, in an age of dumb terminals and phones, traffic flows to smart networks full of intricate software. In an age of ever-multiplying computer power, impelled by Metcalfe's Law, traffic flows to the dumbest networks that gain their intelligence from the variety of powerful machines attached to them. A corollary is that, along with traffic, capital flows to the dumbest and most broadband nets with the most computer intelligence on their edges.

Perhaps most important of all is the cultural law of the telecosm. Networks promote choice, choice enhances quality and quality favors morality. Television is culturally erosive because its small range of offerings requires a broad, lowest-common-denominator appeal. Linking to millions of cultural sources, global networks provide a cornucopia of choices, like a Library of Congress at your fingertips. On the Net, as at a giant bookstore, you always get your first choice rather than a lowest-common-denominator choice. A culture of first choices creates a bias toward excellence and virtue.

The critics of the Internet are mostly skeptical about the value of choice. But choice validates freedom and substantiates individuality. Choice accords with the inexorable genetic diversity of humans. It makes possible individual aspiration and creativity. It is the lowest-common-denominator offerings of mass-broadcast media that lower humans to the animal level, eclipsing the differences that make us human, cutting off the higher aspirations and inspirations that elevate us beyond our appetites, reducing us to an impressionable crowd, zapping through the channels looking for a splash of blood or flash of nudity or demagogic spiel of hate.

In prophesying centralization and tyranny, the Cassandras miss the centrifugal forces of the Law of the Microcosm, overthrowing all monopolies, hierarchies, pyramids and power grids of established industrial society and endowing individuals with the power to be transcendent and free.

17

Goliath at Bay

Microsoft suddenly sees itself beset by broadband rebels and its own middle age.

Goliath in the Vale of Elah roared his contempt at the weapons and zeal of David: "Do you think me a dog that you contest me with sticks and stones?"

Bill Gates, the Goliath of software, sees himself similarly beset by zealous rivals with risible weapons. Entering his modest second-floor office on the edge of the Microsoft campus on a twilight evening in late November, I find him irked and addled by what he sees as a siege of slingshots from irrational media and capital markets in his industry.

Microsoft entered November on an autumnal blaze of upside news-earnings up 53%, sales up 63%, a double gigabuck quarter. But now, amazingly, people were speaking of a "crisis" at Microsoft. "That's an emotional word," says Gates, twisting uncomfortably in his chair.

It was bad enough when Netscape came on with 9,000 lines of code for a World Wide Web browser that took six weeks to build and that was given away free, and people began talking of his company's downfall. Gates had pulled that trick himself in 1976, with a few thousand lines of code for the Basic programming language for the PC and then again in 1980 with MS-DOS. But to do it to Goliath seemed lèse-majesté.

Then comes Sun Microsystems with a new programming language called Java, and people like me, who by Microsoft standards don't know anything about programming, who have never written a single line of code, presumed to tell him about its virtues. It's safe, secure, interpreted, platform independent; it collects your garbage (automatic garbage collection). It compiles as if by incantation. It builds market cap as by magic. Give poor Bill a break.

"Yeah, right," says Gates. "I have to wonder who screwed your head around. . . ." Oh, he knows, he knows. " The Internet" makes everything different. You can make any claim you want, however bizarre or ludicrous, that would ordinarily be laughed off the stage, and if you add the mantra "on the Internet" at the end you can morph yourself from a typical media clown into a visionary, a prophet, a guru. "Nobody pauses to say, 'Huh?' "

Even the analysts will nod and the market will bow. It's "on the Internet."

One day in November, three days before my visit, Rick Sherlund, the Goldman Sachs analyst who helped bring Microsoft public in 1986 and had touted the stock for a decade, downgraded Microsoft's shares from buy to "moderately outperform" on the basis of Internet incantations from Sun and Netscape. Sherlund also replaced Microsoft with Netscape on his recommended list. Indeed, Goliath's net worth was shrinking by the minute as Microsoft's market cap sank by $9 billion, and Sun's and Netscape's surged by $9 billion in a matter of weeks.

Does Bill Gates know Rick Sherlund, by any chance? Sure, Gates answers, "extremely well." "He's your man, he's great," says Gates, "if you want to run a spreadsheet."

In this world of manias and emotions, "I have to make rational decisions," Gates says, glaring at me. "Somebody who thinks that because of a browser that anyone can clone, because of a language that is magic, they [Netscape and Sun, the unmentionables] can overthrow the world—that person can't even think two chess moves ahead. You're not even in the game I'm playing."

Okay, thinking forward a couple of moves, what is the big thing bearing down on Microsoft on that road ahead?

It's middle age.

No, in Redmond, they have another name for it. Throughout the company, wherever you go—from hummus on pita bread at the cafeteria with a glib former Hollywood agent hired to handle publicity, to a Starbucks latte at the Microsoft model "home" with software sage Rick Rashid incandescent on a couch, or off to Rover's Restaurant where Nathan Myhrvold spiels refulgently at a corner table through 12 courses of rococo "fatware" and my two missed flights—the word is middleband. From the top down, Microsoft is becoming a middleband company.

Gates, Myhrvold, James Allchin, Craig Mundie—nearly anyone in Redmond will step you through it. The future is not broadband, not narrow-band; it is some middle way. It takes Excel and Word and PowerPoint presentation graphics and multimedia CD-ROMs and the new Video ROMs—indeed all the front and back Office suites that are the core of the company, all the teeming towers of legacy code—and attaches that to the Internet. It's Encarta and Baseball and digital TV all tied to the Web over middle-band circuits.

Gates explains: "We will translate Encarta into many languages and make it a front end to the Internet, so that whenever you look up a topic in the encyclopedia, we can link you into what there is in the Internet on that topic.

"Now the Internet is not fast enough when you just want to go pure Internet, so every year you can buy the CD that holds the bulk of the material." It will be a middleband world. I see the millennium at hand: People are all queuing up at Egghead for their Encarta update CDs.

From Gates on down, however, Microsoft leaders do grasp the essence of the change. Myhrvold trenchantly points out that communications standards no longer rise from the center out, from the LAN to the WAN. They begin on the Net and move inward to the LAN and transform it. "The LAN is dead," as Myhrvold says.

But these same Microsoft leaders seem to believe that the transforming power of the Net stops short of the PC and operating system. Sun will set, but Windows will open wide on the World Wide Web (up to ISDN speeds). After all, as Allchin puts it, "We see the Internet as an extension of the operating system."

I ask Gates how we can have a middleband world in the face of a rising tide of bandwidth. Gates in the past has spoken of virtually "infinite bandwidth." But he does not see it today.

Twenty years from now we will have broadband in homes, he explains, but until then middleband is the best you can expect. Indeed, in his presentation to the press the week after my visit, on December 7, he strangely declared "broadband is the holy grail, [but] it's much further away than ever before."

I ask about cable modems. But to Gates, cable modems are mere middleband: "Don't get me wrong—you can do a lot in middleband. But cable is a shared medium. Cable modems are middleband. You get 10 megabits per second and share it with 500 homes and you are back to ISDN speeds."

But, I protest, Netscape has a different view. It has joined with @Home (the Kleiner Perkins-TCI joint venture) to supply browsers and servers for a new scalably broadband Internet based on cable.

Gates's voice reaches a new pitch. "I assure you Netscape has no relationship with @Home that Microsoft does not have. I didn't spend three years talking with John Malone for nothing—three years with Bruce Ravenel [Tele-Communications Technology Ventures' senior vice-president and chief operating officer]. In the first place, browsers are trivial. We will have cable browsers. And we will have cable servers. We will do anything with @Home that Netscape does." After all, TCI Technology Ventures invested $125 million in MSN (Microsoft Network).

So it went in the Redmond gloaming. I deeply admire Gates. The guts to leave Harvard at the end of his junior year and launch a new industry; the tenacity to build it into a planetary utility; the audacity and ingenuity of the original deal with IBM; the entrepreneurial confidence to cut loose from OS/2. The vision to be the only major software company to embrace Macintosh and save Apple by endowing the Mac with the leading GUI spreadsheet and word processor, Excel and Word, while at the same time gaining the graphics skills to create Windows. The bold challenge to Unix through Windows NT.

There is no doubt that Gates has been the exemplary business leader of our era. Compared with the leaders of IBM, heavy with "NIH" (not-invented-here) and degrees in business administration and finance, who could not even grasp the concept of sunk costs or the rule of self-cannibalization well enough to burke OS/2, who could not even see the huge opportunity to embrace the Mac OS, Gates is indeed a giant.

A week later, in an announcement emblazoned in *Computerworld* as "Capitulation," Gates showed his superiority to the NIH syndrome at IBM. He declared that he was licensing Sun's Java Internet animation language, in which he seemed suddenly to have discovered new virtues, and was essentially abandoning Microsoft Network as a proprietary paid service. It would serve as an attractive Internet entry point, open to all, with content and advertising prepared with anyone's available software. Beyond that, Microsoft announced an array of impressive-sounding new Internet products: Blackbird publication tools for the Net; Gibraltar Internet server products four times as fast as Netscape's; Visual Basic as a scripting language for the Net already far easier and more familiar than Java; upgrades of current Word versions that allow direct creation of HTML documents; and an array of other announcements.

But all the brave talk, the bestselling book, the stilted TV appearances, the announcement of a news channel with NBC, the stream of new products, the bold embrace of an Internet strategy, the spread of Windows 95, could not disguise the rising confusion in Redmond.

All of a sudden, Gates seemed to have lost his bearings. The man who elbowed aside an on-air Connie Chung as if she were a bothersome gnat and shunned NBC as a nuisance, now was clutching the old network, of all things, as a source of news and investing in it, as if it had a future. It was as if old NBC with its Max Headrooms of smiling anchor faces and two-minute splashes of "news" could morph into an information resource simply by invoking the mantra "on the Internet."

As in his long romance with Warren Buffett, Gates seemed to be reaching out to old money, power and prestige to bolster his company as it whirled in the vortex that he had described as the "Internet tidal wave." It was as if he no longer trusted the PC to sustain his growth as an $8 billion revenue company, as if he needed sustenance from mass media.

With Netscape, Sun, @Home and other firms, Silicon Valley is in the ascendant again. But the software colossus is still losing ground on the road ahead, so Gates pivots on his peerless pinnacle simultaneously at the summit of the *New York Times* bestseller list and the *Forbes* 400 and looks back with a Macaulay Culkin smile from the cover of a book that is mostly news of yesterday.

INTEL OUTSIDE?

Two weeks later, back in Silicon Valley from the Vale of Elah, I visit Goliath's prime mover, Andrew Grove of Intel. With revenues more than twice as large as Microsoft's and a price/earnings ratio less than half as high, and commanding the world's most awesome manufacturing facilities for the world's most complex and portentous product, Intel seems to stand on firmer foundations.

Grove opens the meeting with jokes about the "tunnel of death" that perpetually menaces his industry in the pages of the media. Ensconced in a small open cubicle on the fifth floor of the Robert Noyce headquarters in Santa Clara at the heart of Silicon Valley, with "Intel Inside" inscribed on the roof to enlighten the planes from nearby San Jose International Airport, Grove effervesces wit and irony and bonhomie where Gates seethed sarcasm and defensiveness.

With Grove, there is no longing for canonization by old money, no sell-sign craving for the sickly glamour of Hollywood and TV, no fashionable yearning for business in "content." Grove grasps that the PC is the ascendant force in the global culture of capitalism and that the Internet consummates the PC. Nonetheless, asked about the possibility of the teleputer—the $500 Internet PC-freed from the coils of Wintel, he echoes Gates in a celebration of current PC culture that somehow misses the point.

Grove associates the teleputer with dumb or static appliances, from set-top boxes to PDAs, in the catalog of PC sub-species that emerged in hype as substitute PCs. Most of them sold a few hundred thousand units, and then expired. "The new device will be produced and it too will sell a few hundred thousand units. But not 10 million units," he says.

As *Forbes ASAP* editor Rich Karlgaard and I prepare to leave his office, he asks us to guess the cycle rate of the upcoming '96 basic home-based PC. I suggest 100 megahertz. Grove shakes his head. He confides that he is headed for a meeting to decide whether the 1996 PC will bear a 120- megahertz or a 133-megahertz Pentium. "Everyone underestimates the progress of PCs," he says with satisfaction.

"You could fix on a special-purpose device today, to satisfy Larry Ellison's mother [who wants a simpler PC], but by the time it came out, the PC will have moved on, powered by incomparably more potent microprocessors, leaving the new machine trivialized and obsolete in its wake." In other words, evolutionary products will suffice in this revolutionary time of exponentially expanding Nets and peripheral CPUs. Nonetheless, moving a few miles north on California's Route 101, out of the hypergravitational fields of Philistea, one can still feel a radical shifting in the spheres of possibility.

"And David took his staff in his hand and chose him five smooth stones." I Samuel 17:40

For the new order, the ultrawideband wireless Sand Hill slingshot—the capitalist conjurer of the forces causing new sleeplessness in Seattle is John Doerr of Kleiner Perkins Caufield & Byers. Shunning Herb Allen's summits of schmooze, where the entrepreneurial big-time is an "audacious" investment in Coke or NBC, Doerr epitomizes the venture capitalist as industrial demiurge.

As technology investor Roger McNamee puts it: "While other venture capitalists say, 'Let's start a company,' John says, 'Let's start an industry.'" So far, beginning at Intel in the early years, he has played a key role in launching industries in electronic design automation, RISC workstations, personal computers, financial software, multimedia and wireless pen appliances (well, let that last one pass). His current new industry will be the biggest yet. It is broadband Internet.

From the vertiginous launch of Sun, Lotus and Compaq in the early 1980s to a fund gushing Go at pens, his career has seen several peaks and valleys. Doerr has even dallied with middle age. He once weighed a mid-life retreat from the madding bustle of Silicon Valley to contemplate the Tantra or the Tao: "I sometimes think," Doerr told the *New York Times* in 1987, "I would like to become a Buddhist monk." Sure, John. But, tell me, what yoga discipline was he brewing two years ago in Palo Alto, at breakfast at Il Fornaio head-to-head with Jim Clark? What karmic rites was he conjuring with Clark and Bill Joy in the winter of 1994 on a three-hour conference call among wildernesses of Marriott on the road? What karass was he kenning in December 1994 among the tacky booths and bins, the barkers and indoor bikinis at the Western Cable Show in Anaheim? What tables were tipping in January 1995 in his Woodside home, among pizzas and pastas with his wife, Anne, and Marc Andreessen, Bill Joy, Andy Bechtolsheim, Jim Gosling and Rick Schell (Netscape's VP of engineering)?

Why, in early 1995, was he lurking around the NASA Ames Research Center at Moffett Field in Mountain View, Calif.? Is he seeking evidence of alien IPOs, or just some hard-core Unix Christian libertarian netbender from outer space to levitate a new industry in Palo Alto?

AT&T venturer Thomas Judge told *Forbes ASAP*'s Nancy Rutter in 1993: "You have to be on the fringes to make money in [Doerr's] business, and that's where he is." Follow Doerr, however, from day to day, call to call, from Sun to Oracle to America Online to Netscape to Macro-mind, and you will find yourself at the fringes just as they invert into the Zen center of the sphere.

A lean figure, with blondish hair, a cowlick and horn-rims, Doerr at 44 is as bashfully all-business and frenetically bitwise as Gates whom he resembles, but he is still flouting the gravity of middle age. On a crisp Sunday in mid-December, I catch up with him at Buck's restaurant, near his home in Woodside in Silicon Valley. Wearing a dark suit from church, he checks for messages on his Skytel pager, greets fellow venturer Bill Davidow passing by and then opens a black briefcase full of technotoys. From across the restaurant, this venture colossus looks to be a frowsy salesman perhaps a little desperate to present his wares. He removes a Mac Power-Book 5300 and Sony speakers and lays them out on the table. Amid empty latte glasses and plates of ravioli pesto and his own half-eaten hamburger, Doerr is ready to give a demo of the new industry—a forecast for next year's Netscape-style IPO.

It takes a minute or so to boot up the Mac, checking through the 32 megabytes of RAM (teleputers, Doerr says, will boot up instantly from flash ROM). But from there on out, it is all immediate gratification. Click to ignite a Java Web page with streaming stock-market data, a c/net talking-head newscaster and a vocano video from Venezuela. "Wow, look at that new PowerBook go," exults a jolly woman observing from the next table.

But Doerr is on a rush through a world of his own. Click again and you have the Sunnyvale Sun, efflorescent with vivid speech, sports clips and classified personals. Newspapers will be hot on the broadband Internet. Click on the classifieds and you can presumably meet their makers in living color.

This is a glimpse of @Home, a mere demo of Doerr's new broadband Internet company. As the service develops you will soon be able to download movies and other programs on demand. Over 28.8 modems or even 128-kilobit-per-second ISDN lines, all such dynamic fare would be agonizingly slow to access. By contrast, Doerr says, in @Home everything is instant, full motion and always on.

How can this be, you ask, on an essentially middleband Internet? "That's the genius of Milo Medin, @Home's network chief," he explains, "linked to the genius of Marc Andreessen of Netscape." NASA Ames's network king, Medin is now building a scalable, extensible architecture for a cable-based World Wide Web. With some help, I might add, from John Doerr and his five smooth stones.

BREAKING WINDOWS AND BOTTLENECKS

Indeed, four of the five companies—Sun, Netscape, Macromind and Intuit-Doerr estimates, "have added more than $10 billion to their market cap in the last six months because of their Internet initiatives," this new model of computing based on the Web, while Microsoft lost a similar total by briefly resisting it. Now @Home is on target to generate another multibillion market cap by exploding the current bandwidth bottlenecks of the Net.

At Intel, Doerr worked at a desk down a corridor from Bruce Ravenel. Then an architect of the 8086 and the 8087, Ravenel is now TCI Technology Ventures' influential chief of technology. Igniting the fuse for @Home were words between Doerr and Ravenel as the two old grads from "Noyce-Moore U" wove their way through the Western Cable Show in the first week of December 1994. "I dare not call it an epiphany," Doerr says, "but Bruce and I were at the Motorola booth where they were showing off a sleek little $300 box the size of a modem that would enable telephone calls over a cable line. 'What would it cost,' I asked, 'to add an Ethernet port to the device, so you could link a computer to the Internet through it at up to 10 megabits per second? ' When the Motorola guy guessed, 'Maybe $30,' our eyes got as big as saucers."

When Doerr sees a hole in the line, he hits it hard and fast. Two weeks later, four days before Christmas 1994, he was in John Malone's office in Denver presenting a plan for a Silicon Valley startup to bring broadband Internet over cable. Likely IPO market value in two years? $3 billion. Malone also hits hard and fast. After a three hour meeting, the TCI chief signed off on the venture without a qualm. Doerr's chief job was to "line up some unique Silicon Valley technical genius to make it work."

Tapping Internet experts at Sun and around the Valley, Doerr found only one name popping up on every list. It was that hard-core Unix Christian libertarian netbender from outer space, Milo Medin. A 32-year-old wunderkind manager of the multiple networks converging at NASA Ames Research Center in Mountain View, Medin had spent the last 12 years making increasingly crucial contributions to the Internet's growth. But uh-oh. For a week or more, Medin refused to answer any calls from Kleiner Perkins. He says, "I thought they were a bunch of lawyers."

Doerr was attacking the key problem of the Internet. With the number of host computers doubling every year since 1970 and the power of the computers doubling every 18 months, the Internet had mastered every challenge of capacity by multiplying cheap local routers and servers. The Net has already overtaken the U.S. Postal Service as a carrier of mail (by one estimate, a trillion e-mail messages compared with 180 billion postal deliveries). And the Net similarly has pushed the number of digital data bits ahead of the total of voice bits on the phone system.

Over the last two years, however, the traffic has taken a turn toward GIFs and graphics, doubling the number of bits every few months. As the Internet careens toward its destined collisions with television and telephony as the prime sources of information, entertainment and communication for the public, the prime obstacle is bandwidth. Many in the industry have begun to blink and bluster in the bright light of optical media and other broadband pipes.

Led by Bill Gates, they believe in middleband and ISDN. They dabble defensively in TV. As a shared medium, even cable, so Gates contends, will dwindle to ISDN rates as the number of customers on the system rises. But at 128-kilobit-per-second or even at 1.54-megabit-per-second T1 rates, ISDN means picture quality inferior to NTSC television. A shared medium linked to slow routers means bottlenecks throughout the system if cable modems yield a thousandfold increase in bit traffic beyond existing modems (up from 28.8 kilobits to close to 30 megabits per second). On-line services will bog down in slow access, sticky searches, jerky movement, blurred faces.

Such a middleband net will not be able to maintain its current momentum of growth and power. It will not be able to challenge television and telephony. Yet the valuations of Internet companies depend on a continued exponential ascent. Thus many people believe the Net is overhyped, overvalued, starved for "content." They believe Doerr's broadband revolution will fail.

Milo Medin is Doerr's weapon to break the bottleneck. He has spent most of his adult life overcoming crises on the Net. Medin's fast rise began in 1987 when he led the creation of NASA's Internet and almost came to an end in 1993, when the swarthy Serb with the spruce mustache and the piping voice and broadband gush had barged into Washington to persuade the entire government to embrace the Internet protocols (TCP/IP). Fueled by this universal language, the Net had grown exponentially up a wall of worry.

The problems did not reach critical mass until 1994, however, when its traffic began doumHere the entire Internet converged in one room in one building at Ames. On one side of the room were the Cisco 7000 routers and Digital gigaswitches and Northern Telecom add-drop multiplexers of the FIX (the Federal Internet Exchange), the government peering-and-exchange point, managed mostly by Medin. On the other side was MAE West, the Internet access exchange point for most of the private Internet, including the pullulating college and university Nets, the regnant Internet service providers such as ANS and Sprint, and the budding local fiefdoms of Netcom and The Well.

Then in April 1994, the government ended its $25 million in annual Internet subsidies and arranged for a private takeover. Among the winning bidders were Pac-Bell and Ameritech, assigned to run two key network access points (NAPs).

Long expecting the withdrawal of government subsidies to throw the Net into chaos, many observers would welcome the ensuing crash. The private sector would flub the job. There would be a tragedy of the commons. As in feudal Britain, when the commonly owned lands were overgrazed and ruined, the commonly owned Internet would suffer a glut of graphics "GIFraff" and traffic jams. Sure enough it was happening.

PacBell's ATM switches from Newbridge Networks, with skimpy buffers designed like a PBX for voice-traffic patterns, choked. California, the source of two-fifths of Internet traffic, was down. The Western NAP jammed, and Ameritech's Chicago NAP was also largely out of commission. Bay Area e-mail from a student on Netcom to a small business on BBN's BARNet had to steer clear of the Ames hub and pinball through routers all the way across the country to Sprint's NAPs in Pennsauken, N.J., or Reston, Va., and then all the way back again. As a result, the Eastern Internet hubs also began to tilt. An obvious solution seemed to be to have FIX West, the government hub at Ames, take over the traffic that was fleeing the Pacific Bell NAP.

Savvy residents of Silicon Valley, the Ames management was sympathetic. Then Medin gained the blessing of NSF networking chief Steve Wolff and enlisted Jack Waters at MCI, a crucial Internet backbone supplier that no longer used its PacBell connection.

Within two weeks, Medin created a system comparable in capacity and reliability to the original FIX, with expanded Net management capabilities, power supplies, communications ports and routing facilities. The result was a broadband national peering- and-exchange point, with a cumulative capacity of some 10 gigabits per second. It combined traffic from all the major commercial Internet suppliers with the bitstreams from government laboratories and agencies.

Meanwhile, throughout this period of crisis and turbulence, no ordinary Internet customer experienced any untoward deterioration of service. Although Medin's contribution was only part of a major national effort, he became the talk of the Net. Doerr had to sign him up.

As Doerr sums it up, "Milo was running the largest IP net in the federal government. When they decided to set up a White House.gov Web site, they asked where to put it. They put it on Milo's server. Milo helped run the fiber ring around Moscow. Internet connections for Australia and Antarctica and for deep space probes ran through Milo. He was supplying IP connectivity for the entire Scandinavian subcontinent. He had some 200 remote nodes. And he ran it all with some 99.98% uptime."

@Home CEO Will Hearst of Kleiner Perkins likes to tell a story that gives some clues as to how this young Net nerd from NASA became a legend in his own time: "In 1988, a Finn call him Lars hacks his way into Milo's computers. Ticks Milo off. He does a trace route and finds his way back to the administrator of the domain in Finland. It's an academic site. Milo already knows Lars's IP address. You can't hide from Milo. He says to the administrator, 'We have a problem. Please have a conversation with Lars.' That upset the Finns, who say, 'We are not going to do that! We respect civil liberties here! You can post a complaint if you like, but we can't tell the guy what to do.' So Milo goes into a slow boil. Says, 'I'll give you about 30 minutes to get that guy's files off our machine.'

"Nothing happens. So Milo issues an order: 'Take down Scandinavia.' The switch is pulled. Three countries go dark. They don't notice it immediately, but pretty soon e-mail messages are not getting returned. At last, three senior administrators go to Lars, so the story goes, and they say: 'We don't care if you hack into the CIA; we don't care if you bring down NSA; and we don't mind if you abscond with all the financial bits in the Federal Reserve. But don't mess with Milo at NASA.'

"The Finns called back Milo, said the situation had been taken care of. Milo said fine and put the service back up."

Now Doerr and Medin are again confronting the perennial doomsday adventists who gather on mountaintops of slightly older money and disparage the future of the Net, talking crisis, overload, overhype, overvaluation. Tragedy of the Commons. The experts are chiming in. From Howard Anderson of the Yankee Group to Andrew Seybold and Bob Metcalfe, leading analysts are prophesying a crash in 1996.

Medin has been there before. The answer to traffic jams on a narrowband Net is creation of a broadband Net. Don't tell him it is not technically possible. Who are you kidding? This is the age of the telecosm.

Bill Gates, though, thinks it is the age of middleband. It is obvious beyond cavil to Gates that his regime, ruling 80% of the world's computers, is destined to prevail. He commands a market share so overwhelming that Washington's antitrusters see it as a monopoly in need of government dissolution. For Gates, among the most ludicrous claims to be validated by the mantra "on the Internet," is the idea that Windows machines are an inferior minority system difficult to digest in the prevailing habitat of Unix and TCP/IP.

To Medin, however, it is a matter of simple fact that Windows and NT are awkward systems, hard to incorporate in his domains except as mere terminals. To Medin, Unix is the heart of the Internet, the matrix of creativity in networking, the bearer of thousands of programs and services and tools and scripts and languages that together comprise the pullulating fabric of the rampantly growing Web. So far, Medin has a strong case.

Sixty percent of the managers of Internet host computers use Macintoshes as their preferred personal machine. On the Internet, as a platform for servers, whether for the World Wide Web, e-mail, FTP, Telnet, Gopher or NeWS, Microsoft's favored NT now ranks seventh, with a 4% share, behind Sun, which commands a 56% share, Apple, Silicon Graphics, IBM, Digital Equipment and Windows 3.1.

Around the time that Gates was assuring me of Microsoft's impregnable position with @Home, Medin was reviewing the Seattle company's software concepts for his new network. The @Home people wanted to adopt Microsoft's Explorer browser if they could (TCI favored its interactive TV ally), but it was simply impossible. Explorer ran on neither Unix nor Macs, and could not handle multicasting.

Netscape's browser already worked with all the existing systems, including the various Windows.

Under the influence of Marc Andreessen, who had learned networking in the broadband 45-megabit-per-second environment of the National Center for Supercomputing Applications (NCSA), Netscape had long ago left behind all the comforts of middleband. Andreessen was eager for broadband connections. Gates was not even in the game that Medin and Andreessen were playing.

All right, suppose that "browsers are a trivial technology," as Gates told me dismissively. It was servers that Microsoft really wanted to sell to @Home. Their Gibraltar system was running Microsoft's somewhat balky internal Internet at a pace some four times faster than Netscape's server might. Here, Microsoft benefited from its homogeneous campus environment. Netscape had to employ the "union" code-using the lowest-common-denominator instructions to coordinate several varieties of Unix, Mac and Windows NT.

Meanwhile, Microsoft could optimize Gibraltar for all the most powerful instructions in Windows NT, so it was much faster.

But the @Home people were perplexed. How could they use Windows NT, an alien system on the Internet, unfamiliar to their employees or to the Internet service-provider personnel who would work the @Home headends and other nodes? Microsoft was behaving in the Internet environment as if the company were still safe in the imperial realms of Windows desktops.

So @Home, which promises to be the most important force in the next phase of Internet evolution, and Medin, the intellectual firebrand at the heart of @Home, seem unlikely to embrace Microsoft's offerings.

MILO'S DARK SHADOW OVER MICROSOFT

As for TCI, its enthusiasm was dented a bit by the collapse of the MSN project, in which Malone invested $125 million. But TCI has recouped its loss. Jim Clark was persuaded to offer TCI a small share of the Netscape IPO. After the initial public offering and the subsequent boom in Netscape shares, TCI's holding was worth $125 million, leaving TCI quite comfortable with its new allies in Mountain View.

A deeper look at Medin's plans casts darker shadows in the path of Microsoft. Asked about the notion of an Internet computer being free of Windows and other Microsoft levies, Gates stops rocking on his chair and gets to his feet. He turns and paces urgently back and forth across his office. He gesticulates, summons the history of past challenges, refers repeatedly to dumb terminals and other unappetizing machines, and hurls forth rhetorical questions: "Do you want to go onto the Internet when you are doing word processing, do you want to go on the Internet when you are using PowerPoint or Excel?" In other words, do you want to forgo all the wonderful new OLE interactions among Microsoft programs and all the new Microsoft hot links and other forthcoming tools when you go on the Net?

Under the pressure of Gates's energy and conviction and hypotheticals, I answer, "Of course not." But the real answer is, "Sure, if in exchange I can have a computer that outperforms a current Wintel machine on the Net and contains linking capabilities comparable to OLE for one-third the price."

Gates himself sketched out the answer in his famous Internet Tidal Wave memo, issued in May to galvanize his company in the face of the new threat. He pointed out that not only could he access far more information on the Internet, he could also find, search and browse it more readily on the Net than on a LAN or, for that matter, he might have pointed out, Gates's own hard drive or CD-ROM.

The error of all the critics of the $500 teleputer is their assumption that it will be inferior to current PCs. It will be, they claim, a PC minus a fast CPU, short a high-resolution monitor, without a fast memory or large drive.

This assumption misses the compounding impact of microcosm and telecosm. The advance of chip technology through Moore's Law, together with the advance of network bandwidth, will endow a machine not inferior but hugely more powerful, than the most supercharged Pentium workstation on a local-area network linked to the Internet at ISDN speeds. The Law of the Microcosm ordains that one-chip systems will be better, not worse, than intersecting boards strewn with devices linked by wires and buses. As Wilf Corrigan, chief of LSI Logic, observes, "From calculators to cellular phones, every time a system has moved onto a sin-gle chip, it has wreaked havoc with the existing industry."

In preparing the way for one-chip teleputers, Medin concedes that the current Internet will not support broadband services. "You link a broadband modem to the existing Internet and what you get is an impedance mismatch"—a bunch of fire hoses attached to a network of garden hoses. In order to accommodate the fire hoses of @Home, Medin will have to enlarge the band-width of the Net, from the humblest service provider to the NAPs at the top of the network hierarchy, where the leading service providers join to "peer and exchange" data.

Leasing capacity from the telephone companies, @Home will create a new broadband network linking to the existing NAPs at MAE East in Tyson's Corner, Va., at the Sprint NAP in Pennsauken, N.J., and at MAE West in Mountain View. This will expand the capacity of the so-called Internet back-bone (in fact, an ever-shifting array of virtual vertebrae), which currently works with maximum pipes running at 45 megabits per second. Over the next two years, Medin plans to upgrade his backbone to 622 megabits a second.

Most important and revolutionary, though, are Medin's plans for the local loops and service providers of the Net. Contrary to the claims of many critics that the Internet PC implies a return to the now-discredited model of the main-frame and dumb terminals, @Home resolutely distributes intelligence and memory through the network.

At the heart of the @Home system is ingenious hierarchical memory management and caching to conceal the mazes of slow routers, sluggish switches and narrowband wires that lurk treacherously among the higher reaches of the Internet. Indeed, when Doerr finally got through to Medin and, with Will Hearst, first proposed cable modems to him, he said they wouldn't work. There would be "impedance mismatches" with the hardware and software in the rest of the network.

"This kind of blew the air out of their tires," says Medin. "But then I told them how the system could work."

"You have to think of it as a distributed computer system. In such systems, every processor cannot access memory at once. You build caches and shared-memory protocols and you mirror and replicate a lot of the data so that it's always available locally. That's what you're going to have to do on the Internet."

In other words, the Internet is a computer on a planet. Like a computer on a chip, its raw bandwidth cannot handle the necessary throughput. Thus its communications depend on ingenious hierarchical memory management, with registers, buffers, latches, caches and direct-memory access controllers.

Studies of Internet use show that some 80% of the traffic is still local. If a particular Web page is popular in a particular locality, you have to have that page in the hard drive or even in RAM on a local server. You have to use the multicast capabilities of cable to broadcast popular information to all addresses. Above all, you have to make the system scalable. You have to phase in bandwidth, moving fiber links and nodes deeper into neighborhoods as demand rises. All this is perfectly possible technically, Medin assured Doerr.

"After I was through, they decided they had to hire me.

"I still thought we would have to build all the software ourselves. I didn't know Netscape was thinking the same way. But I went down to Netscape and got together with Marc Andreessen, who is a friend, and we had a real mind-meld on all this stuff. They were doing the software already. Netscape became our main software partner. It turned out that their browser is designed for multicast. And their proxy server is great for caching information and delivering it to users on demand."

Medin thinks that a key to making the system work is to distribute lots of cache through all the local points of presence. With this kind of network, the teleputer might become not only far cheaper but also far superior to today's PC. A now famous Gartner Group study shows that the average office PC costs $40,000 over five years when you factor in software and network maintenance.

Perhaps 75% of cumulative PC costs now come from staff support. @Home will supply tech support, maintenance and storage more efficiently, whether centrally by phone or at local headends.

For a glimpse of the future, visit Boston College, where cable modems supplied by Continental Cablevision are already becoming "addictive" to many students and professors. On the basis of this experience, Forrester Research is now predicting sales of some 7 million cable modems by the turn of the century. Medin thinks this estimate is conservative.

With cable modems you will come to demand wireless connectivity throughout your home or small office, so that your teleputers can link to the Net wherever they are without plugging them in to a connector or dialing up a connection. Only cable can accomodate such demands. "Internet PCs fit with @Home like ice cream and hot fudge," sums up Medin.

Now the big question: Is it possible to build such a machine? "Sure it is," says Medin. "Just take a Sony PlayStation, essentially based on a one-chip ASIC, and replace the CD-ROM connector with an Ethernet adapter. You'll get 3D graphics, Dol-by III sound, a 30-megahertz CPU controller, a memory-access controller, and a 10-megabit-per-second 10BaseT link to your cable headend."

CONSTERNATION INSIDE INTEL

Here the new paradigm begins to threaten the cause and complacency not only of Bill Gates but also of the other master of Wintel, Andy Grove. When I ask him about such an ASIC solution to the problem of the $500 PC, consternation breaks briefly through the surface of his bonhomie.

He snaps: "I won't comment on the fantasies of Brian Halla," the former Intel manager now executive vice-president of product marketing at LSI Logic. Yet LSI Logic offers precisely Medin's PlayStation so-lution to the problem of cheap teleputers, free of Wintel code.

LSI Logic is the supplier of the workhorse chip for the PlayStation. Using some 2 million transistors, this integrated chip combines a 30-megahertz Silicon Graphics MIPS processor, a 60-MIPS geometry transfer engine, a direct-memory access unit, and Sony's proprietary MDEC device (for hybrid MPEG and JPEG decompression) for full-screen video playback.

For a Netstation, the MDEC would be replaced with the appropriate decompression engines, and added to those would be Reed-Solomon and Viterbi error correction together with a cable modem module that receives 64-QAM signals and sends QPSK. Based on its experience with the PlayStation chip, which LSI Logic will be producing in volume on the world's first commercial 0.25-micron fabrication lines, LSI Logic estimates that it could sell a teleputer on a chip for around $50 in volume.

This machine is the consummation of a long LSI Logic strategy. In the mid-1980s, the company suffered a serious crisis as NEC, Fujitsu and Toshiba all opened fast-turnaround design centers in the U.S. to deliver high-speed, high-density gate arrays. At the same time, LSI launched a spinoff, Headland Technology, to make chipsets for PCs in competition with Chips & Technologies and VLSI Technology.

"Supporting Headland," says Halla, "was like walking around with an open artery. Intel remorselessly sucks out all the margins in PC hardware." Chastened by the Japanese in gate arrays, LSI learned from Grove not to take on Intel in PC markets.

To a company specializing in gate arrays and chipsets, these lessons were not inspiring. Then Wilf Corrigan, LSI's salty founder and CEO-a Silicon Valley legend from Liverpool who previously played key roles at Fairchild and Motorola—underwent a triple bypass.

People talked of retiring him, giving him a title with a new consortium, U.S. Memories, where he might have learned not to compete with the Koreans in DRAMs.

Two weeks after surgery, however, Corrigan returned to work at LSI and developed a new strategy that would transcend the strategies of both Intel and the Japanese. Under the new plan, LSI built state-of-the-art fabrication facilities and design tools that could enable creation of a software library of "CoreWare." CoreWare programs would generate a large variety of key functions, from CPU kernels to signal processors and graphics engines, that could be deployed in weeks on single special-purpose chips tailored to high-volume applications mostly outside the Wintel ambit.

By 1995, this strategy was bearing rich fruit. The company announced it had developed a fab process that could place some 49 million transistors on a single sliver of silicon some 200 millimeters square. LSI released a series of bellwether high-volume devices that moved the company beyond the path of the PC, out into the network and into the consumer appliance. The Sony PlayStation chip ran 1995's most successful CD game machine. LSI's MPEG-2 decoder will go in the next version of RCA-Thomson's hugely successful direct-broadcast satellite receiver. LSI also supplied the first ATM segmentation and reassembly chip for several key equipment companies, and the first 100-megabit switched-Ethernet solution for a fast Ethernet pioneer.

Looking beyond Intel, this experience led Corrigan and Halla to conclude that their company commanded all the crucial CoreWare ready to deploy a teleputer on a single device manufacturable in volume for about $50. Attesting that Halla's view is not fantasy is the success of the Sony PlayStation, now on sale for $299, leaving room to buy a monitor and still stay under $500. LSI also has several as-yet-unannounced design wins for cable modem chips aimed at the markets to be opened by @Home.

Intel's response to such capabilities is its currently embattled program for native signal processing. NSP allows software implementation of real-time functions performed in special-purpose hardware under the "CoreWare" model. As Grove points out, DSPs and compression chips may be getting cheaper all the time, but from Indeo video to Proshare teleconferencing to Intel's new Vertical Blanking Interval webware, NSP comes free of charge—if you are already buying a Pentium (and you probably are).

But no sooner will the CPU suck in another real-time role than a new virtual temptation will glimmer on the horizon. For reaching the ever-receding real-time goals—from continuous speech recognition to 3D rendering-the CoreWare approach will prevail, at least until the arrival of the new super broadband mediaprocessors from MicroUnity and other Silicon Valley firms.

Regardless of what happens on these far frontiers of technology, John Doerr will launch his five smooth stones as the foundation for a new industry. With Intuit leading the move to Internet financial services, Netscape pioneering Internet software, Macromind supplying the authoring tools for multimedia, @Home providing the bandwidth and Sun offering Java and UltraSPARC, the entente is on its way.

But perhaps Doerr's most important stone is Sun. Asked to name the key influences in TCI's shift toward the Net, John Malone mentions Doerr first, hesitates and then stresses the role of Scott McNealy, chairman and CEO of Sun Microsystems. Relentlessly, year after year, McNealy would travel to Denver and give his pitch to Malone: Buy sets of Sun servers and link them to your headends in order to supply data services. At first Malone resisted. "Two-way data," he used to say, "is not a business that I want to be in." But as the Internet grew, McNealy's argument gained new force. In late 1994, it triumphed.

Malone now believes that two-way broadband communications is the heart of his business. For a total in-vestment of less than $188 million, Doerr claims @Home can launch a business yielding at least $500 million in cumulative revenues by the year 2000. Later this year, the Sunnyvale system will be up and running. Weeks later, depending on cooperation from other cable companies, the entire state of Connecticut will move onto broadband two-way cable.

At that point, all the other cable companies will accelerate their drive to upgrade their facilities to accommodate the gold rush. By the turn of the century, @Home hopes to extend service to all the major urban and suburban centers.

With Sprint, TCI leads a cable group that is paying $2 billion for wireless personal communications service (PCS) spectrum across the country. Through New York-based Teleport Communications and other bypass providers, TCI and other cable firms already command fiberoptic rings through most major metropolitan areas. With cable providing broadband backhaul for PCS, @Home's founders think the company will emerge as the backbone for a full-service digital communications network, including high-resolution teleconferencing, on-demand films and other pay-per-view video, local news and school listings, classified advertisements, World Wide Web resources, and multimedia programming. TCI itself is furiously upgrading and streamlining all its billing systems to accommodate this rich transactional environment.

ZERO MARGINAL MAGIC

Perhaps most important, as Nathan Myhrvold explains, is the extension of the computer model of flat-rate pricing into the field of communications. When you buy a PC, you purchase its MIPS and bits essentially at a flat rate. The average cost per MIP or bit of memory you use is determined by how much you use the machine. The marginal cost is zero. As a result, people have a powerful incentive to use computers as intensively and creatively as possible.

This flat-rate pricing effect—where incremental costs are essentially zero—largely explains the huge success of the general-purpose PC and the companies supplying it with software and peripherals. Faced with a zero marginal cost of incremental use, PC owners channel as much of their information processing, education and entertainment as possible through the PC. Flat-rate pricing makes the PC a dire threat to all contiguous industries and related functions.

Similarly, on the Internet model, you will pay a flat rate for bandwidth. Again marginal costs will be zero. Average cost will respond to the extent of usage rather than to a Public Utilities Commission tariff or some per-minute charge. As Myhrvold points out, this approach will give you a tremendous incentive to exploit bandwidth as fully as you can, channeling as much communication as possible away from systems that charge incrementally and toward flat-rate systems. In the end, nearly all communications will gravitate toward the Internet model, and companies will prosper to the extent that they can ally themselves with this tremendous force of creativity and economy.

Myhrvold now says that bandwidth is growing at the same pace as Moore's Law. Gates, too, though long alert to the effects of exponentials in semiconductors, is strangely blind to the faster trajectory of communications. He finds the Internet a big surprise: "Who predicted it?" he asks. "Let's find the guy and make him king."

But by any measure-nodes, total bandwidth, traffic—the Internet has been doubling every year since 1970, and many people have predicted that it would come to dominate communications. I prophesied in 1989 that it would usurp television.

Today I believe the bandwidth tidal wave will sweep away the notions of Gates and Myhrvold of a smooth middleband transition for Microsoft and its boob-tube collaborators.

Increasingly released from regulatory restrictions, bandwidth is now expanding far faster than MIPS and bits (see *Forbes ASAP*, "The Bandwidth Tidal Wave," Dec. 5, 1994).

Over the next five years, for example, @Home will increase the bandwidth to home and small-business computers by a factor of thousands. While Moore's Law doubles computer power every 18 months, the law of the telecosm, by the most conservative possible measure, doubles total bandwidth every 12 months. This adds up. Over the next decade, computers will improve a hundredfold while bandwidth will expand a thousandfold.

Until this year, the computer and software industries have drafted behind Moore's Law, while hiding behind what Roger McNamee has dubbed "Moron's Law"—the telecom regulations that stifle bandwidth expansion. The industry thus has thrived by employing MIPS and bits as a replacement for bandwidth by using compression, decompression, switching speed, and logic circuitry to make up for the constrained bandwidth of public networks.

Grove capped off this tradition in early October, in a memorable keynote address, following South African president Nelson Mandela to the podium, at the Telecom 95 quadrennial exposition in Geneva. Grove wowed the large audience of telco potentates with an on-stage real-time demonstration of Intel's Proshare teleconferencing technology. And yet, what chiefly struck the viewer was the mediocrity of the partial-screen facial images. They were far lower in resolution than ordinary television.

As long as the pictures are inferior to TV images, PC teleconferencing will remain chiefly a niche or a stunt. As bandwidth expands powerfully over the next decade, it will seem increasingly perverse to substitute processing for bandwidth, and more and more inviting to substitute bandwidth for processing.

The logic of MIPS and bandwidth works both ways. Not only can processing make up for bandwidth, but bandwidth, as Claude Shannon pointed out in 1948, can serve as a substitute for switching and other computer functions. With bandwidth now expanding faster than processing speeds, new architectures will prevail by substituting bandwidth for MIPS and bits. Today, the bulk of bandwidth to homes is coaxial cable laid over the last 25 years by the cable television industry. Exploiting that bandwidth for the Internet is the single greatest opportunity in the history of information technology.

Having ascertained that Doerr had been meeting regularly with all the pioneers of the new paradigm that Andreessen was "mind-melding" with Medin, and that Malone had been consulting with Doerr and McNealy, I ask McNealy whether he has talked to Medin.

"No," he answers, "I have not talked with Medin at all . . . since lunch on Wednesday. But back then he and I had sore necks from basically agreeing with what the other was saying. We're fighting like crazy to become the standard platform for Medin's environment. Our companies are incredibly well aligned. We have a list of about 12 engineering efforts that we are undertaking and driving at Medin's request. The power of a network comes from the number of nodes times the bandwidth. By this measure, the @Home opportunity is as big as there is." McNealy revealed that the day before in his office at Sun, he saw the demo of "a diskless, CD-less, floppyless, OS-less computer, and it was great. It had just about every bus, serial and parallel and S-bus, and every kind of interface you can imagine. With connectors on all four sides, it was a model for what I call a zero-administration client.

"Consider: If you give a user a disk drive, a CD, a floppy, an OS and 16 megabytes of memory, you have made him, whether he wants it or not, a system administrator. He has so many resources to manage. What they showed me yesterday was a virtual machine written in Java, and it booted up instantly off flash ROM and ran like crazy because the virtual machine rides so close on the hardware."

Echoing Medin and Corrigan, McNealy evoked the future of the teleputer: "Put a touch screen on it and make it a kiosk, put a large screen on it and make it a workstation, put in an infrared detector and make it a set-top box, put a joystick on it and make a game machine, put a cable modem or an ISDN port on it and make it a PC or a digital phone. You never run out of disk space; you never have to back it up; it's mirrored so you never lose your files. You have an uninterruptible power supply. Your phone or cable line is much more reliable than your hard drive on your PC. You get used to the security of the system with no disks to corrupt and with Java programs that execute only in a virtual machine and cannot invade your system."

McNealy might have added, in ecumenical concern for Larry Ellison's mother, "Put in some Oracle code and you have a terrific, cheap database client in an emerging world of far-flung databases."

All the participants in the new regime agree. Combined with a broadband network, the teleputer will be more flexible and powerful than existing PCs. Rolling out both the network and the teleputer will be the central activity in the industry over the next two years. Responding to it will be the principal challenge to Gates and Grove, and possibly a route of redemption for their companies. All the leading figures in this Silicon Valley renaissance have endured recent periods of trial and failure. Malone suffered the collapse of his Bell Atlantic merger in 1994 and the long stagnation of his stock. Corrigan suffered physical collapse and the slump of his company. McNealy endured a long tunnel of shrinking market share as his SuperSPARC processor proved too complex to keep pace with rivals. Clark of Netscape lost influence at Silicon Graphics, the company he had founded, and finally had to leave in order to retain his self-respect. Even Doerr lost his touch for several years.

For Bill Gates, however, business life has been an almost unrelenting ascent toward riches untold for one so young. In the end, his success has made him seem a bionic business leader leached of his humanity.

His company has appeared to government and to competitors alike as a monopoly threat, targeting existing rivals and systematically suppressing them, rather than creating new products and industries. Much the same is said of Intel.

Perhaps this is the time for the Wintel team to face a domestic challenge. From it they may well emerge stronger. Without them, it is clear, the Internet will be weaker. Only from the crucible of competition between paradigms can emerge a robust and redemptive new economy of information.

18

Feasting on the Giant Peach

WILL THE INTERNET COLLAPSE? NO WAY!

What is all this commotion in Massachusetts? The very source of the Arpanet at Bolt, Beranek & Newman—the cradle of the Internet—Massachusetts is falling to the forces of Auntie Spiker and Aunt Sponge.

These are the mingy ladies in the Roald Dahl story who rejoiced in James's Giant Peach as long as it didn't take flight. Now Massachusetts—the state that once barred Apple shares as a likely West Coast levitation scam—looks askance at the Giant Peach of the Internet, aloft in Silicon Valley and around the globe, with James Clark, James Gosling, Netscape and a series of thin-air IPOs.

Howard Anderson of Boston's Yankee Group, long an Internet tout, thinks those wired yahoos on Wall Street and Sand Hill Road are blind to the inevitable sine waves of advance: What goes up must come down, he sternly avers, trying to bring some simple physics to the scene, as if the Internet has to obey the law of gravity.

And now Bob Metcalfe—Metcalfe himself!—inventor of Ethernet, pioneer of Arpanet and the founding father of the networking era. Here he is, prophesying lugubriously into every megaphone he can grasp, from the *New York Times Magazine* and PBS to *U.S. News & World Report* and *InfoWorld*, that the Internet will collapse in 1996. Metcalfe now predicts a general retreat to Intranets, shielded from the public system and unavailable to it.

Metcalfe was striking a blow against the very solar plexus of my prophecies. I had founded my confidence in the Internet on the continuing power of the law of the telecosm, an edict adapted from Metcalfe's very own law of networks. Metcalfe's Law ordains that the value of a network rises by the square of the number of terminals attached to it.

Et tu, Bob?

In its most basic form, this law merely captures the exponential rise in the value of any network device, such as a telephone, with the rise in the number of other such devices reachable by it. Metcalfe, however, shrewdly added in the declining cost of Ethernet adapters and other network gear as the Net expanded. In the law of the telecosm, I summed up these and other learning-curve factors by incorporating into Metcalfe's Law the law of the microcosm.

Based on the power-delay product in semiconductors, the law of the microcosm ordains that the cost-effectiveness of the terminals will rise by the square of the number of additional transistors integrated on a single chip. Amplified by the law of the microcosm, the law of the telecosm signifies the rise in the cost-effectiveness of a network in proportion to the resources deployed on it and the number of potential nodes and routers available to it.

As the network expands, each new computer both uses it as a resource and contributes resources to it. This is the secret of the stability of the Internet. The very process of growth that releases avalanches of new traffic onto the Net precipitates a cascade of new capacity at Internet service providers (ISPs). They supply new servers and routers, open new routes and pathways for data across the Web, and buy new terminals and edge switches to upgrade their connections to the Network Access Points (NAPs), the Internet supernodes that in turn exert pressure on the backbone vendors to expand their own bandwidth.

Because all these routes and resources are interlinked, they are available to absorb excess traffic caused by outages, crashes or congestion elsewhere on the Net. Because all these resources are growing in cost-effectiveness at the exponential pace of the law of the microcosm, and total available bandwidth on the Net is rising at the still-faster pace of the law of the telecosm, the Internet has been able to double in size annually since 1970 and increase its traffic two times faster still, without suffering any crippling crashes beyond the Morris worm of 1988.

Impelling the growth of the largest interconnected network, the law of the telecosm means that the most open computer networks will prevail. Proprietary networks lose to a worldwide web.

LOADED FOR BEAR

I wanted to answer Metcalfe's challenge. As the apparent winner of a previous argument over ATM and Ethernet [see *Forbes ASAP*, "Metcalfe's Law and Legacy," Sept. 13, 1993], I thought I might have an edge (after all, Fast Ethernet outsells ATM at least 20 to 1). But when he met me on a rainy day late in May at his Boston townhouse on Beacon Street, where he looks benevolently across the Charles at the MIT campus, Metcalfe was loaded for Internet bear. At the peak of his influence, this smiling cover boy of June's IEEE *Spectrum*, winner of the 1996 IEEE Medal of Honor, was ready to explain.

"I am way out on a limb here," he says over sushi and wasabi at a restaurant near his house. "I actually told a World Wide Web conference I would eat my column if the Internet didn't collapse. . . ."

"What do I mean by a collapse? Well, the FCC requires telcos to report all outages that affect more than 50,000 lines for more than an hour. I mean something much bigger than that." I suggested that with enough raw tuna and wasabi, his column would go down well. But Metcalfe was dead serious.

The Internet will collapse and it will be good for us, and for the Net. "The collapse has a purpose. The Internet is currently in the clutches of superstition, promoted by a bio-anarchic intelligentsia, which holds that the Net is wonderfully chaotic and brilliantly biological, and homeopathically self-healing by processes of natural selection and osmosis. The purpose of the collapse will be to discredit this ideology.

"What the Internet is—surprise, surprise—is a network of computers. It needs to be managed, engineered and financed as a network of computers rather than as an unfathomable biological organism."

Metcalfe's intellectual targets are not hard to find. He dubs them the "*Wired* intelligentsia, epitomized by Nicholas Negroponte," and, one supposes, author/editor Kevin Kelly and hippie mystic seer John Perry Barlow, celebrating a "neo-biological civilization out of control."

For example, at a recent meeting of NANOG (North American Network Operations Group), whenever Metcalfe brought up the problems of Internet management—the need for a settlements-and-payments process so that people who invest in the Net backbone can get their money back—"they kept telling me to get lost.

"They'd tell me, 'You just don't get it, do you?' This is the worst possible charge of the politically correct: 'You just don't get it.' The implication is that I am a clueless newbie.

"But I am not a newbie and I do get it: an accelerating pattern of wild behavior on the Internet [caused by] a breakdown of any relationship between supply and demand for Internet services, any way of metering usage, any method of paying back people who invest in the backbone. One thing is sure: They will not be paid by biofeedback loops.

"The result is bad—the deterioration of the public Internet and the rise of private Intranets. These are not really part of the Internet at all. Many of them use 'hot potato routing,' throwing any messages from nonsubscribers back into the pot. It is a tragedy of the commons, a shrinkage of the public network on which we all ultimately depend."

Since I had frequently cited Metcalfe's Law as an answer to "The Tragedy of the Commons" argument, this charge hit home.

Metcalfe warns that "back when Internet backbones carried 15 terabytes of traffic per month, the world's Ethernet capacity was 15 exabytes per month, a million times higher." (Exabytes, if you wonder, add up. While a terabyte is a 1 with 12 zeros after it, an exabyte commands 18 zeros.) But those were last year's numbers. Carrier of some 40% of backbone traffic, MCI now reports 250 terabytes per month. Just a small shift in local traffic onto the public Net can create catastrophic cascades of congestion.

With private networks increasingly becoming TCP/IP Intranets that can use the Internet but shield their resources from it by "firewalls," the likelihood of a crippling cascade from private to public Nets grows more acute every day. According to Metcalfe, one way or another, such a disaster is now at hand.

His primary evidence is data from the Routing Arbiter at Merit (the Michigan group that commands routing servers at every NAP and collects Internet statistics by "pinging" routers across the Net every few minutes). Merit's pings yield an echo of chaos: "a dramatic, accelerating rise of packet losses, delays and routing instability. This data is available on the Net. But the Merit people are afraid of making waves, offending the big carriers, so they don't really tell anyone how bad it is.

"I ask my readers [at *InfoWorld*], and they tell me they think the Net has already collapsed."

As the North American guild of network operators, what does NANOG need? I asked. "One thing NANOG definitely needs," sums up Metcalfe, "is more people in suits." The trouble with NANOG is that it is full of biomystics with big beards and Birkenstocks who look like Bob Metcalfe did when he finally got his Ph.D. from Harvard after a dramatic setback the year before, when his thesis board flunked him at the last minute.

(Perhaps it was because he "hated Harvard" and spent all his time at MIT and Bolt, Beranek & Newman, laying the foundations for the Internet with Larry Roberts rather than sitting humbly at the feet of Crimson computer scientists refining their professorial perks and queues. Republished in June under the title *Packet Communication*, with a new introduction from the author, Metcalfe's thesis is now recognized as a classic text on networking that anticipated most of the evolution from the Arpanet to the Internet. In the front of the new edition is a picture of Metcalfe as a newbie at the Harvard commencement, with a big beard and a weird shirt and jacket, looking kind of like a bio-anarchic, Harvard-hating Hawaiian homeopath himself, ready to help start the Internet movement back in 1973.)

What does this all mean? The conversion of Bill Gates into an Internet obsessive. The jeremiads of Metcalfe, one of my favorite people in the industry, both as a technical seer and conservative economic voice in a webby-minded wilderness. What do I make of the descent into vapor of several of my favored technologies and the admitted biodegradation of the Net?

NEW SCARCITY, NEW ABUNDANCE

Rather than debating this apparent jumble of conjectures—and for a second time jousting with the Olympian Metcalfe—I would instead transcend the details in a larger theme: Marking every industrial and economic transformation are new forms of scarcity and new forms of abundance.

Economics has been termed the dismal science of scarcity. Indeed, scarcity is at the heart of most economic models; many of my critics still live in the grip of the dismal scarcities and zero sums of pre-Netic economics. But what is the controlling scarcity of an information age? In the Industrial Age, natural resources and real estate were scarce. But Julian Simon of the University of Maryland has shown that, as manifested by falling real prices, all natural resources, such as foodstuffs, minerals, clean air and available water and energy, have been increasing in abundance over the last century.

If conventional resources are becoming more abundant, what is the ruling scarcity of the information era? Is it information? Hardly. The information glut has become a ruling cliche. As all resources—from energy to information—become more abundant, the pressure of economic scarcity falls ever more heavily on one key residual, and that single shortage looms ever more stringent and controlling. The governing scarcity of the information economy is time: the shards of a second, the hours in a day, the years in a life, the latency of memory, the delay in aluminum wires, the time to market, the time to metastasis, the time to retirement.

The ruling scarcities in the economy of time, however, can be distilled to two commanding limits: the speed of light and the span of life. They form the boundaries of all enterprise.

The speed of light is the most basic constraint in information technology. As a key limit, the speed of light shapes the future architectures and topologies of computers and communications. For example, the light-speed limit dictates that the fastest computers will tend to be the smallest computers. Electrons move nine inches a nanosecond (a billionth of a second). As computers move toward gigahertz clock rates—a billion cycles a second—the longest data path must be decisively smaller than nine inches. Pulses of electromagnetic energy—photons—take some 20 milliseconds to cross the country and one-quarter second to reach a satellite in geostationary orbit (as you notice in a satellite phone call). At a gigabit per second, this means that as many as 250 megabits of data—many thousands of IP packets, for example—can be latent (or lost) in transit at any time, thus playing havoc with most prevalent network protocols, such as TCP.

Thus light speed is a centrifuge. It abhors concentration in one place, ordains that these small supercomputers will be distributed across the globe and will always be near to a network node. Although the networks will be global in reach, they will depend on the principle of locality: the tendency of memory or network accesses to focus on clusters of contiguous addresses at any one time. Light speed imposes limits on the pace of any one processor or conduit, and pushes both computer and communications technologies into increasingly parallel and redundant architectures.

As a governing scarcity in the new economy, no less important than the speed of light is the span of life. Just as light speed represents the essential limits of information technology, lifespan defines the essential shortage of human time. Although medical and other health-related advances have increased the span of life in the United States some 5 years in the last 25—while the media focused on aids and cancer, and zero-sum pundits declared that our descendants, the scions of our science, will live less well than we do—the ultimate lifespan remains limited. Indeed, the modal economic activity of the information economy is exploitation of the technologies of the speed of light to increase the effective span of life by increasing efficiency in the use of time.

GDP and other economic numbers from the National Income and Product Accounts (NIPA) totally miss the minting of new time through innovation: the opening of parallel universes of choice in ideas, courses, arts, letters, entertainments, therapies and communities. Finding stagnation and poverty and agonizing over new wealth, Morgan Stanley gapologist Stephen Roach plumbs the shallows of NIPA for all the world like the CIA economists who found the Soviets exceeding the United States in growth for 17 years. Video teleconferencing, telecommuting, teleputing, digital wireless telephony, Internet mail, cybercommerce, telemedicine and teleducation all are in the process of compressing the span of life toward the increasingly thronged channels of the speed of light.

If time is scarce, what is the growing and defining source of abundance among all the material abundances in the information economy? Signifying the definitive abundance in any economic era is the plummeting price of a key factor of production. In order to grow fast, every new-era company must exploit the drop in the cost of the newly abundant resource. Companies that use the resource that is plummeting in cost will gain market share against all other companies and will come increasingly to dominate the economy.

FROM WATTS TO MIPS AND BITS

Over the last hundred years, there have been three such economic eras. The industrial era fed on the plummeting price of physical force or energy, best measured in watts. Some 30 years ago, with the regulatory sclerosis of the nuclear and natural gas industries, the price of watts began to plateau, dropping less than 0.7% per year for the last 35 years. The last 30 years brought the reign of the microcosm, which fed on the plummeting price of transistors, manifested in the exponential drop in the cost of computer MIPS (millions of instructions per second) and memory bits. For the last 30 years, the price of a bit of semi-conductor memory has dropped 68% per year. With this year's decline in DRAM prices, the trend line is being resumed after a four-year hiatus. The likely result is a sharp upside surprise in PC sales—and thus in chips—through 1997.

As fast as the price of MIPS and bits continues to drop, however, this Moore's Law trend line will no longer dominate the economy. Like a great river headed for a falls, a new factor of production is racing toward a historic cliff of costs. Over the next 30 years, the spearhead of wealth creation will be the telecosm, marked by the plummeting cost of bandwidth—communications power—measured in gigabits per second.

This result means that the growth of bandwidth will outpace the growth of processor power. After an entire career keyed on Moore's Law, Bill Gates remains skeptical, foreseeing an era of middleband nets, with shared cables bogging down in gigabytes from tomcruise. com/vrml and fiber gushing into twisted copper cul-de-sacs. The usually savvy *Network Computing* columnist Bill Frezza believes that bandwidth is inherently a slower-moving technology than processing, because bandwidth has to be delivered at once to an entire area while processors can be sold one at a time. Robert Lucky, Bell system laureate, and Paul Green of IBM debated these points two decades ago. Stressing the dependence of bandwidth on the labor-intensive digging of trenches and stretching of wires across continents and under seabeds, Lucky doubted that communications could ever be truly cheap. Paul Green, a computer network man, thought that digital computer communications could join the Moore's Law learning curve.

The evidence mounts that Green was more than right. Impressed by Green's own achievements in fiber optics, Lucky now acknowledges that communications power will grow at least tenfold more than computing power over the next decade. Using the rough metric of Moore's Law, computer power doubles every 18 months. Bandwidth is now doubling at least every year. Over a 10-year period, this means a hundredfold rise in computer power and at least a thousandfold rise in bandwidth, measured at any point in the network from the home to the backbone.

The reason communications power has lagged behind computer power is not the difference in technology but in regulation. Moore's Law in bandwidth has given way to what venture capitalist Roger McNamee calls Moron's Law, the labyrinthine tangle of tariffs and rulings and FCC dockets that frustrate the implementation of communications advances. With an acceleration of technology and a tsunami of new Internet demand for bandwidth, this bottleneck is breaking at last.

Backbone capacity is leaping upward today. As TCP/IP coinventor Vinton Cerf of MCI told *Forbes ASAP* in December, his company correctly predicted its backbone bandwidth would increase from 45 megabits per second to 155 megabits per second this year, or by a factor of nearly four. But on March 11, MCI Vice-President of Enterprise Marketing Stephen VonRump told Gordon Cook of the *Cook Report* on the Internet that MCI will jack up the speeds to 622 megabits per second before the end of the year, or nearly fifteenfold in one year. Meanwhile, cable modems, telco Digital Subscriber Line technologies (from HDSL to ADSL and SDSL) and digital wireless advances promise even larger factors of expansion in the bandwidth to homes, though unlike the backbone expansion, the impact will be incremental.

Shaping the future, however, will be breakthroughs in laboratories. As "Into the Fibersphere" maintained, the ultimate source of bandwidth expansion is the immense capacity of optical fiber. Now comprising a global installed base of 40 million miles (some 25 million miles in North America), each optical fiber, as Paul Green of IBM estimated to *Forbes ASAP* four years ago, commands an intrinsic available bandwidth of 25,000 gigahertz. At the time, the world record transmission over a significant distance was still approximately 20 gigabits per second, and the highest deployed capacity was just 2.5 gigabits per second. Moreover, the light pulses had to be converted to electronic pulses every 50 to 70 kilometers to amplify and regenerate the signal. This electronic bottleneck restricted the speed of long-distance transmission to the maximum speed of the optoelectronics, or some 10 gigahertz. So Green's projections provoked incredulity in many quarters.

Early this year, however, Green's visions were becoming more plausible. On Feb. 26, 1996, at the conference on Optical Fiber Communication (OFC '96) in San Jose, Calif., papers from Lucent Technologies' Bell Labs, Fujitsu and NTT Labs all reported successful transmissions at a landmark rate of a terabit per second, one twenty-fifth of Green's limit. For these terabit rates, Fujitsu and Bell Labs used between 50 and 55 separate bitstreams or wavelengths, each some 20 gigabits per second. NTT, which employed 10 separate bitstreams, also reported diffraction grating receivers that could resolve 64 different wavelengths at once.

At the same time, erbium-doped fiber amplifiers were smashing the electronic bottleneck. Impelled by a pump laser (light amplification by stimulated emission of radiation), these all-optical amplifiers are now being deployed in networks around the world. They open a new era. Simple broadband amplifiers made of a coiled fiber thread, they replace optoelectronic repeaters comprising nine custom bipolar microchips that must be duplicated for every frequency or modulation scheme used in the fiber. Thus the new amplifiers make possible the creation of vast broadband fiber networks bearing hundreds or even thousands of separate carriers, and permit the sending of thousands of separate messages around the globe or under the seas entirely on wings of light. The bandwidth of these all-optical amplifiers is now up to 4.5 terahertz, or close to 20% of Green's estimated limit.

The ultimate capacity of fiber is not a merely academic issue. At a rate of 4,000 miles a day, fiber deployment is beginning to make a dent in neighborhoods. David Charlton of Corning estimates that over the past five years, the top 10% of U.S. households, comprising most of the early technology adopters, have drastically improved their access to fiber. Five years ago these homes were, on average, 1,000 households away from a fiber node; this year, they are just 100 households away. Milo Medin of @Home estimates that 15% of U.S. cable TV subscribers had systems directly connected to fiber nodes at the beginning of 1996. By the end of the year, that number will be close to one-third.

Hostility to cable TV remains high and politically useful; many city governments subsist on cable TV franchise fees and regulate these companies into a stupor. Eerily mimicking computer experts of the 1960s who attested that telephone wires were too beset with noise and interference to carry digital data, telco experts today pronounce cable plant entirely unsuited for Internet bits. But the fact remains that cable TV coax is the only truly broadband link already in most U.S. homes.

Flaws in the transmission of analog video, in which every glitch of interference is visible on the screen, fall away in digital systems that can deliver flawless images at a signal-to-noise ratio more than 1,000 times lower. DirecTV, for example, does not outperform cable TV because it is harder to send a signal a few thousand feet down a coaxial cable than to zap it to a satellite 23,600 miles away, beam it to an 18-inch dish on a roof, then send it down a coaxial cable to your TV. The superiority of DirecTV derives from its digital nature. Essentially, the picture is created in the set rather than at the station. Using a variety of new cable modems, possibly including Cisco and Terayon's CDMA for upstream signals (CDMA finesses interfering frequencies by spreading codes through them all), cable TV plant will prove to be entirely adequate for digital transmissions, both upstream and downstream.

But what about switching, ask the critics of cable? Claude Shannon of MIT and Bell Labs, the inventor of information theory, had the answer in 1948: Bandwidth is a replacement for switching. Rather than performing the processing at some central point, you use routers in the Net and filters in the terminals. If you have adequate bandwidth, you can emulate any switching topology you want. Cable commands a potential of some

8 gigabits per second of two-way bandwidth. Linked to the potential terabits of fiber bandwidth, cable plant has as much chance of accommodating the explosive growth of the Internet as the telcos do.

The two essential models for the distribution of information are select and switch or broadcast and select. Select and switch is based on intelligence in central servers that search databases for desired material, and on intelligence in switches that channel the material to the desired address. Select and switch uses computer power at the servers and switches to compensate for the lack of bandwidth on the network and the lack of storage and processing power in the terminals. By contrast, broadcast and select is based on bandwidth in the network and on intelligence and storage in the terminals.

Envisaging video servers, information warehouses and other centralized schemes, select and switch is the model pursued by much of the industry today. In some schemes, agents from networked terminals search through large banks of data looking for specified items, which are switched through the network to the terminals. Computers reach out and grab data they need from servers with large storage facilities.

Epitomized by the World Wide Web today, the marvels of this select-and-switch model are evident to us all. It is far superior for personal two-way communications and one-to-one file transfers. But it is not superior for everything, as companies trying to send movies point-to-point over ATM switches discovered in Orlando and elsewhere. The success of select and switch, using the storage of servers, has been too total for the health of the Internet.

In its extreme form, select and switch contravenes the laws of the microcosm and telecosm. These laws will increase storage at the terminals far faster than at the centralized server and will expand the network's bandwidth faster than its switching capability. For many uses, the broadcast-and-select method is appropriate—indeed, inevitable—and its spread will relieve many of the pressures on Internet capacity.

Broadcast and select is the system used in wavelength division multiplexing systems in the new multi-bitstream terabit-per-second fiber tests. Broadcast and select conforms closely with the strengths of the cable system. In late April, for example, Wave Systems (where I serve as a director) launched its CablePC project in the heart of Silicon Valley with the Palo Alto Cable Co-op. Supporting the test are 26 other companies with equipment and services, including cable modems from Com21 and En Technology; a merchandising engine from Zero.one; the Destination PC/TV from Gateway 2000; game machines from MAK Technologies; and content from Simon & Schuster Interactive, Network News, William Morris Agency, Microsoft's interactive software arm and an array of CD-ROM publishers.

This system uses cable bandwidth to broadcast huge amounts of digital information and entertainment. Originating anywhere from the World Wide Web and DirecTV satellites to CD-ROMs on a PC, the rush of bits will be filtered and downloaded by the PC at the programmable specifications of the viewer. Customers pay for material by the piece and only when they choose to decrypt it through an onboard "credit chip" or WaveMeter that may be periodically tapped over telephone lines from a transaction center. Rather than millions of people downloading new versions of Netscape one at a time over 28.8

modems, for example, you can program your machine to download all new Netscape browser releases to your hard drive when they are broadcast, probably late at night. The next day you can decide whether to buy, save or delete the program. Explains new Wave Systems president Steven Sprague, "This system creates a new channel where the customer pays only for what is used, when it is used, and the owner of intellectual property benefits from each use."

Together with systems of mirroring, replicating and local buffering being pioneered by @Home, the CablePC project is one of many ways to use cable bandwidth to relieve pressure on the Net and to exploit the ever-rising intelligence and storage in the terminals. Other broadcast-and-select systems include PointCast for the PC, which uses the screen-saver as a way to display programmably filtered news and other information. Another large contribution of broadcast-and-select bandwidth for the WWW will come from digital satellite systems, such as DirecTV, that devote channels to Internet services.

Meanwhile, coming to the rescue of the Net backbone are an array of technologies incorporating asynchronous transfer mode (ATM), an elaborate set of standards for broadband switching. Supported by some 800 companies in the ATM Forum, ATM resembles RISC (reduced instruction set computer), which accelerates speeds by making all instructions the same length and processing them in silicon. Similarly, ATM breaks all data into 53 byte cells, small enough to be processed in a semiconductor chip at speeds fast enough to accept voice, video or data at once. Conceived as an end-to-end system from your phone or PC through the "cloud" to your Internet service provider and beyond, ATM seems a panacea for the protocol zoo emerging in data communications.

ATM to the desktop faces dire challenges, however. Paul Green noticed that the most popular booth at the early May ATM Year '96 conference in San Jose was by a company called Ipsilon. Now partnering with Hitachi, Ipsilon makes an IP switch that dispenses with all ATM software and uses ATM cells only for fast hardware switching. Similarly, NetStar [see *Forbes ASAP*, "Angst and Awe on the Internet," Dec. 4, 1995], now being purchased by Ascend Communications for $300 million in stock, offers an IP crossbar switch in gallium arsenide with a backplane throughput of 16 gigabits per second. Meanwhile, vendors of Fast Ethernet and Gigabit Ethernet attracted increasing attention. Why transform your network when you can get most of the advantages of ATM through new forms of Ethernet and TCP/IP? But in one form or another, ATM switches are still the fastest switches and use their advantage in silicon integration to dominate the top-of-the-line slots in the backbone of the Internet.

REVENGE OF BEARDS AND BIRKENSTOCKS

The readers of *Forbes ASAP* will recall Gordon Jacobson and Avi Freedman, East Coast ISPs who have graced these pages contemplating a national network. Tonight, in New York, they are debating the future of the Net with each other and with two executives from a San Diego company called AtmNet who have similar ambitions. I am there to get a view from the pits of the Internet on Metcalfe's lament.

Jacobson has a problem, though. He wants to take us to Le Colonial on East 57th Street, which he describes as the hottest bar and best French-Vietnamese restaurant in the city. But the bearded Avi Freedman has shown up in a green T-shirt and Birkenstock sandals, which won't cut it at Le Colonial.

A second-floor hideaway, Le Colonial looks like Rick's place in *Casablanca*, so they say, and it sounds like a bar on the Champs-Élysées. More important to guru Gordon, it allows him to flaunt a tycoon's cigar, unlike P. J. Clarke's, his other favored haunt, which has succumbed to nicotine correctness since Dan Jenkins's novel on the Giants, *Semi-Tough*, celebrated its smoke and grit. Unlike P. J. Clarke's with its elderly Irish trolls, Gordon tells us, Le Colonial offers "the most beautiful bartender in all New York. You got to see her."

Avi, though, has more important things on his mind. Polynomials.

They're a dilemma, those polynomials. But Gordon decides to act anyway. We will start out with dinner at Clarke's and then move on to Le Colonial for after-dinner drinks. At the bar, Le Colonial will tolerate the T-shirt, and perhaps, with adequate lubrication, we will be able to relieve the pressure of the polynomials.

The Internet is in the process of a horizontal explosion, with new network exchange points popping up everywhere—two in L.A., one each in Tucson, Phoenix, Atlanta, Cincinnati—you name it, a hundred or more network exchange facilities coming online. AtmNet is beginning one in San Diego and has plans to participate in those in L.A.

Meanwhile, the P. J. Clarke's waiter, delivering salad with home fries well done and a Diet Pepsi, is struggling with the demands of serving different meals to five customers (that's 25 different possibilities). With mental buffers overflowing and packet losses mounting, he resolves on a polling algorithm, offering the plate to each of us around the table before settling on Avi. Gordon is looking worried; Avi is questioning his confidence that ATM switching can resolve most of the complexity problems on the Internet.

SEX AND POLYNOMIALS AT LE COLONIAL

I ask whether the problem arises from scanty RAM buffers in the Cisco routers. Avi says no. An entire global routing table still takes just 14 megabytes and virtually everyone on the Net can now handle that. Soon they will be able to handle a gigabyte of routes, no sweat, enough to deal with any foreseeable growth of the Net. Yes, I observe, it's exponential; I talk about it all the time. No, Avi corrects me, complexity growth is not exponential. It is polynomial.

This problem will have to wait, however, says Gordon, hailing the waiter. It's time to leave for Le Colonial. Gordon wants Jim Browning and John Mevi of AtmNet to explain how their ATM systems can transcend all these complexities.

AtmNet is visiting New York to consult with Gordon and Avi about AtmNet's plans to create a new national 155-megabit backbone across the country. AtmNet already has a

155-megabit-per-second backbone on the West Coast connecting San Diego, L.A. and San Francisco. But they are dependent on the caprices of long-distance carriers to cross the country. Gordon pays the waiter and we're off to Le Colonial.

After dinner, Avi's T-shirt and sandals pass. But upon arrival, Gordon is crestfallen: The exponential bartender is off for the night. When Gordon recovers, we all troop to a table in the corner. Thronging the room are models in miniskirts—tall, lithe and pneumatic. Across the table, in front of a large framed photograph with a wraithlike image of Ho Chi Minh in a Huey Newton chair, a sleek young couple in black hungrily writhes through hot kisses. A sultry Asian waitress in a red kimono blouse emerges from behind palm leaves to take orders of port, Courvoisier and Diet Pepsi. Avi is worried that we still don't get his point about the polynomials.

He wants to correct me: Strictly speaking it is not exponential (that's when the exponent rises), it is polynomial (the variable n rises). In this case, the complexity of the network rises by n nodes times n-1, which is not even quite the square of n. I got it. The growth of Internet complexity is polynomial. But the growth curve still rises toward the sky, okay?

Avi ignores my comment and cruises on. Cisco is selling 60,000 routers a month. It's the low end of the Net that is exploding. Hierarchical segmentation through routers is the answer, reducing the n squared factor to the logarithm of n. "Log n is wonderful," Avi says. "It shears off complexity." The curves are relatively flat. But what about Metcalfe's prediction of a whopping Internet crash in 1996? Avi will get to that. And what is the role of AtmNet's ATM switches?

Indeed. Apparently joining Avi in ignoring these tantalizing questions, the girl across the table raises her legs and hooks them sinuously around the body of the sleek young man. The waitress leans forward to deliver the drinks, suffusing the table with exotic perfumes. The two AtmNet promoters insist that the router problem can be overcome through the interposition of ATM switches.

Avi dismisses the ATM argument. The complexity curve is still polynomial, he says. Whether routed or switched, the messages have to follow the same physical routes. The complexity is the same. Moreover, Avi's cell phone is on the blink and he has been out of reach for three hours. Gordon offers a show-off Audiovox the size of a pack of cards, only lighter. Avi manages to put through a call.

The girl across the table shudders with pleasure as the man reaches out and cups her breasts in his hands. "The FIX is down," Avi sighs. "What does that mean?" I ask. That means, so I learn, a 45-megabit line is out of service and the Federal Internet Exchange, a Washington NAP, cannot trade routes or data with MAE East, Metropolitan Fiber Systems's Fiber Distributed Data Interface exchange point in Vienna, Virginia. This glitch ramifies, creating certain problems for some of Avi's new customers in Washington. The young man whispers something in the ear of the girl. She balks. "No, I'm getting embarrassed," she says. "Let's leave." "I'll call back in 10 minutes," says Avi. The pair unwrap their entangled limbs and staggers up from the table. Avi and the rest of us get up to go.

Thus ends the visit to the palmy domain of Le Colonial. Before I can pry in a question about Metcalfe, Avi is on the road back home to his wife and an Internet crisis at 11 p.m., enjoying life as a Diet Pepsi bon vivant polynomial ISP. Anyway, it was time for fresh air. John Mevi of AtmNet needs a break. "Avi talks so fast it makes my ears ring," he explains. "You've got to understand. I'm from a telco environment."

So it was that on a steamy evening in New York, on June 17, I returned to consult Avi again on Metcalfe's predictions of a network crash. We met with Gordon Jacobson at Martini's, an Italian restaurant near the Sheraton Hotel on the west side of Manhattan. While Avi and Gordon consume a lox pizza and several orders of pasta, I question these men who live on the Net from minute to minute, day to day, who live in a world of routing tables, TCP/IP address resolutions, and BGP (Border Gateway Protocol) and Gate Daemons, about what they make of the doom scenario.

Avi believes that Metcalfe has ascended to an elevation in the industry that takes him out of the loop. He really doesn't get it. The Merit data is mostly irrelevant. Pings from the Routing Arbiter are weighted as lowest-priority packets. It is predictable and unimportant that many are dropped and re-sent. "That's the way the Internet works. Like Ethernet, it is tolerant of failure. Undelivered packets are re-sent; they show up as a few milliseconds of delay."

Metcalfe makes much of Merit's index of router instability, measured by the number of routes announced and withdrawn. In the extreme, instability brings "route flaps," in which waves of announcements and withdrawals spread across the Net in positive feedback loops that congest the system. Avi dismisses this effect. "There have been no significant route flaps in the last six months or more."

A large portion of the instability problems is attributable to a bug in Cisco router software that is in the process of being fixed. He confirms the findings of Ken Ehrhart of Gilder Technology Group that shows little correlation between the router instability number and performance of the Net measured by throughput at NAP switches. While all this "wild statistical behavior" went on, the Net continued to perform stably by using other routes, circumventing the congested paths. "That's how the Internet works."

Avi sums it up: "Metcalfe has become an elder statesman and now he is doing more harm than good, spreading fear and doubt while the rest of us solve the problems." As Ehrhart puts it, "These Merit numbers bear bad names like 'instability,' 'packet loss' and 'delay.' Metcalfe says these bad things are growing wildly. But in back of these numbers what is really growing wildly is the Internet and that is a good thing." Richard Shaffer's ComputerLetter, for example, reports that MCI's backbone traffic has risen fivefold in the last year. MCI reports that its traffic has grown a total of 5,000% since it opened the backbone in 1994.

Like Howard Anderson, Bill Gates, Andy Grove and other bandwidth skeptics, Metcalfe seems to find the explosive growth of his intellectual progeny—Ethernets and Internets—too good to be true. All the sages and titans seem to seek obsessively the worms in the Giant Peach as it hurtles through the air. The message from Avi, Gordon and the AtmNet crew is "Let them eat worms. We'll feast on the peach."

Metcalfe's economics arguments are largely true. As Michael Rothschild's *Bionomics* shows, growth in natural and economic systems depends on running a surplus in every cell. But the cells of the Internet are thriving today. From the creators of the backbone who lease their facilities, to the ISPs who are madly multiplying their points of presence, the leading companies are attracting so much investment and support that laggard behemoths such as AT&T, TCI and the RBOCs are rushing in.

The law of the telecosm depends on the principle that new computers and routers on the Net not only use its resources but also contribute new resources to it. If the recent upsurge in Intranets is parasitical to some degree (because these newcomers use the resources of the Net without contributing resources of their own), the ultimate parasite on the scene may be AT&T, which commands perhaps the world's largest Intranet.

AT&T has attracted some 6 million orders from newcomers for Net service, with plans to have 20 million by the end of the year, while lagging far behind MCI and Sprint in contributing to the Internet system. Until recently, AT&T's vast fiber backbones carried just 2% of Internet traffic. AT&T preens as the largest and lowest-cost ISP, but its traffic mostly travels the backbones of MCI, Sprint and other national Internet carriers. A key to clearing the current bogs and bit pits of the Internet and preventing a Metcalfe collapse is the enlisting of the full-fiber and switching resources of AT&T to relieve the pressure on the existing NAPs and backbones and to accommodate the Internet's growth. AT&T is currently moving to supply such support.

The Intranets criticized by Metcalfe are crucial to the Internet's growth. Like the corporate PCs that spearheaded the advance of PC technology, Intranets spread Internet technology through business, expand the market for high-powered gear, lower component prices, enlarge bandwidth, and bring new users and buyers onto the Net.

As for Metcalfe's prediction of Internet crashes from private network overflows, the fact is that no computer memory system could work without the principle of locality—the tendency of memory accesses to focus on a contiguous region of addresses. The Internet is similar. Internal corporate e-mail, for example, is about 10 times as voluminous as remote e-mail. Metcalfe's private Net overflow cascade is mostly a theoretical chimera. Like Ethernets, "the Internet works in practice but not in theory."

A second key fact of the Internet is that nothing in modern computer systems could survive the combinatorial explosions of multimillion-line software programs and multimillion-node circuitry without the magic of the microcosm. Semiconductors sink the complexity into silicon, where it gives way to the exponential boon of the power-delay product. The performance of the circuit—measured by its speed and low power—improves roughly by the square of the number of transistors on the chip.

A microprocessor using separate components would be taller than the Empire State Building and cover most of New York state. Most of the problems of Internet complexity must be solved the same way that the microprocessor solves its complexity explosion, sucking the complexity into semiconductors and taming it on the chip. This means that Internet nodes would ideally be single-chip systems. Avi is correct; it makes little difference whether these systems are routers or switches. Today the backbone is being renewed by ATM switches because these devices integrate more of the process onto silicon than any other switches. In the future, broadband optics will likely prevail by integrating entire communications systems onto seamless webs of glass.

THE INTERNET AS LIFE EXTENDER

The internet is a human contrivance requiring finance and physical renewal. In practice, this means capital from phone companies and other large institutions. In the real world, self-organizing systems rely on market incentives rather than bio-analogies. Metcalfe is right that these incentives must be protected and extended in order for the law of the telecosm to conquer the laws of entropy.

The key remaining obstacle to the fulfillment of the promise of the Internet is government regulation. This obstacle is being overcome at last by the brute force of bandwidth abundance, stemming from breakthroughs in fiber optics, smart radios, satellites and cable modems.

In every industrial transformation, businesses prosper by using the defining abundance of their era to alleviate the defining scarcity. Today this challenge implies a commanding moral imperative: to use Internet bandwidth in order to stop wasting the customer's time. Stop the callous cost of queues, the insolence of cold calls, the wanton eyeball pokes and splashes of billboards and unwanted ads, the constant drag of lowest-common-denominator entertainments, the lethal tedium of unneeded travel, the plangent buffeting of TV news and political prattle, the endless temporal dissipation in classrooms, waiting rooms, anterooms, traffic jams, toll booths and assembly lines, through the impertinent tyranny of unneeded and afterwards ignored submission of forms, audits, polls, waivers, warnings, legal pettifoggery.

All these affronts once were tolerable in an age when the customer's time seemed abundant—an available economic externality in an economy of material scarcity. All are intolerable in an age of compounding abundance, pressing down on the span of life as the irreducible scarcity.

For all this abusive waste of the most precious resource, the remedy is the Net. Businesses must use its defining abundance—MIPS, bits and gigahertz—to redress the residual scarcity of time. A key way to save time is to economize on space—geography. In practical terms, there is only one way to collapse time and space together. That is to relegate more and more of the routine functions of life to microchips, where room expands as space contracts, and where operations cycle in nanoseconds, and then to interconnect the chips through the technologies of the speed of light. This is the promise of the Internet and it will keep the Giant Peach aloft and ascendant in the new global economy of bandwidth abundance.